Parallel Population and Parallel Human

Parallel Population and Parallel Human

A Cyber-Physical Social Approach

Peijun Ye and Fei-Yue Wang
Institute of Automation, Chinese Academy of Sciences
Beijing, China

IEEE Press Series on Systems Science and Engineering
MengChu Zhou, Series Editor

WILEY

Published by John Wiley & Sons, Inc., Hoboken, New Jersey.
Published simultaneously in Canada.

For general information on our other products and services or for technical support, please contact our Customer Care Department within the United States at (800) 762-2974, outside the United States at (317) 572-3993 or fax (317) 572-4002.

Wiley also publishes its books in a variety of electronic formats. Some content that appears in print may not be available in electronic formats. For more information about Wiley products, visit our web site at www.wiley.com.

Library of Congress Cataloging-in-Publication Data Applied for:

Hardback ISBN: 9781394181896

Cover Design: Wiley
Cover Image: Courtesy of Fangfang Li

Set in 9.5/12.5pt STIXTwoText by Straive, Chennai, India

To Jenny and Ryder.

Contents

Preface

Parallel Population of Parallel Human in Metaverses

This book is a result of an ambitious research agenda I made for myself almost 30 years ago after reading Karl Popper's **The Open Society and its Enemies**. To me, the open society should have no enemies, we must find a way to build the bridge between Popper's utopian social engineering and piecemeal social engineering, perhaps through the *Cyber-enabled Social Movement Organizations and Operations* (**CeSMO**), and that would be my research for the rest of my professional career. I had promised myself to write a book entitled **The Open Society and its Friends**, and even created a new name for my ambition, **Bemonad**, for *Becoming* and *Being* Gottfried Leibniz's *Monad*, which was redefined as the atom of intelligence for Popper's Artificial World in the sense of ancient Greek philosopher Democritus' atom for matters in the Physical World. Of course, I realized very soon that it is simply a dream and a mission impossible. However, this had dramatically changed my career path from intelligent control for robotic systems to a mixture of science, technology, engineering, and social studies for complex intelligent systems, or an interdisciplinary approach by today's term, starting from my technical report at *NASA/UA Space Engineering Research Center* (SERC) on *Shadow Systems* in 1994 and ending up with the creation of the *Program for Advanced Research in Complex Systems* (PARCS) at the University of Arizona, Tucson, Arizona in 1999.

During the late 1990s and entire 2000s, I spent all my energy and enthusiasm in building Sino-US research collaboration projects and programs for coming and future *Intelligent Science and Technology*, from the *US-China Joint Research Center on Intelligent Control and Systems* to *US-Sino Center for Advanced Research and Education* (US-CARE), including projects such as **FPGA** (*Foundational Platforms and Gateways for All*) to support start-ups and intelligent industries, **CASIA** (*Complex Adaptive Systems for Intelligence Analytics*) for Academic Intelligence to be used for graduate students around the world for writing their theses and dissertations, and **PUREST** (*Parallel Universities for Research and Education in Science and Technology*) for helping future students in high schools and universities. Those efforts made me realize that we need to move fast and far beyond our conventional thinking on technology such as agents, robots, or shadow systems, and far beyond our general desire for virtual, mixed or enhanced reality, we must develop digital human technology for our sustainability. My vision for future is simple and straight: The world population would be 5% biological human, 15% robotic human, and 80% digital human. To this mission, over the last two decades, our research has been focused on *Artificial Societies, Computational Experiments, and Parallel Execution* (ACP), *Cyber-Physical-Social Systems* (CPSS), as well as their derivatives such as *Parallel Intelligence, Parallel Systems, Parallel Management, Parallel Economics, Parallel Manufacturing, Parallel Control, Parallel Agriculture, Parallel Transportation, Parallel Services, Parallel Energy, Parallel Mining, Parallel Medicine, Parallel Ecology, ...,* spanning over 100 fields and leading to the establishment of the *State Key Laboratory for Management and Control of Complex Systems* in 2011.

Today, our vision for the future is more closing than ever and has becoming the past in quite a few places in our industries and societies. Digital twins, foundational or Big AI models, metaverses, web 3.0 or web3, DAO for decentralized autonomous organizations or operations, DeSci, DeEco, or DeSoc for decentralized autonomous sciences, economies, or societies, are emerging fast and receiving tremendous attention from researchers and entrepreneurs around the world. Therefore, I think the time is ready for publishing some of our research in the past decade on parallel human and parallel population for CPSS, we need more people to work and study in this field.

The central theme of this book concentrates on how to computationally model human individual's deliberation and thinking so that her/his behavior is prescribed to achieve the expected goal of management in cyber physical social systems. Our discussion will address the basic theory and methodology for modeling as well as some implementation techniques. Potential acceleration technologies will be also exploited in our prototype systems due to the high computational cost. Some application cases from different fields are also included to show preliminary validations. Though some chapters may concern about implementations, we generally follow the technological path rather than system component details to introduce our work concisely. Our discussion begins with the synthesis of basic population, which includes Chapters 2 and 3. These two progressive chapters elucidate how to generate a "static" set of virtual individuals with their personal attributes and mutual social relationships according to statistical results and optional micro samples. Chapter 2 only considers the individuals, while Chapter 3 further addresses social organizations. The resulting basic population plays as a start state in the subsequent artificial population evolution. Next, we move to the micro level, concentrating on the individual cognition and behavioral modeling. This part includes four chapters, Chapters 4–7, where we address three intercoupling aspects of human intelligence and cognition: the representation of human knowledge, the acquisition of an individual's knowledge in a static/dynamic way, and the exploitation of one's knowledge to elicit a specific decision/action. These three aspects are also fundamental questions in general intelligence. Chapter 4 presents the cognitive architecture for agent decision cycle. It provides a unified container or framework that organizes knowledge segments and data flow in decision process. On the basis of such framework, Chapters 5 and 6 address the learning and reasoning which offer rudimentary solutions for knowledge acquisition and application. To model the mental heterogeneity in a time-variant human-in-loop environment specifically, we put our emphasis on adaptive learning through detected individual actions. The decision making based on reasoning via one's knowledge base adopts an evolutionary paradigm rather than classic reasoning in artificial intelligence (AI) research. This is in line with the philosophy from science of complexity and cognition where the deliberation results from a bottom-up emergence. We do not organize a separate chapter to the knowledge representation because existing relevant techniques are directly exploited. Instead, a brief introduction is included in Chapter 5. Interested readers can easily find corresponding details in other related literature. The last but not least problem for artificial human modeling is the parameter calibration and validation, which is essential for the reliable use of models. For a large-scale social system in particular, model calibration seems more important, since compared with a few agents, parameter values in such systems are difficult to be fully measured in a wide range. This sampling bias may cause the obtained parameters not representative enough and thus impacts the accuracy of the model. Several calibration methods have been be described in Chapter 7 in order to avoid such a dilemma. After establishing learning and reasoning mechanisms for artificial human, next we turn to their implementation. In Chapters 8 and 9, we consider acceleration approaches for a large-scale knowledge base that is computationally expensive. This is almost inevitable in practice since one's mental repository is usually complicated. Distributed reasoning and active strategy prescription via cloud computing are illustrated. Some theoretical foundations on the completeness and optimality in such a reasoning mode are also analyzed in these two chapters. The book concludes with some applications in Chapter 10, ranging from computational demography, urban transportation management and control, to evacuation in emergency. Some ethical and legal issues of parallel population/human are further discussed in Chapter 11.

I would like to take this opportunity to express my sincere thanks to my co-author Dr. Peijun Ye, a former PhD of mine and my colleague now at Chinese

Academy of Sciences. He did his project and dissertation on Intelligent Transportation Systems under my supervision, but was persuaded by me into doing research in parallel population and parallel human 10 years ago, starting from zero background in an area that was not "cold," but "frozen" at the time. It was really a tough choice (yes, a bad decision in the short term) for a young researcher then, especially considering the fact that he had to work alone since he was the only person I talked into this direction. I have graduated more than 100 PhD students in my career so far, but no one else is willing in working with me in this "dark" or even "crazy" field. I really appreciate Peijun's patience, dedication, and hard work. I am also extremely happy to see our efforts are very productive and, in addition to this book, our works on parallel cognition, digital personality of digital person, as well as CPSS are emerging with encouraging attraction and attention as promising and important new directions for research and development in intelligent science and technology.

Fei-Yue Wang
Institute of Automation
Chinese Academy of Sciences
Beijing, China

Acknowledgments

The work in this book is supported in part by the National Key R&D Program of China under Grant 2018AAA0101502; the Science and Technology Project of SGCC (The State Grid Corporation of China): the fundamental theory of human-in-the-loop hybrid-augmented intelligence for power grid dispatch and control; the National Natural Science Foundation of China under Grant 62076237, Grant T2192933; and in part by the Youth Innovation Promotion Association of Chinese Academy of Sciences under Grant 2021130.

1

From Behavioral Analysis to Prescription

1.1 Social Intelligence

The virtual reality (VR), augmented reality (AR), artificial intelligence (AI), 5G, mobile social media, block-chain, and other emerging technologies have been pushing the development of our society faster than ever. Since almost everyone plays a terminal in the huge network weaved by such techniques, we are driven to elevate our capacity of perception and information processing, to expand our scope of information access, and to speed up our interactions with other remote citizens. Assume that Lily planned to meet her client 10 miles away from her company. She was supposed to travel by subway for six stations and then by walk for about nine minutes for that face-to-face talk. However, due to the spread of the epidemic (like COVID-19) these days, the government has called on people to stay indoors as much as possible. Lily then arranged the talk online, which saved her one hour for commuting. The online video conference also brought her subsequent activities ahead of her original schedule so that she could have an additional social meeting with her friend Betty. This mundane but trivial example shows us that new technologies have drastically accelerated the social process nowadays. Such facilitation of information dissemination, together with its customized content, has greatly influenced the human society and, ultimately, results in a faster and more volatile emergence of social choices. Consequently, how to analyze the formation of social choices has become a central topic in the related research. And that is one of the primary questions of social intelligence: why and how the group intelligent behaviors could emerge. Accordingly, this basic question involves two levels – personal and social, which are sequentially focused in its two-phase history. In an early stage, psychological scholars first concerned with this field, treating social intelligence as a fundamental part of human intelligence. They referred it to the capacity to understand others according to your own similar experience in social contexts. Yet, in recent years, the tide has shifted to the focus on the intelligence of social collective behaviors

Parallel Population and Parallel Human: A Cyber-Physical Social Approach,
First Edition. Peijun Ye and Fei-Yue Wang.
© 2023 The Institute of Electrical and Electronics Engineers, Inc. Published 2023 by John Wiley & Sons, Inc.

as a whole, where the interactions within modern society are seamlessly connected.

Social intelligence was explicitly studied as early as the 1920s when Thorndike [1] postulated his framework of human intelligence by differentiating ideas, objects, and people that someone has to deal with. He did this in such a way that he could distinguish intelligence as academic, mechanical, and social dimensions. Social intelligence is further defined as "the ability to understand and manage men and women, boys and girls, and to act wisely in human relations." This basic idea clearly laid the foundation of the research scope and played as a guideline in later studies. Unlike the distinction between cognitive (understand others) and behavioral (act wisely in human relations) components from Thorndike, Vernon [2] defined social intelligence as "knowledge of social matters and insight into the moods or personality traits of strangers" (cognition) and as the ability to "get along with others and ease in society" (behavior). Different from the two definitions that involve both cognition and behavior, other studies mostly focus on one of them, such as "the ability to get along with others" for Moss and Hunt [3], "judge correctly the feelings, moods, and motivation of individuals" for Wedeck [4], "ability to judge people with respect to feelings, motives, thoughts, intentions, attitudes, and so on" for O'Sullivan et al. [5], and "individuals' fund of knowledge about the social world" for Cantor and Kihlstrom [6]. By summarizing, studies in the early stage tend to investigate one's ability to understand and interpret other people's psychological states and to interact with them for better emotional and mental supports.

Though some dispute might still exist in academic community, psychologists were mainly concerned about five cognitive aspects in traditional studies: social understanding, social memory, social perception, social creativity, and social knowledge. As a central part among all these facets, social understanding specifically refers to one's comprehension during social interaction with others. It requires individuals to interpret given surrounding social stimuli that are represented as the implications for the situation and their underlying features. The point is well illustrated by a sample test requirement: understand correctly what a person wants to express via verbal communications as well as nonverbal hints. Researches mostly concentrate on measurement methods such as George Washington Social Intelligence Test [7], Chapin Social Insight Test [8], the broad test batteries [9], and nonverbal decoding skills [10]. Social memory maintains both episodic and semantic memory contents with one's intention. Its performance is determined by the conscious recall of objectively and explicitly given a variously complex social circumstance. A representative study comes from Kosmitzki and John who discovered the factor for names and faces in laypersons' implicit theories [11]. Social perception, the ability to perceive social information in an agile way, could determine further information processing that is essential for social intelligence behaviors. Wong et al. selected several predesigned tasks to operationalize the measure of social perception [12]. Their experiments also involved interpretational demands that cannot be categorized into pure perceptual abilities. Analogous to the perceptual speed in models of academic intelligence, Carroll further specified the perceptual speed in social perception [13]. Social creativity, also called social flexibility, is the divergent production of individual's behavioral content. It is also reflected as the fluent production of possible interpretations of, or solutions for, a particular social situation. For quantitative evaluation, the participant's performance is not based on the correct answer but on the number of diversity of ideas [14]. This measure is able to successfully distinguish the domain of social cognitive flexibility from academic intellectual abilities. Social knowledge has been operationalized by the knowledge of good etiquette on the one hand, and by the social skills on the other hand. The latter is a concept similar to the taxonomy in AI, where knowledge is recognized as procedural and declarative parts according to its contents [15]. Procedural knowledge refers to the skills or tactics for specific tasks that could not be taught or recalled explicitly, whereas declarative knowledge reflects the world's facts and states and is stored in episodic and semantic memory. Social knowledge, in this sense, refers to the procedural part, which is distinct from social memory.

As alluded, social intelligence is defined at the micro individual level in the early stage. In particular, it investigates what cognitive facets together with their measurements support people's interaction to make themselves more popular. One of the best summaries might be Goleman's famous book which has been selling million copies worldwide [16]. In recent years, however, academic communities turned to analyze the collective social behavior as a whole. In this sense, social intelligence is redefined as the rational decision making that emerged from the whole society [17, 18]. Since the process stems from a bottom-up aggregation of social members' decisions, the macro emergent intelligence is also grounded on one's micro cognitions as well as behaviors. However, as most social members are self-interested and only have access to local information, their "myopic" decisions may not lead to the optimal choice overall. Thus, scholars concentrate on the modeling and analyzing social behavior by capturing individual social dynamics, the interaction between actual social and physical systems, and on the mechanism design that can guide the maximal utility of the society.

The new definition has endowed social intelligence with more comprehensive connotations, expanding such fields as an interdisciplinary research. For modeling and analyzing, studies involve individual behavior [19], social networks [20], or both of them [21]. Combined with the electronic commerce and mobile social media, user online behavior, commodity recommendation, social network evolution, social topic propagation, etc. are the most concerning issues.

For the interaction of social and physical systems, researchers have proposed Cyber-Physical-Social System (CPSS) as a promising direction [22]. Followed by such concept, related work on urban transportation [23], intelligent manufacturing [24], smart cities [25], block-chain [26], etc. have been conducted. We refer the reader to [27] for a detailed review. The mechanism design for an "optimal" social choice is originally from game theory, where each member is modeled as a "greedy" agent that maximizes his own utility. Yet with the increase of computational power and various social sensing technologies, agent-based social computing is introduced for complex problems. For instance, social trust mechanism [28], incentive design [29], and supply chain [30] are main areas of applications.

1.2 Human–Machine Interaction

Not only in social management but also similar things happened in the area of human–machine interaction (HMI). On the one hand, new technologies have endowed rigid machines with higher level of autonomy and intelligence. This undoubtedly releases human labor force from trivial and tedious work. On the other hand, technologies have also fiercely promoted the complexity of systems where several human operators participate to jointly undertake complicated tasks with "smart" machines. Representative cases come from the manipulation of aerospace craft, surveillance of nuclear power plant, control of high-speed railway, driving of intelligent vehicles, etc. In particular scenarios, these real-time human-in-loop systems (can be viewed as a small-scaled CPSS as well) usually involve fast exchange of information or control instructions between machines and operators. For instance, manual rendezvous and docking of spacecraft is still retained as an alternative for emergent situations, though the automated way has become sufficiently mature. Manual rendezvous process, often lasting for several hours, requires operator to constantly monitor the current position of spacecraft and fine tune its attitude for accurate alignment. Such a long period of concentration may probably lead to a cognitive fatigue for human individual and thus a decrease of his perception ability. In addition, cognitive fatigue and cognitive overload may also stem from inappropriate task allocation [31]. They are very likely to result in the inconsistency of HMI that causes human–machine conflicts. Predictably, such incompatible coordination of human–machines will lead to the failure of the task, even with multiple sorts of safety accidents [32, 33].

In essence, the fundamental reason for potential human–machine conflicts is that traditional design paradigm internalizes operators as a part of the system and strictly regulates their operations according to the predetermined operational rules or instructions. This design principle mainly characterizes coarse requirements of human operator and assumes that they can "perfectly" undertake their assigned subtasks. Yet by contrast, different operators have different physiological and psychological foundations such as cognitive load, distraction, and knowledge level. The distinct cognitive status may result in different decision-making styles, or even unsafe operations [34]. To avoid such potential conflicts, researchers have been focusing on many promising directions, one of which is the adaptive or adaptable automation [35]. The main goal is to develop an adaptive mechanism that is capable of dynamic allocation of suitable tasks/functions to both humans and machines so that their incompatibility is reduced to a minimum level. For this goal, it is necessary to establish a reliable model for a human operator to investigate his operational style, preference, or possible errors. As the dynamic allocation usually takes place during fast interaction, the computational model seems appropriate. It can fully exploit the elevation of computing power from contemporary hardware. Moreover, due to the difference and time-variant cognitive status of individuals, the model needs to monitor and "learn" the operator's physiological and mental states (like the fatigue or risk preference) from his constant interactions, and further prescribe his actions to avoid human errors.

Yet how to provide a customized prescription to a specific operator? Solutions may come from the conquering of heterogeneity in complex systems. As alluded before, traditional design paradigm deems participated human operator as a system "component" and regulates him via deterministic rules and instructions. It neglects individual's heterogeneity. Unlike the complex social system where heterogeneity usually refers to individual behavioral patterns, it concentrates more on the diversity in cognition and deliberation of different people (which are complex biological systems). Such diversity is our intrinsic characteristic and, in turn, drives our civilization forward. As indicated by Prof. Marvin Minsky, a father of Artificial Intelligence, it is vast individual diversity that causes the emergence of intelligence [36, 37]. One important source of the cognitive heterogeneity lies in the different mental beliefs of the world. It can ultimately result in the emergent dynamics of human–machine system (from same initial states and operational rules), sometimes chaotic, sometimes oscillating, and sometimes in a nice order. Description, analysis, and even prescription of such cognitive heterogeneity demand distinct computational models or, at least, distinct parameter levels. Classic psychology conforms to the "Experiment—Induction—Modeling—Validation" modeling path. However, this may not be applicable again for highly time-variant systems. On the one hand, subjects in psychological or neural biological experiments usually account for quite a small part of the whole studied group. This often brings sampling bias, leading to the inaccurate cognitive models that do not reflect behavioral differences among individuals. On the other hand, the final cognitive models from traditional approach are "static." They can hardly model the dynamic cognitive process: human's reasoning and decision-making patterns may evolve as his knowledge and skills gradually accumulates (such accumulation usually comes from his learning, imitation, socialization, etc.). Therefore, to analyze and prescribe one's heterogeneous behavior, new paradigm of cognitive modeling is required to simulate various possible actions or responses to investigate potential errors and safety problems, especially in different interactive environments.

1.3 From Behavior Analysis to Prescription

The broader definition of social intelligence and new challenges faced by HMI have linked the promising fine-grained human behavioral research with several related traditional studies, such as game theory, mechanism design, complex networks, and so on. Yet, it does not mean that the specific area is reinventing wheels. Admittedly, game theory and mechanism design – perhaps the most representative methodologies from those studies – have provided us a strict prototype to analyze distributed systems from the perspectives of agent's optimal strategy selection and exogenous rule making. But when it comes to the real system, things could be worse. On the one hand, even a local part of the human group involves multiple participants, and the complicated dynamics among all these components are usually not able to be analytically modeled. For those clearly established game or mechanism models (if it has), they usually include too many decision factors that are sensitive to initial conditions and highly inter-dependent. Consequently, analysis by equilibrium computation for a large-scale population seems impossible in practice. On the other hand, members in a system are inclined to be "bounded rational." That is, given a specific circumstance, they tend to choose an "acceptable" strategy rather than the "optimal" one, without comparing every candidate's response accurately. Such phenomenon may not be strictly explained by the game model.

Limitations from all these aspects have brought the research on social and human–machine hybrid systems to the bottom-up methodology where the group behaviors, as mentioned before, are "grown" from individuals. The virtual individuals are usually called agents that react to their surrounding environment signals according to their predefined rules. Such a multiagent paradigm is adopted by comprehensive studies ranging from computational social science [38], computational economics [39], urban transportation analysis [40, 41], contagious disease propagation [42], to recent anticrime and terrorism [43]. By contrast with other components, agent-based individual/population plays the central part of those computational systems. Clearly, it is the aggregation of each individual's behavior (represented as agent's behavior in simulation) that determines the whole system's dynamics and thus distinguishes different systemic evolutionary paths. Yet unlike the environmental elements (vehicles and traffic infrastructure in urban transportation, for example) where many analytical or numerical models can be exploited, agent behavioral models are much more difficult to establish. This is because our behaviors in real hybrid system are subjective and uncertain. We have not recognized ourselves quite well. Therefore, the indispensable task of how to build "accurate" and reasonable computational models of human behaviors receives constant research from various disciplines.

Traditionally, human behavior is viewed as a result of decision making. And three approaches are used to model the decision-making process. The first type is simple stochastic sampling. In this approach, human decision making is deemed as a selection process among several behavioral candidates. For instance, the migration behavior is modeled as a binary variable and a selection for potential destination cities if the variable gets "True." The selection result is determined by the sampling probability from a particular distribution (such as the uniform distribution) [44]. The second type considers decision making as optimization and uses greedy methods to simulate such process. In practice, agent's selected behavior comes from the maximization of his expected utility function. To model different goals from different groups of individuals, various types of utility functions are introduced in particular scenarios. For instance, in travel mode selection, users usually concentrate on the travel time, travel cost, familiarity of the route, etc. Thus, agents may choose to maximize one of them when they are contradictory with each other. Utility maximization is mainly adopted by the computational economics like disaggregate selection model [45, 46], game theory [47], to name a few. The third type of decision making comes from AI (called the production rule systems), which uses "If…Then…" rules to model individual selections. In such an implementation, agent's external perception signal is mapped as the rule's condition (the "If …" part), while the corresponding behavior is mapped as the rule's conclusion (the "Then …" part). Different rules may have identical conditions but different conclusions, so that same input signals are able to fire multiple rules. To avoid multiple behaviors, conflict resolution mechanisms must be introduced [48–50]. A typical mechanism is to assign each rule with a preference degree. Then all the fired rules are ranked according to their preferences, and the candidate with top preference is adopted as his final action. This operation, in essence, can be also viewed as a utility maximization, leaving that utility function implicitly defined as the preference quantitatively. Generally, simple stochastic sampling and greedy methods are easy to implement. Yet they have not considered human reasoning process. The production rule systems mapped the environment input to a specific action. It treats the reasoning as a "black box." Such myopic one-step behavior is weak to simulate real human activities.

Though computationally simple, the utility function and "black" decision process have brought us some obvious dilemmas for real applications.

First, "black box" model severely depends on the training data, while the reasons behind the final decisions are not understandable. Researchers are not able to dig into social phenomena to analyze how the specific individual as well as group behavior is formed and propagates. It is this vagueness that leads to large deviations between real social systems and simulation results. Thus, computational experiments for management policies grounded on such agent behaviors seem not convincing. Second, modern complexity and computational social science not only require the traceable analysis of existing dynamics but also expect further "soft" management for the human society by prescribing individual behaviors, so as to ease social conflicts from various groups. In the environment of free market, only by clearly understanding people's thinking and decision making can we fundamentally guide their expectations and ultimately exert influence on their behavior patterns.

Both of the above dilemmas have motivated us to conduct a constant research that is contained in this book. More essentially, the granularity of current main behavioral models does not support the agent's endogenous deliberation. We need models at a finer level. To achieve such a goal, however, we are facing great challenges. One difficulty comes from the high heterogeneity of actual social system that extremely stochastic individual behaviors are not represented by a universal model. It makes us develop specific models for each type of social members. Such modeling approach is not operational since there are numerous behavioral patterns in reality. A second difficulty lies in the huge search space when each type of agent behavioral models available. As the number of model variables increases, the combinations of different decision rules form a huge reasoning space. Searching for a "plausible" reasoning path in such a huge space is computationally non-deterministic polynomial hard (NP hard). And effective strategies need to be developed to overcome the challenges.

Situations are not that bad. Recent breakthroughs in AI have ignited our inspiration. For the high heterogeneity of different social individuals, a potential solution to build corresponding virtual agents might be using machine learning techniques. Specifically, a few general behavioral templates can be constructed at first, and interactive learning can be introduced based on a particular template to imitate the detailed behavioral dynamics of its related actual user host [51, 52]. The long-term interaction and imitation will adaptively fine-tune the general agent model, capturing one's specific decision patterns automatically. By that way, building thousands of heterogeneous agent models can be avoided. For the huge reasoning space, Alpha Go from DeepMind may provide a feasible direction [53, 54]. Given the environment and agent internal states, the system's evolutionary paths are self-computed via cooperation and games among agent groups. The evolution will autonomously explore certain decision sequences with high probabilities in the reasoning space. And reinforcement learning could also be exploited to iteratively update the probability of each action. By doing this, we are able to prune the "impossible" system evolutionary paths so that the NP-hard computation could be conducted within an acceptable time.

1.4 Parallel Population and Parallel Human

Breakthroughs from AI have directly led to the work in this book, that is, the AI-based parallel population/parallel people for behavioral prescription. The overall structure of the system is a tiered (or nested) bi-closed loop, as illustrated in Figure 1.1. We will explain its details in two levels. For social management, the outer two loops establish a parallel population system which consists of the real population and its virtual counterpart – artificial population (represented as real and artificial "Environment, Population System, System Metrics," respectively). Including virtual individuals as well as their social relationships (like family, friends, schoolmates, and colleagues), artificial population plays the virtual society that is a digital mapping of the reality. As two autonomous systems, artificial and real populations keep running independently for self-evolution. At the same time, they have also formed an interactive setting to prescribe real

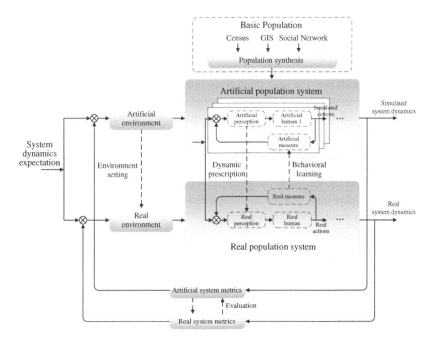

Figure 1.1 Structure of parallel population and parallel human systems.

system's evolutionary trajectories in a macro scope. Such prescription relies on the comparative evaluation between the two systems' running dynamics and on the active environment setting from artificial to real ones. The building of artificial population starts from a basic population synthesis, which provides initial individual states with social network patterns. For a clear organization, this part is separately drawn in the figure and will be discussed later.

As system dynamics are aggregations of multiple individuals, it is natural to decompose the behavioral prescription into a micro level where a group of artificial individuals are developed for a particular real individual. The real individual with its virtual counterparts constitutes a many-to-one parallel human system (the inner two closed loops in Figure 1.1), with every artificial individual standing for a probable representative evolutionary state. Similar to a parallel population, local control for each real–artificial human runs independently in an autonomous way. And their constant interaction will dynamically describe, predict, and prescribe one's specific actions based on sufficient computational experiments by the artificial groups. In particular, the interaction involves behavioral learning from real to artificial individual, to adaptively calibrate the digital human model, and dynamic prescription from artificial to real individual, to adjust the actual perception signal as expected. In the implementation, AI-based agent technology is a suitable path for the modeling and computation of parallel human.

Although the parallel population shows a nested structure, it should be noted that the outer two peer closed loops can be tailored and simplified when it is not applied for the smart management of complex social systems. This is determined by the specific task that the system aims to complete. For example, in a scenario of spacecraft manipulation concerning multiple human operators, there are no complicated social network patterns as real social systems. Artificial population system, at this time, degenerates into only a few agents. When such a process involves only one operator, artificial population system vanishes, leaving only one parallel human loop. Note that the machines are implicitly contained in the control loops and not illustrated in the figure. It is because the modeling for humans is far more complex than that for machines, and our focus lies much more on the human analysis as well.

In contrast with traditional analytical models, individual models for a specific person can sufficiently investigate various possible evolutionary states as well as his responded actions. This is proved to be effective for individual heterogeneity in the science of complexity. More deeply, such individual heterogeneity derives from differences in personal cognition, which we call it mental heterogeneity. Therefore, the ultimate goal of parallel human (with its aggregation – parallel people) is to computationally model and simulate mental heterogeneity. We will investigate this problem from AI and cognitive computing later in this book.

1.5   Central Themes and Structure of this Book

As alluded before, the central theme of this book concentrates on how to computationally model a human individual's deliberation and thinking, so that his behavior is prescribed to achieve the system's expected control objective. Our discussion will address the basic theory and methodology for modeling as well as some implementation techniques. Potential acceleration technologies will be also exploited in our prototype system due to the high computational cost. Some application cases from different fields are also contained to show preliminary validations. The overall organization of the book is shown in Figure 1.2. Though Chapter 8 may be concerned about with implementations, we generally follow the technological path rather than system components to introduce our work. Our discussion begins with the synthesis of basic population (as shown in

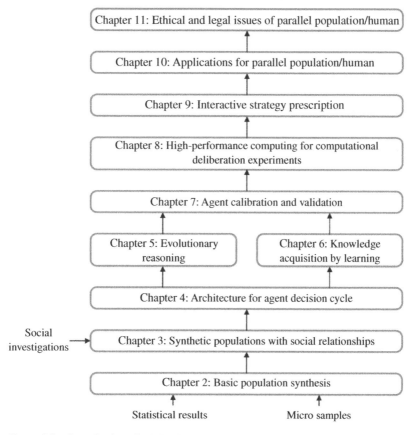

Figure 1.2   Organization of this book.

the upper dashed box in Figure 1.1), which includes Chapters 2 and 3. These two progressive chapters elucidate how to generate a "static" set of virtual individuals with their personal attributes and mutual social relationships according to statistical results and optional micro samples. Chapter 2 only considers the individuals, while Chapter 3 further addresses social organizations. The achieved basic population plays a start state in the subsequent artificial population evolution. Next, we move to the micro level, concentrating on the individual cognition and behavioral modeling. This part includes four chapters, Chapters 4–7. Generally, the central problem for such an issue lies in three intercoupling aspects: the representation of human knowledge, the acquisition of an individual's knowledge in a static/dynamic way, and the exploitation of one's knowledge to elicit a specific decision/action. These three aspects are also fundamental questions in human-like intelligence. Chapter 4 talks about the cognitive architecture for agent decision cycle. It provides a unified container or framework that organizes knowledge segments and data flow in decision process. On the basis of such framework, Chapters 5 and 6 address the learning and reasoning, which provide rudimentary solutions for knowledge acquisition and application. To model the mental heterogeneity in a time-variant human-in-loop environment specifically, we put our emphasis on adaptive learning through detected individual actions. The decision making based on reasoning via one's knowledge base adopts an evolutionary paradigm rather than classic reasoning in AI research. This is in line with the philosophy from science of complexity and cognition where the deliberation results from a bottom-up emergence. We do not give a separate chapter to the knowledge representation because existing relevant techniques are directly exploited. A brief introduction is included in Chapter 5. Interested readers can easily find corresponding details in other related literature. The last but not least problem for artificial human modeling is the parameter calibration and validation, which is essential for the reliable use of models. For a large-scale social system in particular, model calibration seems more important, since compared with a few agents, parameter values in such systems are difficult to be fully measured in a wide range. This sampling bias may cause the achieved parameters not representative enough and thus impacts the accuracy of the model. Several calibration methods will be presented in Chapter 7, trying to avoid such a dilemma. After establishing learning and reasoning mechanisms for artificial human, we next turn to their implementation. In Chapters 8 and 9, we consider acceleration approaches for a large-scale knowledge base that is computationally expensive. It is almost inevitable in practice since one's mental repository is usually complicated. Distributed reasoning and active strategy prescription via cloud computing are elucidated. Some theoretical foundations on the completeness and optimality in such a reasoning mode are also analyzed in these two chapters. The book concludes with some applications in Chapter 10, ranging from computational demography to urban transportation management and control, to evacuation in emergency. Some ethical and legal issues of parallel population/human are further discussed in Chapter 11.

References

1 E. L. Thorndike. Intelligence and Its Uses. Harper's Magazine, 1920, 740: 227–235.

2 P. E. Vernon. Some Characteristics of The Good Judge of Personality. Journal of Social Psychology, 1933, 4(1): 42–57.

3 F. A. Moss and T. Hunt. Are You Socially Intelligent? Scientific American, 1927, 137(2): 108–110.

4 I. Wedeck. The Relationship Between Personality and Psychological Ability. British Journal of Psychology, 1947, 37(3): 133–151.

5 M. O'Sullivan, J. P. Guilford and R. de Mille. The Measurement of Social Intelligence. Reports from the Psychological Laboratory, University of Southern California, 1965.

6 N. Cantor and F. Kihlstrom. Personality and Social Intelligence. Prentice-Hall, Englewood Cliffs, NJ, USA, 1987.

7 F. A. Moss, T. Hunt, K. T. Omwake, et al. Manual for the George Washington University Series Social Intelligence Test. The Center for Psychological Service, Washington, DC, 1955.

8 F. S. Chapin. The Social Insight Test. Consulting Psychologists Press, Palo Alto, CA, 1967.

9 M. O'Sullivan and J. P. Guilford. Four Factor Tests of Social Intelligence: Manual of Instructions and Interpretations. Sheridan Psychological Services, Orange, CA, 1976.

10 M. L. Barnes and R. J. Sternberg. Social Intelligence and Decoding of Nonverbal Cues. Intelligence, 1989, 13: 263–287.

11 C. Kosmitzki and O. P. John. The Implicit Use of Explicit Conceptions of Social Intelligence. Personality and Individual Differences, 1993, 5: 11–23.

12 C.-M. T. Wong, J. D. Day, S. E. Maxwell, et al. A Multitrait-Multimethod Study of Academic and Social Intelligence in College Students. Journal of Educational Psychology, 1995, 87(1): 117–133.

13 J. B. Carroll. Human Cognitive Abilities: A Survey of Factor-Analytic Studies. Cambridge University Press, New York, 1993.

14 J.-E. Lee, J. D. Duy, N. M. Meara, et al. Discrimination of Social Knowledge and Its Flexible Application from Creativity: A Multitrait-Multimethod Approach. Personality and Individual Differences, 2002, 32: 913–928.

15 I. F. Kihlstrom and N. Cantor. Social Intelligence. In R. J. Sternberg (Ed.), Handbook of Intelligence. Cambridge University Press, New York, 2000: 359–379.

16 D. Goleman. Social Intelligence: The New Science of Human Relationships. Bantam, 2006.

17 R. Dai, Science of Social Intelligence. Shanghai Jiao Tong University Press, 2006.

18 F.-Y. Wang, K. M. Carley, D. Zeng, et al. Social Computing: From Social Informatics to Social Intelligence. IEEE Intelligent Systems, 2007, 22(2): 79–83.

19 S. Zhang, X. Liang, X. Zhang, et al. On Identification of Organizational and Individual Users Based on Social Content Measurements. IEEE Transactions on Computational Social Systems, 2018, 5(4): 961–972.

20 T. Gao, F. Li, Y. Chen, et al. Local Differential Privately Anonymizing Online Social Networks Under HRG-Based Model. IEEE Transactions on Computational Social Systems, 2018, 5(4): 1009–1020.

21 D. Perna, R. Interdonato and A. Tagarelli. Identifying Users with Alternate Behaviors of Lurking and Active Participation in Multilayer Social Networks. IEEE Transactions on Computational Social Systems, 2018, 5(1): 46–63.

22 F.-Y. Wang. The Emergence of Intelligent Enterprises: From CPS to CPSS. IEEE Intelligent Systems, 2010, 25(4): 85–88.

23 L. Chen, X. M. Hu, W. Tian, et al. Parallel Planning: A New Motion Planning Framework for Autonomous Driving. IEEE/CAA Journal of Automatica Sinica, 2019, 6(1): 236–246.

24 R. Lei and R. Ming-Lun. The Organizational Model Smart Manufacturing Resources Based on Social Information Physics System. China Science Technology Forum, 2017, 2017(7): 118–125.

25 C. G. Cassandras. Intelligent City in the Perspective of Information Physical-Social Systems. Engineering, 2016, 2(2): 20–26.

26 F.-Y. Wang, Y. Yuan, J. Zhang, et al. Blockchainized Internet of Minds: A New Opportunity for Cyber-Physical-Social Systems. IEEE Transactions on Computational Social Systems, 2018, 5(4): 897–906.

27 J. J. Zhang, F.-Y. Wang, X. Wang, et al. Cyber-Physical-Social Systems: The State of the Art and Perspectives. IEEE Transactions on Computational Social Systems, 2018, 5(3): 829–840.

28 N. Sardana, R. Cohen, J. Zhang, et al. A Bayesian Multiagent Trust Model for Social Networks. IEEE Transactions on Computational Social Systems, 2018, 5(4): 995–1008.

29 Z. Hu and J. Zhang. Toward General Robustness Evaluation of Incentive Mechanism against Bounded Rationality. IEEE Transactions on Computational Social Systems, 2018, 5(3): 698–712.

30 H. K. Nguyen, R. Chiong, M. Chica, et al. Contract Farming in the Mekong Delta's Rice Supply Chain: Insights from an Agent-Based Modeling Study. Journal of Artificial Societies and Social Simulation, 2019, 22(3): 1.

31 A. Haarmann, W. Boucsein and F. Schaefer. Combining Electrodermal Responses and Cardiovascular Measures for Probing Adaptive Automation during Simulated Flight. Applied Ergonomics, 2009, 40(6): 1026–1040.

32 P. Johnston and R. Harris. The Boeing 737 MAX Saga: Lessons for Software Organizations. Safety and Automation, 2019, 21(3): 4–12.

33 W. Bi, Q. Feng, K. Qi, et al. Failure Evolution Analysis for Complex Human–Machine System: A Case for Nuclear Power System. The 2nd International Conference on Reliability Systems Engineering (ICRSE), Beijing, China, 2017: 1–8.

34 M. L. Walters, K. Dautenhahn and R. te Boekhorst. The Influence of Subjects' Personality Traits on Personal Spatial Zones in A Human–Robot Interaction Experiment. IEEE International Workshop on Robot and Human Interactive Communication, Nashville, TN, USA, Aug. 13–15, 2005.

35 S. G. Lakhmani, J. L. Wright and J. Y. C. Chen. Transparent Interaction and Human–Robot Collaboration For Military Operations. In R. Pak, E. J. de Visser and E. Rovira (Eds.), Living with Robots. Academic Press, 2020: 1–19.

36 M. Minsky. The Society of Mind. Simon & Schuster, 1987: 308.

37 F.-Y. Wang. A True Scientific Thinker: Professor Marvin Minsky, the Father of AI. http://blog.sciencenet.cn/blog-2374-962496.html.

38 D. Lazer, A. Pentland, L. Adamic, et al. Computational Social Science. Science, 2009, 323(5915): 721–723.

39 M. Gallegati, A. Palestrini and A, Russo. Introduction to Agent-Based Economics. Amsterdam, Elsevier, 2017.

40 P. Ye and D. Wen. A Study of Destination Selection Model Based on Link Flows. IEEE Transactions on Intelligent Transportation Systems, 2013, 14(1):428–437.

41 F.-Y. Wang. Parallel Control and Management for Intelligent Transportation Systems: Concepts, Architectures, and Applications. IEEE Transactions on Intelligent Transportation Systems, 2010, 11(3): 630–638.

42 R. A. Nianogo and O. A. Arah. Agent-Based Modeling of Non-Communicable Diseases: A Systematic Review. American Journal of Public Health, 2015, 105: e20–e31.

43 European Union. The PROTON project. 2016. https://www.projectproton.eu.

44 L. Riccetti, A. Russo and M. Gallegati. An Agent Based Decentralized Matching Macroeconomic Model. Journal of Economic Interaction and Coordination, 2015, 10: 305–332.

45 D. McFadden. Conditional Logit Analysis of Qualitative Choice Behavior. In Z. Paul (ed), Frontiers in Econometrics. Academic Press, New York, 1974: 105–142.

46 Z. Sandor and M. Wedel. Heterogeneous Conjoint Choice Designs. Journal of Marketing Research, 2005, 42(2): 210–218.

47 Y. Shoham and K. Leyton-Brown. Multiagent Systems: Algorithmic, Game-Theoretic, and Logical Foundations. Cambridge University Press, 2008.

48 M. Schmotzer. Reactive Agents Based Autonomous Transport System. In: P. Sincak, J. Vascak, V. Kvasnicka, et al (eds), The State of the Art in Computational Intelligence—Advances in Soft Computing, Physica. Heidelberg, 2000, 5: 390–391.

49 K. Rabuzin. Agent By Example—A Novel Approach to Implement Reactive Agents in Active Databases. International Journal of Advancements in Computing Technology, 2013, 5(10): 227.

50 J. E. Laird. The SOAR Cognitive Architecture. MIT Press, Cambridge, MA, USA, 2012.

51 Z. Wang, J. S. Merel, S. E. Reed, et al. Robust Imitation of Diverse Behaviors. Advances in Neural Information Processing Systems, 2017, 30: 5320–5329.

52 J. A. Bagnell. An Invitation to Imitation. Technical Report, CMU-RI-TR-15-08, Robotics Institute, Carnegie Mellon University, March, 2015.

53 D. Silver, A. Huang, C. J. Maddison, et al. Mastering the Game of Go with Deep Neural Networks and Tree Search. Nature, 2016, 529: 484–489.

54 J. Schrittwieser, I. Antonoglou, T. Hubert, et al. Mastering Atari, Go, Chess and Shogi by Planning with a Learned Model. Nature, 2020, 588: 604–609.

2

Basic Population Synthesis

Basically, two categories of typical scenarios are most concerned by the multi-agent social computing. One is about the short-term systemic dynamics, which focuses on how the individual and group decisions arise and through what measures can we guide the people's behavioral modes. Agent in this scenario usually has to make decisions based on his own knowledge in a limited time. Thus, he may not be always right or optimal. Such near-optimal actions led by temporal and other constraints can be also viewed as a form of "bounded rationality." The other typical scenario addresses the long-term systemic evolution, which seeks to investigate the potential equilibrium, if it has, among the interaction of multiple agents. In this situation, each agent, standing for an individual or a certain group, plays much more rationally, since he usually has enough time to deliberate and decide. Thus, he mostly chooses his optimal strategy in each decision cycle.

The two typical scenarios also lead to different requirements of the agent-based modeling. For the analysis of short-term dynamics, detailed decision knowledge needs to be established. It should consider as many probable responses to various environment inputs as possible, since humans are very inclined to increase the uncertainty of behaviors with temporal constraints. By contrast, the long-term systemic evolution could incorporate fewer action candidates, as rationality, to some extent, means an optimal or suboptimal process. To endow the evolutionary results with realistic sense, this scenario also needs a virtual basic population that plays as an initial start of the systemic evolution. In Chapter 2 and Chapter 3, we will focus on the reliable population synthesis. The synthesis starts with a generation of baseline population where each agent independently stands for an individual in reality and contains a set of internal attributes determined by particular algorithms. Then, multiple social relationships are added in Chapter 3 to model different social networks quantitatively. The final synthetic population is expected to be one of the most plausible start points of the subsequent evolutions.

Parallel Population and Parallel Human: A Cyber-Physical Social Approach,
First Edition. Peijun Ye and Fei-Yue Wang.
© 2023 The Institute of Electrical and Electronics Engineers, Inc. Published 2023 by John Wiley & Sons, Inc.

2.1 Problem Statement and Data Sources

The primary objective of population synthesis can be summarized as generating an individual dataset in full compliance with the statistical characteristics of various input data. In other words, the synthetic process must generate a population list, or sometimes with its corresponding instances, which conformed to the aggregate indicators. This sort of population is deemed among the "best possible" estimates of the actual one. It retains particular demographic properties with actual personal details ignored, thus can be treated as an alternative to micro data acquisition and social phenomenon demonstration and prediction. Generally, the individual record is depicted by several personal characteristics according to a specific profile. Different application scenarios may concentrate on different attributes. For example, in computational demographics, it is very common to investigate *Gender*, *Age*, *Dwelling Place*, *Type of Residence*, and so on. Whereas in traffic micro-simulation, the attribute *Has Driving License* is usually considered. The values of the studied attributes can be discrete, enumerate, binary, and even continuous. For convenience, continuous values are often split into several intervals in order to reduce the computational complexity.

Input data sources of population synthesis include census, traffic survey, labor force survey, tax record from revenue agency, real estate cadaster, etc., though some of them are rarely used in practice. Household registration information in China also provides a supplement of micro individual data. Among all of the data sources, census has attracted most of the concentrations since it reflects the status of target population directly. In most countries, census is conducted periodically, ranging from every 5 years (e.g. Canada) to every 10 years (e.g. United States, Switzerland, China, etc.). The ultimate data officially published by Bureau of Statistics and other corresponding ministries are generally in two forms: sample of individuals and cross-classification table. As mentioned before, the disaggregate sample is usually used as a seed directly, whereas the cross-classification tables are the basis of conditionals and marginals. The Public Use Microdata Samples (PUMS) in the United States and the Sample of Anonymized Records (SAR) in the UK are representatives of disaggregate samples, while typical aggregate tables include the Summary Files (SF), Standard Type File 3A (STF-3A) in the United States and the Small Area Statistics (SAS) in the UK. Here, we mainly focus on the population data available in China.

2.1.1 Cross-Classification Table

Like many other countries, China conducts its national census for entire population every 10 years. Between two adjacent censuses, a 1% population sample survey is conducted. In this paper, we only consider the national census. The most recent two censuses are in 2000 and 2010. The whole target populations are investigated through questionnaire under guidance of census takers. Two kinds of questionnaires are applied in the census. One is called the Short Table which involves several basic characteristics, whereas the other is the Long Table which not only contains all the content of the short one but also includes additional detailed features like migration pattern, educational level, economic status, marriage and family, procreation, housing condition, etc. The Long Table is filled by particular individuals stochastically selected in advance (about 9.5% according to the official sampling rule), while the rest of people are recorded by the Short Table. Results from these two kinds of questionnaires are the original individual records. They are usually confidential and will be further summarized over a few variables to get marginal frequencies. For instance, if the original records concern about (*Gender* × *Residential Province* × *Age* × *Educational Level*), the processed marginal frequencies may contain partial attributes like (*Gender* × *Residential Province*) or *Educational Level*. This operation is referred as the data aggregation. Some but all marginal frequencies are published on the website of National Bureau of Statistics (NBS) in the form of cross-classification tables [1, 2]. Tables 2.1–2.3 give three examples of them. This sort of data for public use is the principal information for population synthesis. Though these tables have not

Table 2.1 (*Gen.* × *Res. Prov.* × *Res. Type*) cross-classification table (city, t0101a).

Province	Beijing	Tianjin	Hebei	Shanxi_1	···
Male	4,975,203	2,710,200	5,815,353	3,692,451	···
Female	4,521,485	2,603,502	5,682,752	3,510,536	···

Table 2.2 (*Gen.* × *Res. Prov.* × *Res. Type*) cross-classification table (town, t0101b).

Province	Beijing	Tianjin	Hebei	Shanxi_1	···
Male	529,781	905,488	3,103,386	2,193,311	···
Female	495,995	870,622	2,958,606	2,035,697	···

Table 2.3 (*Gen.* × *Res. Prov.* × *Res. Type*) cross-classification table (rural, t0101c).

Province	Beijing	Tianjin	Hebei	Shanxi_1	···
Male	1,569,534	1,400,687	25,017,594	10,914,996	···
Female	1,477,196	1,358,232	24,106,728	10,124,251	···

revealed the joint distribution concerning the whole attributes, they present its partial views in various dimensions.

In this chapter, we use the data of year 2000 to generate a synthetic population. The overall cross-classification tables concern about a number of characteristics including population scale, gender, residential province, ethnic group, age, educational level, household scale and structure, dead people information, migration, housing condition, etc. Several instructions should be put forward about these tables. According to the NBS post-enumeration survey for quality check, about 1.81% population are omitted in the survey.[1] It may slightly change the joint distribution. In addition, the census result does not contain information of military forces and organizations which are around 2,500,000 people. These two groups of people are also ignored in our synthetic process. In other words, our target population is those investigated in the overall dataset. Since the objective of our study is to generate nationwide synthetic population, and the overall cross-classification tables cannot provide detailed attributes as the sample and Long Table, we concentrate on the basic individual attributes shown in Table 2.4 (Where city refers to the municipality with the population density over $1500/km^2$. Town, outside the city, refers to the borough where the town government locates in. Rural refers to the area other than city and town.). The corresponding partial distributions given by cross-classification tables are listed in Table 2.5. Note that the Table Codes are the ones used by the NBS.

Table 2.4 Individual attributes considered for nationwide population.

Attributes	Values	Number of values
Gender	Male, female	2
Age Interval	0–4, …, ≥100	21
Ethnic Group	Han, MengGu, …	58
Residential Province	Beijing, Tianjin, …	31
Educational Level	Infant, not educated, …	10
Residence Type	City, town, rural	3
Registration Province	Beijing, Tianjin, …	32
Registration Type	Agricultural, non-agricultural	2

---

1 In order to evaluate the quality of the fifth census, the NBS conducted a post-enumeration survey for quality check. Six hundred and two nationwide census blocks were stochastically determined by the Stratified Sampling and were investigated two weeks after the census. Results of these blocks from the survey and the census were compared to calculate deviations. The missing rate for the total recorded population is estimated from the weighted summary of the deviations.

Table 2.5 Partial distributions used in population synthesis.

No.	Distributions	Table codes
1	*Gen. × Res. Type × Res.Prov.*	t0101a–t0101c
2	*Gen. × Res. Prov. × Reg. Type*	t0102, t0105
3	*Gen. × Res. Type × Res.Prov. × Eth. Group*	t0106a–t0106c
4	*Gen. × Res. Type × Res. Prov. × Age Inter.*	t0107a–t0107c
5	*Gen. × Res. Prov. × Edu.Lv*	t0108
6	*Gen. × Res. Type × Age Inter. × Eth. Group*	t0201a–t0201c
7	*Gen. × Edu.Lv × Eth. Group*	t0202
8	*Gen. × Res.Type × AgeInter. × Edu.Lv.*	t0401a–t0401c
9	*Res.Type × Res.Prov. × Reg.Prov.*	t0701(2)a–t0701(2)c

In contrast with Short Table, the Long Table includes additional details as the sample shown, which reflects the structure and composition of target population much more concretely. People surveyed through this type of table are stochastically determined by NBS and each provincial government. Their scale accounts for 9.5% of total population. Statistical results, in the form of cross-classification tables, can be also accessed from the official website. Since we do not have any other data in this study, these tabulations are treated as our criterion for the evaluation of each synthetic population.

2.1.2 Sample

While total statistical characteristics can be easily acquired, original results directly from questionnaire are strictly protected by the government. They are never accessible for the general public due to national security concerns and individual privacy protection. The whole input data available for the researchers is a set of statistical indicators extracted from original data published by the Bureau of Statistics and a small proportion of detailed sample with some attributes concerning personal privacy omitted. In the worst case, the small proportion of sample is even deficient. Fortunately, we have collected a small proportion of sample of the year 2000. The dataset includes 1,180,111 records, which accounts for 0.095% of the total population. These records all come from Long Table, each of which gives detail information of a particular individual. The attributes provided by the sample can be categorized into two types. One is the basic household information such as household type (family or corporate), number of members, housing area, number of rooms, etc., while the other is personal

Table 2.6 Individual attributes of sample and Long Table.

For each person		For citizens ≥6-year-old	For citizens ≥15-year-old	For female ≥15-year-old
Attr.	Attr.	Attr.	Attr.	Attr.
Name	Reg. type	Literate or not	Employ status	Num. of children
Relation to householder	Place of birth	Edu. lv	Industry	Num. of survival children
Gen.	Date of dwelling in current place	Academic completion	Occupation	Gen. of children
Age	Ancestral native place		Marital status	
Eth. group	Ancestral native place type			
Reg. condition	Reason of migration			

detailed attributes that involve employment status, occupation, marital status, number of children, etc. Individual attributes contained in sample and Long Table are illustrated in Table 2.6. Original questionnaire templates can be referred to the website [3].

2.1.3 Long Table

The indicator adopted in our evaluation is the modified overall Relative Sum of Squared Z-scores (RSSZm). That is, for a given similar scaled subset of population being compared to the corresponding tabulations of Long Table, it is

$$RSSZm = \sum_k \sum_i F_{ki}(O_{ki} - E_{ki})^2$$

where

$$F_{ki} = \begin{cases} \left(C_k O_{ki} \left(1 - \frac{O_{ki}}{N_k} \right) \right)^{-1}, & \text{if } O_{ki} \neq 0 \\ \frac{1}{C_k}, & \text{if } O_{ki} = 0 \end{cases}$$

O_{ki} is the generated count for the ith cell of the kth tabulation;
E_{ki} is the given (known) count for the ith cell of the kth tabulation;
N_k is the total count of tabulation k;
C_k is the 5% χ^2 critical value for tabulation k (where degrees of freedom are treated as $n-1$ for a table with n cells).

Details of the attributes in the Long Table are identical to the sample. It should be pointed out that the statistical results from Long Table have not provided us the information about Registration Province and Registration Type. Thus, our evaluation is only established on the rest of six characteristics.

2.2 Sample-Based Method

As explained in Section 2.1, the available data for basic population synthesis are often a set of statistical indicators extracted from original data published by the Bureau of Statistics and a small proportion of detailed sample with some attributes concerning personal privacy omitted (in some worse cases, the detailed sample is even deficient). These two types of input information are called aggregate and disaggregate data. According to the essential input data type, major methods are categorized into two classes – sample-based methods and sample-free methods, which will be discussed in Sections 2.2 and 2.3.

2.2.1 Iterative Proportional Fitting Synthetic Reconstruction

The Synthetic Reconstruction method, published by Wilson in 1976, is the first population synthesis approach. It is most important and extensively used. The central task of this method is composed of two steps: estimating the joint distribution of the target population and realizing the individual dataset. Thus, the synthetic process can be separated as two phases called "Fitting" and "Allocation," respectively. Usually, the iterative proportional fitting (IPF) procedure is adopted to calculate the sample distribution in the former stage. Thus, this method is also expressed as iterative proportional fitting synthetic reconstruction (IPFSR). In the "Fitting" phase, the IPF procedure requires both a set of disaggregate sample as the seed and the statistical indicators as the marginals associated with all the attributes we are interested in. Obviously, IPFSR is a sample-based method. The basic hypothesis that lies behind this approach is straightforward and clear. It deems that the joint distribution from the sample is consistent with the true correlation structure of the target population. Therefore, we only need to fit the frequency under each attribute combination into the marginal constraints. Operationally, the joint distribution is represented as a contingency table (CT) when the attribute number is relatively small. But in a higher-dimensional case, CT is not able to describe the joint distribution intuitively. It is more convenient to mathematically denote the distribution as $f\{X_1 = x_1, X_2 = x_2, \ldots, X_n = x_n\}$, where n is the number of attributes we are interested in and x_i are the values of the ith attribute. The initial frequencies are the individual counts from the input sample under each attribute combination. During the kth iteration, the frequency under each attribute combination is updated according to

$$f^{(1)}(k) = \frac{f\{X_1 = x_1, \ldots, X_n = x_n\}(k-1)}{\sum_{x_1} f\{X_1 = x_1, \ldots, X_n = x_n\}(k-1)} \cdot N_1$$

$$f^{(2)}(k) = \frac{f^{(1)}\{X_1 = x_1, \ldots, X_n = x_n\}(k)}{\sum_{x_2} f^{(1)}\{X_1 = x_1, \ldots, X_n = x_n\}(k)} \cdot N_2$$

$$\vdots$$

$$f^{(n)}(k) = \frac{f^{(n-1)}\{X_1 = x_1, \ldots, X_n = x_n\}(k)}{\sum_{x_n} f^{(n-1)}\{X_1 = x_1, \ldots, X_n = x_n\}(k)} \cdot N_n$$

$$f\{X_1 = x_1, \ldots, X_n = x_n\}(k) = f^{(n)}(k)$$

where N_i is the marginal of the ith attribute. The convergence of two-dimensional IPF procedure is proved by Pukelsheim and Simeone in 2009 [4]. A necessary condition is the marginal sum should be all equal. And we will give a proof of multivariate case in Section 2.3. Among all the tables that satisfy the marginal constraints, the result that IPF yields is the one that most resembles the initial sample [5, 6]. Once the joint distribution of the target population estimated, the "Allocation" phase seems much easier. The synthetic population can be simply drawn via Monte Carlo method. The pseudocode of IPFSR is given in Algorithm 2.1.

2.2.2 Combinatorial Optimization

Combinatorial optimization (CO) is another sample-based method of population synthesis. It is proposed by Williamson et al. in 1998. When using this method to generate population, it is essential to divide the studied area into several mutually exclusive regions similar to the census block or traffic analysis zone. The input data includes a survey sample of the studied area consisting of all the attributes (called the overall sample) and a statistical investigation table of each region that contains part of the attributes (called the distribution table). For instance, if the population attributes include gender, age, and height, then the overall sample must entail the three attribute values and the distribution table should contain at least one of them.

The CO synthetic process is iterative: starting from an initial set of population chosen randomly from the overall sample, an assessment is conducted after randomly replacing one of the selected individuals with a fresh one from the overall sample. If the replacement improves the fitness, the two individuals are swapped. Otherwise the swap is not made. This process is repeated many times, with the aim

Algorithm 2.1 Algorithm of Iterative Proportional Fitting Synthetic Reconstruction

Require:
    Each marginal frequency $M(x_i = v_i)$, where $v_i \in V_i$. Disaggregate sample D. Synthetic population scale *PopSize*.

Ensure:
    Synthetic population dataset.

1: Calculate initial frequencies under each variable combination:
    $f^{(0)}(x_1 = v_1, \ldots, x_n = v_n), \forall v_1 \in V_1, \ldots, \forall v_n \in V_n$

2: **repeat**

3:     **for** $i = 1$ to n **do**

4:         Update x_i: $f^{(i)}(x_1 = v_1, \ldots, x_n = v_n) = \dfrac{f^{(i-1)}(x_1 = v_1, \ldots, x_n = v_n)}{\sum_{\forall v_i \in V_i} f^{(i-1)}(x_1 = v_1, \ldots, x_n = v_n)} \cdot M(x_i = v_i)$

5:     **end for**

6:     Let $f^{(0)}(x_1 = v_1, \ldots, x_n = v_n) = f^{(n)}(x_1 = v_1, \ldots, x_n = v_n)$

7: **until** Convergence

8: **for** $i = 1$ to *PopSize* **do**

9:     Use Monte Carlo simulation to draw an individual record, *IndRec*, according to the obtained distribution.

10:     Save *IndRec* to the dataset.

11: **end for**

12: **return** dataset

of gradually improving the fitness between the regional synthetic populations and the statistical investigation table. Given the search space, the final combination arrived is normally the best achievable in a given time, rather than the guaranteed optimal solution. Clearly, the basic idea behind CO is somewhat similar to the genetic algorithm without crossover and mutation. Some important contributions about this method come from National Center for Social and Economic Modeling (NATSEM) in the University of Canberra [7–11].

The CO method has several derivatives and is more suitable for generating a small range of synthetic population via a larger amount of sample [12–14]. It is because when the scale of target population is large, fitness variation during swap will be overwhelmed due to the computational truncation. To avoid this, target population is usually divided into several smaller parts with each generated in turn. In addition, as a sample-based method, CO is also dependent on the input sample like IPFSR. The omitted groups in the sample will not be included in the final received population as well. The pseudocode of CO is given by Algorithm 2.2.

Algorithm 2.2 Algorithm of Combinatorial Optimization

Require:

Each marginal frequency $M(x_i = v_i)$, where $x_i \in V_i$. Disaggregate sample D. Synthetic population scale *PopSize*.

Ensure:

Synthetic population dataset.

1: Divide the studied area into several regions (in this paper, we set 100 parts). The region number is denoted as *RegNum*.
2: **for** each region **do**
3:    Extract a random sample from D with the scale of *PopSize/RegNum* as the initial population *Pop*
4:    Calculate the fitness F of the initial dataset *Pop*
5:    Swap two random individuals from *Pop* and D, respectively
6:    **if** $F(beforeswap) > F(afterswap)$ **then**
7:      let $Pop = Pop(beforeswap)$
8:    **else**
9:      let $Pop = Pop(afterswap)$
10:    **end if**
11:    **if** F reaches the stop condition **then**
12:      save *Pop* to the dataset
13:    **else**
14:      go to 5
15:    **end if**
16: **end for**
17: **return** dataset

2.2.3 Copula-Based Synthesis

Copula function is used to estimate associations among random variables. It is extensively applied in economics and statistics. Following Sklar [15], a joint distribution function F with marginal distribution functions $F_1, F_2, \ldots, F_n$ can be written as:

$$F(x_1, \ldots, x_n) = C(F_1(x_1), F_2(x_2), \ldots, F_n(x_n))$$

where C is called copula function, which indicates the association among variables. When $F_1, \ldots, F_n$ are strictly monotonically increasing, so that the margins are continuous, C is known to be unique. Currently, several copula functions are proposed, such as Gaussian copula [16] and logit copula [17]. However, when one or more marginal distribution is discrete, this is no longer the case [18]. The copula function is not unique, and it is more complicated than the continuous case.

Nevertheless, there are still several candidates for applications like independence copula, minimum copula, and so on [19]. In contrast with Pearson's correlation coefficient that only represents linear associations among variables, copula function is applicable for any type of distributions. It is more general and widely used. Thus, in the following, we will discuss how to create a synthetic population via copula functions.

In the population synthesis, the studied attributes can be discrete, enumerate, binary, and even continuous. However, continuous values are often split into several intervals in order to reduce the computational complexity. Therefore, it can be safely assumed that all the variables are discrete. For each frequency distribution represented by cross-classification table, it can be converted into a probabilistic distribution through dividing each cell by the total number of target population. Therefore, the basic problem is to estimate the joint probabilistic distribution. Given a set of marginal and partial joint distributions, our method starts by investigating the two with highest disaggregate level. Disaggregate level means the number of variables that a specific partial joint distribution contains. For example, the disaggregate levels of *Res. Type* × *Res. Prov.* × *Eth. Group* × *Gen.* and *Age Inter.* × *Eth.Group* × *Gen.* are 4 and 3, respectively. If two partial joint distributions have the same disaggregate level, it is preferred to select the one that contains more attribute values. This is because more direct details from partial views will lead to a more accurate estimation. For example, when considering *Gen.* × *Res. Type* × *Res. Prov.* × *Eth. Group* (58 values) and *Gen.* × *Res. Type* × *Res.Prov.* × *Age Inter.* (21 values), we should choose the former in priority. Another pre-operation is to fold the mutual dimensions of the two selected partial joint distributions. For example, if the most disaggregate distributions are *Res. Type* × *Res. Prov.* × *Eth. Group* × *Gen.* and *Age Inter.* × *Eth. Group* × *Gen.*, then we need to fold the mutual dimension *Gen.* in one of them, like

$$P\left(AgeInter,\ EthnicGroup\right) = \sum_{Gender} P(AgeInter, EthnicGroup, Gender)$$

This operation is able to guarantee that the two selected partial joint distributions do not include mutual variables. That is, the two distributions can be represented by: $F(X_1, \ldots, X_m)$ and $F(X_{m+1}, \ldots, X_n)$, and $X_i \neq X_j (i \neq j, i, j \in 1, \ldots, n)$.

When the two partial distributions of target population determined, say $F(X_1, \ldots, X_m)$ and $F(X_{m+1}, \ldots, X_n)$, we introduce a transform:

$$(X_1, \ldots, X_m) \rightarrow X$$

and

$$(X_{m+1}, \ldots, X_n) \rightarrow Y$$

to convert multidimensional into one-dimensional variables. Such transform can be easily implemented by mapping each value combination of $(X_1, \ldots, X_m)$

into an ordinal value. For convenience, the values of X and Y are denoted as $I_X = (x_1, \ldots, x_m)$ and $I_Y = (y_1, \ldots, y_n)$. Furthermore, without loss of generality, it can be assumed that $x_1 < x_2 < \cdots < x_m$ and $y_1 < y_2 < \cdots < y_n$.

The second step of our method is to estimate the association between X and Y. Let $F(x, y) := P(X \leq x, Y \leq y)$ be the joint cumulative distribution function (cdf), $F_X(x) := F(x, +\infty) = P(X \leq x, Y \leq +\infty)$, and $F_Y(y) := F(+\infty, y) = P(X \leq +\infty, Y \leq y)$ be the marginal cdf. Following Sklar's theorem, there is a copula function that

$$F(x, y) = C\left(F_X(x), F_Y(y)\right)$$

where C is not unique. Here, we propose to use empirical copula function, which is computed via disaggregate sample. Let $S = \{\langle x^{(1)}, y^{(1)} \rangle, \langle x^{(2)}, y^{(2)} \rangle, \ldots, \langle x^{(K)}, y^{(K)} \rangle\}$ be the sample records. The empirical copula $\mathbb{C} : I_X \times I_Y \to \mathbb{R}$ is defined as:

$$\mathbb{C}(x, y) = \begin{cases} 0 & \text{if } x < x_1 \text{ or } y < y_1 \\ \frac{\#\{\langle x^{(k)}, y^{(k)} \rangle \in S | x^{(k)} \leq x, y^{(k)} \leq y\}}{K} & \text{otherwise} \end{cases} \tag{2.1}$$

The notation # means the number of samples that satisfy the conditions in the brace. The empirical copula above manifests the dependence between X and Y. However, it may probably not be compatible with $F_X(x)$ and $F_Y(y)$ when using original disaggregate samples. This is because in most cases, the samples are extracted randomly from original census data, which probably brings a bias to the achieved results. Thus, they do not accurately reveal the correlation structure of the target population. To deal with this problem, we use bootstrap alternatively. Bootstrap is a resampling technique that is used in R-copula computation [20]. But it does not suffer restrictions from marginal cdfs there. In our application scenario, the bootstrap steps are as follows:

1. Initialize bootstrap sample S' as null;
2. Get a random individual record *Ind* from original samples and compute marginal distributions $\hat{F}_X(x)$ and $\hat{F}_Y(y)$ of $S' \cup Ind$;
3. If $\hat{F}_X(x)$ and $\hat{F}_Y(y)$ are "closer" to $F_X(x)$ and $F_Y(y)$, then include *Ind* into S';
4. Repeat steps 2 and 3 until convergence.

In essence, the obtained S' is a modified sample set consistent with marginal constraints from target population. It is an appropriate candidate to calculate empirical copula given in Eq. (2.1). The main algorithm for joint cdf estimation is shown in Algorithm 2.3, where function *ComputeError* calculates the fitness of S' (shown in Algorithm 2.4) and function *ReplicateRandInd* replicates a random individual from samples. The notation *Card*($*$) represents the number of elements in set $*$.

As explained above, the obtained joint distribution only includes variables $(X_1, \ldots, X_n)$. If they do not cover all the studied attributes, then we select another marginal distribution with new attributes and repeat the process. Such repeat will bring expansion of at least one new attribute into our current variable set. Thus at

---

Algorithm 2.3 JointCDFEstimation($F_X(x)$, $F_Y(y)$, S)

Input:

    $F_X(x)$, $F_Y(y)$, marginal cdfs;

    S, original samples;

Output:

    Joint cdf $\mathbb{C}(x, y)$.

1: $S' \leftarrow \{\ \}$;

2: $(e_x, e_y) \leftarrow$ ComputeError($F_X(x), F_Y(y), S'$);

3: **repeat**

4:     $Ind \leftarrow$ ReplicateRandInd(S);

5:     $(\hat{e}_x, \hat{e}_y) \leftarrow$ ComputeError($F_X(x), F_Y(y), S' \cup Ind$);

6:     **if** $\hat{e}_x < e_x$ and $\hat{e}_y < e_y$ **then**

7:        $S' \leftarrow S' \cup Ind$;

8:        $(e_x, e_y) \leftarrow (\hat{e}_x, \hat{e}_y)$;

9:     **end if**

10: **until** $e_x + e_y <$ *threshold* or reaches maximum iteration

11: **return** $\mathbb{C}(x, y)$ computed via Eq. (2.1) using S'.

Algorithm 2.4 ComputeError($F_X(x)$, $F_Y(y)$, S)

Input:

    $F_X(x)$, $F_Y(y)$, marginal cdfs;

    S, samples;

Output:

    Errors (e_x, e_y).

1: $(e_x, e_y) \leftarrow (0, 0)$;

2: **for** each (x, y) **do**

3:     **if** $Card(S) = 0$ **then**

4:        $(e_x, e_y) \leftarrow (e_x, e_y) + (|F_X(x)|, |F_Y(y)|)$;

5:     **else**

6:        $e_x \leftarrow e_x + \left| F_X(x) - \frac{\#\{\langle x^{(l)}, y^{(l)} \rangle \in S | x^{(l)} \leq x\}}{Card(S)} \right|$;

7:        $e_y \leftarrow e_y + \left| F_Y(y) - \frac{\#\{\langle x^{(l)}, y^{(l)} \rangle \in S | y^{(l)} \leq y\}}{Card(S)} \right|$;

8:     **end if**

9: **end for**

10: **return** (e_x, e_y).

---

last, we are able to get the distribution of all attributes. The joint distribution acquired by empirical copula can be converted into frequency distribution by multiplying each probability with the total number of target population. Furthermore, an arbitrary total number is eligible instead of real target population number so that any scale of population can be synthesized easily.

2.3   Sample-Free Method

Disaggregate sample provides an association among multiple variables which plays a direct population structure from micro level. However, this micro-level sample is difficult to acquire in most countries. Thus, algorithms that do not essentially require this data are developed later. The first sample-free method is proposed in 2010, which is called sample-free fitting here [21, 22]. This method only adopts marginals or/and conditionals of partial attributes from various data sources as its input and gives more flexibility in terms of data requirements (see Figure 2.1). In the synthetic process, an individual pool with the scale of target population is firstly generated according to the most disaggregate data source.

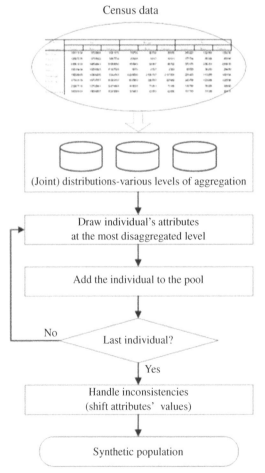

Figure 2.1   Flow chart of sample-free fitting.

Then, the missing attributes are estimated from other conditionals or partial joint distributions associated with them. Once all the interested characteristics are defined, the initial individual pool has been constructed (see the pseudocode in Algorithm 2.5). In an ideal case, this individual set should satisfy all the conditionals and marginals, which are determined by the unique joint distribution of the target population. However, it does not always happen due to the distinctions of conditionals/marginals from different data sources. When the conditionals/marginals are not consistent, an attribute shift of some individuals needs to be performed further. Note that the shift is for the discrete attributes only. In essence, this type of techniques also conducts a fitting process. In contrast with IPF that fits a unique marginal of all the attributes, this sample-free fitting attempts to find an approximate joint distribution conformed to various conditionals. Objectively, sample-free fitting has overcome a strong limit of the sample requirements. Yet, it does not reveal the internal correlations between individual attributes.

Algorithm 2.5 Algorithm of Sample-Free Fitting

Require:

    Partial frequencies *ParFre* (cross-classification tables listed in Table 2.5).

    Synthetic population scale *PopSize*.

Ensure:

    Synthetic population dataset.

1: Construct an individual pool *indPool* with the scale of *PopSize* from the table in *ParFre* at most disaggregated level.

    (*Gender* × *ResidenceType* × *ResidentialProvince* × *EthnicGroup*/$t0106a$ − $t0106c$, in this study)

2: **for** each other variable x_i: **do**

3:    Update x_i of each record according to its marginal from the table at most disaggregated level.

    (*AgeInterval*/$t0107a$–$t0107c$, *EducationalLevel*/$t0401a$–$t0401c$,

    RegistrationType/$t0102$, $t0105$,

    RegistrationProvince/$t0701a$–$t0701c$, $t0702a$–$t0702c$ sequentially)

4: **end for**

5: **for** each rest table T in *ParFre* **do**

6:    Update *indPool* by shifting its individuals with problematic attribute values to match T.

7: **end for**

8: **return** dataset

The second sample-free method is Markov chain Monte Carlo (MCMC) simulation, which is a stochastic sampling technique to estimate the overall distribution when the actual joint distribution is hard to access. The theoretical foundation of MCMC is that a sequence of observations from a specified multivariate probability distribution can be obtained approximately through a Markov chain, if its stationary distribution equals to the specified distribution mentioned before. When applied in population thesis, it firstly constructs a Markov chain, with its conditional transfer probabilities of each interested attribute [23]. Then samples are extracted from the chain at a particular interval, which is called Gibbs sampling. This process is deemed as an individual drawing from the actual population when the Gibbs sampler runs for an extended amount of iterations and reaches a stationary state. Thus, the individual dataset obtained can be directly used as a synthetic agent. Mathematically, the main idea of Gibbs sampler is to simulate drawing from the joint distribution of individual attributes $f_X(x)$ by using the conditionals $f(X_i|X_j = x_j, \text{for } j = 1, \dots, n \text{ and } i \neq j) = f(X_i|X_{-i})$, where $x = (x_1, \dots, x_n)$ is a specific value of X and X_i is the ith variable of X. The key challenge here is to prepare all the conditional distributions according to the available data about the individual attributes. In the straightforward case, these conditionals can be counted by category for each attribute, either from the census zonal statistics table or the disaggregate sample. When the disaggregate sample is not available, the conditional distributions are usually constructed by integrating partial views of the joint distribution of actual population from various data sources. As a particular census cross-classification table rarely covers the whole individual attributes, there may be cases that not enough data are available to construct the full conditional for an attribute over all the other attributes. Assume that in $f(X_1|X_{-1}) = f(X_1|X_{2,\dots,k}, X_{(k+1),\dots,n})$, only the incomplete conditional $f(X_1|X_{2,\dots,k})$ is available. In such a case, we introduce the conditional independence of X_1 on $X_{(k+1),\dots,n}$, given $X_{2,\dots,k}$. As a consequence, we have $f(X_1|X_{-1}) = f(X_1|X_{2,\dots,k})$. In the worst case where only marginals are available, this approximation degenerates into $f(X_1|X_{-1}) = f(X_1)$. Note that additional domain knowledge about the incomplete part of the conditional can be exploited to construct full conditionals. It may result in a coarse case like $f(X_1|X_{2,\dots,k}, X_{(k+1),\dots,n} = \alpha) = f^\alpha(X_1|X_{2,\dots,k})$ and $f(X_1|X_{2,\dots,k}, X_{(k+1),\dots,n} = \beta) = f^\beta(X_1|X_{2,\dots,k})$. For example, if there are no data about the head of household conditioned upon age, it is reasonable to safely assume that the probability of a child to be head of the household as zero, while making a different assumption for adults.

Given the constructed full conditional distributions, Gibbs sampler can extract individuals after reaching a stationary state. At that point, any draw will be as if the draw was from the joint distribution $f_X(x)$. Hence, we can realize a synthetic population by simply drawing the number of individuals equaling the size of the target population (or any size of population). Since the input disaggregate sample is not essentially required, MCMC simulation is another sample-free synthetic technique (see the pseudocode in Algorithm 2.6). MCMC simulation can deal with both discrete and continuous attributes. It extends the scope of characteristics investigated. However, when the conditionals from different data sources are inconsistent, the Gibbs sampling may never reach a unique stationary state, which prevent the valid population drawing.

Algorithm 2.6 Algorithm of Markov Chain Monte Carlo Simulation

---

Require:

Partial frequencies *ParFre* (cross-classification tables listed in Table 2.5). Number of transfer, *TranNum*. Sample interval, *Interval*. Synthetic population scale *PopSize*.

Ensure:

Synthetic population dataset.

1: For each x_i, construct the incomplete conditional distribution at most disaggregated level, $Px_i|x_{(-i)}$.

2: Generate an individual record as the initial seed randomly: *SeedInd*.

3: **repeat**

4:    **for** each x_i: **do**

5:       Update x_i of the *SeedInd* according to $Px_i|x_{(-i)}$.

6:    **end for**

7: **until** *TranNum* times. (in this paper, we set *TranNum* = 1, 000, 000)

8: Let $k = 0$.

9: **repeat**

10:    **for** each x_i: **do**

11:       Update x_i of the *SeedInd* according to $Px_i|x_{(-i)}$.

12:    **end for**

13:    $k \leftarrow k + 1$.

14:    **if** $k\%Interval == 0$ (in this paper, we set *Interval* = 10) **then**

15:       Save *SeedInd* to the dataset.

16:    **end if**

17: **until** the scale of dataset reaches *PopSize*

18: **return** dataset

Sample-free fitting and MCMC simulation do not require disaggregate sample as input. This relaxes strict constraints from sample-based methods and makes them easy to use. However, these two approaches directly operate on individuals and are much computational expensive when the scale of the synthetic population is large. So a new efficient method called joint distribution inference (JDI) is proposed. In general, JDI has the following highlights:

1. Infers the joint distribution of the target population directly. This could avoid the manipulation of individuals each time one attribute is adjusted.

2. Uses marginals and partial joint distributions as much as possible. It needs to maximally use total target population information acquired.

3. Not necessarily requires disaggregate samples. This makes it possible to apply the approach to general cases even if samples are not available.
4. Has a solid statistical and mathematical basis.

Starting from these objectives, JDI method is composed of two steps: independence test and association inference. Figure 2.2 shows the main steps of the method, in which the association inference is most crucial.

Independence test aims to validate whether two variables are independent of each other. According to probability theory, two random variables, X and Y, are called independent if and only if

$$F(x,y) = F_X(x) \cdot F_Y(y), \quad \forall x, y \in \mathbb{D}$$

where $\mathbb{D}$ is the field of probability definition, F is the cdf, and F_X and F_Y are the marginal distribution functions. Suppose the studied individual attributes are $(X_1, X_2, \ldots, X_n)$. For convenience, only discrete cases are considered here because the continuous variables can be spilt into several intervals and converted into discrete ones. Consequently, the definition of independence can be written in the form of probability mass function:

$$f(x,y) = f_X(x) \cdot f_Y(y), \quad \forall x, y \in \mathbb{D}$$

At the beginning of the synthesis, independence test is conducted between every two attributes. Chi-square testing is usually introduced to complete this task. For any two attributes X_i and X_j, as shown in Table 2.7, let the null hypothesis be

$$f(x_i, x_j) = f_{X_i}(x_i) \cdot f_{X_j}(x_j)$$

and the alternative hypothesis be

$$f(x_i, x_j) \neq f_{X_i}(x_i) \cdot f_{X_j}(x_j)$$

Chi-square value can be computed by:

$$\chi^2 = \sum_{r=1}^{R} \sum_{s=1}^{S} \frac{(A_{rs} - \frac{A_{r\cdot}}{A_{r\cdot}} \cdot \frac{A_{\cdot s}}{A_{\cdot s}} \cdot A_{\cdot\cdot})^2}{\frac{A_{r\cdot}}{A_{r\cdot}} \cdot \frac{A_{\cdot s}}{A_{\cdot s}} \cdot A_{\cdot\cdot}} = \sum_{r=1}^{R} \sum_{s=1}^{S} \frac{(A_{r\cdot} \cdot A_{\cdot s} - A_{rs} \cdot A_{\cdot\cdot})^2}{A_{r\cdot} \cdot A_{\cdot s} \cdot A_{\cdot\cdot}} \tag{2.2}$$

where A_{rs} stands for the statistical individual number of $X_i = x_i^{(r)}$ and $X_j = x_j^{(s)}$. The corresponding degree of freedom is $(R-1) \cdot (S-1)$. According to the hypothesis testing theory, given a significance level, if the Chi-square value is in the acceptance region of $\chi^2((R-1) \cdot (S-1))$ distribution, X_i and X_j are deemed to be independent; else, they are associated.

If we separate the studied attributes into two sets and have validated that $\forall X_i \in \{X_1, X_2, \ldots, X_m\}$ is independent with $\forall X_j \in \{X_{m+1}, X_{m+2}, \ldots, X_n\}$, the joint distribution can be denoted as:

$$f(x_1, \ldots, x_n) = f(x_1, \ldots, x_m) \cdot f(x_{m+1}, \ldots, x_n)$$

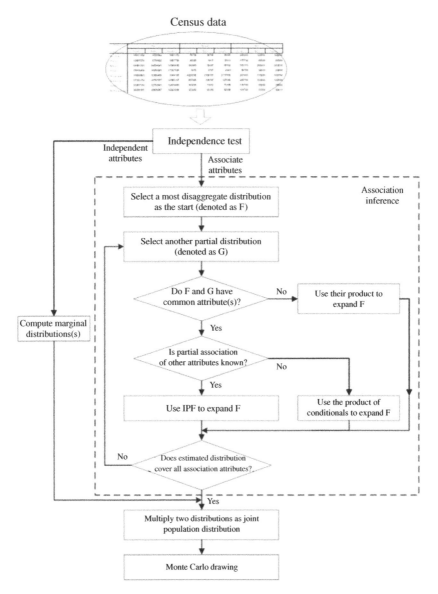

Figure 2.2 Flow chart of joint distribution inference.

In other words, the joint distribution can be directly computed from partial distributions. Specifically, if one set degenerates into a variable, that is, X_i is independent with $\forall X_j \in \{X_1, X_2, \ldots, X_n\} \backslash \{X_i\}$, then we have

$$f(x_1, \ldots, x_n) = f_{X_i}(x_i) \cdot f(x_1, \ldots, x_{i-1}, x_{i+1}, \ldots, x_n) \tag{2.3}$$

Table 2.7 Partial joint distribution of two variables.

X_i \ X_j	$x_j^{(1)}$	$\cdots$	$x_j^{(s)}$	$\cdots$	$x_j^{(S)}$	Row sum
$x_i^{(1)}$	A_{11}	$\cdots$	A_{1s}	$\cdots$	A_{1S}	$A_{1\cdot}$
$\vdots$	$\vdots$	$\ddots$	$\vdots$	$\ddots$	$\vdots$	$\vdots$
$x_i^{(r)}$	A_{r1}	$\cdots$	A_{rs}	$\cdots$	A_{rS}	$A_{r\cdot}$
$\vdots$	$\vdots$	$\ddots$	$\vdots$	$\ddots$	$\vdots$	$\vdots$
$x_i^{(R)}$	A_{R1}	$\cdots$	A_{Rs}	$\cdots$	A_{RS}	$A_{R\cdot}$
Col. sum	$A_{\cdot 1}$	$\cdots$	$A_{\cdot s}$	$\cdots$	$A_{\cdot S}$	$A_{\cdot\cdot}$

Consequently, joint distribution can be represented as the product of a marginal and a partial distribution. It reduces the dimension of our problem, and we need only focus on the last partial probability item.

The second step is association inference. Without the loss of generality, we assume the last $(n - m)$ attributes are independent and rewrite Eq. (2.3) as:

$$f(x_1, \ldots, x_n) = f(x_1, \ldots, x_m) \cdot f_{X_{m+1}}(x_{m+1}) \cdot f_{X_{m+2}}(x_{m+2}) \cdots f_{X_n}(x_n)$$

The following task is to estimate the $f(x_1, \ldots, x_m)$ from its marginals and partial joint distributions. Here, we assume that the information related to each variable is contained in the known partial and marginal distributions (this is always satisfied). For a particular distribution, the disaggregate level is defined as the number of variables it contains. The partial distribution with the highest disaggregate level should be selected as the start point. Once the start point is determined, we need to investigate other partial distributions. In the following, we will use a simple example to illustrate the method.

Suppose the start distribution is $f(x_1, x_2)$. Consider another distribution $f(x_1, x_3)$ where x_1 is the common variable. Our objective is to estimate $f(x_1, x_2, x_3)$. In theory, this contains infinite solutions if we do not have any further information. Thus, the basic idea is to construct one particular joint distribution that conforms to both of the partial views. The problem is categorized into two cases.

Case 1: $f(x_2, x_3)$ is known. Then,

$$f(x_1, x_2, x_3) = f_{X_1}(x_1) \cdot f(x_2, x_3 \mid x_1) \tag{2.4}$$

where $f_{X_1}(x_1)$ can be easily calculated from $f(x_1, x_2)$ or $f(x_1, x_3)$. Since x_2 and x_3 are not independent, their associations should be estimated. This task could be completed via IPF procedure. The CT involves two variables, (x_2, x_3), and its initial seed is set according to $f(x_2, x_3)$. For each given x_1, IPF procedure is conducted and the corresponding marginals are computed as follows:

$$f(x_2 \mid x_1) = \frac{f(x_1, x_2)}{f_{X_1}(x_1)}, \; f(x_3 \mid x_1) = \frac{f(x_1, x_3)}{f_{X_1}(x_1)}$$

The result that IPF yields is denoted as $f'(x_2, x_3)$, and its marginals will conform to the above two conditional distributions. That is,

$$f'_{X_2}(x_2) = \sum_{x_3} f'(x_2, x_3) = f(x_2 \mid x_1)$$

$$f'_{X_3}(x_3) = \sum_{x_2} f'(x_2, x_3) = f(x_3 \mid x_1)$$

The joint distribution is estimated by:

$$f(x_1, x_2, x_3) = f_{X_1}(x_1) \cdot f'(x_2, x_3) \tag{2.5}$$

Comparing Eqs. (2.4) and (2.5), it is easily to find that the conditional probability $f(x_2, x_3 \mid x_1)$ is approximated by $f'(x_2, x_3)$. The reason for this operation is $f'(x_2, x_3)$ not only retains the associations between x_2 and x_3 but also satisfies the marginal constraints. It should be noted that the input $f(x_2, x_3)$ may be acquired from a more complicated partial distributions by summarizing other unconsidered dimensions. This is a more general case which will be discussed later in this section.

Case 2: $f(x_2, x_3)$ is unknown. In this case, all of the distributions do not contain associations between x_2 and x_3. It prevents us from estimating their joint distribution. Thus, we can only simply construct the associations as a product of their conditionals. That is,

$$f(x_1, x_2, x_3) = f_{X_1}(x_1) \cdot f(x_2, x_3 \mid x_1) = f_{X_1}(x_1) \cdot f(x_2 \mid x_1) \cdot f(x_3 \mid x_1)$$

Clearly, operations of the two cases above have extended the joint distribution. When this extension repeats until all the interested variables are included, the ultimate distribution is inferred. Theoretical convergence of JDI algorithm is proved in the Appendix. The pseudocode is in Algorithm 2.7.

2.4 Experiment Results

In this section, we will show the experiment results using the methods in this chapter. As illustrated in Section 2.1, our data source mainly comes from the fifth national census of China. The experiments will concentrate on copula-based approach and JDI algorithm, with comparative analysis with other methods.

2.4.1 Copula-Based Population Synthesis

We consider the attributes *Gender*, *Residential Province*, *Residence Type*, *Household Type*, and *Age Interval* as the studied variables and select the most disaggregate distributions as the constraints. The attribute values, input, and evaluation

---

Algorithm 2.7 Algorithm of Joint Distribution Inference

Require:

    Partial frequencies *ParFre* (cross-classification tables listed in Table 2.5).

    Synthetic population scale *PopSize*.

Ensure:

    Synthetic population dataset.

  1: Conduct independence test to determine associated variable sets.

  2: **for** each associated variable set: **do**

  3:     Select the most disaggregated table in *ParFre* as the initial distribution F. (*Gender* × *ResidenceType* × *ResidentialProvince* × *EthnicGroup*/t0106a–t0106c, in this study)

  4:     **repeat**

  5:         Select the most disaggregated table in the rest of *ParFre* as the partial distribution G.

  6:         **if** F and G have common variables **then**

  7:             **if** *ParFre* contains a table H that covers the different variables between F and G **then**

  8:                 Use H as the initial distribution, F and G as two marginal distributions.

  9:                 Adopt IPF to obtain a partial distribution $\hat{H}$.

10:                 Expand F with $\hat{H}$. (in this paper, we sequentially expand: *AgeInterval* with t0201a–t0201c (G) and t0107a–t0107c (H), *EducationalLevel* with t0108 (G) and t0401a–t0401c (H))

11:             **else**

12:                 Expand F with G by multiply F and $PG|F$. (in this paper, *RegistrationType* with t0102, t0105, *RegistrationProvince* with t0102, t0702a–t0702c)

13:             **end if**

14:         **else**

15:             Use the product of F and G to expand F.

16:         **end if**

17:     **until** F covers all the variables.

18: **end for**

19: Multiply each F to get the final joint distribution.

20: **for** $i = 1$ to *PopSize*: **do**

21:     Use Monte Carlo simulation to draw an individual record, *IndRec*, according to the final joint distribution.

22:     Save *IndRec* to the dataset.

23: **end for**

24: **return** dataset

Table 2.8 Population attributes and values.

Attributes	Values	Numberof values
Gender	Male, female	2
Residential Province	Beijing, Tianjin, …	31
Residence Type	City, town, rural	3
Household Type	Family, collective household	2
Age Interval	$\{0-5, ..., 96-100, \geq 100\}$	21

cross-classification tables are listed in Tables 2.8 and 2.9. Both the copula-based method and IPF are applied to conduct five independent experiments. Relative error of each attribute value is computed as:

$$RE = \frac{|Count_{LT} - Count_{syn}|}{Count_{LT}}$$

where $Count_{LT}$ and $Count_{syn}$ stand for the frequencies from the Long Table and sampled synthetic population, respectively. Since all the frequencies in the Long Table are not zero, the formula above always makes sense. For every attribute combination, average RE of the five independent experiments are reported as follows.

The first evaluation indicator is one-dimensional marginal frequencies. We investigate each attribute. Figures 2.3–2.5 gives the results of the studied five variables. In the first subfigure, copula-based method gets a larger deviation in the total number of population than IPF. But the total relative error is less than 1%, which is acceptable in most applications. In addition, proportions of different groups are recovered well by both methods. Specifically, copula-based method keeps a similar accuracy with IPF for Gender and Residence Type and even performs slightly better than the latter for Household Type. The second and third subfigures clearly illustrate that our method is able to reconstruct a more accurate population. However, differences between the two methods are not

Table 2.9 Input and evaluation benchmark cross-classification tables.

Input marginal dis. (Short Table)		Benchmark (Long Table)	
Attr. of dis.	Tab. codes	Attr. of dis.	Tab. codes
Gen. × *Res.Prov.* × *Res.Type* × *HhType*	*t0101a–c*	*Gen.* × *Res.Prov.* × *Res.Type* × *HhType*	*l0101a–c*
Gen. × *Res.Prov.* × *Res.Type* × *AgeInter.*	*t0107a–c*	*Gen.* × *Res.Type* × *AgeInter.*	*l0102a–c*

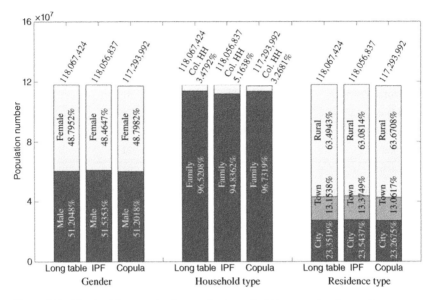

Figure 2.3 Marginal frequencies for gender, household type, and residence type.

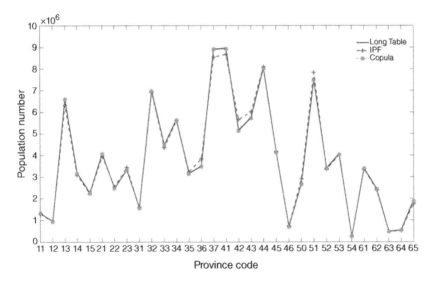

Figure 2.4 Marginal frequencies for residential province.

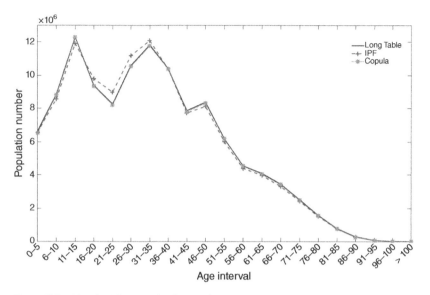

Figure 2.5 Marginal frequencies for age interval.

significant. Therefore, we are inclined to conclude that for one-dimensional marginal frequencies, the copula-based method can achieve the same level of accuracy as IPF.

Our second evaluation indicator concentrates on partial joint frequency distributions. Figure 2.6 shows the results of two distributions. Figure 2.6a treats the first Long Table given in Table 2.9 as the benchmark (zero line). To illustrate more clearly, we draw frequency deviations for male and female separately. For each zero line, frequency deviations from IPF method are placed above the line, whereas deviations from copula-based method are marked below the line. Each frequency deviation is an absolute value, computed as:

$$Dev = \left| Count_{LT} - Count_{syn} \right|$$

As can be seen, the data points from copula-based method are more clustered near zero lines in general, both for male and female. Quantitatively, copula-based method gets a 13.20% average relative error, while IPF receives 50.03%. Also, similar deviation computation is applied to the second Long Table, which led to Figure 2.6b. In this subfigure, error differences seem more obvious. But the average relative errors are 8.71% (copula) and 6.78% (IPF), which is quite surprised. This indicates IPF may bring large deviations in some attribute combinations. In contrast, copula-based method performs much more stably. In summary, it can be concluded that our copula-based method is able to recover partial joint population structure better than IPF.

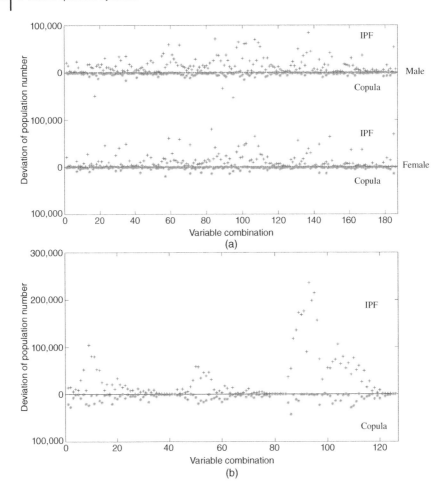

Figure 2.6 Partial joint frequency distributions for Long Tables. (a) *Gen.* × *Res.Prov.* × *Res.Type* × *HHType* and (b) *Gen.* × *Res.Type* × *AgeInter*.

For further evaluation of the partial joint distributions, we consider Freeman–Tukey statistic (FT^2) [24]. The FT^2 indicator is calculated as:

$$FT^2 = 4 \cdot \sum_k \sum_i \left(\sqrt{O_{ki}} - \sqrt{E_{ki}} \right)^2$$

where O_{ki} is the generated count corresponds to the ith cell of the kth table; E_{ki} is the given (known) count for the ith cell of the kth table. In our evaluation, there are only two Long Tables for benchmark, thus $k = 1, 2$. After computation, the total FT^2 values are 1,773,721 (IPF) and 189,386 (copula). Clearly, the error of our method only accounts for 10.68% of IPF. This also proves that the copula-based method brings much lower variations in partial joint distributions.

2.4.2 Joint Distribution Inference

Five methods, IPFSR, CO, SFF, MCMC, and JDI, are compared in this part in the population synthesis of China. Before showing the evaluation of generated synthetic populations, independence test results are presented according to Eq. (2.2). Table 2.10 shows Chi-square values between every two attributes. These results all come from cross-classification tables of the total population. Note that the first line in each box is the Chi-square value whose magnitude is 104, and the two items in the second line of each box are degree of freedom and p-value (significance level $\alpha = 0.1$), respectively. As can be seen, no attribute is independent from others. This causes us to infer associations among all variables.

In our study, all the tables listed in Table 2.5 are used as the inputs of the sample-free methods. The scale of synthetic population generated by the five methods is 1,242,612,226 (total Chinese population). According to the Long Table scale, 9.5% of the synthetic populations are stochastically extracted for quantitative evaluations. In order to reduce the impacts of randomness, each experiment is conducted five times and averaged to obtain the final results. The indicator adopted in our evaluation is the modified overall RSSZm mentioned before. Details of the attributes in the Long Table are identical to the sample. It should be pointed out that the statistical results from Long Table have not

Table 2.10 Independence test results.

	Gender	Age inter.	Ethnic group	Res. prov.	Edu. level	Res. type
Age inter.	179 20/28	—				
Ethnic group	4 57/71	534 1140/1079	—			
Res. prov.	19 30/40	2677 600/645	281145 1710/1635	—		
Edu. level	3315 9/15	5897 96/114	2959 513/554	7310 270/299	—	
Res. type	2 2/5	1436 40/52	1763 114/134	11879 60/74	18373 18/26	—
Reg. prov.	54 31/41	—	—	3493451 930/985	—	605 60/74
Reg. type	32 2/5	—	—	7257 60/74	—	—

The first number is χ^2 value ($\times 10^4$); the two in parenthesis are degree of freedom and p-value (significance level $\alpha = 0.1$).

Table 2.11 Partial distributions used in population evaluation.

No.	Distributions	Table codes
1.	*Gen. × Res.Type × Res.Prov.*	l0101a–l0101c
2.	*Gen. × Res.Type × AgeInter.*	l0102a–l0102c
3.	*Gen. × Eth.Group*	l0201, l0203
4.	*Gen. × Res.Type × Edu.Lv*	l0301a–l0301c

provided us the information about *Registration Province* and *Registration Type*. Thus, our evaluation is only established on the rest of six characteristics. The evaluations are composed of two parts. Firstly, marginal consistency of the rest six attributes from Long Table (*Gender, Age Interval, Ethnic Group, Residential Province, Educational Level*, and *Residence Type*) are investigated. Secondly, partial joint distributions of specific attributes are also given in the Long Table results. These can be used to calculate RSSZm value in a more detailed way. The RSSZm indicator has been introduced in Section 2.1, and the partial joint distributions adopted as our reference criterion are shown in Table 2.11.

The population sizes derived from Long Table and five methods are 118067424 (Long Table), 118051339 (IPFSR), 118000428 (CO), 118042198 (SFF), 118051699 (MCMC), and 118049388 (JDI), respectively. The minor difference stems from the stochastic sampling according to 9.5%. Figure 2.7 gives the statistical result of gender marginal. As can be seen, all errors are below 400,000 which accounts for

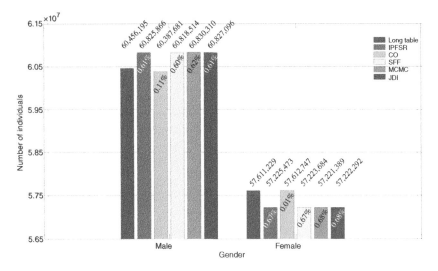

Figure 2.7 Comparison of gender (frequencies and relative errors).

0.66% (male) and 0.69% (female). The sample-based method CO performs the best with its error 68,514 (male) and 1518 (female). The age interval marginal comparison is shown in Figure 2.8. Similarly, the two sample-based methods result in more accurate match with the Long Table data, while the three sample-free ones have brought minor deviations. The proposed JDI method shows a similar performance with other sample-free methods. The trend of lines also indicates two "baby booms" in Chinese history.

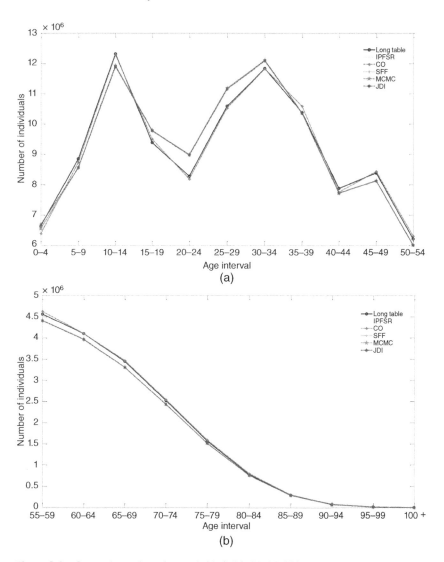

Figure 2.8 Comparison of age interval. (a): 0-54; (b): 55-100.

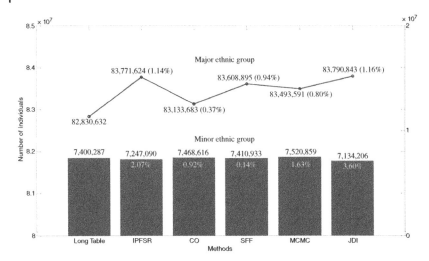

Figure 2.9 Comparison of ethnic group (frequencies and relative errors).

Figure 2.9 gives comparison of ethnic groups, among which the major – Han group – accounts for over 90% and is shown by the line with 1.14%, 0.37%, 0.94%, 0.80%, and 1.16% relative errors. Individual numbers of other 55 minor ethnic groups are summarized and shown by the bar figure. Their relative errors are all below 5%. Unrecognized ethnic group and foreigners are calculated in Table 2.12. It is important to note that IPFSR and CO do not contain individuals from the unrecognized group. The reason of this phenomenon is our input sample does not include this type of person. This "zero element" problem cannot be solved by the sample-based methods. Thus, under this condition, the limitations of the sample-based methods are apparent.

The populations for the 31 provinces of China are compared in Figure 2.10. Absolute deviations between the sampled synthetic populations and the Long

Table 2.12 Numbers of unrecognized ethnic group and foreigner.

	Unrecognized ethnic group	Foreigner
Long Table	47,523	110
IPFSR	0	65
CO	0	51,114
SFF	47,786	68
MCMC	51,307	79
JDI	33,191	27

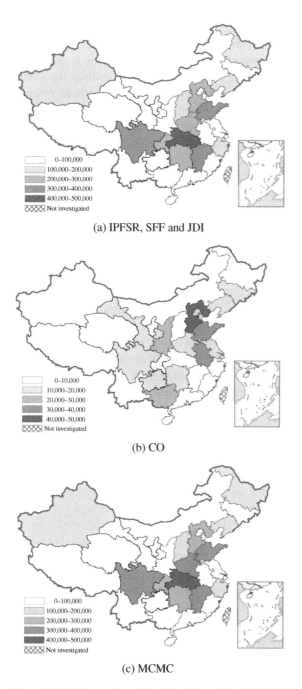

(a) IPFSR, SFF and JDI

(b) CO

(c) MCMC

Figure 2.10 Comparison of residential province. (a) IPFSR, SFF, and JDI, (b) CO, and (c) MCMC.

Table data are represented by the different color in the map. Note the numerical range represented by each type of color in Figure 2.10b is different from others. As can be seen, the CO result always outperforms others. This is due to its generation mechanism. Different from other methods, CO partitions the whole population into several parts and generates it one by one in its synthetic process. This accurately controls synthetic population in smaller scales. Thus, CO brings the best results. The figure also shows the rest of the methods have similar errors.

For the educational level, the census only investigates individuals over six years old. Thus, our evaluation also focuses on these populations. The Long Table and five synthetic results are drawn in Figure 2.11. As can be seen, each educated group percentage of these methods is nearly the same. Quantitatively, the average relative errors are 3.20% (IPFSR), 1.49% (CO), 3.69% (SFF), 3.68% (MCMC), and 3.68% (JDI). It seems that the sample can elevate the accuracy of this marginal indicator. The last marginal attribute is residence type, the results of which are presented in Figure 2.12. From the figure, about two-thirds of the people are living in rural areas in 2000, and each residence type has a similar percentage. It shows the five methods all have good results when measured by this marginal.

The marginal mean absolute errors (MAEs) and root mean squared errors (RMSEs) are computed in Table 2.13. Generally, the CO method has better performance than the others. And all of them show a relative worse result in ethnic group, especially CO. The large MAE and RMSE deviations are also caused by the deficiency of specific type of individuals in sample. The three sample-free methods have a similar accuracy in marginal consistencies.

Table 2.14 gives the RSSZm results which have been introduced before. The main deviation comes from *Gender × Ethnic Group* distribution, and the three sample-free methods generated better population databases than the sample-based ones. The reason for this phenomenon is that the sample-free methods treat associations among individual attributes reflected by partial joint distributions as their inputs, and these associations are derived from the whole target population. Thus, the sample-free methods are able to directly manipulate total population associations rather than the sample which most likely carries deviation in sampling process. The results also show that SFF and JDI have relatively smaller RSSZm values.

MAE and RMSE of partial joint distributions are also calculated in Table 2.15. We can see that CO and MCMC get the largest MAE and RMSE (most come from *Gender × Ethnic Group* and *Gender × Residence Type × Educational Level* distributions), and IPFSR and SFF perform the best. Among the three sample-free methods, SFF is a little better than JDI and they both outperform MCMC.

In summary, the population databases synthesized by the sample-based methods, especially CO, have better performances on marginal indicators, while the sample-free methods generated populations that match partial joint distributions

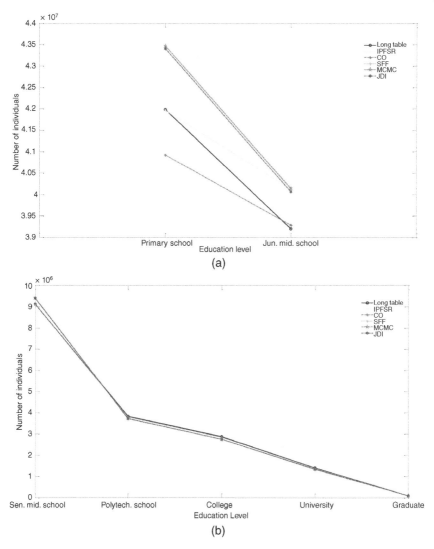

Figure 2.11 Comparison of educational level. (a): Primary and Junior Middle School; (b): Other levels.

more precisely. The SFF and JDI methods have similar accuracy among the sample-free methods, both of which are a little higher than MCMC.

Synthesizing nationwide population database of China is a large project. Consequently, computational performance is another important metric that should not be ignored. To achieve meaningful comparison from the computational cost point of view, we implemented all the five methods in the same

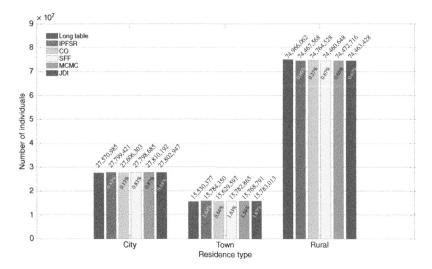

Figure 2.12 Comparison of residence type (frequencies and relative errors).

Table 2.13 MAE (%) and RMSE of marginals.

	Gender		Age inter.		Ethnic group	
	MAE	RMSE	MAE	RMSE	MAE	RMSE
IPFSR	0.64	377,799	3.69	268,701	12.68	123,982
CO	0.06	48,459	2.34	90,971	820.03	40,975
SFF	0.64	375,144	3.78	268,892	6.29	102,547
MCMC	0.65	382,058	3.90	269,218	7.52	87,432
JDI	0.64	380,026	12.88	266,461	27.18	126,592

	Res. prov.		Edu. level		Res. type	
	MAE	RMSE	MAE	RMSE	MAE	RMSE
IPFSR	3.25	178,383	3.20	372,811	1.04	348,894
CO	0.43	17,239	1.49	402,998	0.35	131,286
SFF	3.24	177,453	3.69	671,501	1.04	351,682
MCMC	0.65	382,058	3.90	269,218	7.52	87,432
JDI	3.26	178,052	3.68	639,449	1.05	351,318

Table 2.14 RSSZm values of partial joint distributions.

	Gen. × Res.Type ×Res.Prov. (I0101a−c)	Gen. × Res.Type × AgeInter. (I0102a−c)	Gen. × Eth.Group (I0201, I0203)	Gen. × Res.Type × Edu.Lv (I0301a − c)	Total
IPFSR	1053	1358	8,020,954	1055	8,024,420
CO	85	275	8,021,125	683	8,022,168
SFF	1097	1297	313	2162	4869
MCMC	1098	8962	310	245,325	255,695
JDI	1101	1312	3446	2109	7968

Table 2.15 M: MAE (%) and R: RMSE ($\times 10^3$) of partial joint distributions.

	Gen. × Res.Type × Res.Prov. (I0101a−c)		Gen. × Res.Type × AgeInter. (I0102a−c)		Gen. × Eth.Group (I0201, I0203)		Gen. × Res.Type × Edu.Lv (I0301a−c)		Total	
	M	R	M	R	M	R	M	R	M	R
IPFSR	3.9	38.9	7.0	58.0	23.3	72.7	5.0	76.8	9.6	57.7
CO	1.7	7.4	6.0	21.3	1006.8	20.7	4.2	95.0	251.1	32.5
SFF	3.4	42.9	4.2	55.0	7.0	72.1	6.5	128.6	4.8	65.6
MCMC	3.5	43.0	9.7	151.0	8.3	68.7	321.0	805.8	34.7	257.0
JDI	3.4	43.1	24.6	54.9	29.0	82.0	6.0	122.4	15.6	67.3

programming environment and run the methods on the same computer. More specifically, we implemented the five methods in C# .net framework environment and run the programs on an Intel Core i7-4790 CPU with 8 GB RAM. The execution time is divided into two parts: distribution computation (if it has) and population realization. The averaged results of the five methods are listed in Table 2.16

It is clear that among the five methods, JDI costs the least amount of execution time. Although CO has relatively accurate results as aforementioned, it is also the most computationally expensive one. During its computation, the total target population is partitioned into 100 parts and generated one by one for its convergence. The MCMC method has the second worst performance when comparing with others. The main reason is that MCMC builds its joint distribution by constructing an individual pool via discrete sampling from the Markov Chain. According to the MCMC theory, after Gibbs sampler achieved its stationary state, successive

Table 2.16 Computational performance.

Method	Dis. computation	Pop. realization	Environment
IPFSR	08 H 01 Min	02 D 08 H 18 Min	Software: C# .net framework
CO	—	08 D 21 H 50 Min	OS: Windows 7 (×64)
SFF	—	06 D 16 H 41 Min	CPU: Intel Core i7-4790
MCMC	06 D 21 H 52 Min	10 H 57 Min	(8 cores, 3.6 GHz)
JDI	03 H 47 Min	02 D 09 H 38 Min	RAM: 8 GB

sampling should be prevented in order to avoid any correlations between two adjacently generated individuals. To this end, synthetic individuals are usually drawn at a particular interval rather than from each chain update. In our study, this interval is set to be 10 iterations. The size of the individual pool is set to be 50 million. Therefore, it costs a large amount of computation. The SFF method is a little better than MCMC. This is mainly due to frequent updates on the individual pool, which causes substantial I/O operations on database. In contrast with RAM access, database manipulation seems much slower. IPFSR is much faster than the above three. It directly fits the joint distribution of the population and draws individuals. This approach, however, usually suffers from rapid growth in calculation as the investigated attributes increase. In our study, the theoretical number of attribute combinations is about 1.4×10^8 (including some zero cells in joint distribution). Fitting these combinations is, undoubtedly, much complicated and soars its computational time. On the other hand, Monte Carlo realization of individual records needs conditional probability rather than the joint distribution itself. Thus in contrast with IPFSR, our JDI method directly calculates conditional distributions after each expansion. To a certain extent, this reduces the computational complexity, since the attribute combinations are much fewer at the beginning of its computation. It should be pointed out that the access to database in all the five methods uses a single-threaded pattern. Multi-threaded techniques are expected to accelerate the programs, but more attention needs to be paid to the data synchronization.

2.5 Conclusions and Discussions

Synthetic population is a vital input of the group intelligence study. This chapter reviews algorithms in main streams by distinguishing their data sources. These methods are applied to generating a nationwide synthetic population database of China by using its overall cross-classification tables as well as a 0.95‰ sample from census. The methods are evaluated and compared quantitatively by measuring marginal and partial joint distribution consistency and computational cost. Results indicates that the two sample-based methods, IPFSR and CO, show a better performance on marginal indicators, whereas the sample-free ones especially sample-free fitting and JDI give a relatively small error on partial distributions. Moreover, the JDI gets a better computational performance among the five methods.

For sample-based methods, the bias of input sample will be retained in the final synthetic population inevitably. This can be avoided to some extent by sample-free techniques which treat the total population features as their start points. However, sample-free methods cannot merit the advantage of disaggregate sample – associations among all the investigated attributes. Multiple data sources other than census data might be a beneficial supplement for the issue. In Chapter 3, social relationships will be added into the basic population database so that full group structures can be considered overall.

References

1 National Bureau of Statistics of the People's Republic of China. The 5-th National Census Data. http://www.stats.gov.cn/tjsj/pcsj/rkpc/5rp/index.htm.

2 National Bureau of Statistics of the People's Republic of China. The 6-th National Census Data. http://www.stats.gov.cn/english/Statisticaldata/CensusData/rkpc2010/indexch.htm.

3 National Bureau of Statistics of the People's Republic of China. The 5-th National Census Questionaire. http://www.stats.gov.cn/tjsj/ndsj/renkoupucha/2000pucha/html/appen4.htm.

4 F. Pukelsheim and B. Simeone. On the Iterative Proportional Fitting procedure: Structure of Accumulation Points and L1-Error Analysis. 2009. http://opus.bibliothek.uni-augsburg.de/volltexte/2009/1368/pdf/mpreprint_09_005.pdf.

5 C. T. Ireland and S. Kullback. Contingency Tables with Given Marginals. Biometrika, 1968, 55(1): 179–188.

6 R. J. A. Little and M.-M. Wu. Models for Contingency Tables with Known Margins When Target and Sampled Populations Differ. Journal of the American Statistical Association, 1991, 86(413): 87–95.

7 P. Williams. Using Microsimulation to Create Synthetic Small-Area Estimates from Australia's 2001 Census. National Center for Social and Economic Modeling (NATSEM), University of Canberra, 2003.

8 O. Hellwig and R. Lloyd. Socio Demographic Barriers to Utilization and Participation in Telecommunications Services and Their Regional Distribution: A Quantitative Analysis. University of Canberra (NATSEM), 2000.

9 T. Melhuish, M. Blake and S. Day. An Evaluation of Synthetic Household Populations for Census Collection Districts Created Using Optimization Techniques. Australasian Journal of Regional Studies, 2002, 8(3): 369–387.

http://search.informit.com.au/documentSummary;dn=028511002039922; res=IELHSS.

10 A. King, R. Lloyd and J. McLellan. Regional Microsimulation for Improved Service Delivery in Australia: Centrelink's CuSP model. National Centre for Social and Economic Modeling (NATSEM), University of Canberra, 2002.

11 A. Harding, R. Lloyd, A. Bill, et al. Assessing Poverty and Inequality at A Detailed Regional Level: New Advances in Spatial Microsimulation. 2004/26. Research Paper. United Nations University, 2004.

12 J. E. Abraham, K. J. Stefan and J. D. Hunt. Population Synthesis Using Combinatorial Optimization at Multiple Levels. 91st Annual Meeting of Transportation Research Board, Washington DC, Jan. 22–26, 2012.

13 L. Ma and S. Srinivasan. Synthetic Population Generation with Multilevel Controls: A Fitness-Based Synthesis Approach and Validations. Computer-Aided Civil and Infrastructure Engineering, 2015, 30(2): 135–150.

14 N. Huynh, J. Barthelemy and P. Perez. A Heuristic Combinatorial Optimization Approach to Synthesizing a Population for Agent Based Modelling Purposes. Journal of Artificial Societies and Social Simulation, 2016, 19(4): 11. http://jasss.soc.surrey.ac.uk/19/4/11.html.

15 A. Sklar. Fonctions de repartition a n dimensions et leurs marges. Publications de l'Institut de Statistique de L'Universite de Paris, 1959, 8: 229–231.

16 I. Zezula. On Multivariate Gaussian Copulas. Journal of Statistical Planning and Inference, 2009, 139(11): 3942–3946.

17 A. Nikoloulopoulos and D. Karlis. Multivariate Logit Copula Model with An Application to Dental Data. Statistics in Medicine, 2008, 27: 6393–6406.

18 J. Neslehova. On Rank Correlation Measures for Non-Continuous Random Variables. Journal of Multivariate Analysis, 2007, 98: 544–567.

19 R. Schefzik. Multivariate Discrete Copulas, with Applications in Probabilistic Weather Forecasting. Publications de l'Institut de Statistique de l'Universite de Paris, 2015, 59(1–2): 87–116. https://arxiv.org/abs/1512.05629.

20 O. P. Faugeras. Probabilistic Constructions of Discrete Copulas. Working paper, 2012. https://hal.archives-ouvertes.fr/hal-00751393/file/copuladiscrete-submitted12-11-12.pdf.

21 F. Gargiulo, S. Ternes, S. Huet, et al. An Iterative Approach for Generating Statistically Realistic Populations of Households. PLoS ONE, 2010, 5(1), e8828.

22 J. Barthelemy and P. L. Toint. Synthetic Population Generation Without a Sample. Transportation Science, 2013, 47(2), 266–279.

23 B. Farooq, M. Bierlaire, R. Hurtubia, et al. Simulation Based Population Synthesis. Transportation Research Part B: Methodological, 2013, 58, 243–263. http://www.sciencedirect.com/science/article/pii/S0191261513001720.

24 J. Ryan, H. Maoh and P. Kanaroglou. Population Synthesis: Comparing the Major Techniques Using a Small, Complete Population of Firms. Geographical Analysis, 2009, 41(2): 181–203.

3

Synthetic Population with Social Relationships

In Chapter 2, several methodologies are explained in detail to generate a synthetic population, which plays initial groups of the agents. However, individual behaviors are not only determined by his endogenous states but also impacted by the "neighbors" in his social network. Typical social relationships derive from people's various roles played in different organizations like corporations, schools, and perhaps the most representative – households. These connections have tied individuals together and will undoubtedly trigger particular behaviors in their daily life. Urban traffic analysis is taken as an example. Members of a family may not act in an entirely independent way. Rather, they share resources and may choose to travel together in a single vehicle, to adjust their travel patterns to suit each other's schedules, or to conduct activities based on all family members' needs. Locations of the affiliated corporations and schools determine the individuals' routine destinations and may seriously affect their travel paths. The strong social links among family members may result in a constrained resource assignment in order to maximally reduce their total travel time or travel cost. Another example comes from tennis match, where two players usually shake hands after the match to express their friendship. Otherwise, they may be condemned by the public. Not as strong as the family travel, the social link seems weak but also leads to a routine action that can acquire approval from others. Hence, the influence of social relationships is not to be neglected.

In this chapter, we incorporate multiple social relationships into the synthetic population. It is not a simple extension of the basic population in Chapter 2. As shown in the following Section 3.1 to Section 3.6, consideration of such social organizations will bring some hard issues in the computational process. We will discuss them step by step. Section 3.1 will address the simplest situation, that is, the population synthesis with only households. Sections 3.2–3.4 will give several algorithms to solve that problem from three categories – individual assignment,

Parallel Population and Parallel Human: A Cyber-Physical Social Approach,
First Edition. Peijun Ye and Fei-Yue Wang.
© 2023 The Institute of Electrical and Electronics Engineers, Inc. Published 2023 by John Wiley & Sons, Inc.

heuristic search, and distribution fitting. In Section 3.5, a new type of methods called deep generative models (DGMs) developed in recent years will be introduced briefly. The problem is extended into a more general situation – population synthesis with multiple social relationships in Section 3.6. This would make the initial agent groups contain any number of social organization types. An optimization algorithm is also introduced, and comparative experiments are conducted in this section.

3.1   Household Integration in Synthetic Population

The original motivation to consider household might stem from the input data source, the census data. In many countries, the official census data provide not only person level attributes but also the family or household frequencies. For example, the aggregated statistics in Canada are released in three distinct forms by persons, census families, or households. The census family is defined by a relationship between cohabiting adults and children (and it is complicated particularly when considering cohabiting multigeneration families), while the household is defined more straightforward – consisting of all persons sharing a "dwelling unit." Clearly, there is a one-to-one relationship between households and occupied dwelling units. The dwelling unit definition is slightly more complicated and is defined as living quarters with a private entrance from the outside or from a common hallway. A more strict explanation between households and families via dwelling is given in the census handbook [1]: "People living in the same dwelling are considered a census family only if they meet the following conditions: (i) they are spouses or common-law partners, with or without never-married sons or daughters at home, and (ii) or a lone parent with at least one son or daughter who has never been married. The census family includes all blood, step-, or adopted sons and daughters who live in the dwelling and have never married. It is possible for two census families to live in the same dwelling; they may or may not be related to each other."

The connection between households and families is also provided in some disaggregate samples like the Public Use Microdata Sample (PUMS) released by Statistics Canada. The PUMS contains 2% sample of all census responses made by a person (and likewise a 1% sample of family responses and a 1–4% sample of household responses). As exampled in Table 3.1, each "private household" occupies one dwelling, in the language of the census. This one-to-one relationship between private households and "occupied private dwellings" means that the household PUMS can be used as a PUMS for dwellings. Occupied private dwellings are only one part of the dwelling universe, but almost no data are available on other types of dwellings. The missing parts of this universe are

Table 3.1 An example household with different families.

Person	Age	Mar. status	Relationship	Cen. fam.	Eco. fam.
John	63	Married	Person 1	1	A
Marie	59	Married	Wife	1	A
Julie	37	Widowed	Daughter	2	A
Robert	12	Single	Grandchild	2	A
Lucie	09	Single	Grandchild	2	A
Marc	25	Separated	Son	—	A
Nicole	12	Single	Niece	—	A
Benjamin	14	Single	Lodger (ward)	—	—
Brian	24	Married	Lodger	3	B
Janet	21	Married	Lodger's wife	3	B
Jerry	03	Single	Lodger's son	3	B

Mar., marital; cen., census; eco., economic; fam., family.

collective dwellings, some marginal dwellings (e.g. cottages that are not occupied year-round), and some dwellings under construction or conversion.

Apart from the link between households and families, disaggregate samples like Table 3.1 also reveal the compositions of each family type. As shown, family 1 consists of a couple without a child or an elder. The census usually categorizes families into several such types (see an example from Australian Bureau of Statistics in Table 3.2 [2]). According to family types, we could infer the family member types via the person's attributes. A possible composition is given in Table 3.3 where the minimum number of individuals in each household type (encoded by arbitrary denotations) are summarized. Any cell with value −1 indicates the household type in that column must not have any individuals of the corresponding individual categories in that row. Other nonnegative values represent the number of individuals in the specific household. For example, cells in row "Married/LoneParent" that have value "2" indicate that the corresponding household types must have two individuals of type "Married." Similarly, cells on this row that have value "1" indicate that the corresponding household types must have one individual of type "LoneParent." It should be noted that in some countries, household and census family are not clearly distinguished such as China. In such cases, a group of people in a household is defined as a census family so that the aggregate statistical results can be processed much easier later. So we do not distinguish household and family later in this chapter.

The compositions of each family type can be viewed as a mapping relationship from household frequencies to individual frequencies. For example, if an "elder"

Table 3.2 Categories of household type in 2006 Australian census data.

Fam. Type	With/without child. under 15	With/without dep. students	With/without non-dep. child.	Notation
Couple fam.	N	N	N	HH1
Couple fam.	Y	Y	Y	HH2
Couple fam.	Y	Y	N	HH3
Couple fam.	Y	N	Y	HH4
Couple fam.	Y	N	N	HH5
Couple fam.	N	Y	Y	HH6
Couple fam.	N	Y	N	HH7
Couple fam.	N	N	Y	HH8
1 parent fam.	Y	Y	Y	HH9
1 parent fam.	Y	Y	N	HH10
1 parent fam.	Y	N	Y	HH11
1 parent fam.	Y	N	N	HH12
1 parent fam.	N	Y	Y	HH13
1 parent fam.	N	Y	N	HH14
1 parent fam.	N	N	Y	HH15
Other fam.	—	—	—	HH16
Non fam. HH	—	—	—	NH

Fam., family; child., child (ren); dep., dependent; HH, household.

is defined as a person whose age is greater or equal to 65 years, and a "child" is defined as a person whose age is lower than 15 years, then we have

$$PerNum(age < 15) = \sum_{ft} PerNum\,(age < 15|FamType = ft)$$

$$= \sum_{ft} ChildNum \times HHNum(FamType = ft)$$

where *PerNum*, *HHNum* are aggregate frequencies of particular persons and households, and *ChildNum* means the number of children in the household of family type *ft*. Similarly, there is

$$PerNum(age \geq 65) = \sum_{ft} PerNum\,(age \geq 65|FamType = ft)$$

$$= \sum_{ft} ElderNum \times HHNum(FamType = ft)$$

Table 3.3 Compositional relationships of each household type.

	Mar./SingPare.	Un15Child	Stu.	Ov15Child	Rel.	SingPerson/ GroupHH
HH1	2	−1	−1	−1	0	−1
HH2	2	1	1	1	0	−1
HH3	2	1	1	−1	0	−1
HH4	2	1	−1	1	0	−1
HH5	2	1	−1	−1	0	−1
HH6	2	−1	1	1	0	−1
HH7	2	−1	1	−1	0	−1
HH8	2	−1	−1	1	0	−1
HH9	1	1	1	1	0	−1
HH10	1	1	1	−1	0	−1
HH11	1	1	−1	1	0	−1
HH12	1	1	−1	−1	0	−1
HH13	1	−1	1	1	0	−1
HH14	1	−1	1	−1	0	−1
HH15	1	−1	−1	1	0	−1
HH16	−1	−1	−1	−1	2	−1
NH	−1	−1	−1	−1	−1	1

Mar., married; pare., parent; stu., student; rel., relative.

and

$$PerNum(15 \leq age < 65) = \sum_{ft} PerNum(15 \leq age < 65|FamType = ft)$$

$$= \sum_{ft} (MemNum - ElderNum - ChildNum)$$

$$\times HHNum(FamType = ft)$$

In this way, the household frequencies can be converted into the individual frequencies. But things could be worse. Since the family types are trivial and complicated, the census results would not show member structures of each family type. Rather, they only provide compositions of major types, with other minor households aggregated into an "Other" category like the "Non family household" in Table 3.2. In addition, the compositions of a specific family type usually do not characterize a detailed member structure, but only a partial constraint of that household (as family of type HH1 in Table 3.3 contains at least a couple with other members' features unknown). This leads to an inconsistency between the aggregated marginal frequencies of household and individual. Therefore, our objective in population synthesis with households is to build a household–individual dataset that conforms to the aggregate marginal frequencies in both household and individual levels. Limited by the inconsistency explained before, this conformation cannot be strictly satisfied, especially when the bilevel constraints come from different data sources. Thus, the synthetic accuracy is usually measured by a sort of "distance" to the constraints.

Currently, three categories of approaches have been developed to tackle the inconsistency between household and individual synthesis. The first one, called the individual assignment, starts by independently generating an individual dataset and a household dataset according to their aggregate marginal frequencies. Then the compositions of each household type are viewed as heuristics to allocate eligible persons to households. The assignment process will assemble every household entity one by one and finally get a total synthetic population with links between the two datasets. The second approach is heuristic search, which deems the population composition as an aggregate state that meets the household and individual controls. With the multiple controls calculated as a total fitness function, this method conducts a trail-and-error search to achieve an acceptable solution. The third approach, referred to be the joint distribution fitting, takes the household and individual as a whole. By treating the marginal frequencies from household and individual as mutual constraints, it computes their joint frequency distributions. Then, Monte Carlo method is exploited to extract households from the achieved distribution. Since the distribution contains both household and individual attributes, we can directly construct the members in every extracted household. These methodologies will be elucidated in detail in Sections 3.2–3.4.

3.2 Individual Assignment

Individual assignment, developed earlier than other methods, may be the most intuitive one to introduce household relationship into synthetic population. It begins with generations of household and individual entity pools. The generation of each entity pool reduces to a classic problem of basic population synthesis and thus can be solved by the approaches elaborated in the Chapter 2 such synthetic reconstruction via iterative proportional fitting (IPF), combinatorial optimization, etc. For iterative proportional fitting synthetic reconstruction (IPFSR), the step requires joint distribution estimations at each level separately, and then the entity drawing. As household and individual usually differentiate in their investigated attributes, the two kinds of distributions can be estimated both through IPF fitting. Based on the entity pools, individuals and households are connected one by one so that the membership can be established. This allocation process assembles each individual into a suitable family on condition that its attributes match the family constraints. As mentioned before, the family constraints usually derive from the compositions of each household type predefined by the census. When one of the two pools has decreased to null in assignment, the population synthesis has reached its stop condition. One merit of individual assignment approach is its relatively low computational complexity due to its separated synthesized households and individuals. It also intuitively reproduces the formation of family in reality. However, since the individual and household distributions may probably be inconsistent as explained in Section 3.1, the two generated entity pools are mostly incompatible as well. Therefore, individual assignment will not run out households and individuals simultaneously. And it will cause the final synthetic population to conform to either household or individual constraints, but not both. To date, the assignment method concerning family relationships has been applied in several projects. Gargiulo et al. presented an iterative method to generate statistically realistic population of households [3]. It is worth pointing out that their method uses aggregated census data only. Barthelemy and Toint proposed another sample-free household selection method based on entropy maximization and tabu search [4]. And they adopted it to Belgian synthetic population generation. Recently, population assignment is used by Huet et al. to create households in French municipalities and to study dynamics of labor status and job changes [5]. Nam Huynh et al. used population assignment to generate the synthetic population of New South Wales most recently [2]. They assigned the basic population according to the household–individual mapping relations as illustrated in Section 3.1.

As already shown, the synthesizer using individual assignment starts with the constructions of an individual pool and a household pool. The construction can exploit either the sample-based or sample-free methods. This problem has been clearly discussed in Chapter 2 and will not be repeated here. The resulted individual pool contains a collection of disaggregated records, with each providing detailed and full studied information of a synthetic individual. This pool is consistent with the aggregated census tables, meaning that the number of synthetic individuals is exactly the size of the target population. Furthermore, its endogenous structure can be deemed as a "best" estimation for the reality, so that the pool, in principle, is able to serve as an alternative to the real micro-population data. Likewise, the household pool similarly contains synthetic household entities with family attributes, with the total number also being equal to the real family groups. By the construction of family attributes, composition of each family type may probably be formed as tabled in Table 3.3. Once the pools are constructed, the next task is to establish links between individuals and households in order that they could be appropriately assembled. This process is usually implemented as an individual assignment to a household one by one. Such assignment is determined by the following conditions:

1. the requirement of individual characteristics for a given household type;
2. the distribution of total number of males and females for each household type;
3. the distribution of households by household size.

These three conditions play as particular constraints to the assemble of households. But the allocation algorithm that simultaneously satisfies these requirements would be computationally inefficient. Thus, we introduce a two-stage method here to avoid such a problem. The first stage concentrates on the requirements of individual members for each household type. This could be viewed as a basic allocation of the essential persons that satisfies each household's composition, without considering the family size. After the allocation, most households still include fewer members than they ought to be. So the second stage would fill each household entity with several unassigned persons from the rest individual pool. This process would also focus on the individual marginal frequencies that are converted from the household frequencies (as shown in Section 3.1). The two stages are described in the following.

3.2.1 Heuristic Allocation

The heuristic allocation stage assigns the fewest persons that are necessary to a given household, according to the compositions of each family type. Take Table 3.3 for example. The allocation is composed of seven steps. The first step is a "Married" couple assignment. Households with types from "HH1" to "HH8" need a couple. Thus, for every family falls into these categories, a married male and a married female are randomly selected from the individual pool to form a married couple. "A male and a female" here can be treated as a constraint for a couple. This constraint may be relaxed on condition that homosexual marriage is admitted in some countries. By contrast, additional constraints on the two selected candidates can be also considered. For instance, the match probability is usually set to follow a predefined distribution related to their age gap, which is represented as a matrix:

$$DAge_{ij} = MarriedMale_i.age - MarriedFemale_j.age$$

where $1 \leq i \leq Num\{MarriedMale\}$ and $1 \leq j \leq Num\{MarriedFemale\}$. Apart from the age gap, the selection of the couple to be allocated into a household is further constrained by the female minimum age. This minimum age is determined based on the types of children entitled to this household type, as elaborated as follows:

1. Households that fall into types "HH2" to "HH4" and "HH6" to "HH8" require at least one "Student" and/or one "Ov15Child." Since either of the two

individual types is more than 15-year-old, the minimum age of the female parent allocated should be older than 15 plus the age of consent (say 16);
2. For households of types "HH1" and "HH5" where on children and at least one "Un15Child" are essential, the female's minimum age to be allocated is the age of consent.

By satisfying the parental minimum age constraint in this step, more accurate allocations child individuals (i.e. "Un15Child," "Student," and "Ov15Child") could be achieved in later steps. The couple that both (i) has a valid corresponding age gap in line with the age gap matrix and (ii) meets the aforementioned conditions of parental minimum age is selected. The selected couples are attached to the list of members of the household being considered and are removed from the pool of synthetic individuals. Allocated individuals will not be considered in the subsequent selections. As eligible couples are iteratively drawn, the individual pool gradually shrinks. When there is no pair satisfying the second condition, the pair with the female age closest to the parental minimum age gap is selected. The allocation may end with a situation that only one "Married" individual remains in the pool. In this case, a new "Married" individual is created for a couple matching. The gender and age group of the created person are determined to minimize the fitness function. In this section, we set the global fitness function to be the root mean square between the marginal frequencies converted by the household compositions from census table and the corresponding marginal frequencies in the resulting synthetic population. But note that any arbitrarily defined "distance" would be applicable here to represent the final accuracy. The "Married" couple assignment stops when the computation meets either of the two conditions: there is no household of type "HH1" to "HH8" remaining in the household pool, or there is no "Married" individual remaining in the individual pool. In both cases, any remaining "Married" individuals (household exhausted) or remaining households (individual exhausted) are forced to be deleted.

The second step is a "SingParent" assignment. Household with type "HH9" to "HH15" needs this step. Similar as Step 1, the allocation of a "SingParent" also considers the minimum parental age, which depends on the types of entitled children:

1. Households that fall into types "HH8," "HH9" to "HH11" and "HH13" to "HH15" require at least one "Student" and/or one "Ov15Child." Since either type is with the minimum age of 15 years, the female parent should be older than 15 plus the age of consent;
2. For households of type "HH12," only one "Un15Child" is essential. So the minimum age of the female parent is set to be the age of consent.

For each of these households, the assignment stochastically chooses a "Sing Parent" from the individual pool and links him to the list of members of the household being considered. The assigned individual is removed from the pool of synthetic individuals and will not be considered in the subsequent allocations. If there is no "SingParent" remaining in the individual pool, a new individual with the "SingParent" attribute is created for each of the remaining households. The gender and age of the created individual are also determined to minimize the global fitness function as defined before. The computation stops when all the corresponding households have been assigned.

The third step is an "Ov15Child" assignment. Households with types "HH2," "HH4," "HH6," "HH8," "HH9," "HH11," "HH13," and "HH15" need a member of such type. After the former steps of assignment, each household in these categories has either a "Married" couple (from Step 1) or a "SingParent" (from Step 2). The allocation of an "Ov15Child" in this step is constrained by the biological law which sets out the range of age gap between a child and his/her parents in a household. For households with a "Married" couple, the age of the female parent is used in this constraint. For the "SingParent" households, the age of that parent is used.

All the households considered in this step are arranged in a descending order, according to the age of the selected parent for the child–parent age gap constraint. The collection of "Ov15Child" individuals in the individual pool is also sorted by their age. For each household in the sorted sequence, the allocation algorithm checks the oldest available "Ov15Child" that satisfies the upper bound and lower bound of the child–parent age gap constraint. This allocation strategy guarantees that such a constraint can be met as much as possible, given the census distribution of "Ov15Child" individuals and the distributions of "Married" and "SingParent" individuals across the age groups in a target area.

When there is no "Ov15Child" satisfies the child–parent age gap constraint, the individual whose age is closest to either the upper or the lower bound is selected. A potential explanation for these cases may be that the selected "Ov15Child" is not a natural child to the parent(s) but either an adopted child, foster child, or step child. If no "Ov15Child" remains in the individual pool while at least one household requiring this type of individuals still remains in the household pool, a new "Ov15Child" is created for each of the remaining households. The age and gender of each of the created individuals are determined by minimization of the global fitness function. The computation stops when all the corresponding households have been assigned.

The forth step is a "Student" assignment. Households with types "HH2," "HH3," "HH6," "HH7," "HH9," "HH10," "HH13," and "HH14" need a "Student" to be their members. The allocation of a "Student" resembles the algorithm that allocates "Ov15Child" in Step 3, which is not re-explained here. The fifth step is an "Un15Child" assignment. Households in types "HH2" to "HH5" and "HH9" to "HH12" need this step. The allocation of an "Un15Child" also resembles the allocation of an "Ov15Child" in Step 3. The sixth step is a pair of "Relative" assignment. This step is applicable to households with type "HH16." Two individuals with "Relative" attributes are randomly drawn from the individual pool for each of these households. If the available "Relative" individuals are insufficient for the remaining households, new individuals of that type are created, on condition that the global fitness is minimized. The computation stops when all "HH16" households have been allocated with a pair of "Relative."

The last step is the "SingPerson" and "GroupHH" assignment. This step is applicable for the "NH" households, where a "SingPerson" individual is stochastically drawn from the individual pool and assigned to each household with one member. In case that the number of "SingPerson" individuals is less than the number of 1-member "NH" households, and new eligible individuals are created on condition that the global fitness is minimized. Individuals with "GroupHH" attributes are stochastically extracted and assigned to "NH" households with more than one member. Such an assignment follows the frequency of nonfamily households (also known as the collective households) by household size as specified in a census table. New "GroupHH" individuals will be created provided that the number of corresponding persons is insufficient. Their attributes like age and gender are designed to minimize the fitness as well. This step stops when all nonfamily households are filled with required members.

3.2.2 Iterative Allocation

The heuristic allocation elaborated in Section 3.2.1, in fact, only assigns the fewest essential members to each household. It can be deemed as the result that meets the minimum requirements of each type of households. Due to the "SingPerson" and "GroupHH" assignment in the last step, the synthetic households with type "NH" should all have been assembled completely with required members following the household size from census data. Thus, this type will not be considered furthermore in this part. The rest individuals contained in the individual pool at this time should only involve categories of "Un15Child," "Student," "Ov15Child," and "Relative." In this stage, iterative allocation aims to assign these remaining individuals into synthetic households with the constraints both from the frequencies of individuals by household type and from the frequencies of family households by household size. Given a remaining individual, the allocation algorithm investigates each feasible synthetic household and calculates the global fitness. Here, a "feasible" household means the one that will not violate the constraints from its composition (as illustrated in Table 3.3) when the considered individual assigned to this household. The global fitness function, as mentioned before, adopts the root mean square error between the individual frequencies by family household type in the census data and in the synthetic population:

$$RMSE_{Per} = \sqrt{\frac{1}{n_{HH\,Type}} \sum_{i=1}^{n_{HH\,Type}} \left(PerC_i - PerS_i\right)^2}$$

where

$$PerC_i = \begin{cases} \dfrac{PerNumC_i}{1+\sum_{j=1}^{n_{HH\,Type}} PerNumC_j}, & i \neq k \\[3ex] \dfrac{1+PerNumC_i}{1+\sum_{j=1}^{n_{HH\,Type}} PerNumC_j}, & i = k \end{cases}$$

and

$$PerS_i = \begin{cases} \dfrac{PerNumS_i}{1+\sum_{j=1}^{n_{HHType}} PerNumS_j}, & i \neq k \\[3ex] \dfrac{1+PerNumS_i}{1+\sum_{j=1}^{n_{HHType}} PerNumS_j}, & i = k \end{cases}$$

PerNumC and *PerNumS* are the person numbers in the census and in the current synthesized population (that is before the individual being investigated is allocated to any household). The subscript i stands for a particular household type, and n_{HHType} is the total number of household type. k is the index in *PerNumS* related to the type of feasible synthetic household being considered. The root mean square error between the household frequencies by household size in the census data and in the synthetic population is analogously defined:

$$RMSE_{HH} = \sqrt{\frac{1}{n_{HHSize}} \sum_{i=1}^{n_{HHSize}} \left(HHC_i - HHS_i\right)^2}$$

where

$$HHC_i = \frac{HHNumC_i}{\sum_{j=1}^{n_{HHSize}} HHNumC_j}$$

and

$$HHS_i = \begin{cases} \dfrac{HHNumS_i}{1+\sum_{j=1}^{n_{HHSize}} HHNumS_j}, & i \neq k \\[3ex] \dfrac{1+HHNumS_i}{1+\sum_{j=1}^{n_{HHSize}} HHNumS_j}, & i = k \end{cases}$$

HHNumC and *HHNumS* are the household numbers in the census and in the current synthesized population (before the individual being investigated is allocated to any household). The subscript i here stands for a particular household size, and n_{HHSize} is the number of valid categories of household size. k is the index in *HHNumS* related to the new household size category of the feasible synthetic household being considered which the current synthetic individual should be allocated to.

Given a possible allocation of a considered individual to a feasible household, the pair of the aforementioned relative mean standard errors (RMSEs) defines a "distance" between census and the current synthetic population. Thus during the iterative allocation, the optimal assignment is the household that leads to the minimal RMSEs both in the individual frequencies by household type and in the household frequencies by household size. If such optimal assignment is not available, which indicates that any of the feasible choices cannot strictly outperform others, it means there is a set of assignments formed the Pareto front of RMSE data points. In this case, the allocation will randomly pick a strategy from the Pareto front. The stop condition of iterative allocation in this stage is that all the remaining individuals are assigned to a particular household in the household pool. Then, we get the final synthetic population.

3.3   Heuristic Search

While the individual assignment tries to build links between persons and households, heuristic search views the synthetic population as an aggregate state that meets multiple controls. Representative method in this category is the fitness-based procedure [6]. Basically, this procedure is a kind of sample-based method. It selects a set of households via a sampling with replacement from the seed data to satisfy both the individual and household controls. In particular, the procedure starts with an initial set of households, which can be either a null set without any household or a random sample from the seed data. Then, the synthesis is conducted as an iterative process. In each iteration, a specific household together with all its members is either added or removed from the current household pool. Marginal count tables are used to control the number of households in each type. These count tables are given by the statistical marginal or partial frequencies of census data and are defined as the control tables. By considering all the control tables both from household and person levels, it enables us to assess whether the multilevel constraints have been satisfied. The nearer between current household pool and control tables, the better that the population matches the target.

The core of the fitness-based procedure is a swap mechanism, determining whether a household is to be added or removed at any iteration. For such a purpose, two "fitness" values are calculated for each household as following:

$$F_I^{in} = \sum_{j=1}^{J} \sum_{k=1}^{K_j} \left[\left(R_{jk}^{n-1} \right)^2 - \left(R_{jk}^{n-1} - HT_{jk}^i \right)^2 \right]$$

$$F_{II}^{in} = \sum_{j=1}^{J} \sum_{k=1}^{K_j} \left[\left(R_{jk}^{n-1} \right)^2 - \left(R_{jk}^{n-1} + HT_{jk}^i \right)^2 \right]$$

The "type I" fitness value, denoted as F_I^{in}, is the reduced sum of squared error in matching the control tables if the ith household is selected to be added into the population pool at the nth iteration. The "type II" fitness value, denoted as F_{II}^{in}, is the corresponding error if the ith household is removed at the nth iteration. j is an index standing for the control tables and J is the total number of control tables. For example, $j = 1$ could represent the joint distribution of household size against residential area. $j = 2$ could represent the joint distribution of age against gender, etc. For each control table j, k is an index standing for the different cells in that table. For example, in table $j = 1$ ("household size against residential area"), k could have values from 1 through 14 representing the 14 different cells (seven categories for household size multiplied by the two categories for residential area). Therefore, K_1 here equals to 14, with $k = 1$ representing the first cell (one person/own household) and $k = 2$ representing the second cell (two person/own household), etc. $R_{jk}^{n-1} = T_{jk} - CT_{jk}^{n-1}$ is the number of households/persons required to satisfy the target for cell k in control table j after iteration $n - 1$. T_{jk} represents the value of cell k in control table j, and it is also the target number of households of a particular type to be synthesized. CT_{jk}^{n-1} represents the value of cell k in count table j after iteration $n - 1$. HT_{jk}^i is the contribution of the ith household in the seed data to the kth cell in control table j. Obviously, $\left(R_{jk}^{n-1} - HT_{jk}^i \right)$ is the number households required to achieve the target in the corresponding cell if household i is added into the pool. $\left(R_{jk}^{n-1} + HT_{jk}^i \right)$ is the required number households to achieve the target cell if household i is removed from the pool. Therefore, as already described, the fitness values capture the reduced sum of squared error in matching the control tables. It is useful to acknowledge that using the fundamental terms R_{jk}^{n-1}, $(R_{jk}^{n-1} - HT_{jk}^i)$ and $(R_{jk}^{n-1} + HT_{jk}^i)$. Note that other functional forms of the fitness can be also introduced. In our case, we assume that all the control tables are equally important. This assumption may also be arbitrarily set if this is not the case. For instance, dominant weights can be assigned to the household size tables when the matching of the household size distribution is more important than that of the individual age.

By starting with a set of households that can be either a null set without any household or a random sample from the seed data, all values of the count tables are set according to the initial population. This metric is zero if the set is NULL or the aggregation of the random sample. The two fitness values defined before are computed for each household in the seed data. All households in the seed with positive type I fitness values are considered as the candidates for addition into the synthetic population pool. By contrast, the households in the seed with positive type II fitness values and already present in the currently synthetic population pool are considered as the candidates for removal. It should be noted that for any household, the two fitness values cannot be both positive at the same time. This is clearly from the following fact that the sum of the two fitness values is negative:

$$F_I^{in} + F_{II}^{in} = -2\sum_{j=1}^{J}\sum_{k=1}^{K_j}\left(HT_{jk}^i\right)^2$$

Once the household candidates for addition and removal determined, a particular one is randomly extracted and is either added or removed according to its candidate type. The adding or removing operation will elicit the change of values of the cells in the count tables. And this procedure has completed one full iteration. By using the new count table values from the updated population pool, the fitness values are recalculated and the procedure continues. Because the fitness value of the household addition and removal is positive, the count table after any iteration will approach to with the control tables more closely than previous iteration. In this way, the algorithm gradually reduces the distances between the synthetic population and the control tables with each iteration. As a consequence, it ultimately leads to one of the best possible populations that matches the control tables as much as possible given a convergence criterion.

In essence, the incremental improvement of fitness values aforementioned provides a heuristic search mechanism to get a population estimation. However, other variants of the selection procedure are also applicable. For example, the greedy heuristic that selects the household with the highest fitness can be used as well. However, such a greedy strategy will bring a sampling bias rather than our stochastic selection. The latter draws a household from all the eligible candidates, maximally preserving the correlations among the investigated attributes. A further improvement may come from the arbitrary configuration of the sample probabilities instead of simple stochastic sampling if it is known that certain household types were over or under sampled in the disaggregate seed such as the PUMS data.

A natural convergence criterion for the computation termination could be a predefined threshold that restricts the final error into a certain extent. This operation can be viewed as a truncation of search and may save computational time. However, even if that threshold is missing, the algorithm will still stop after certain iterations. It is because with a finite household pool, the computation will always reach a state that no households in seed data have positive values for either type I or type II fitness. To theoretically estimate the computational complexity, we assume that the sequence of selected households are $(s_1, \ldots, s_l, \ldots, s_n)$ and $T_{jk} = R_{jk}^0$. Define the operation performed on household s_l as u_l where $u_l = 1$

if the household is added and $u_l = -1$ if the household is removed. Then, we have

$$\sum_{j=1}^{J}\sum_{k=1}^{K_j}\left(R_{jk}^{n}\right)^2 = \sum_{j=1}^{J}\sum_{k=1}^{K_j}\left(T_{jk}\right)^2 - \sum_{l=1}^{n}\sum_{j=1}^{J}\sum_{k=1}^{K_j}\left[\left(R_{jk}^{n-1}\right)^2 - \left(R_{jk}^{n-1} - u_l \cdot HT_{jk}^{s_l}\right)^2\right]$$

$$= \sum_{j=1}^{J}\sum_{k=1}^{K_j}\left(T_{jk}\right)^2 - \sum_{l=1}^{n}F^{s_l l}$$

where $F^{s_l l} = \max\{F_I^{s_l l}, F_{II}^{s_l l}\}$. In the aforementioned equation, $F^{s_l l}$ is the positive fitness value of household s_l at iteration l. As a consequence, there is

$$n \le \sum_{l=1}^{n}F^{s_l l} = \sum_{j=1}^{J}\sum_{k=1}^{K_j}\left(T_{jk}\right)^2 - \sum_{j=1}^{J}\sum_{k=1}^{K_j}\left(R_{jk}^{n}\right)^2 \le \sum_{j=1}^{J}\sum_{k=1}^{K_j}\left(T_{jk}\right)^2$$

This manifests that our algorithm will stop after $\sum_{j=1}^{J}\sum_{k=1}^{K_j}\left(T_{jk}\right)^2$ iterations in the worst case. In practice, this upper bound is extremely conservative as the fitness value of each household is much large than 1. Empirical results indicate that the number of iterations is about twice the number of households to be synthesized.

3.4 Joint Distribution Fitting

The individual assignment assembles each household by iteratively allocating eligible members from the individual pool. This process seems quite intuitive as we are in reality first ourselves and then the social roles. However, as the individual and household pools can be guaranteed to match each other when generated independently, the subsequent allocation may probably result in the households are all "filled," while a few persons still remained. Usually, such a result is not optimal (with the minimum overall errors). Thus, researchers have considered this problem in a different way – from the statistical perspective. The main idea is to optimize the overall error during the computation of individual-household joint distribution. Then each household with its members can be extracted directly by using Monte Carlo realization or other typical methods. In essence, this approach, called joint distribution fitting, does not solve the inconsistency between marginal constraints from household and individual levels. It only deals with the problem ahead, at the beginning of the synthesis. This is quite different from the individual assignment where inconsistency is optimized when the persons are allocated as shown in Section 3.3. Therefore, in the fitting stage, the joint distribution cannot conform to the marginals of mutual properties provided by household and individual. Thus, how to obtain the particular joint distribution with the smallest deviations between both household and individual constraints becomes the primary issue.

Currently, several techniques have emerged to tackle this issue. Melhuish et al. adopted three linked convergence algorithms to create synthetic households of the Australian capital territory by adjusting the household weights marginally [7]. In each round, the procedure involved an overall evaluation of all target variables and a multidimensional search for convergence by changing a pair of weights in a positive and/or negative direction. The evaluation measure was set to be the absolute residual between disaggregate household data derived from Household Expenditure Survey and aggregate census targets. Ballas et al. used a deterministic reweighting approach to generate households of small areas in Great Britain [8]. In their study, the weights were fitted on the basis of British Household Panel Survey and applied to compensate for nonresponding households and those individuals in a responding household who failed to give a full investigation. Guo and Bhat combined household and individual distributions and designed a recursive procedure to merge marginal tables of each mutual attribute [9]. Their procedure computed the merged distribution by selecting from a disaggregate dataset. To our knowledge, Guo's method has firstly considered the unified distribution explicitly, which is much intuitive. However, during each household selection, the household- and individual-level counts must be updated dynamically. It seems much time-consuming and computational expensive. Pritchard has studied the problem of inconsistency carefully in his master's thesis [10]. After investigation of its sources, he provided an easily operational approach to try to deal with this issue. In brief, when the person population fitted with IPF algorithm, the slice distribution of households can be applied as its marginal constraints rather than that of individuals. This process can be also conducted reversely – using slice distribution of individuals to constraint the household fitting. Objectively, Pritchard's method only involves one direction adjustment. As he said in his paper, "it is possible that the family population will still not be able to fit the total margin from the individual population" and "the two PUMS could be cross-classified using the shared attributes and forced to agree" [11]. Auld and Mohammadian developed another technique to determine how both household- and person-level characteristics can jointly be used as controls when synthesizing populations [12]. They introduced Bayesian method to assemble the constraints from two levels and calculate selection probability of each sample household. Like Guo's approach, their method still needs to recalculate selection probability in each iteration. And if there are still households remaining to be generated in the final iteration, the program will disregard all person-level controls and generate the remaining households based only on the household constraints. It can be seen that Auld's method does not solve the inconsistency completely. They tackled this problem by forcing the population to the household marginal compulsively. Another technique called iterative proportional updating (IPU) was proposed by Ye et al. [13]. Their algorithm aims at iteratively adjusting and reallocating weights among households of a certain type until both household- and person-level attributes are matched.

To clearly elucidate the joint distribution fitting, here we take the IPU algorithm as an example. IPU is a sample-based method which means it requires a set of disaggregate sample records. It is developed to fit the weights of different types of households so that households and individuals can simultaneously satisfy the statistical marginals in both levels. Consider a target population that contains two household types and three individual types. Here, a household/individual type is defined by a particular combination of its attributes. For instance, (*Number of Members=3, Type of Residence=urban*) and (*Number of Members=3, Type of Residence=rural*) are two different household types. Table 3.4 gives the compositions of each household. Household type 1 contains three possible cases indicated by the top three rows. The first row means that in this composition, the household consists of one person of each individual types 1, 2, and 3. The compositions of each household shown in the table actually depict the mapping relations from household to persons. They are determined from the input sample. In this example, there are eight households with 23 individuals. All initial household weights are set to be one arbitrarily. The "weighted sum" row represents the sum of each column weighted by the "weights" column. The "constraints" row provides the marginal distributions of household and individual types that must be matched. The δ_a and δ_b rows calculate the absolute value of the relative difference between the weighted sum and the given constraints so that the "goodness-of-fit" of the algorithm can be assessed at each stage of the algorithm and convergence criteria can be set. Typical objective functions are

$$\sum_j \left[\frac{\sum_i d_{i,j} \cdot \omega_i - c_j}{c_j} \right]^2 \text{ or } \sum_j \frac{\left[\sum_i d_{i,j} \cdot \omega_i - c_j\right]^2}{c_j} \text{ or } \sum_j \frac{\left|\sum_i d_{i,j} \cdot \omega_i - c_j\right|}{c_j} \quad (3.1)$$

where $w_i \geq 0$; i stands for the household ($i = 1, \ldots, 8$); j stands for the constraint ($j = 1, \ldots, 5$); $d_{i,j}$ is the frequency of household or person of type j in household i; w_i is the weight of the ith household; c_j is the value of constraint j.

The IPU algorithm starts by setting initial weights for all households according to the disaggregate sample. It then proceeds by adjusting weights for each household/person constraint in an iterative fashion until the constraints are matched as closely as possible for both household and person attributes. As in the table, the weights for the first household level constraint are adjusted by dividing the number of households in that category (i.e. the constraint value) by the weighted sum of the first household type column. That ratio is $35/3 = 11.67$. The weights for all households of household type 1 are multiplied by this ratio to satisfy the constraint. The weights for all households of household type 1 become equal to 11.67, and the weighted sum for household type 1 will be equal to the corresponding constraint, as shown in the row titled "weighted sum 1." Similarly, the weights for households

Table 3.4 An example of the iterative proportional updating (IPU) algorithm[a].

HH ID	Wei	HHT 1	HHT 2	IndT 1	IndT 2	IndT 3	Wei 1	Wei 2	Wei 3	Wei 4	Wei 5	FWei
1	1	1	0	1	1	1	11.67	11.67	9.51	8.05	12.37	1.36
2	1	1	0	1	0	1	11.67	11.67	9.51	9.51	14.61	25.66
3	1	1	0	2	1	0	11.67	11.67	9.51	8.05	8.05	7.98
4	1	0	1	1	0	2	1.00	13.00	10.59	10.59	16.28	27.79
5	1	0	1	0	2	1	1.00	13.00	13.00	11.00	16.91	18.45
6	1	0	1	1	1	0	1.00	13.00	10.59	8.97	8.97	8.64
7	1	0	1	2	1	2	1.00	13.00	10.59	8.97	13.78	1.47
8	1	0	1	1	1	0	1.00	13.00	10.59	8.97	8.97	8.64
Weighted Sum		3.00	5.00	9.00	7.00	7.00						
Constraints		35.00	65.00	91.00	65.00	104.00						
δ_b		0.9143	0.9231	0.9011	0.8923	0.9327						
Weighted Sum 1		**35.00**	5.00	51.67	28.33	28.33						
Weighted Sum 2		35.00	**65.00**	111.67	88.33	88.33						
Weighted Sum 3		28.52	55.38	**91.00**	76.80	74.39						
Weighted Sum 4		25.60	48.50	80.11	**65.00**	67.68						
Weighted Sum 5		35.02	64.90	104.84	85.94	**104.00**						
δ_a		0.0006	0.0015	0.1521	0.3222	0.0000						
FWei Sum		35.00	65.00	91.00	65.00	104.00						

a) HH, HouseHold; HHT, HouseHold Type; Ind, Individual; IndT, Individual Type; Wei, Weight; FWei, Final Weight. The bold values mean that after each fitting step, the weights are fitted to align one column.

of household type 2 are adjusted by an amount equal to $65/5 = 13.00$. The updated weights are shown in the "weights 2" column of Table 3.4, and one notes that the household-level constraints are perfectly satisfied at this point (see the row titled "weighted sum 2").

In next stage, the weights of households are updated to satisfy the constraints from person level. For the first person-level constraint, the adjustment is calculated as the ratio of the constraint for person type 1 to weight sum of the person type 1 column after the completion of household-level adjustments. This ratio is equal to $91/111.67 = 0.81$. Then the value is used to update the weights of all households that have individuals of person type 1. As the fifth household (household ID 5) does not have any persons of type 1, the weight for this particular household remains unchanged. The resulting adjusted weights are shown in the column entitled "weights 3." The constraint corresponding to person type 1 is now perfectly matched. The process is repeated for constraints of the other two person types, and the corresponding updated weights are shown in the columns entitled "weights 4" and "weights 5" in Table 3.4. The corresponding weighted sums are shown in the various rows entitled "weighted sum."

The completion of two-stage adjustments to weights for one full set of constraints is defined as one iteration. It can be seen from the table that the difference between the weighted sums and the corresponding constraints for the household/person types of interest has been considerably reduced after one complete iteration. If the absolute value of the relative difference between the weighted sum and the corresponding constraint may be used as a goodness-of-fit measure and is defined as:

$$\delta_j = \frac{\left| d_{i,j} \cdot w_i - c_j \right|}{c_j}$$

where all notations are as denoted earlier in the context of Eq. (3.1). The average value of this measure across all constraints is denoted by δ and serves as an overall goodness-of-fit measure after each complete iteration. Prior to any adjustments being made to the weights, the value of δ, denoted as δ_b, is found to be 0.9127. After the completion of one full iteration, the value of δ, denoted as δ_a, is found to be 0.0954, representing a substantial improvement in the matching of the weighted sample against known population numbers. The gain in fit between two consecutive iterations can be calculated as:

$$\Delta = \left| \delta_b - \delta_a \right|$$

In this particular example, the gain in fit after one iteration is 0.8173. The entire process is continued until the gain in fit is negligible or below a preset tolerance level. This tolerance level serves as the convergence criterion at which the algorithm is terminated. The weights are thus adjusted iteratively until the value of

Δ is less than a small threshold, ε (say, 10^{-7}). Convergence criteria can be set as a reasonable compromise between desired goodness-of-fit and computation time. As the fitting iteration goes on, the δ value reduces. After certain iterations (about 80), the fitness across all constraints comes very close to 0.01, after about 250 rounds, the δ value reduces to 0.001. When the δ value is small enough to show that the weighted sums almost perfectly match the household-type and person-type constraints, we can say that the algorithm finds an acceptable solution. At this moment, the weights for households belonging to a particular household type may be no longer identical. Essentially, households with their individual members can be directly generated according to the fitted weights, and the final synthetic population would match both the given household and person constraints (in this case, perfectly). The final weights are listed in the row entitled "final weighted sum" in the table.

3.5 Deep Generative Models

While the individual assignment and distribution fitting synthesize population by explicitly investigating combinations of personal attributes, DGMs developed in recent years provide a novel path for that task. Unlike the two previous methods that deal with the constraints of attribute combinations in the assignment or distribution fitting stages, DGMs treat them in an implicit way when drawing a person as the output. Generally, DGMs, usually implemented as generative adversarial network (GAN) or Variational Auto-Encoder (VAE), learn a latent distribution from given population samples and then iteratively extract the synthetic individuals/households by getting the output from their direct reasoning. This process essentially performs a sampling in the hidden space. And constraints of attribute combinations are applied as a condition part in the input or sometimes as a criterion for acceptance of the output. In the following, two major models, GAN and VAE, are discussed in detail.

Let X be the disaggregate sample (represented as an attribute combination) and $P(X)$ be the joint probability distribution elicited by X. A GAN is composed of two artificial neural networks, called a generator and a discriminator. It estimates the joint probability distributions of population attributes based on the iterative training of the two networks. These two networks play a min-max two-player game where the generator tries to cheat the discriminator by generating as realistic data as possible, while the discriminator tries to distinguish the generated fake data from the real one. When the two-player game reaches an equilibrium, the training is over. Mathematically, the generator referred to as $G(z; \phi_g)$ parameterized by ϕ_g estimates $P_\phi(\hat{X})$, with a z sampled from a prior random distribution (say a multivariate normal distribution $P(z)$). In other words, it forms mapping from z

to $\hat{X}$. Here, $\hat{X} = G(z)$ is the output of generator. The parameterized discriminator $D(X; \phi_d)$ judges whether the attribute combination is from the real data X or the fake data $\hat{X}$. For an easy computation, its output usually gives a probability that the input X is sampled from the real data. The network parameters ϕ_g and ϕ_d are learned by optimizing the following value function:

$$\min_{\phi_g} \max_{\phi_d} \mathbb{E}_{X \sim P(X)}[\log D(X)] + \mathbb{E}_{z \sim P(z)}[\log(1 - D(G(z)))]$$

The inner optimization means that the discriminator in each training epoch tries to maximize the value by imposing a higher $D(X)$ and a lower $D(G(z))$, which aims to elevate the ability to distinguish the two kinds of inputs. The outer optimization trains the generator to minimize $\log(1 - D(G(z)))$ by deceiving D with generated data.

An equilibrium is achieved when the Jensen–Shannon divergence (JSD) between the generated distribution $P_\phi(\hat{X})$ and the real distribution $P(X)$ is minimized. When the generated data are multi-categorical, however, $P(X)$ is discrete on a K-dimensional set of simplex ($\{p_i \geq 0, \sum p_i = 1\}$), but $P_\phi(\hat{X})$ is continuous over this simplex set. This discrepancy will bring an instability of equilibrium because it may lead to an infinite JSD. Therefore, a Wasserstein generative adversarial network (WGAN) with a gradient penalty (GP) is usually employed [14]. Instead of JSD, the training of WGAN minimizes the Wasserstein distance (WD) between $P_\phi(\hat{X})$ and $P(X)$ and thus does not suffer from the instability problem as WD is continuous and differentiable almost everywhere. The GP is further used to restrict the parameter search space of discriminator to stabilize the training. The final loss function is

$$\mathcal{L} = \mathcal{L}_d + \mathcal{L}_g + \lambda \cdot \mathcal{L}_{GP}$$

where

$$\mathcal{L}_d = \frac{1}{m} \sum_{i=1}^{m} -D(X_i) + D(G(z_i))$$

$$\mathcal{L}_g = \frac{1}{m} \sum_{i=1}^{m} -D(G(z_i))$$

$$\mathcal{L}_{GP} = \frac{1}{m} \sum_{i=1}^{m} (\|\nabla_{\tilde{X}_l} D(\tilde{X}_l)\|_2 - 1)^2$$

and

$$\tilde{X}_l = \alpha \hat{X}_i + (1 - \alpha)X_i, \quad \alpha \sim Uniform[0, 1]$$

m is the size of mini-batch sampled from training data. $\| \cdot \|_2$ is an Euclidian norm. $\hat{X}_i$ and X_i are the generated and real data, respectively. $\tilde{X}_l$ is a weighted average of

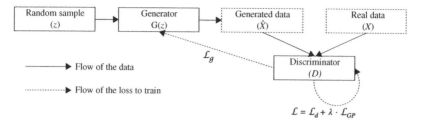

Figure 3.1 Training procedure of GAN.

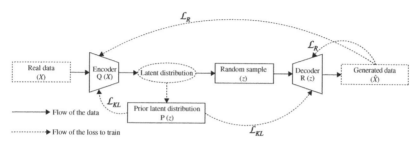

Figure 3.2 Training procedure of VAE.

them with λ being the weight for GP term. Clearly, $\mathcal{L}_d$ corresponds to maximizing the value function, and $\mathcal{L}_{GP}$ regularizes it based on D's gradients. $\mathcal{L}_g$ indicates minimizing $\log(1 - D(G(z)))$ to train G (see Figure 3.1).

In contrast with GAN that involves two separated artificial neural networks, a VAE includes two sequentially connected networks, called the encoder and decoder. As shown in Figure 3.2, the encoder $Q(X; \theta_e)$ converts the input data (X) into the parameters of latent prior distribution $P(z)$, say, a vector that encodes the mean and standard deviation of a multivariate normal distribution. The decoder $R(z; \theta_d)$ tries to recover X from the latent z sampled from $P(z)$. Using a reparameterization trick, the decoder parameter θ_d is trained together with the encoder parameter θ_e [15]. The training of VAE aims to minimize the discrepancy between the input and generated data. And the output of encoder is regularized near $P(z)$, which usually adopts a multivariate normal distribution. The final loss function is

$$\mathcal{L} = \mathcal{L}_R + \beta \cdot \mathcal{L}_{KL}$$

where

$$\mathcal{L}_R = \frac{1}{m} \sum_{i=1}^{m} X_i \cdot \log(\hat{X}_i)$$

$$\mathcal{L}_{KL} = -D_{KL}[Q(X)\|P(z)]$$

$\mathcal{L}_R$ indicates the cross-entropy between the recovered and input multi-categorical data, which elicits minimization of the discrepancy between these two vectors. $\mathcal{L}_{KL}$ is the Kullback–Leibler (KL) divergence between the prior and estimated latent distributions, which measures the distance between these two distributions. β is a regularization weight for $\mathcal{L}_{KL}$.

3.6 Population Synthesis with Multi-social Relationships

Sections 3.3 and 3.4 have elaborated the most two representative paradigms. Though the IPU algorithm may reach an acceptable solution, it does not, unfortunately, converge to the global optimum in a general case. In addition, most of the existing approaches just consider the household only, ignoring other typical social relationships like the links from colleagues, school mates, etc. This is mainly because the census data source usually lacks investigation of other social entities. To our knowledge, the only representative work that takes multiple social organizations into account comes from Wheaton et al., who used Census Bureau TIGER (Topologically Integrated Geographic Encoding and Referencing) data, SF3 (Summary File 3), and PUMS of United States to synthesize the basic dataset of 50 states and the District of Columbia in the year 2000 [16]. For social relationship formulation other than household, they further referred to NCES (National Center for Education Statistics) public and private school data for 2005–2006, STP64 (US Census Bureau Special Tabulation Product 64), InfoUSA Business Counts, SF1 (US Census Bureau Summary File 1), HSIP (Homeland Security Infrastructure Program) database and Group Quarters Age Distributions to construct schools, corporations and group quarters. In the generation of various social organizations, Wheaton et al. adopted direct assignment according to the data sources, making their approach not applicable to other cases. Therefore, in this section, we will first analyze the IPU algorithm in theory, showing its computational limit, and then expand the population synthesis into a more general situation by considering any sorts of social entities.

3.6.1 Limitations of IPU Algorithm

As illustrated in Section 3.4, the IPU algorithm runs two IPF procedures to fitting household and individual constraints, respectively. In a general case, however, it may probably encounter fatal problems: it cannot converge to a global optimal solution when such a solution does exist. Before giving a theoretical proof, we firstly construct the mathematical model that IPU operates. Table 3.5 shows the

Table 3.5 The general case of IPU.

HH type 1	HH type 2	$\cdots$	HH type m	Ind type $(m+1)$	$\cdots$	Ind type $(m+n)$	Weights
$d(1,1)=1$	0	$\cdots$	0	$d(1, m+1)$	$\cdots$	$d(1, m+n)$	h_1
$\vdots$	$\vdots$		$\vdots$	$\vdots$	$\vdots$	$\vdots$	$\vdots$
$d(R_1,1)=1$	0		$\vdots$	$\vdots$	$\vdots$	$\vdots$	$\vdots$
0	$d(R_1+1,2)=1$	$\vdots$	$\vdots$	$\vdots$		$\vdots$	$\vdots$
$\vdots$	$\vdots$		$\vdots$	$\vdots$	$\vdots$	$\vdots$	$\vdots$
$\vdots$	$d(R_2,2)=1$	$\vdots$	0	$d(i, m+1)$	$\cdots$	$d(i, m+n)$	h_i
$\vdots$	0		0	$\vdots$		$\vdots$	$\vdots$
$\vdots$	$\vdots$		$d(R_{m-1}+1, m)=1$	$\vdots$		$\vdots$	$\vdots$
$\vdots$	$\vdots$		$\vdots$	$\vdots$		$\vdots$	$\vdots$
0	0		$d(R_m, m)=1$	$d(R, m+1)$	$\cdots$	$d(R, m+n)$	h_R
$H(x_1)$	$H(x_2)$		$H(x_m)$	$P(y_{m+1})$		$P(y_{m+n})$	

general mathematical model of IPU. Let A_1 and A_2 be the frequency matrices of households and individuals coming from disaggregate samples ($R_m = R$). The total frequency matrix in Table 3.5 is

$$A = (A_1 \mid A_2) = \begin{pmatrix} d(1,1) & \cdots & 0 & \mid & d(1, m+1) & \cdots & d(1, m+n) \\ \vdots & \ddots & \vdots & \mid & \vdots & \ddots & \vdots \\ 0 & \cdots & d(R_m, m) & \mid & d(R, m+1) & \cdots & d(R, m+n) \end{pmatrix}$$

Let $H(x_i)$ ($i = 1, \ldots, m$) and $P(y_j)$ ($j = m+1, \ldots, m+n$) be the constraints of household and individual, $h = (h_1 \ h_2 \ \cdots \ h_R)^T$ ($i = 1, \ldots, R$) be the relevant weights. During the tth ($t \geq 1$) iteration, the weights are updated through the household fitting and individual fitting:

$$h_i^{(1)}(t) = \frac{h_i^{(m+n)}(t-1)}{\sigma_i^{(1)}(t)}, \quad h_i^{(2)}(t) = \frac{h_i^{(1)}(t)}{\sigma_i^{(2)}(t)}, \quad \ldots, \quad h_i^{(m)}(t) = \frac{h_i^{(m-1)}(t)}{\sigma_i^{(m)}(t)}$$

$$h_i^{(m+1)}(t) = \frac{h_i^{(m)}(t)}{\sigma_i^{(m+1)}(t)}, \quad h_i^{(m+2)}(t) = \frac{h_i^{(m+1)}(t)}{\sigma_i^{(m+2)}(t)}, \quad \ldots, \quad h_i^{(m+n)}(t) = \frac{h_i^{(m+n-1)}(t)}{\sigma_i^{(m+n)}(t)}$$

$$(3.2)$$

where ($i = 1, \ldots, R$) and $h_i^{(j)}(t)$ ($j = 1, \ldots, (m+n)$) represents the weights after the jth constraint fitted in the tth iteration. In Eq. (3.2), the update factors are

$$\sigma_i^{(j)}(t) = \begin{cases} \dfrac{\sum_r d(r,j) \cdot h_r^{(j-1)}(t)}{H(x_j)}, & d(i,j) > 0 \\ 1, & d(i,j) = 0 \end{cases} \quad j \in \{1, \ldots, m\}$$

$$(3.3)$$

$$\sigma_i^{(j)}(t) = \begin{cases} \dfrac{\sum_r d(r,j) \cdot h_r^{(j-1)}(t)}{P(y_j)}, & d(i,j) > 0 \\ 1, & d(i,j) = 0 \end{cases} \quad j \in \{m+1, \ldots, m+n\}$$

In order to investigate the convergence, we have to consider the objective functions in Eq. (3.1). Note that the three objective functions are equivalent. If there exists a solution vector w (represented as h in Table 3.5) that satisfy all personal and household constraints, the objective functions are zeros. Specifically, the third indicator:

$$L = \sum_j \left[\left| \sum_i d_{ij} \cdot w_i - c_j \right| / c_j \right]$$

$$(3.4)$$

is investigated but the conclusion can be applied to the other two analogically. Our discussions start from two different cases according to the feature of A_2.

Case 1. A_2 does not contain zero elements. It means that for a given i, $\sigma_i^{(m+1)}(t), \dots, \sigma_i^{(m+n)}(t)$ are all determined by the weights. The following proposition reveals the trend of objective function.

Proposition 3.6.1 *Suppose the IPU algorithm starts from any feasible initial solution and updates the weights according to Eq. (3.2). $\forall d(i,j) > 0$ in A_2. Then,*

$$\prod_{k=1}^{m+n} \sigma_i^{(k)}(t) = 1$$

holds for $t > 1$, $\forall i \in 1, 2, \dots, R$.

Proof: From Eq. (3.3), there is

$$\sigma_i^{(m+2)}(t) = \frac{\sum_r d(r, m+2) \cdot h_r^{(m+1)}(t)}{P(y_{m+2})} = \frac{1}{P(y_{m+2})} \sum_r d(r, m+2) \cdot \frac{h_r^{(m)}(t)}{\sigma_r^{(m+1)}(t)}$$

Since $\forall d(i,j) > 0$, the

$$\sigma_i^{(m+1)}(t) = \frac{\sum_r d(i, m+1) \cdot h_r^{(m)}(t)}{P(y_{m+1})}$$

holds for $\forall i$. Thus, $\sigma_i^{(m+1)}(t)$ is a constant that does not depend on i and

$$\sigma_i^{(m+2)}(t) = \frac{1}{P(y_{m+2})} \sum_r d(r, m+2) \cdot \frac{h_r^{(m)}(t)}{\sigma_r^{(m+1)}(t)}$$

$$= \frac{1}{P(y_{m+2})} \cdot \frac{1}{\sigma_i^{(m+1)}(t)} \sum_r d(r, m+2) h_r^{(m)}(t)$$

$$\Rightarrow \sigma_i^{(m+1)}(t) \sigma_i^{(m+2)}(t) = \frac{1}{P(y_{m+2})} \sum_r d(r, m+2) h_r^{(m)}(t)$$

Inductively, we have

$$\prod_{k=m+1}^{m+n} \sigma_i^{(k)}(t) = \frac{1}{P(y_{m+n})} \sum_r d(r, m+n) \cdot h_r^{(m)}(t) \tag{3.5}$$

For a given $i \in 1, \dots, m$, the ith row in A_1 only has one nonzero element. Suppose, it emerges in the $k_{i,0}$th column and $d(i, k_{i,0}) = 1, (1 \leq k_{i,0} \leq m)$. Therefore,

$$\sigma_i^{(k)}(t) = 1, \quad \forall k \in [1, m], k \neq k_{i,0}$$

Note that during household fitting, the weight cells are actually partitioned into m disjoint subsets and each update only involves one of them. This elicits

$$\sigma_i^{(k_{i,0})}(t) = \frac{\sum_r d(r, k_{i,0}) \cdot h_r^{(k_{i,0}-1)}(t)}{H(x_{k_{i,0}})} = \frac{\sum_r d(r, k_{i,0}) \cdot h_r^{(m+n)}(t-1)}{H(x_{k_{i,0}})}$$

which does not depend on i as well. Thus, Eq. (3.5) can be written as:

$$\prod_{k=m+1}^{m+n} \sigma_i^{(k)}(t) = \frac{1}{P(y_{m+n})} \sum_r d(r, m+n) \cdot h_r^{(m)}(t)$$

$$= \frac{1}{P(y_{m+n})} \sum_r d(r, m+n) \cdot \frac{h_r^{(m+n)}(t-1)}{\prod_{k=1}^{m} \sigma_i^{(k)}(t)}$$

$$= \frac{1}{P(y_{m+n})} \sum_r d(r, m+n) \cdot \frac{h_r^{(m+n)}(t-1)}{\sigma_r^{(k_{i,0})}(t)}$$

$$= \frac{\sum_r d(r, m+n) \cdot h_r^{(m+n)}(t-1)}{\sigma_i^{(k_{i,0})}(t) \cdot P(y_{m+n})}$$

So we have

$$\prod_{k=1}^{m+n} \sigma_i^{(k)}(t) = \prod_{k=1}^{m} \sigma_i^{(k)}(t) \prod_{k=m+1}^{m+n} \sigma_i^{(k)}(t) = \sigma_i^{(k_{i,0})}(t) \cdot \prod_{k=m+1}^{m+n} \sigma_i^{(k)}(t)$$

$$= \frac{1}{P(y_{m+n})} \sum_r d(r, m+n) h_r^{(m+n)}(t-1) = 1$$

The last equation sign holds because

$$\sum_r d(r, m+n) \cdot h_r^{(m+n)}(t-1) = P(y_{m+n})$$

after the last constraint fitted when $t > 1$. □

Proposition 3.6.1 indicates after the first iteration, the weights will remain unchanged in subsequent computation. Specifically, consider the first iteration where $t = 1$

$$\prod_{k=1}^{m+n} \sigma_i^{(k)}(1) = \frac{1}{P(y_{m+n})} \sum_r d(r, m+n) h_r(0) \tag{3.6}$$

If the IPU converges to an optimal solution, it will be completed in the first round, which elicits

$$\sum_r d(r,j) \cdot h_r^{(m+n)}(1) = H(x_j), \quad \forall j \in [1, m]$$

$$\sum_r d(r,j) \cdot h_r^{(m+n)}(1) = P(y_j), \quad \forall j \in [m+1, m+n] \tag{3.7}$$

when there exists positive solutions. Equations (3.6) and (3.7) lead to

$$\sum_i \left[d(i,j) - \frac{H(x_j)}{P(y_{m+n})} \cdot d(i, m+n) \right] \cdot h_i(0) = 0$$

$$\sum_i \left[d(i,j) - \frac{P(y_j)}{P(y_{m+n})} \cdot d(i, m+n) \right] \cdot h_i(0) = 0 \tag{3.8}$$

where $\forall j \in [1, m]$ and $[m + 1, m + n]$, respectively. Note Eq. (3.8) holds automatically for $j = m + n$. Therefore, Eq. (3.8) is usually an under-determined system with R variables and $(m + n - 1)$ equations. The aforementioned analysis manifests that, if the optimization problem shown in Table 3.5 has feasible positive weights, only when the initial solution $h(0)$ satisfies Eq. (3.8) that can the IPU find one. This type of $h(0)$, however, cannot always be guaranteed by the input sample, which may contains errors.

Case 2. A_2 has some zero elements. In contrast with the previous one, this case is more complicated. If the ith row of A_2 contains zero(s), then the $\sigma_i^{(m+1)}(t), \ldots, \sigma_i^{(m+n)}(t)$ are no longer constants and we cannot receive Eq. (3.5) now. In the following, we will prove by contradiction.

Assume that IPU converges to a positive solution of Table 3.5 for the first time after the tth iteration, then we have error:

$$
\begin{aligned}
L^{(m+n)}(t - 1) = \sum_{1 \leq j \leq m} & \frac{\left| \sum_i d(i,j) h_i^{(m+n)}(t - 1) - H(x_j) \right|}{H(x_j)} \\
+ \sum_{m+1 \leq j \leq m+n} & \frac{\left| \sum_i d(i,j) h_i^{(m+n)}(t - 1) - P(y_j) \right|}{P(y_j)} > 0
\end{aligned}
\tag{3.9}
$$

and

$$
\begin{aligned}
L^{(m+n)}(t) = \sum_{1 \leq j \leq m} & \frac{\left| \sum_i d(i,j) h_i^{(m+n)}(t) - H(x_j) \right|}{H(x_j)} \\
+ \sum_{m+1 \leq j \leq m+n} & \frac{\left| \sum_i d(i,j) h_i^{(m+n)}(t) - P(y_j) \right|}{P(y_j)} = 0
\end{aligned}
\tag{3.10}
$$

The superscript $(m + n)$ means after fitting the $(m + n)$th constrain. For convenience, let $L^{(0)}(t) = L^{(m+n)}(t - 1)$. Then consider the error sequence:

$$
\{ L^{(0)}(t), L^{(1)}(t), \ldots, L^{(m+n)}(t) \}
$$

Let $L^{(c)}(t)$ be the last positive error $(1 \leq c \leq m + n - 1)$. Thus

$$
\begin{aligned}
L^{(c)}(t) = \sum_{1 \leq j \leq m} & \frac{\left| \sum_i d(i,j) h_i^{(c)}(t) - H(x_j) \right|}{H(x_j)} \\
+ \sum_{m+1 \leq j \leq m+n} & \frac{\left| \sum_i d(i,j) h_i^{(c)}(t) - P(y_j) \right|}{P(y_j)} > 0
\end{aligned}
\tag{3.11}
$$

and

$$L^{(c+1)}(t) = \sum_{1 \le j \le m} \frac{1}{H(x_j)} \left| \sum_i d(i,j) h_i^{(c+1)}(t) - H(x_j) \right|$$
$$+ \sum_{m+1 \le j \le m+n} \frac{\left| \sum_i d(i,j) h_i^{(c+1)}(t) - P(y_j) \right|}{P(y_j)} = 0 \tag{3.12}$$

Note that Eqs. (3.11) and (3.12) are both the sum of $(m+n)$ items with absolute value signs. Therefore, each item in Eq. (3.12) equals to zero. And there is at least one positive item in Eq. (3.11) (if not, the greater sign cannot hold). Again, consider the last positive item, represented as the kth one.

1°: If the last positive item in Eq. (3.11) comes from individual constraints, we first investigate the situation that $m + 1 \le k < m + n$, which means

$$\frac{1}{P(y_k)} \left| \sum_i d(i,k) h_i^{(c)}(t) - P(y_k) \right| > 0 \Rightarrow \sum_i d(i,k) h_i^{(c)}(t) \ne P(y_k) \tag{3.13}$$

Since the kth item is the last positive one, there is

$$\frac{1}{P(y_{k+1})} \left| \sum_i d(i,k+1) h_i^{(c)}(t) - P(y_{k+1}) \right| = 0$$
$$\Rightarrow \sum_i d(i,k+1) h_i^{(c)}(t) = P(y_{k+1}) \tag{3.14}$$

From Eq. (3.12), we have

$$\frac{1}{P(y_k)} \left| \sum_i d(i,k) h_i^{(c+1)}(t) - P(y_k) \right| = 0 \Rightarrow \sum_i d(i,k) h_i^{(c+1)}(t) = P(y_k) \tag{3.15}$$

$$\frac{1}{P(y_{k+1})} \left| \sum_i d(i,k+1) h_i^{(c+1)}(t) - P(y_{k+1}) \right| = 0$$
$$\Rightarrow \sum_i d(i,k+1) h_i^{(c+1)}(t) = P(y_{k+1}) \tag{3.16}$$

According to Eq. (3.15), we know

$$\sum_i d(i,k) h_i^{(c+1)}(t) = \sum_i d(i,k) \frac{h_i^{(c)}(t)}{\sigma_i^{(c+1)}(t)} = P(y_k)$$

This indicates that at least one $\sigma_i^{(c+1)}(t)$ does not equal to 1 (if not, Eq. (3.13) will turn into an equation), denoted as $\sigma_r^{(c+1)}(t) \ne 1$. On the other hand, from Eqs. (3.14) and (3.16), we have

$$\sum_i d(i,k+1)[h_i^{(c)}(t) - h_i^{(c+1)}(t)] = 0$$
$$\Rightarrow \sum_i d(i,k+1) h_i^{(c)}(t)[1 - 1/\sigma_i^{(c+1)}(t)] = 0 \tag{3.17}$$

Recall that

$$
\sigma_i^{(c+1)}(t) = \begin{cases} \frac{\sum_i d(i,c+1)h_i^{(c)}(t)}{P(y_{c+1})}, & d(i,c+1) > 0 \\ 1, & d(i,c+1) = 0 \end{cases}
$$

This means for $\forall i \in \{1, \dots, R\}$, each $\sigma_i^{(c+1)}(t) \geq 1$ or each $\sigma_i^{(c+1)}(t) \leq 1$. Therefore, each $[1 - 1/(\sigma_i^{(c+1)}(t))] \geq 0$ or each $[1 - 1/(\sigma_i^{(c+1)}(t))] \leq 0$. Since all $d(i,k+1)$ $h_i^{(c)}(t) > 0$, Eq. (3.16) indicates that each $\sigma_i^{(c+1)}(t) = 1$. Specifically, $\sigma_r^{(c+1)}(t) = 1$. Now, we have a contradiction. If $k = m + n$, define $P(y_{m+n+1}) = H(x_1)$ and $d(i, m+n+1) = d(i,1)$, the proof is similar.

2°: If the last positive item of Eq. (3.15) comes from household constraints, replace $P(y_k)$ with $H(x_k)$, and the proof is similar.

3.6.2 Population with Multi-social Relationships

A part from IPU algorithm, most existing approaches are applied in the household–individual scenarios and are difficult to be extended to more levels, especially for large-scale computation. For the household–individual case, classic methods (such as fitness-based method and combinatorial optimization) are able to improve the fitness of household frequencies, while evaluating the individual fitness by converting the household into individuals according to its member types. However, if controls from two (or more) social relationships included, say the household and enterprise, they may fail to compute the enterprise's fitness since the relations between such two organizations are not explicit. Therefore, to generate an integrated population system with multiple social organizations, we seek to directly assign the person to each type of social entities. To model multi-social relationships, it is required to expand the current household–individual bilevels to multiple levels. For simplicity, we concentrate on three levels of constraints: individual and two social relationships (e.g. household and enterprise). Please note that our formulation can easily be expanded to more social constraints as well. Our restricted problem is illustrated in Figure 3.3. Let $\underline{X} = (x_1, x_2, \dots, x_n)$ be the individual attributes we care about in the population (such as *Gender*, *Age*, etc.). These attributes can respectively take on $I_1, I_2, \dots, I_n \in \mathbb{N}$ possible values. $\underline{Y} = (y_1, y_2, \dots, y_h)$ and $\underline{Z} = (z_1, z_2, \dots, z_m)$ are the social relationship attributes of interest (such as *Household Type*, *Household Residential Province*, *Enterprise Type*, *Enterprise Scale*, etc.) with $J_1, J_2, \dots, J_h$ and $K_1, K_2, \dots, K_m$ possible values. A distribution over individual attributes will map each possible set of characteristics $(x_1, x_2, \dots, x_n)$ to a nonnegative integer that represents the number of individuals in that type. This frequency distribution is represented by a multi-dimensional array called a tensor and is denoted by $\underline{X} \in \mathbb{N}^{I_1 \times I_2 \times \cdots \times I_n}$. Similarly, $\underline{Y} \in \mathbb{N}^{J_1 \times J_2 \times \cdots \times J_h}$ and $\underline{Z} \in \mathbb{N}^{K_1 \times K_2 \times \cdots \times K_m}$ are tensors for social relationships. In the

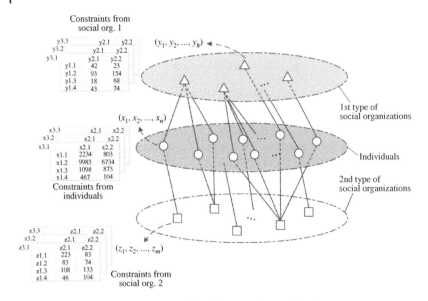

Figure 3.3 Synthetic population with multiple social relationships.

rest of this part, we introduce our tensor decomposition method, which involves individual/organization synthesis and population assignment.

The first step is to generate a synthetic population and social organizations. Basically, for the individual level and each type of organizations, we are facing the same problem. Here, we give a new sample-based method to generate basic population. When the sample is available, we have two types of data sources. The first one is the sample distribution $X_s \in \mathbb{N}^{I_1 \times I_2 \times \cdots \times I_n}$. Same as the unknown actual population denoted by $\underline{X} \in \mathbb{N}^{I_1 \times I_2 \times \cdots \times I_n}$, it is a full-dimensional tensor. For example, suppose we have three attributes to study ($n = 3$) and they have 3, 4, and 5 categories, respectively. The sample and actual population can be represented as $X_s \in \mathbb{N}^{3 \times 4 \times 5}$ and $\underline{X} \in \mathbb{N}^{3 \times 4 \times 5}$, which look like the left side of Figure 3.4. The gray boxes stand for already known individual frequencies and the white boxes stand for the unknown ones.

The synthesis begins with Tucker decomposition of X_s:

$$\underline{X}_s = \underline{g} \times_1 U_1 \times_2 \cdots \times_n U_n \tag{3.18}$$

where $\underline{g} \in \mathbb{R}^{r_1 \times r_2 \times \cdots \times r_n} (r_n \leq I_n)$ is the core tensor and $U_n \in \mathbb{R}^{I_n \times r_n}$ is the factor matrix. $\times_n$ is the n-mode product of the tensor and matrix. For the three-dimensional example, the bottom right subfigure in Figure 3.4 illustrates the decomposition result. Here, we set $r_i = I_i$ in Tucker decomposition; thus, the factor matrices are square. The 1-mode product of $\underline{g} \times_1 U_1$ is calculated as: (i) unfold

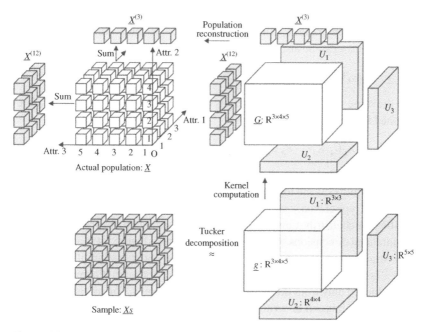

Figure 3.4 An example of $3 \times 4 \times 5$ tensor decomposition.

$\underline{g}$ to a 3×20 matrix, denoted as $\underline{g}_{(1)}$ (called the 1-mode unfolding/flattening/matricization). That is, arranging the four horizontal (3×5) slices one by one; and (ii) compute $U_1 \cdot \underline{g}_{(1)}$ and then reversely fold the result matrix as a $3 \times 4 \times 5$ tensor. Generally, if a tensor is $r_1 \times \cdots \times r_n$ dimension, and a matrix is $I \times r_m$ dimension, their m-mode product is a $r_1 \times \cdots \times r_{m-1} \times I \times r_{m+1} \times \cdots \times r_n$ tensor. Specifically, if the matrix degenerates to a vector, that is $I = 1$, the m-mode product will be a $r_1 \times \cdots \times r_{m-1} \times r_{m+1} \times \cdots \times r_n$ tensor, which means dimension m collapses.

Mathematically, Tucker decomposition tries to solve the optimization problem:

$$\min_{\hat{X}_s} \|\underline{X}_s - \hat{X}_s\|$$

where

$$\hat{X}_s = \underline{g} \times_1 U_1 \times_2 \cdots \times_n U_n$$

There are classic algorithms for this problem, such as Higher-Order Singular Value Decomposition (HOSVD) and Higher-Order Orthogonal Iteration (HOOI) [17]. To improve the accuracy, we set $r_n = I_n$, which means each factor matrix U_n is square and $\underline{g}$ has the same size of $\underline{X}_s$ (as the bottom right part of Figure 3.4). In addition, to guarantee each frequency positive, we add a group of constraints as:

$$\underline{g} \geq 0, \quad U_i \geq 0 \ (i = 1, \ldots, n)$$

Tucker decomposition can be viewed as a high-dimensional principle component analysis (PCA). Factor matrices are the principle components. Similarly, the actual population tensor can be also decomposed as: kalpana

$$\underline{X} = \underline{G} \times_1 V_1 \times_2 \cdots \times_n V_n$$

$\underline{G}$ is in the same size with $\underline{g}$. We use U_n as the approximation of V_n and the aforementioned formula is converted into

$$\underline{X} = \underline{G} \times_1 U_1 \times_2 \cdots \times_n U_n \tag{3.19}$$

Since U_n are already known, the problem is to estimate the core tensor $\underline{G}$, under certain constraints (as the top right part of Figure 3.4).

The second type of data source is marginal/partial joint distributions from actual population. Such distributions are obtained by summing up the original tensor in other unrelated dimensions. As the top left subfigure in Figure 3.4 shows, there are two constraints: one marginal distribution $\underline{X}^{(3)}$ and one partial joint distribution $\underline{X}^{(12)}$. $\underline{X}^{(3)}$ is achieved by aggregating the full $3 \times 4 \times 5$ tensor in dimension 1 and 2. $\underline{X}^{(12)}$ is achieved only from the aggregation in dimension 3. The marginal and partial joint constraints can be written as:

$$\underline{X}^{(3)} = \underline{X} \times_2 e_2 \times_1 e_1 = e_1 \cdot (e_2 \cdot \underline{X}_{(2)})_{(1)}$$
$$\underline{X}^{(12)} = \underline{X} \times_3 e_3 = e_3 \cdot \underline{X}_{(3)}$$

where $e_n = (1, \ldots, 1) \in \mathbb{N}^{1 \times I_n}$ is an I_n-dimensional vector of ones. By substituting Eq. (3.19) into the aforementioned constraints (here $n = 3$), we have

$$\underline{X}^{(3)} = (\underline{G} \times_1 U_1 \times_2 U_2 \times_3 U_3) \times_2 e_2 \times_1 e_1$$
$$\underline{X}^{(12)} = (\underline{G} \times_1 U_1 \times_2 U_2 \times_3 U_3) \times_3 e_3$$

This can be rewritten as:

$$\underline{X}^{(3)} = \underline{G} \times_1 (e_1 \cdot U_1) \times_2 (e_2 \cdot U_2) \times_3 U_3$$
$$\underline{X}^{(12)} = \underline{G} \times_1 U_1 \times_2 U_2 \times_3 (e_3 \cdot U_3)$$

Therefore,

$$\underline{G} \times_1 (e_1 \cdot U_1) \times_2 (e_2 \cdot U_2) = \underline{X}^{(3)} \times_3 U_3^{\dagger}$$
$$\underline{G} \times_3 (e_3 \cdot U_3) = \underline{X}^{(12)} \times_1 U_1^{\dagger} \times_2 U_2^{\dagger} \tag{3.20}$$

where $U_n^{\dagger}$ is Moore–Penrose (MP) pseudo-inverse of U_n. Note that in Eq. (3.20), $(e_n \cdot U_n)$ is a vector for $n = 1, 2, 3$, and our task is to determine $\underline{G} \geq 0$ with all the other items known. In this three-dimensional example, it means we need to solve an under-determined system with $3 \times 4 \times 5 = 60$ variables and $5 + 3 \times 4 =$

17 equations. Many optimization algorithms can be exploited to complete such task. Here, we use Gradient Decent to do this. Define the total error as:

$$
J = \sum \left[\underline{G} \times_1 (e_1 \cdot U_1) \times_2 (e_2 \cdot U_2) - \underline{X}^{(3)} \times_3 U_3^{\dagger} \right]^2
$$
$$
+ \left[\underline{G} \times_3 (e_3 \cdot U_3) - \underline{X}^{(12)} \times_1 U_1^{\dagger} \times_2 U_2^{\dagger} \right]^2
$$

(3.21)

On the right of equation sign, the two items inside square brackets are 5×1 matrix and 3×4 matrix, same sizes as the constraints $\underline{X}^{(3)}$ and $\underline{X}^{(12)}$. The summation and square signs mean each element of the matrix is squared and then summed together. Thus, Eq. (3.21) sums $5 \times 1 + 3 \times 4 = 17$ quadratic items to compute the total error. Using the sample decomposition kernel g as an initial solution, Gradient Decent algorithm will minimize the total error and finally achieve an estimation of $\underline{G}$. By substituting the estimation into Eq. (3.19), we will get the population distribution.

In a general case, there may be more than two marginal and partial joint constraints, and Eq. (3.21) will have more quadratic items as well. In addition, we may set $r_n < I_n$ so that factor matrix U_n is no longer square. This means we use principal components with lower ranks to approximate the original tensor. General pseudocode is provided in Algorithm 3.1. The tensor decomposition method is also applicable for other social organizations' synthesis. If the disaggregate sample of such type of organizations is not available, the initial solution can be set arbitrarily or from other sample-free methods.

Algorithm 3.1 TensorDecomPopSyn $(\underline{X}_s, \underline{X}^{con})$

Input:

$\underline{X}_s, I_1 \times I_2 \times \cdots \times I_n$ sample tensor;

$\underline{X}^{con}$, lower-dimensional constraint tensors, represented as $\underline{X}^{(l_1, l_2, \ldots, l_c)}$, $\{l_1, l_2, \ldots, l_c\} \subset \{I_1, I_2, \ldots, I_n\}$;

Output:

Population Tensor.

1: $[g, U_1, \ldots, U_n] \leftarrow Tucker\_Decom(\underline{X}_s, I_1, I_2, \ldots, I_n)$;

2: $\overline{CoreCons} \leftarrow \{ \}$;

3: **for** each constraint $\underline{X}^{(l_1, l_2, \ldots, l_c)}$ **do**

4: $\quad con(l_1, l_2, \ldots, l_c) \leftarrow \underline{X}^{(1,2,\ldots,m)} \times_1 U_1^{\dagger} \times_2 \cdots \times_m U_m^{\dagger}$; /* $U_m^{\dagger}$ is Moore–Penrose pseudo-inverse of U_m */

5: $\quad CoreCons \leftarrow CoreCons \cup con(l_1, l_2, \ldots, l_c)$;

6: **end for**

7: $\underline{G} \leftarrow GradDecent(g, U_1, \ldots, U_n, CoreCons, error)$;

8: **return** $\underline{G} \times_1 U_1 \times_2 \cdots \times_n U_n$.

After basic individual and social organization synthesized, the second step is to assign each individual to specific organizations. The objective is to establish the assignment probability to each organization type. To avoid unreasonable assignment (means the assignment probability equals to zero), we need to establish the mapping relations between social organizations and individuals. Two sources of information can be exploited. One is called data-based assumption. If the input data from different levels have overlapped attributes (such as the locations in both individual and enterprise levels, as discussed later in this paper), or some member features (such as members' age structure from the organization survey), we can establish some mapping relations based on reasonable assumptions. For instance, if individual and enterprise levels both contain locations, we can safely assume that in a coarse-grained level, employed person works in an enterprise that has the same location as his residence. The overlapped attributes can lead to a conditional assignment probability as:

$$P(\underline{X}, \underline{Y} \mid \underline{X}) = P(\underline{Y} \mid \underline{X})$$
$$= P(y_1, \ldots, y_u, y_{u+1}, \ldots, y_h \mid x_1, \ldots, x_u, x_{u+1}, \ldots, x_n)$$
$$= P(y_1, \ldots, y_u, y_{u+1}, \ldots, y_h \mid x_1, \ldots, x_u)$$
$$= P(y_1, \ldots, y_u, y_{u+1}, \ldots, y_h \mid y_1, \ldots, y_u)$$
$$= P(y_{u+1}, \ldots, y_h \mid y_1, \ldots, y_u)$$
$$= \frac{IndNum(y_1, \ldots, y_u, y_{u+1}, \ldots, y_h)}{IndNum(y_1, \ldots, y_u)}$$

where

$$\underline{X} = (x_1, \ldots, x_u, x_{u+1}, \ldots, x_n)$$
$$\underline{Y} = (y_1, \ldots, y_u, y_{u+1}, \ldots, y_h)$$

are individual and social organization attributes, respectively, and $x_i = y_i (i = 1, \ldots, u)$ are the overlapped attributes. $P(\underline{X}, \underline{Y} \mid \underline{X})$ stands for the probability that the individual of type X is assigned to the organization of type Y. It is computed from the individual number required by eligible organizations. Considering the denominator is possibly zero, the assignment probability is

$$P(\underline{X}, \underline{Y} \mid \underline{X})$$
$$= \begin{cases} \frac{IndNum(y_1, \ldots, y_u, \ldots, y_h)}{IndNum(y_1, \ldots, y_u)} & \text{if } IndNum(y_1, \ldots, y_u) > 0 \\ 0 & \text{otherwise} \end{cases} \tag{3.22}$$

where

$$IndNum(y_1, \ldots, y_u)$$
$$= \sum_{y_{u+1}, \ldots, y_h} IndNum(y_1, \ldots, y_u, y_{u+1}, \ldots, y_h)$$

Algorithm 3.2 PopAssigment (Pop, Orgs, Heurs)

Input:
    Pop, basic population;
    Orgs, set of social organizations with S levels, represented as $\{org_1, \ldots, org_S\}$;
    Heurs, heuristics;
Output:
    Population with Social Relationships.
1: $AssPop \leftarrow \{\}$;
2: **while** Pop is not empty **do**
3:     $Ind(x_1, \ldots, x_n) \leftarrow GetRandInd(Pop)$;
4:     $OrgCand \leftarrow \{\}$;
5:     **for** each org_i in a given sequence /*The sequence (if has) is determined by the assignment dependencies of different levels*/ **do**
6:       **for** each $Y = (y_1, \ldots, y_h)$ in org_i **do**
7:         $IndNum(y_1, \ldots, y_h) \leftarrow ComMemNum(org_i, Ind(x_1, \ldots, x_n), Heurs)$;
        /*Compute required number of Ind by organization Y in level org_i*/
8:         $OrgCand \leftarrow OrgCand \cup$
            $\{(y_1, \ldots, y_h), IndNum(y_1, \ldots, y_h)\}$;
9:       **end for**
10:     **if** OrgCand is not empty **then**
11:       $ObjOrg \leftarrow GetRandOrg(OrgCand)$;
      /* Get a random organization according the distribution by normalizing OrgCand*/
12:       $Ind \leftarrow LinkOrg(Ind, ObjOrg)$;
      /*Assign Ind to ObjOrg */
13:       $ObjOrg \leftarrow LinkInd(ObjOrg, Ind)$;
14:       **if** the member number of ObjOrg reaches its maximum **then**
15:         $or_i \leftarrow org_i \backslash ObjOrg$;
16:       **end if**
17:     **else**
18:       $Ind \leftarrow LinkOrg(Ind, null)$;
      /* There is no suitable organizations */
19:     **end if**
20:     **end for**
21:     $AssPop \leftarrow AssPop \cup Ind$;
22:     $Pop \leftarrow Pop \backslash Ind$;
23: **end while**
24: **return** $AssPop$.

Note that overlapped attributes do not always exist, and the assumptions should be made reasonable. For organization member features such as the age structure mentioned before, the assignment probability can be also computed by Eq. (3.22). In this case, the numerator is the number of individual X required by organization Y, and the denominator is the total number of individual X required by the whole organizations. In essence, the problem is converted into the overlapped attribute case.

The second source of information for establishing the mapping relations is implicit heuristic rule. This type of heuristics is set according to the rules that are not reflected by the input data. For example, normal non-single family has a couple as its members. This is not mandatory, but we usually give priority to assemble such family. General pseudocode of assignment is provided in Algorithm 3.2. The loop from lines 5 to 20 sequentially assigns the randomly generated individual to each level organization. The assignment sequence relies on the dependence of different social relationships.

To validate the proposed method, we conduct experiments of Chinese national population synthesis by considering two social relationships – household and enterprise. Individual and household constraints come from the census results, which directly reflect basic features of target population. Enterprise constraints come from national economic investigation. The final synthetic population is composed of three databases: individuals, households, and enterprises. Some record samples are listed in Table 3.6. As can be seen, there are two males and

Table 3.6 Example records of synthetic population database.

Synthetic individual			
Ind. ID	1100000067	1100000082	1100000099
Gender	Female	Male	Male
Res. prov.	Beijing	Beijing	Beijing
Res. type	City	City	City
Age interval	65–69	60–64	35–39
HH type	Family	Family	Family
HH ID	320322	320322	320322
Enter. ID	−1	7	29

Synthetic household and enterprise			
HH ID	1100320322	Enter. ID	1100000007
Res. prov.	Beijing	Res. prov.	Beijing
Res. type	City	Enter. type	Corporation
HH type	Family	Enter. scale	8–19
Member num.	3	Employee num.	9
Elder num.	1		

one female. Their ages are in the 65–69, 60–64, and 35–39 intervals. All the three people belong to the household with ID 320322. The household is recorded in Synthetic Household table (the ID is slightly different with its province code ahead), and it has three members including one elder person. The Enter ID of the female is −1, which means she is retired and not affiliated with any enterprise. The other two people are employed and affiliated with enterprise 7 and enterprise 29, respectively. The enterprise 7 is recorded in Synthetic Enterprise table. We refer the readers to Ref. [18] for detailed comparative results.

3.7 Conclusions and Discussions

Social relationships among individuals are of great significance in modeling personal behaviors, since they probably impact one's decisions and usually cannot be ignored in a simple way. Typical social relationships derive from people's various roles in different organizations like corporations, schools, and perhaps the most representative – households. These connections tie individuals together and will undoubtedly trigger particular behaviors in their daily life. Many micro or agent-based models have considered the influence of households. This is because census data, which is typically used as the input of population synthesis, provides statistical information about both individuals and households. However, given the diversity and increasing complexity of social activities, it is essential to consider additional social relationships beyond households. For example, the geographic locations of corporations and schools determine the routine destinations of many affiliated individuals. These individuals may account for a large proportion of urban travel in rush hours. Therefore, how to generate a synthetic population that conforms to constraints from all those social relationships requires to be essentially considered. To our knowledge, only a report from the Research Triangle Institute, United States, has explicitly concerned this issue [16]. Unfortunately, it does not provide a general method that seeks to handle this problem.

In this chapter, we talk about the issue by first distinguishing four classic paradigms of methodology – individual assignment, heuristic search, joint distribution fitting, and DGMs. After analyzing limitations of a representative IPU algorithm, the problem is extended to a more general case by incorporating multiple social relationships. A tensor decomposition method is provided to compete such a consistent population synthesis, minimizing the inconsistencies from individual and multi-social relationship constraints while keeping the associations among population structure from disaggregate samples.

Generally, when the multilevel assignments involve dependencies, considering each level as an explicit layer (as shown in Figure 3.3) is advantageous. For instance, in most municipalities of China, the teenager whose parent has a local registration can enroll the nearest school in priority. Other immigrant children will be randomly assigned after such enrollment. Therefore, we need to investigate his family members before assigning one to school. This can be only achieved after his assignment to household completed. Even though the personal attributes, household attributes, and family member list can be stored in one record to merge the household and individual levels, the data structure would be much more complicated especially when the dependencies involve many social organizations. As a consequence, it is more convenient to treat the multilevel social organizations separately. The sequence of assignments to different levels is also determined by such dependency, as encoded in Algorithm 3.2.

In Algorithm 3.2, the main "while" loop assigns synthetic individual into each type of organizations one by one. The algorithm scans the synthetic populations as well as organizations to dynamically choose eligible candidates. When the scale is large, as the Chinese scenario that involves billions of people, such scanning may take a long time. This is unacceptable in real applications. One solution is to only maintain joint distributions of individuals and organizations and dynamically draw candidates during iteration. For instance, if the current individual to be assigned is in type X (also can be dynamically drawn from joint distribution) and one eligible enterprise type is Y. The number of X required by Y is

$$IndNum(X) = IndNum(X \mid Y) \cdot EnterNum(Y)$$

$IndNum(X \mid Y)$ means the individual number of X in each enterprise of the type Y. During iteration, organization candidates can be dynamically drawn according to normalization of the above frequencies for each type Y and complete the assignment. When the assigned organization is "full," it is deleted from memory and saved into database. In the worst case, the algorithm only needs to maintain one organization entity for each type, rather than the whole organization set. This improvement can reduce the memory cost extensively.

Another approach to accelerate the computation of Algorithm 3.2 is parallel computing. Such operation is effective provided that assignments among different individual groups and different levels are independent. As assumed in our case where *Residential Province (RP)* is the conditional attribute between individual and enterprise, the assignment probability is

$$P(y \mid RP = Beij.) = \begin{cases} \frac{IndNum(y, RP = Beij.)}{IndNum(RP = Beij.)} & \text{if } IndNum(RP = Beij.) > 0 \\ 0 & \text{otherwise} \end{cases}$$

That is to say, any person with $RP = Beijing$ can only be assigned to an organization with the same RP value. Thus, we can deploy such assignment in an independent CPU or core without influencing other provinces. Note that this parallel deployment is applicable only when all types of organizations can be partitioned. If there is at least one exception, we will unavoidably face the data synchronization.

References

1 Statistics Canada. 1996 Census Handbook. Report 92-352-XPE, Ottawa, June, 1997.

2 N. Huynh, J. Barthelemy and P. Perez. A Heuristic Combinatorial Optimization Approach to Synthesizing a Population for Agent Based Modelling Purposes. Journal of Artificial Societies and Social Simulation, 2016, 19(4): 11.

3 F. Gargiulo, S. Ternes, S. Huet and G. Deffuant. An Iterative Approach for Generating Statistically Realistic Populations of Households. PLoS ONE, 2010, 5(1), e8828.

4 J. Barthelemy and P. L. Toint. Synthetic Population Generation without a Sample. Transportation Science, 2013, 47(2), 266–279.

5 S. Huet, M. Lenormand, G. Deffuant, et al. Parameterisation of Individual Working Dynamics. In S. Alexander and B. Olivier ed.), Empirical Agent-Based Modelling - Challenges and Solutions: Volume 1, The Characterisation and Parameterisation of Empirical Agent-Based Models. New York, Springer: 2014: 133–169.

6 L. Ma and S. Srinivasan. Synthetic Population Generation with Multilevel Controls: A Fitness-Based Approach and Validations. Computer-Aided Civil and Infrastructure Engineering, 2015, 30(2): 135–150.

7 T. Melhuish, M. Blake and S. Day. An Evaluation of Synthetic Household Populations for Census Collection Districts Created using Optimization Techniques. Australasian Journal of Regional Studies, 2002, 8(3): 369–387.

8 D. Ballas, G. Clarke, D. Dorling, et al. *SimBritain*: A Spatial Microsimulation Approach to Population Dynamics. Population, Space and Place, 2005, 11(1): 13–34.

9 J. Y. Guo and C. R. Bhat. Population Synthesis for Microsimulating Travel Behavior. Transportation Research Record, 2007: 92–101.

10 D. R. Pritchard. Synthesizing Agents and Relationships for Land Use/Transportation Modeling. Master's Thesis, Department of Civil Engineering, University of Toronto, 2008.

11 D. R. Pritchard and E. J. Miller. Advances in Population Synthesis: Fitting Many Attributes per Agent and Fitting to Household and Person Margins Simultaneously. Transportation, 2012, 39: 685–704.

12 J. Auld and A. Mohammadian. An Efficient Methodology for Generating Synthetic Populations with Multiple Control Levels. Transportation Research Record, 2010: 138–147.

13 X. Ye, K. Konduri, R. M. Pendyala, et al. A Methodology to Match Distributions of Both Household and Person Attributes in the Generation of Synthetic Populations. Transportation Research Board Annual Meeting, 2009, 9601(206): 1–24.

14 I. Gulrajani, F. Ahmed, M. Arjovsky, et al. Improved Training of Wasserstein GANs. Advances in Neural Information Processing Systems, Long Beach, CA, USA, Dec. 3–9, 2017: 5767–5777.

15 D. P. Kingma and M. Welling. An Introduction to Variational Autoencoders. arXiv, 1906.02691, 2019. [Online] URL: http://arxiv.org/abs/1906.02691.

16 W. D. Wheaton, J. C. Cajka, B. M. Chasteen, et al. Synthesized Population Databases: A US Geospatial Database for Agent-Based Models. RTI Press publication No. MR-0010-0905, Research Triangle Institute, 2009.

17 S. Rabanser, O. Shchur and S. Gunnemann. Introduction to Tensor Decompositions and their Applications in Machine Learning. Eprint arXiv:1711.10781, 2017. https://arxiv.org/pdf/1711.10781.pdf.

18 P. Ye, F. Zhu, S. Sabri, et al. Consistent Population Synthesis with Multi-Social Relationships Based on Tensor Decomposition. IEEE Transactions on Intelligent Transportation Systems, 2020, 21(5): 2180–2189.

4

Architecture for Agent Decision Cycle

The two chapters before have introduced methods and algorithms for a basic population synthesis. Such a virtual population, together with its total social relationships, determines an initial state of each agent, which plays a start point of subsequent evolution. From this chapter, we begin to talk about the agent behavioral model. That is, we shift our focus from the macro-systemic level to the micro-individual level. Unfortunately, this shift will bring us much more difficulties because it involves how to model human behaviors in a reliable way, and solving such a problem has always been one of the primary goals of artificial intelligence. Different from many other technologies such as game theory, behavioral science, and statistics, this book attempts to enter this field from cognitive computing. The basic idea behind is that an individual's behavior is the result of his deliberation. And it is only by the grasp of one's mental state as well as deliberative features that we can reasonably describe and predict his upcoming actions. Therefore, our concentration is mainly on the analysis of one's decision making, trying to infer the gradual change of his mental states.

In cognitive science, individual's decision stems from one's perception of the surrounding world and the reasoning based on his own cognition. Complex reasoning process requires plenty of knowledge from different fields, different scenarios, and different stages of particular cases, which is supported by a large and intricate knowledge base. This paradigm is consistent with the real situation of human decision-making where the intelligence in various environments benefits from his abundant knowledge repository. In technical implementation, it is a challenge to manage such an intricate knowledge base for an efficient reasoning. This chapter tries to use the cognitive architecture (CA) as a container to maintain agent's cognitive knowledge and simulate the information flow of his decision process. Section 4.1 provides the structure of parallel humans with their related users in human–machine interactive systems. Section 4.2 selects CA as an implementation framework and explains why the CA is appropriate for such a goal. From Sections 4.3–4.8, we comparatively retrospect classic architectures

Parallel Population and Parallel Human: A Cyber-Physical Social Approach,
First Edition. Peijun Ye and Fei-Yue Wang.
© 2023 The Institute of Electrical and Electronics Engineers, Inc. Published 2023 by John Wiley & Sons, Inc.

according to their applied fields. Section 4.9 shows our new hybrid architecture for agent decision cycle. A few examples of using the decision cycle to model individual's behavior are also demonstrated in the section. Then, the chapter concludes at last with some additional discussions.

4.1 Parallel Humans in Human–Machine Interactive Systems

Let us return to the central goal of this book: to computationally model human individual's deliberation and thinking, so that his behavior is prescribed to achieve the system's expected control objective. The overall structure of parallel population is given in Section 1.4, where the artificial and real population systems form a two-closed loop framework. For each user in the micro-scope, we build three artificial humans to complete his behavioral prescription. The parallel human system is illustrated in Figure 4.1, which aims to establish interactive cognitive systems. Note that the artificial cognitive system uses plural forms, indicating that there is more than one artificial system corresponding to a real system. As discussed later, we actually build three artificial cognitive systems for each user in our implementation.

The artificial system will sequentially run in three different stages to prescribe one's behaviors. The first stage is called generative intelligence, in which we first build a cognitive agent named as descriptive agent to represent one's mental state. The descriptive agent needs to characterize its corresponding user's basic attributes (like age, risk preference style, and personality) and knowledge structure as much as possible. It provides a reliable basis for subsequent reasoning by approximating the user's mental state. The construction of descriptive agent needs various techniques. First, knowledge representation is required to encode the cognitive knowledge. Since human knowledge can be differentiated into explainable knowledge and experience knowledge, it is recommended to exploit multiple ways for encoding. Second, the descriptive agent needs to reflect the heterogeneity of different individuals. This particularly refers to the heterogeneity

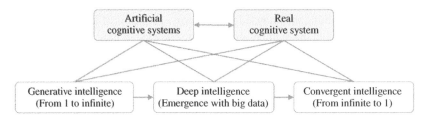

Figure 4.1 Organizations of parallel cognitive systems for individuals.

of mental deliberation in cognitive science. Two possible implementations can characterize such heterogeneity. One is using different knowledge repositories in descriptive agents for different users, where the heterogeneity between persons is fundamentally modeled as different knowledge structure, composition, etc. The other is using various levels of parameters while given the same knowledge for descriptive agents. For the latter case, a refined user-dependent calibration method is required to determine the parameter values of heterogeneous individuals. Third, the descriptive agent is expected to be endowed with the ability of dynamic learning. Learning ability is indispensable because it simulates the continuous accumulation and growth of individual's knowledge. Therefore, machine learning, especially incremental learning, could be adopted to update the knowledge repository. Starting with the descriptive agent, various techniques (such as generative adversarial networks, and knowledge automation) can be introduced to generate multiple reasoning paths.

The second stage is deep intelligence, in which the reconstruction of knowledge brings numerous reasoning paths. Here, "deep" refers to the degree of knowledge evolution. Given a collection of knowledge, rational decision-making relies on one's mental reasoning that images future state by recombining his related knowledge. This is also called planning in some literature. Result of planning can be viewed as a state-action sequence from current world state to the desired goal state. It also gives an action path that the individual may sequentially adopt. Ideally, all feasible paths from current world state to the desired goal can be traversed to get all possible action sequence candidates. Yet it does not seem biologically plausible in such a way. On the one hand, people tend to consider only a few choices rather than all possible candidates, due to the existence of "Bounded Rationality." Their decision-making greatly relies on their individual experience and personal habits. Thus, if they find a solution acceptable for the goals, then they are not inclined to make a change even if the solution is not optimal. On the other hand, when the number of possible reasoning paths is large, the searching process will be quite time-consuming. This dilemma, however, is partially solved with the elevation of computing power. We call the mental planning process as computational deliberation experiments and will address this issue in detail later. Through computational deliberation experiments, multiple decision patterns will emerge as a new type of "Big Data" to support the final decision recommendation. Evolution of deliberation is conducted by an explorative agent called predictive agent.

The third stage is called convergent intelligence. The main goal in this stage is to extract the most suitable deliberation trajectory that reaches a desired state from massive experiments. Naturally, we have to set a criterion to evaluate which emergent decision pattern is most suitable. The criterion can be a performance function or a user-defined "distance" between the investigated reasoning path and an expert decision pattern. The final desired mental state is also represented as a cognitive agent called prescriptive agent. Given the extracted deliberation trajectory, its perception environment is returned to the realistic user for the prescription of his behaviors. Strategy prescription will be discussed in detail later as well.

4.2 Why and What Is the Cognitive Architecture?

In early years, agent's behavior is simply deemed as a reactive response to its perceptions of the surrounding (virtual or actual) environment. Such type of agents, mostly designed in artificial intelligence, is usually called reactive agents, which is typically applied in production rule systems [1]. Though reactive agents are able to effectively handle particular tasks such as data processing, they are often criticized for their greedy and myopic strategies. These strategies are too simple to delineate actual human behavior that often concerns thinking about and planning for several future steps. Therefore, to understand individual behavior patterns more insightfully, the later emerged deliberative agent grounds human decision-making in multiple cognitive processes and introduces cognitive functions into the agent model [2]. In contrast with the reactive one, deliberative agent attempts to reconstruct the beliefs/concepts in mind and form the perception, reasoning, learning, etc., to achieve a particular decision. Parts of psychologically and neurologically inspired deliberative models can even emulate the "mental state" of individuals to some extent, as well as the state transferring accompanied by heterogeneous selection. Therefore, by simulating main components of human thinking and decision-making with their inter-relationships, CA is a most fundamental abstract framework for a deliberative agent.

Originally, the study of CA, to a large extent, came from the research of intelligent control. But some of them have been applied in behavioral simulation. This line of work attempts to model the main factors participated in our thinking and decision and concentrates on the relationships among them. Generally, CA research is an interdisciplinary field, ranging from psychology, neurology, philosophy to sociology. But in computer science particularly, CA mostly refers to the computational model (usually called agent) simulating human's cognitive and behavioral characteristics. The ultimate goal of CA study, which dates back to the 1950s, is to achieve human-level intelligence at the level of a computational model. Such intelligence might be realized in four different patterns: systems that think like humans, systems that think rationally, systems that act like humans, and systems that act rationally [3]. Here, the "rationality" refers to achieving consistent and correct conclusions (given its available information) for arbitrary tasks. On the one hand, parallel population in most cases concentrates on the evolution of social systems for a period of time. The result emerges from massive individual rational behaviors, not the "low-level" reflexive actions that are activated by specific stimuli. In this sense, the rationality of individual behaviors just conforms to the definition aforementioned. On the other hand, individual rational behaviors are correlated in the temporal dimension. For example, to achieve a goal, people usually decompose it into sub-goals and take several steps sequentially. When the task is partially completed, they are inclined to continue even though their surroundings turn detrimental (of course, it depends on the personality and endurance). At this point, people can bear the negative impact and persist in conducting their original plans. Obviously, deliberative agent is more appropriate than reactive agent for such typical paradigm. And CA is the most suitable framework to model such plan execution. Furthermore, CA is able to simulate people's internal deliberation, concerning not only planning but also other functions like reasoning, emotion, learning, etc., and their connections. Since rational behaviors are the results of human decisions, they originally stem from human deliberation in essence. Based on this perspective, the generation of rational behaviors is naturally modeled as the cycle – perception (or communication), thinking, and action – that are constantly repeated through the agent's whole "life."

The concept of CA is general, and there is no clear definition theoretically. However, consensus of current CA research is reached, to some extent, in that specific aspects should be considered practically. In an early stage, Newell proposed a functional criterion, including flexible behavior, real-time operation, rationality, large knowledge base, learning, development, linguistic abilities, self-awareness, and brain realization [4]. Sun broadened the scope in his desiderata later. He took ecological, bio-evolutionary, cognitive realisms into account and argued that reactivity, sequentiality, routines, trial-and-error adaptation need to be captured. Based on these notions, CA should carry essential features such as dichotomy of implicit and explicit processes, synergistic interaction, bottom-up learning, and modularity [5]. Adams et al. explicitly categorized the human-level intelligence into 14 aspects that are covered by multiple scenarios [6]. They are namely perception, memory, attention, social interaction, planning, motivation, actuation, reasoning, communication, learning, emotion, modeling self/other, building/creation, and quantitative. Most of these aspects are further spilt into subareas. For example, memory is divided into working memory (WM), episodic memory, implicit memory, etc., and social interaction involves social communication, cooperation, competition, etc. Obviously, these aspects are comprehensive. As will be seen in this chapter later, most studies and applications only concentrate on some of them.

As the scope of CA is highly comprehensive, it needs to be noted that CAs in this chapter mainly focus on the sense of mathematics and philosophy, which means two types of systems are not contained. The first one is the structure at the implementation level, such as the agent's communication module, the database, and the graphical user interface. Despite being similar to the CA at times, these components, in essence, are the software structure. Therefore, they will not be discussed from Sections 4.3–4.9. The second type of system is usually referred to as the simulation environment. Although a part of these simulation environments certainly includes CAs, they are not generally essential. Rather, these systems are computational platforms for the implementation and validation of various agent models.

To show the extensive CAs more clearly, it is required to give a classified glimpse to show their distinct features. One popular criterion for the classification is the cognitive mode. For instance, the CAs applied in problem solving or reasoning are mostly based on symbol processing, which is often called the symbolic CA. Whereas, those for computer vision usually emulate our neural dynamics via artificial neurons and are called the emergent CA. Hybrid CA refers to the combination of the two. However, this categorization, drawn in Figure 4.2, seems a little coarse so that many CAs in the same category will not be distinguished clearly. Thus from Sections 4.3–4.9, CAs are organized according to their original or primary application domains elucidated in the related references. What we should always keep in mind is that these domains are not stringently distinguished from each other. Rather, they are possibly overlapping, an example of which is some architectures in artificial general intelligence (AGI) are also used in robot control and pattern recognition.

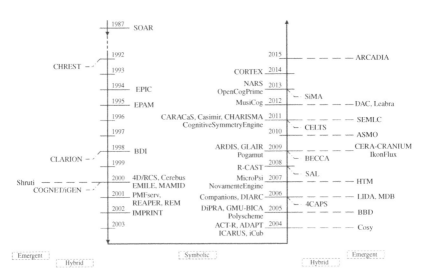

Figure 4.2 Categorization of cognitive architecture according to cognitive mode.

4.3   Architecture for Artificial General Intelligence

AGI aims at modeling the general mechanism of human intelligence emergence and the overall parts with their connections of cognitive systems. This type is mainly symbolic CAs. Adaptive Control of Thought-Rational (ACT-R). ACT-R is a well-known architecture and oriented for simulating and understanding human cognition [7]. It aims to understand how people organize knowledge and produce intelligent behavior. Still active currently, ACT-R is one of the most popular architectures that is studied and applied in multi-fields. Its implication is based on Common Lisp. The latest version is organized into a set of modules, including sensory modules for visual processing, motor modules for action, an intentional module for goals, and a declarative module for long-term declarative knowledge (Figure 4.3). Each module has an associated buffer that holds a relational declarative structure (often called "chunks," but different from those in State, operator, and result [Soar], which will be discussed later). These chunks are deemed as the

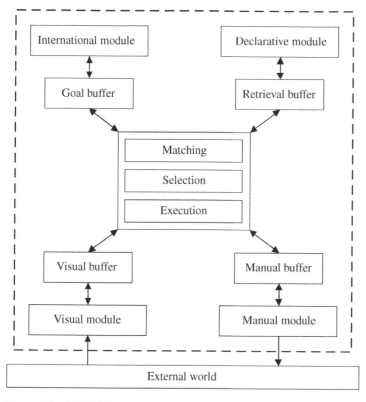

Figure 4.3   ACT-R 6.0.

agent's short-term memory (STM). In contrast, a long-term production memory coordinates the processing of the modules, which records the past usage and influences of declarative chunks and can be used to calculate the expected cost as well as the probability of success. During each cycle, the agent selects the production with the highest utility and executes its actions.

Belief–Desire–Intention (BDI). BDI is one of the most popular models of agent decision making in the agents community, particularly for constructing reasoning systems for complex tasks in dynamic environments [8]. BDI deems that agents have a "mental state" as the basis for their reasoning. As suggested by its name, this architecture is centered around three mental attitudes, namely beliefs, desires, and, especially, intentions (Figure 4.4). It is therefore typically referred to as an "intentional system." Beliefs are the internal view that the agent has about the world. They are not required to correspond with reality. Rather, they could be outdated or distorted. But they are deemed absolutely correct by the agent. Desires are all the possible states of affairs that the agent would like to accomplish. They stand for the motivational state of the agent. Another concept is goals, which has a close relation with desires. The main difference is that desires only present options that may not be all acted upon. They only represent the potential influence on an agent's actions. While goals are the states that an agent actively desires to achieve. An intention, also usually referred as a plan, is a particular course of action for achieving a goal. In computation, each reasoning round starts with the update of the agent's beliefs according to its perception. The goals to be achieved are pushed into a stack that contains all the goals that are pending achievement. Then the agent searches through its plan library to find plans (in the form of first-order logic) with post-conditions matching the top intention in the stack. In the obtained

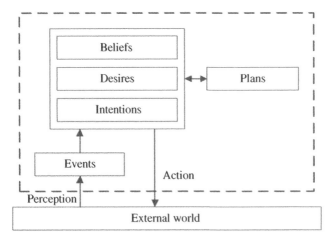

Figure 4.4 BDI.

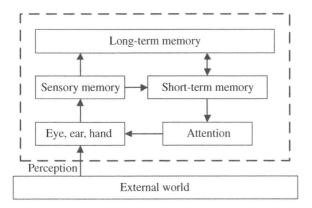

Figure 4.5 CHREST.

plans, those pre-conditions satisfied the agent's beliefs are considered possible options. The agent finally selects the plan with the highest relevance to its beliefs.

Chunk Hierarchy REtrieval Structures (CHREST). CHREST is a symbolic CA like ACT-R and Soar, with an emphasis on perception and learning (Figure 4.5). It is composed of short-term memory, long-term memory (LTM), and Input/Output mechanism [9]. Patterns (visual, action, and verbal) are encoded by the agent's input/output system from its field of vision and actions prescribed by the agent's production-rule system. Chunks are retrieved by sorting input patterns generated by the agent through familiarization and discrimination. These chunks of patterns are held in STM and LTM for differing modalities. The size of STM is limited, whereas the size of LTM is unlimited. Unlike other CAs such as ACT-R and Soar, CHREST does not discriminate between types of LTM memory such as procedural, declarative, or semantic.

Connectionist Learning with Adaptive Rule Induction Online (CLARION). CLARION, another popular CA, is intended for capturing all the essential cognitive processes within an individual cognitive agent in its routine, everyday activities, in accordance with the ecological functional perspective [10]. It focuses on the representational differences and learning differences of two different types of knowledge: implicit and explicit. These two types of knowledge differ in terms of accessibility and attentional requirement. CLARION is divided into four subsystems: Action-Centered Subsystem (ACS), Non-Action-Centered Subsystem (NACS), Motivational Subsystem (MS), and Meta-Cognitive Subsystem (MCS) (Figure 4.6). The ACS contains procedural knowledge concerning actions and procedures; thus, it serves as the procedural memory. The NACS contains declarative knowledge and serves as the declarative memory, both semantic and episodic. Both of these two subsystems are composed of explicit knowledge (easily accessible, requiring more attentional resources) and implicit knowledge

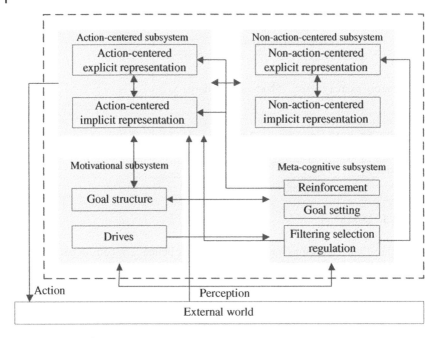

Figure 4.6 CLARION.

(harder to access, more automatic), respectively. The MS includes goal structure and drives, while the MCS involves reinforcement learning, goal setting, and filtering selection regulation. The ACS manages the action control regardless of whether the actions are for external physical movements or internal mental operations. The NACS maintains general knowledge (ultimately in the service of action decision making by the ACS). The MS provides underlying motivations for perception, action, and cognition. The MCS monitors, directs, and modifies the operations of the other subsystems for the sake of better performance.

Elementary Perceiver And Memorizer (EPAM). EPAM is a general CA involving immediate memory, short-term memory, and long-term memory [11, 12]. At the core is a discrimination net, which can have access to the LTM through the encoded index much as that of an encyclopedia. The discrimination net itself is also a part of the LTM. Other components of the LTM are the declarative memory and procedural memory, the concrete knowledge and algorithms that the indexes pointed to. In STM, auditory and visual modalities associated to various stimuli are stored to conduct particular actions. The immediate memory recognizes the stimulus pattern from the auditory and visual sensors. EPAM is applied in a wide variety of experimental paradigms including classification learning, serial anticipation learning, distractor task, and articulatory-loop paradigms.

IMproved Performance Research INtegration Tool (IMPRINT). IMPRINT is a hybrid CA. It consists of a set of automated aids to conduct human performance analyses built on top of the Micro Saint task network modeling environment [13]. Different behavioral levels are handled by different parts. The top task level, which is concentrated by IMPRINT, seeks how high-level functions can be decomposed into smaller-scale tasks and the logic by which those tasks follow each other to accomplish those functions. The bottom atomic level of thought is targeted by ACT-R, which is embedded in the architecture to handle the individual cognitive. Goals in ACT-R are derived directly from tasks in IMPRINT, providing a natural integration level. Certain tasks in IMPRINT can be implemented as ACT-R models, combining the cognitive accuracy of a CA with the tractability and ease of design of task networks.

Learning Intelligent Distribution Agent (LIDA). LIDA is a comprehensive, conceptual, and computational model covering a large portion of human cognition [14, 15]. Primarily based on the Global Workspace Theory that is widely accepted both in psychological and neurobiological fields, LIDA involves Perceptual Associative Memory (enables agents to distinguish, classify, and identify external and internal information), Workspace (holds perceptual structures both from perception and previous percepts that have not yet decayed away and local associations from episodic memories), Episodic Memory (memory for events), Attentional Memory (a collection of a particular kind of attentions), Procedural Memory, Action Selection, and Sensory-motor Memory (initiate schemes for the next decisions), Action Selection (chooses actions among the schemes), Sensory-motor Memory (responsible for deciding how tasks will be performed) (Figure 4.7). The LIDA cognitive cycle can be divided into three phases, namely understanding, consciousness, and action selection. Agent first tries its best to make sense of the current situation by updating its representation of the world, both external and internal. It then decides what portion of the represented situation is most in need of attention, through a competitive process. Broadcasting this portion, the current contents of consciousness, enables the agent to finally choose an appropriate action and execute it. This cycle keeps going all through the agent's "life." LIDA is one of the most popular architectures concerning about AGI.

Novamente Engine. The main innovation of the Novamente Engine is that it confronts the problem of "creating a whole mind" in a direct way that has not been done before. It incorporates aspects of many previous AI paradigms such as evolutionary programming, symbolic logic, agent systems, and probabilistic reasoning [16]. In Novamente, nodes, links, mind agents, mind OS, maps, and units are the major elements. Nodes are the symbols of abstract concepts or concrete entities in the external world. They may embody simple executable processes and may serve as components in relationship-webs signifying complex concepts or procedures. Links embody various types of relationships between concepts, percepts,

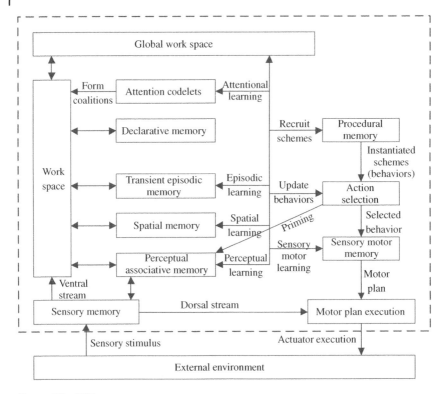

Figure 4.7 LIDA.

or actions by pointing at nodes or other links. Mind agents are carriers encapsulating dynamical processes such as importance updating, concept creation, or first-order logical inference. Mind OS is a support framework that enables diverse mind agents to act efficiently on large populations of nodes and links distributed across multiple machines. A map represents declarative or procedural knowledge, as a pattern distributed across many nodes and links. A unit is a collection of nodes, links, and mind agents, living on a cluster of machines, collectively devoted to carrying out a particular function such as vision processing, language generation, highly-focused concentration. Novamente Engine is implemented in the Second Life virtual world [17].

Performance Moderator Functions server (PMFserv). PMFserv is an agent CA that attempts to reflect the state of the art in human behavior modeling with particular attention to the impact of personality/cultural values, biology/stress, and social relations upon individual coping and group decision-making [18]. The biology module keeps decision strategies for coping under stress, time pressure, and risk. Effectiveness under stress in combat situations is also integrated in this module. The personality/cultural module includes 11 pairs of opposing fundamental emotions such as pride-shame and hope-fear. The personality/cultural module is able to perform a continual two-way interaction with the biology, perceptual, and decision-making modules. The agent uses its perception module constrained by coping mode and emotive needs to see what is going on in the world. Its perception is based on the affordance approach as well as the physiology, coping styles, prior emotional needs, and any memory elements that might have been created before the current cycle. The social module simulates the impact of social influence on an agent's decision-making based on a trust degree. The cognitive module serves as the point where diverse emotions, stressors, coping style, memories, and object affordances are all integrated into a decision for action (or inaction) to transition to a new state (or remain in the same state). At the tick of the simulator's clock, a decision style is selected and all of the information commented above is processed to produce a best response that maximizes expected, discounted rewards or utilities in the current iteration of the world.

State, operator, and result (Soar). Soar is a symbolic CA that characterizes agent's decision achievement as a goal-oriented search through problem spaces [19]. The search generates knowledge in the form of chunks that describe which operator (the operation that one needs to perform to reach the goal) to use in a certain state. Therefore, the architecture is capable of learning from experience. Apart from the perception and action modules, the architecture primarily contains a working memory (WM), a long-term memory (LTM), and a decision procedure (Figure 4.8). The WM contains information that describes the current situation or state in the

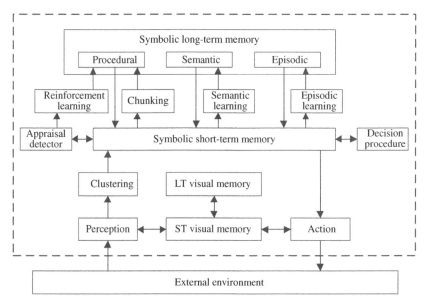

Figure 4.8 Soar.

problem-solving cycle. The information elements stored in WM are called working memory elements, which form statements or properties of an object. The LTM incorporates procedural memory, world facts in the semantic memory, and experienced situations in the episodic memory. Each execution cycle of Soar consists of five steps, namely input, proposal, decision, application, and output. The input adds elements to the WM, which can result in the firing of production rules. The fired production rules suggest one operator each. The decision procedure chooses one operator according to its knowledge information. In the application step, the selected operator is run. If there are no operator candidates or such kind of knowledge information, an impasse will be created. To solve an impasse, Soar will create a selection state that tries one of the possible operators at random and then try to run it to create a new switch state. This process is recursive until the goal state has been reached or Soar has run out of options. Soar is widely used, and the research on this architecture is still active.

4.4 Architecture for Control

CAs used for agent control are primarily emerging in the field of robotics. They try to construct computational architectures for machines that can perform humanoid reasoning, coordination, and communication for particular tasks. To achieve this goal, they usually integrate multiple cognitive modules like perception, planning, interaction, etc. This type of CA is in the majority and is mostly implemented in actual robot entities.

Adaptive Dynamics and Active Perception for Thought (ADAPT). ADAPT is a CA specifically designed for robotics [20]. It manipulates a hierarchy of perceptual and planning schemas that include explicit temporal information and that can be executed in parallel. Different from many other CAs, ADAPT treats perception as an active process that is goal-directed and context-sensitive, even down to the raw sensory data. It also assumes that true parallelism is necessary and that a robot must be able to reason about a hierarchy of concurrent real-time actions.

Conscious and Emotional Reasoning Architecture-Cognitive Robotics Architecture Neurologically Inspired Underlying Manager (CERA-CRANIUM). As stated by its name, CERA-CRANIUM is a joint framework for the development and testing of cognitive models of consciousness [21]. CERA is a control architecture structured in layers, while CRANIUM is a tool for the creation and management of high amounts of parallel processes in shared workspaces [22]. CERA is structured in four layers: sensory-motor services layer (comprises a set of interfacing and communication services which implement the required access to both sensor readings and actuator commands); physical layer (encloses agent's sensors and actuators low-level representations); mission-specific layer (produces and manages elaborated sensory-motor content related to both agent's vital behaviors and particular missions); and core layer (the highest control level in CERA, encloses a set of modules that perform higher cognitive functions). CRANIUM provides a software library in which CERA can execute thousands of asynchronous but coordinated concurrent processes. CERA uses the services provided by CRANIUM with the aim of generating a highly dynamic and adaptable perception processes orchestrated by a computational model of consciousness.

CORTEX. CORTEX is a robotics cognitive architecture for social robots. Its early version is called RoboCog [23]. It is a three-layer structure, with action execution, simulation, and perception intimately tied together, sharing a common motor representation [24]. The core of CORTEX is an integrated and dynamic multi-graph object named as Deep State Representation (DSR). DSR can hold several levels of abstraction, from basic geometry and sensorial state to high-level symbols and predicates describing the state of the robot and the environment during a short time lapse. Perceptual agents can edit the graph by changing the truth value of symbolic predicates or by updating the numerical value of metric attributes. An explicit validation by the executive agent can bring structural changes to the graph. Deliberative agent can write a plan obtained from a new mission into the graph as sequence of desired action/states pairs that are recognizable by the action generation agents. These agents can collaborate with each other through the DSR and let the robot interact with its human counterparts in open-ended tasks. CORTEX is integrated into a robot called Gualzru.

Cognitive Systems for cognitive assistants (CoSy). CoSy is a European project that attempts to build human-like, autonomous, and integrated physical (e.g., robot) systems, including research on architectures, forms of representation, perceptual mechanisms, learning, planning, reasoning, motivation, action, and communication. The general architecture schema contains several components called sub-architecture for separate competences (Figure 4.9). These sub-architectures

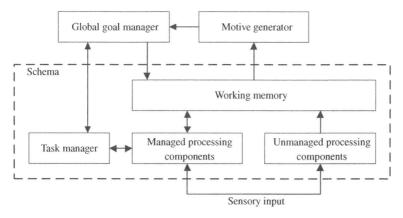

Figure 4.9 CoSy.

are loosely coupled to reduce complex inter-dependencies, so that the system could complete motor control, vision, action, planning, language, etc., concurrently. Some sub-architecture can be recursively decomposed. The components of each sub-architecture share information via its specific working memory. Two classes of goals are distinguished, namely global goals (goals of various kinds that require coordination across sub-architectures) and local goals (goals of various kinds that originate from a processing component within a single sub-architecture); (also can be written by a single global process for the global goal). Knowledge within sub-architecture is defined by a set of ontologies. CoSy architecture is applied in the PlayMate System and Explorer System [25, 26].

Distributed Adaptive Control (DAC). DAC is a single framework to solve real-world and simulated robot tasks. This architecture integrates the interactions between prediction, anticipation, attention, and memory [27]. From bottom to top, four layers are setup in the architecture (Figure 4.10). The somatic layer stands for the body of the agent, an interface with the world. It describes low-level processes such as sensing (perception of the environment) and actuation. The reactive layer is in charge of mapping sensory states into prewired action. This layer includes computational elements mimicking the reflex-like sensory-motor transformations performed by some brainstem components. The adaptive layer manages associative sensory-motor learning, encoding of motivation and reward and action selection. It simulates partial function of the cerebellar microcircuits. The contextual layer is the highest one that performs in spatial representation,

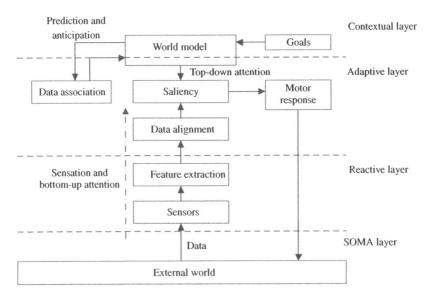

Figure 4.10   DAC.

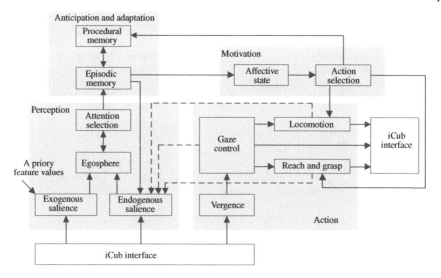

Figure 4.11 iCub.

decision-making, and planning. This layer includes a computational model of brain cortex together with a LTM structure for goal-place couplets storage.

Integrated Cognitive Universal Body (iCub). The architecture of iCub is designed for a humanoid robot platform to support collaborative research in cognitive development through autonomous exploration and social interaction. Several key capabilities like gaze control, reaching, and locomotion are focused in its initial development (Figure 4.11). Episodic and procedural memories are also included to facilitate a simplified version of internal simulation in order to provide capabilities for prediction and reconstruction, as well as generative model construction bootstrapped by learned affordances. Basically, seven modules with 13 components are contained [28]. It is comprehensive, and most other CAs can be mapped to some of the seven modules. Based on this architecture, extensive research and experiments are carried out [29].

4.5 Architecture for Knowledge Discovery

In contrast with the former two, the third category is more specific – focusing primarily on the reasoning and learning mechanism in problem solving. Similar to the AGI CAs, this type is mainly symbolic ones as well and takes a remarkable amount.

Brain-Emulating Cognition and Control Architecture (BECCA). BECCA is loosely based on the structure and function of the human brain and is referred

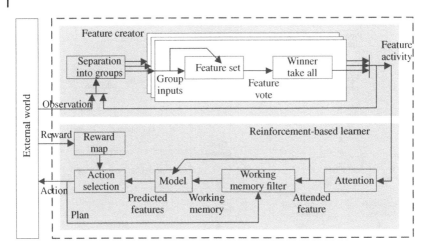

Figure 4.12 BECCA.

to optimistically as a BECCA [30]. It is composed of two parts: feature creator and reinforcement-based learner (Figure 4.12). Feature creator learns feature representation of its state space. Reinforcement-based learner learns a model of its environment and how to behave in order to receive reward. At each round, the BECCA agent conducts one sensing-learning-planning-acting loop, consisting of six major steps: reading in observations and reward; updating its feature set; expressing observations in terms of features; predicting likely outcomes based on an internal model; selecting an action based on the expected reward of likely outcomes; and updating its world model.

Conscious Emotional Learning Tutoring System (CELTS). CELTS is a biologically plausible cognitive agent model based on human brain functions [31]. This model includes the mechanisms of learning and remembering events and any related information such as corresponding procedures, stimuli, and their emotional valences (Figure 4.13). It gives the emotion a central role in the encoding and remembering of events and thus improves the agent behavior from its emotional simulation. CELTS involves eight main components, namely perception, Amygdala (emotion codelets), behavior network, attention, declarative memory, working memory, access consciousness, and learning. The cognitive cycle of CELTS proceeds in sequential steps: agent perceives its environment; the percept enters working memory; memories are probed and other unconscious resources contribute; coalitions assemble; the selected coalition is broadcasted; unconscious behavioral resources (action selection) are selected; action execution occurs.

Distributed Practical Reasoning Architecture (DiPRA). DiPRA is another architecture designed for robots. It refers to BDI but lays more stress on division of labor between offline planning and online action, regulation of epistemic

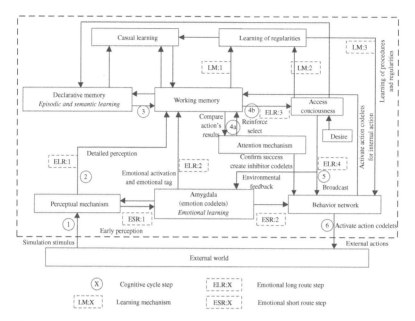

Figure 4.13 CELTS.

processes with a loop between different modules, bounded resource allocation and realization of reasoning and deliberation as intertwined processes [32]. The earlier version of DiPRA is the Artificial Knowledge Interface for Reasoning Applications (AKIRA), which is designed for parallel, asynchronous, distributed computation and fully implements the perception-action loop. Two layers are introduced in the DiPRA architecture, namely the intentional layer and the sensorimotor layer (Figure 4.14). The components of the former are reasoner, goals, plans, beliefs, and actions. This layer selects the current intention by choosing among multiple goals on the basis of current beliefs, and selects a plan to adopt for the purpose of realizing the current intention. The sensorimotor layer consists of various specialized schemas, each realizing an action with an anticipatory mechanism to predict the actual or potential effects of its actions. The schemas run concurrently, but a variable, activity level (like the thread's priority), can determine the speed of execution and priority over sensors and actuators.

FOr the Right Reasons (FORR). FORR, another achievement in the early stage of AI, is an architecture for learning and problem solving that models expertise at a set of related problem classes [33]. Hypothesis behind this architecture is that broad general knowledge applicable within certain domains theoretically exists and that it provides a natural framework from which specific expertise develops. FORR categorizes the knowledge into three layer structure – commonsense, weak theory, and problem class. It contains a problem class definition that delimits the

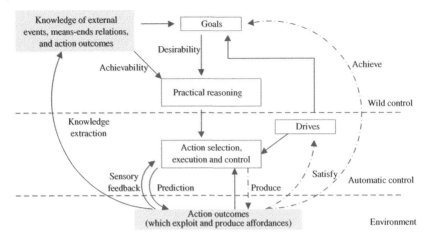

Figure 4.14 DiPRA.

domain and is part of a human expert's start-up knowledge, a behavioral script that represents the human expert's problem-solving knowledge for how to proceed in the skill domain, useful knowledge, an advisor that seeks a good reason for taking or not taking an action, an expert model that concerns about human or programmed exemplar of performance, and a learner that simulates the human expert's discovery procedures.

Non-Axiomatic Reasoning System (NARS). Based on the assumption that intelligence is the ability for a system to adapt to its environment while working with insufficient knowledge and resources, NARS is very different reasoning system from the traditional ones. It depends on finite capacity in information processing, works in real time, and is open to novel tasks and knowledge [34]. NARS can accept three types of tasks: a piece of new knowledge to be absorbed, a question to be answered, and a goal to be achieved. The major components of NARS involve a memory containing all beliefs and tasks, an inference engine deriving new tasks from a given task-belief pair, a task buffer keeping new (input or derived) tasks, one or more input/output channels connecting the task buffer and the outside environment, and a control center managing the working process.

4.6 Architecture for Computational Neuroscience

CAs from computational neuroscience consider the biological basis of human intelligence and try to simulate the neural dynamics of the brain. Generally, they adopt a large number of independent (hierarchical) storage units – called the "neurons" – to keep the knowledge repertoire of an agent. Cognitive process is modeled as the information transfer and feedback among these "neurons." Intelligence is deemed as the result of competition of various "neurons" that store different information. Therefore, this type of CA is also referred to as emergent models.

Brain-based device (BBD). Compared with other architectures, BBD is more like a computational model for simulating the activities at the nervous level [35]. Mainly deriving from computational neuroscience, BBD attempts to model the mammalian nervous system but, obviously, with far fewer neurons. BBD is designed with several principles: the device needs to engage in a behavioral task; the behavior must be controlled by a simulated nervous system having a design that reflects the brain's architecture and dynamics; the device needs to be situated in the real world; and the behavior and the activity of its simulated nervous system must allow comparisons with empirical data. Generally, BBD contains a morphology, or body plan, that allows for active exploration in a real environment; a brain simulation embedding detailed neuroanatomy, based on vertebrate nervous systems to control the BBD's behavior and shape its memory; and a value system that signals the salience of environmental cues to the BBD's nervous system, causing change in the nervous system that results in modification of the device's behavior.

Cognition and Affect (CogAff) project. CogAff has been studying to understand the "higher level" mental concepts applicable to human beings. Its mental concepts such as believe, desire, intention, mood, emotion are grounded in assumptions about information processing architectures, not merely in concepts based solely on "intentional stance" [36]. CogAff proposes a three layer architecture including reactive process, deliberative process, and meta-management process (Figure 4.15). Reactive process refers to mechanisms that are permanently dedicated to specific functions. Deliberative process can generate new behaviors, evaluate and compare options for novel combinations. It also needs a long-term associative memory. Meta-management can help to control the deliberative strategies by recording deliberative processes and noticing which planning strategies or attention switching strategies work well in which conditions.

Copycat. Copycat is an early emergent architecture that seeks to make a fluid model of the process of analogical thought. Its basic thought behind is that analogy is the driving force of cognition [37]. Three major components are included: Slipnet (distances between the LTM types are stored here for slippage, and these can change over time), Workspace (instances of types from the Slipnet and has temporary perceptual structures), and Coderack (agents who want to act on stuff in workspace reside here). In the analogic problem solving, seven phrases will be conducted sequentially. At first, codelets will scan the semantic concepts in the syntactic Scanning Phase, and then the concepts activated try to instantiate themselves. Rules will be formulated, and world-mapping will be discovered.

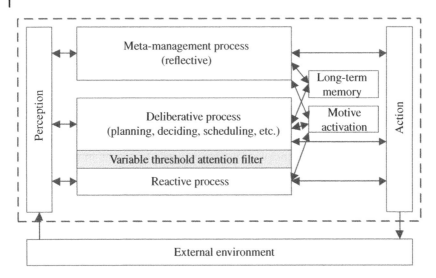

Figure 4.15 CogAff.

Finally, Rule-Slipping, Rule Execution, and Closure Checking will adjust the generated rules and recognize a potential answer. Copycat can recognize numbers of letters, but resists numbers.

Hierarchical Temporal Memory (HTM). HTM is based on biologically inspired techniques. It imitates human neocortex for recognition and categorization tasks [38]. The organization of this architecture is a tree-like hierarchical network of elementary units, called nodes (neurons) (Figure 4.16). All nodes in the HTM network embody the same learning, inferring, and prediction process that uses an internal memory which serves for storing information about a node's environment. Each node is with a set of connections (synapses). Perceptive signal arrives at the bottom level of nodes and then transmits to the upper levels. The action output is given by the uppermost node, which covers the entire input field. HTM is not a deep learning or machine learning technology, but a machine intelligence framework strictly based on neuroscience and the physiology and interaction of pyramidal neurons in the neocortex of the mammalian brain.

Leabra. Leabra is an additional architecture from computational neuroscience for object recognition (Figure 4.17). It based on the biologically-based computational model of working memory, which emulates the roles of three regions in the brain – posterior cortex, frontal cortex, and hippocampus [39]. The Leabra architecture consists of tiered feature processing layers that roughly correspond to areas within the ventral stream of the brain: primary visual cortex (V1), extrastriate cortex (V2/V4), inferotemporal cortex (IT) as well as higher-level layers that represent a modal semantic properties and named output responses. Grayscale bitmap images are pre-processed by capturing the response properties of the retina and

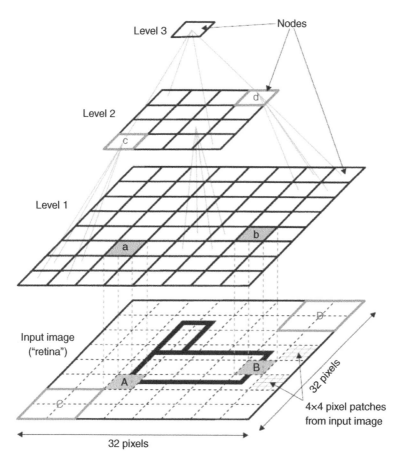

Figure 4.16 HTM.

lateral geniculate nucleus of the thalamus. The output signal is sent to the V1 layer as input, where V1-like features at multiple spatial scales are represented via a retinotopic grid of many units. This recognition process takes place sequentially in the V2/V4 and IT, where contexts of the object are different and the numbers of encoded units decrease. Leabra can be viewed as an expansion on a large class of hierarchical feed-forward models of visual processing in the brain. Its primary innovation is that hierarchically adjacent layers are recurrently connected, which provides top-down feedback connections within the brain's ventral stream.

Simulation of the Mental Apparatus and applications (SiMA). SiMA attempts to construct human motivation factors that impact the particular decisions and actions. The motivational system is based on the psychoanalytic model of human personality, presented in the psychoanalytic drive theory [40]. SiMA is a symbolic and emergent architecture, containing three layers (Figure 4.18). The lowest one

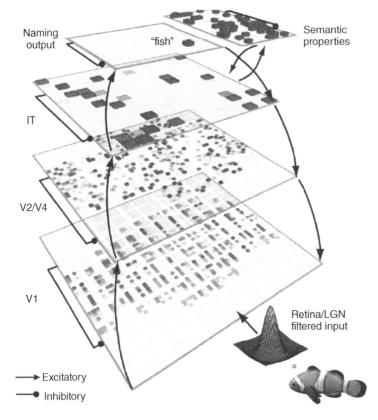

Figure 4.17   Leabra.

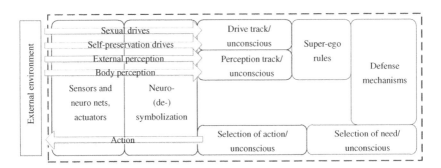

Figure 4.18   SiMA.

comprises the neural activities, i.e. the perception from sensors and the actions from the higher layers. The middle layer has to build neurosymbols from the neural input and, in the other direction, neural actuator signals from the symbolic results of the topmost layer. The top layer, the psyche, is understood as a symbol processing machine and incorporates several components like super-ego rule base, defense mechanism, perception track, action selection, etc. SiMA is applied in case-driven, agent-based simulations.

4.7 Architecture for Pattern Recognition

Objectively, pattern recognition can be viewed as knowledge acquisition and is more or less concerned with the previous categories. The reason that we treat the following CAs as a separate sort is they place a remarkable stress on the domains of object recognition through image or speech.

Architecture for Real-time Dynamic Inspection Systems (ARDIS). ARDIS is a knowledge-based architecture designed for configuration of visual dynamic surface inspection systems in the industry of laminated materials [41]. Following the CommonKADS methodology, it embeds a hierarchy of representations and components to perform information abstraction. Its computation involves three processes: the initialization which generates an initial skeleton that behaves as a seed for its subsequent extension into a more complex skeleton, the extension of the initial inspection skeleton which configures an inspection considering all the specific requirements, and the revision that validates the configuration by means of the acquired images.

Executive-Process/Interactive Control (EPIC). The EPIC architecture is developed to support an active vision approach to visual search and provides a general framework for simulating a human interacting with an environment to accomplish a task [42]. Conceptually, it consists of a set of interconnected processors that operate simultaneously and in parallel (Figure 4.19). EPIC uses an event-driven simulation approach implemented with Object-Oriented Programming methodology. At each round, an event object containing a pointer to the receiver and the arriving time is collected by the auditory or visual processor. A global Coordinator sequentially assigned the event objects in the event queue to their destination processors, specifically, the cognitive processor, to fire its matched production rules. The production rules can be updated during executions and are stored in the Long-Term Memory and Production Memory. Vocal processor and manual processor get the movements command from the cognitive processor and send

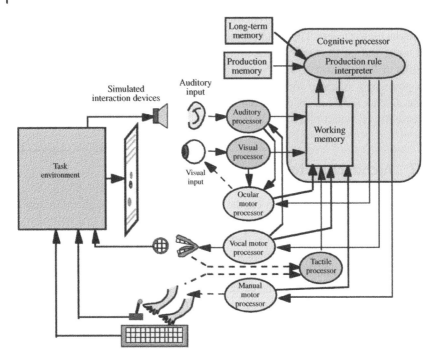

Figure 4.19 EPIC.

event objects to simulate the actions. Software of EPIC can now be achieved freely for further research.

Selective Tuning (ST). The ST model of visual attention starts from the "first principles" that formulate vision as a search problem, and the complexity theory that is concerned with the cost of achieving solutions to such problems. Research on ST focuses on both neurobiological predictive power and utility in practice [43]. The architecture is pyramidal in structure, a layered representation characterized by successively coarser spatial representations. The units within this network receive both feed-forward and feedback connections. When a stimulus is presented to the input layer, it activates in a feed-forward manner all of the units within the pyramid with receptive fields mapping to the stimulus location. The result is a diverging cone of activity within the processing pyramid. The response strength of units in the network is a measure of goodness-of-match of the stimulus within the receptive field to the model that determines the selectivity of that unit. Selection relies on hierarchical optimization and recursive pruning, taking the winner-take-all form. With substantial behavioral and neurophysiologic experimental support, the architecture is implemented and tested in several labs applying it to guide computer vision and robotics tasks.

Ymir. Ymir is a broad, generative model of psychosocial dialog skills that incorporates multimodal perception, decision, and multimodal action in a coherent framework [44]. It is a three-layered feedback-loop architecture, both descriptive (based on descriptive results from the psychological and linguistic literature) and generative (specifies how a conversant can construct dialog in real-time). The main elements in Ymir are perception, decision, action, inter-process communication, knowledge, and organization. The perception component includes unimodal perceptors that encode features related to a single mode and multimodal integrators that aggregate the information from unimodal perceptors. Decision making is conducted about what to do from moment to moment by checking the agent's up-to-the-millisecond knowledge state. Like production rules, each decider sends out a behavior request, changes its state, and waits for a reset condition when it is fired. The behavior request from each decider can be viewed as an intention to perform, and the action module will select a set of postures stored in a library for that act. Knowledge base contains task and declarative knowledge about a particular topic, specifically, the information on high-level interpretation of a person's multimodal acts, responses to those acts, and communication to other parts of the system.

4.8 Other Representative Architecture

Apart from the previous CAs, some other architectures used in specific domains are summarized in this section. These domains involve human–machine system, music composition, air-traffic control, 3-D game modeling, and so on.

Cognitive architecture, specification, and implementation of mental image-based reasoning (Casimir). Casimir is a CA designed for computationally modeling human spatial knowledge processing relying on spatio-analogical or quasi-pictorial knowledge representations [45]. The main parts of this architecture are the long-term memory, working memory, and a diagram interaction component that realizes the interactions between internal working memory representations and external visualizations (Figure 4.20). Abstract knowledge is stored in a tree-like ontology structure and it is accessed by current task interpretation. Working memory combines the spatial information from LTM and current perceptions to establish a representational basis for further exploring and reasoning. Diagram interaction involves image externalization and diagram inspection that are beneficial to complement the properties of internal mental representations.

Context Hierarchy based Adaptive ReasonIng Self-Motivated Agent (CHARISMA). CHARISMA CA is proposed for the agents within the Civilization-Inspired Vying

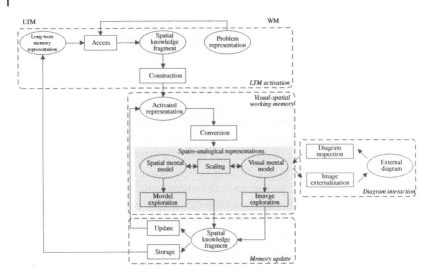

Figure 4.20 Casimir.

Societies (CIVS) system [46]. Compared to other available ones, this architecture has two distinct features. First, its basic idea is that agent intrinsic motivation in a social context is vital to the self-sustaining development of knowledge, skills, and adaptations, especially if they are novel or unforeseen by the user. Second, a dynamic knowledge representation mechanism in the CHARISMA architecture allows the agents to learn not only from their own experiences but also from social interactions with other agents. Generally, CHARISMA consists of sensory memory, active and passive perception, reflex, working memory (conscious focus and unconscious focus), intrinsic motivation, preservation drives, and memory subsystem (Figure 4.21). Its knowledge is represented as sematic network.

Man–machine Integration Design and Analysis System (MIDAS). MIDAS is a dynamic, integrated human performance modeling and simulation environment that helps facilitate the design, visualization, and computational evaluation of complex man–machine system. It includes a cognitive structure to represent human capabilities and limitations [47]. The cognitive component is comprised of a perceptual mechanism, memories, attentions, and an output behavior module (Figure 4.22). The perceptual mechanism has visual and auditory processors which get the objects in view as well as signal and messages in surrounding environment. The memories are composed of an LTM that contains both declarative and procedural knowledge and a working memory that captures the current context (retrieved from LTM and initiated from perceptions) and the task agenda,

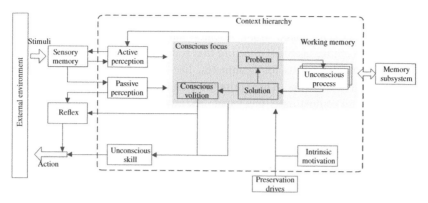

Figure 4.21 CHARISMA.

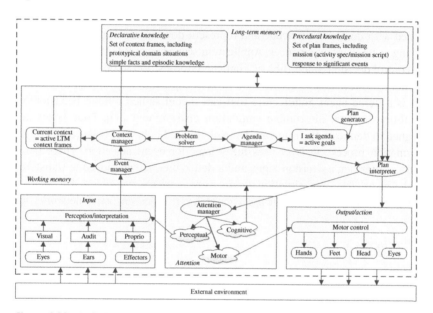

Figure 4.22 MIDAS.

which indicates active goals. The output behavior is regulated by the motor control process and conducts activities when the required resources are available. MIDAS adopts probabilistic fixations and the Salience, Effort, Expectancy, and Value (SEEV) approach to model the attentions. The former drives the eyeball toward a particular area of interest based on a known scan pattern and a statistical distribution of fixation times, while the latter breaks down relevant flight deck display features into the four parameters.

Recognition-primed-decision-enabled Collaborating Agents Simulating Teamwork (R-CAST). Originated from research on human-centered teamwork, R-CAST is a cognitive agent architecture that is designed to be able to anticipate relevant information needs for teammates, like a human team member of a high performance team [48]. Three principles, architectural flexibility, teamwork adaptability, and context reasoning capability, are conformed in its designation. The key components of R-CAST are "RPD-based Decision Making" module (domain knowledge, past experiences, and the current situation awareness are used to produce a new, or adapt to, an existing decision), "Teamwork manager," and "Taskwork manager" modules (coordinate the fulfillment of a decision that involves inter-agent and intra-agent activities) (Figure 4.23). R-CAST is cognitively inspired, supports context awareness, and provides a framework for agents to work as teams. Two major steps are required to develop a multi-agent system using this architecture: implement a domain adapter for the problem studied with domain knowledge and represent domain expertise about decision making in terms of experiences. Application scenarios of R-CAST are command and control decision-aided, 3-block challenge studies, and so on.

Situation Awareness Model for Pilot-in-the-Loop Evaluation (SAMPLE). SAMPLE is a tiered agent architecture that can model skilled human behaviors in a real-time tactical air combat simulation environment [49]. Four layers are designed to delineate the rule-based and skill-based behaviors (Figure 4.24). The information processing layer uses fuzzy logic for event detection. Three main blocks, a fuzzifier, a decision logic, and a defuzzifier, are employed to transform fused sensor data into situationally relevant semantic variables. The second processing stage, the situation assessment layer, relies on belief networks for

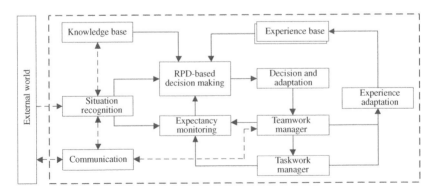

Figure 4.23 R-CAST.

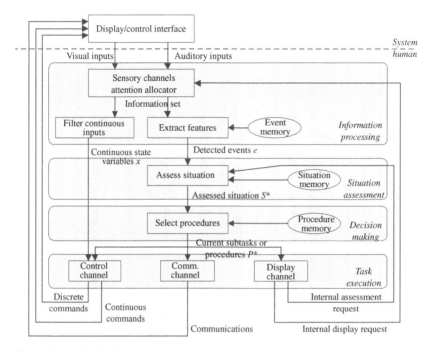

Figure 4.24 SAMPLE.

probabilistic reasoning in the presence of uncertainty to generate a high-level interpretation of the operational situation. This layer emulates a skilled human's information fusion and reasoning process in a multi-task environment. The third stage, decision-making, is implemented by a cascade of a procedure selection layer and a task execution layer. Decision-making behavior is in the form of a production rule system, with a general structure of "If (situation) Then (procedure set)" maintained by a knowledge base. SAMPLE also uses a special language called Command and Control Simulation Interface Language to establish the inter-agent communications. And its simulation scenario of a four-ship fighter sweep mission is implemented as well.

Some of the CAs mentioned before have established their websites, which collect the related research achievements such as project introductions, publications, source codes, and forums. These open sources have tied scholars and engineers from different areas together and facilitated the further research as well as application to a great extent. Thus, we have summarized them in Table 4.1.

Table 4.1 Classic cognitive architectures with websites

Abbreviation	Perception	Actuation	Memory	Reasoning	Learning	Attention	Emotion	Planning	Interaction	Motivation	Proposed year	Website
4CAPS	✓		✓	✓	✓						2006	http://www.ccbi.cmu.edu/4CAPS/index.html
ACT-R	✓	✓	✓	✓	✓						2004	http://act-r.psy.cmu.edu/
CHREST	✓		✓	✓	✓	✓					1992	http://chrest.info/
CLARION	✓	✓	✓	✓	✓	✓					1998	http://www.cogsci.rpi.edu/~rsun/clarion.html
CogAff	✓	✓	✓	✓	✓		✓			✓	1991	http://www.cs.bham.ac.uk/research/projects/cogaff/
Cosy	✓	✓	✓	✓	✓			✓	✓		2004	https://www.societyofrobots.com/robottheory/cosy-short.pdf
DiPRA	✓	✓	✓	✓				✓			2005	www.akira-project.org/
EPAM	✓	✓	✓		✓						1995	http://www.chrest.info/epam.html
EPIC	✓	✓	✓	✓	✓	✓					1994	http://web.eecs.umich.edu/~kieras/epic.html
GLAIR	✓	✓	✓	✓				✓			2009	http://www.cse.buffalo.edu/sneps/Projects/sneps3.html
HTM	✓		✓		✓						2007	www.numenta.org/
iCub	✓	✓	✓	✓	✓	✓	✓			✓	2004	http://macsi.isir.upmc.fr, www.icub.org/
MicroPsi		✓	✓	✓	✓		✓			✓	2007	www.micropsi-industries.com/
MIDAS	✓	✓	✓			✓					1993	http://hsi.arc.nasa.gov/groups/midas/
MusiCog	✓		✓		✓						2012	(Not available)
NARS			✓	✓	✓						2013	http://opennars.github.io/opennars/
OpenCogPrime	✓	✓	✓	✓	✓		✓	✓	✓	✓	2013	http://wiki.opencog.org/w/The_Open_Cognition_Project
OSCAR			✓	✓	✓			✓	✓		1999	http://johnpollock.us/ftp/OSCAR-web-page/oscar.html
PMFserv							✓		✓		2001	http://www.seas.upenn.edu/~barryg/HBMR.html
Pogamut	✓	✓	✓								2009	http://pogamut.cuni.cz/main/tiki-index.php
Soar		✓	✓	✓	✓						1987	http://soar.eecs.umich.edu/
ST	✓		✓	✓	✓	✓					1995	http://laav.eecs.yorku.ca/index.php/test/visual-attention/

4.9 TiDEC: A Two-Layered Integrated Cycle for Agent Decision

The architecture reviewed from Sections 4.3–4.8 mainly follow two mainstream paradigms – symbolic processing and emergent cognition. Roughly, the former involves those for AGI, Control and Knowledge Discovery, while the latter are for Computational Neuroscience and Pattern Recognition. With the breakthrough of artificial intelligence in recent years, particularly the deep learning techniques, we are able to integrate these two paths to exploit both of their benefits. To this end, we propose a novel cognitive model called Two-layered integrated DEcision Cycle (TiDEC). The model, compared with most of previous architecture, characterizes fine-grained cognitive components as well as the information flow in decision-making process. As shown in Figure 4.25, the model is a hybrid structure and intended to capture all the essential cognitive elements. The cognitive components are organized in two layers, and they form two parallel decision cycles.

Perception, interaction, and actuation. Perception, interaction, and actuation may be the most basic components that an agent has. These components are

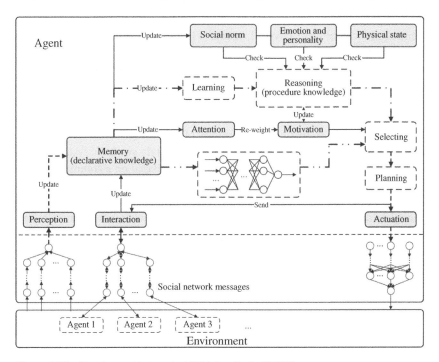

Figure 4.25 Two-layered integrated DEcision Cycle (TiDEC).

located at the bottom, implemented by an artificial neural network (ANN) layer that represents the agent's biological sensory and motor systems. The perception ANN (proactively or passively) receives low-level sensory signals from the environment and converts them into symbolic concepts or numerical values for the high-level deliberative system. A primary kind of ANN that shows remarkable perception ability is the deep neural network (DNN). It can proactively or passively transform raw sensory signals like images, audio, or sentences in different languages into formal representations for the upper-level deliberative layer. Typical DNNs including convolutional neural network (CNN), recurrent neural network (RNN), generative adversary network (GAN) and their derivatives are used to simulate one's visual, auditory, et al. perceptions. Interaction refers to the communication and information exchange with other agents. Since group dynamics and systemic behaviors are mostly studied in social management, it is a very important facet that deserves extensive research. This is because the interaction among heterogeneous agents reflects the sociality, and complex social phenomena also emerge from the interactions. Usually, the interaction is implemented by passing messages among different agents. The received messages from other agents (actively or passively) are sent to working memory and learning procedure. And the information that an agent would like to "tell" or "show" his "friends" is dispatched through the interaction DNN. Protocols developed by the Foundation for Intelligent Physical Agents (FIPA), an international organization that is dedicated to promoting the interoperability of intelligent agents by openly developing specifications, are often adopted to guarantee efficient and regular communications. At the end of each "observe, decision, act" loop, the actuation DNN controls the agent's actuators according to the input parameters provided by his deliberative results. Parameters of the controller are adaptively passed through the DNN to simulate the uncertainty of execution.

The upper layer of the cognitive model is an uncertain symbolic system, which simulates the human deliberative decision-making. Based on a common perception and actuation, the decision-making may involve two parallel cycles (drawn in dot dashed lines in the figure). One is the logic reasoning that simulates human's rational deliberation. According to classic cognitive science, such rational deliberations are called System 2 where knowledge is stored in an explainable way and reasoning is conducted with explicit semantics (the cycle formed by the uppermost dot dashed line in the figure). A good example comes from the mathematical theory proving. When doing that task, we need to understand every proof step in a logic thinking from the assumptions to the final conclusions. This requires a common knowledge set among agents with each concept unambiguously referring to a specific kind of entity. The reasoning path can be also recognized by comprehensive people and can be taught to novices who have not completed that task before. The cycle of System 2 logic reasoning is composed of perception, memory, learning, reasoning, planning, and actuation and will be discussed in the following paragraphs.

Memory. Memory usually includes two parts, working memory (or short-term memory) and long-term memory, which incorporates the main beliefs of an agent and forms the foundation of his reasoning. Beliefs in the memories are the internal view that the agent has about the world. They are not required to correctly reflect reality but could be out-dated or distorted. Every agent deems his beliefs (including negative recognitions of the world) as absolutely correct knowledge. Working memory can be switched to the LTM when it is not relevant to the current problem any longer. Similarly, when the agent encounters a new problem that cannot be solved only by his working memory, he will search the LTM and read the concerned beliefs to expand his current working memory. LTM has a mechanism of decay, leading to some beliefs gradually vanished if they are not applied for a long period. Belief is also referred to as declarative knowledge and is generated via the output of perception/interaction DNN that maps environment signals into uncertain facts with confidence levels. A popular pattern to encode such uncertain facts is using fuzzy logic like

$$IF\ x_1 = s_1\ \text{``and''}\ x_2 = s_2\ \text{``and''}\ \ldots\ \text{``and''}\ x_n = s_n\ THEN\ D(\underline{s}) - fs$$

where $\underline{x} = (x_1, \ldots, x_n)$ is the input data from universe $U \subset \mathbb{R}^n$, $\underline{s} = (s_1, \ldots, s_n) \in S_1 \times S_2 \times \cdots \times S_n$ is the linguistic value defined on U. fs stands for the firing strength of the rule. In each computational iteration, agent updates his beliefs by comparing current environment state and historical knowledge. The inconsistency between current state and his expectations may result in learning, updating the firing strengths of common reasoning rules that are stored in the reasoning module [50]. According to the time and importance, beliefs in the two memories also impact the agent's attention.

Social norm, emotion and personality, and physical state. The three modules are the reflection of the agent's internal states. Social norm refers to a collection of constraints that impose significant impacts on one's behavior to adapt to cultural or expectations of the whole society or an organization. These constraints are neither obligatory nor in the legislative level. Yet an agent will probably receive a punishment such as being isolated by others if it does not comply with them. For example, shaking hands to express a friendly attitude after sports is a widely used social norm. Almost every athlete adopts this behavior. Otherwise he will incur drastic critics and successive detriments in his future career. Social norm can be acquired by directly teaching from others as well as learning from the interactions. Emotion and personality are another two factors influencing one's decision. Emotion refers to temporary feelings characterized by intense mental activity and a high degree of pleasure or displeasure, while personality means the individual style or preference of behavior. The two aspects are distinct from each other in that emotion plays a more influential role in decisions with limited time and uncertainty, whereas personality determines the long-term strategies. In this sense, personality is more "rational" than emotion. Since our cognitive model not only focuses on the macro equilibrium of social systems but also on the investigation of the local human–machine dynamics in a short period of time, emotion is incorporated to consider the agent's temporary actions. As a Bayesian learning example in the upcoming paragraph, emotion, and personality may affect the learning process. The basic emotion contains anger, disgust, fear, happiness, sadness, and surprise. And personality is represented in various forms such as dominance, influence, conscientiousness, and steadiness. Emotion can be dynamically updated through the agent's perception and physical state, while personality is not as erratic as the emotion by contrast. However, it is the personality that greatly determines the heterogeneity of individuals. The physical state module includes one's physiological conditions and social characteristics. In contrast with the social norm and personality which lie on the psychological and cognitive levels, physical states can be viewed as a low-level state. Physical state is determined by the actuation and the actual situation of environment. It also impacts the agent's reasoning and emotion in turn. A fatigue physical condition may give the agent a stressful mood very likely.

Learning. Learning is a process that an agent converts his received information (from perception and/or interaction) into his knowledge. Its primary output is to adjust the reasoning mode. Note that this adjustment is only based on local observation or communication thus is possibly incorrect. Social norms, which can be viewed as a specific type of LTM, are also obtained and updated through learning. The agent's learning style is influenced by emotion and personality as mentioned before. For example, in the Bayesian learning, the agent will calculate his opponents' previous strategy frequencies and choose his best response that may be very different from his historical measures. If the agent has an easy-to-change personality, this shift seems natural. But if it is "stubborn" enough, the transition may consider the past to a certain extent.

Reasoning. Reasoning is perhaps the most central part of the decision-making. As can be seen in the figure, it is a procedure based on multiple inputs. Beliefs in the working-memory and long-term memory are the foundation of reasoning, while social norm, emotion and personality and physical state impose constraints on this process. Many decision algorithms or mechanisms can be adopted in the reasoning module. One of the most representative instances may be the utility maximization, which is very popular in economic studies. For a specific problem, the agent gives each solution candidate a utility value according to the current percept, the knowledge stored in his LTM, and the constraints from other modules. If a candidate does not satisfy some "hard" constraints such as violating a compulsive norm or cannot be conducted by the restriction of current physical conditions, its utility will set to be zero thus this solution will be excluded from the agent's considerations. Finally, the candidate with the highest utility will be selected as the ultimate determination. Common reasoning rules are also called procedural knowledge. And multiple reasoning results (probably conducted in a parallel way) are selected by motivations that are sorted in different priority by attention to satisfy the most urgent needs.

Motivation and Attention. Motivation includes the purposes that an agent pursuit in various aspects. It can be seen as a concrete form of desires. In the daily life, one may concentrate on multiple problems of different fields as he is endowed with multiple social roles. He may expect to complete a project as well as his can, and also look forward to keeping a compatible relationship with the customers. For each field, one pursuit (or some near optimal alternatives) is maintained in the motivation module until it is fully achieved. The motivation can be dynamically adjusted as the reasoning result may change in different cycles. Attention reflects an agent's focus or the degree of the importance of the problems he tackles. In our model, attention is updated by the beliefs in memory according to their time (such as a deadline) and significance. Attention acts on the motivations updated by the reasoning procedure, and arranges the motivations in a specific sequence, usually by attaching an urgence level to each goal. The motivation with highest urgence will be arranged at the top position and will be conducted in priority.

Planning. After the motivation generated and sorted, each motivation will be realized through a sequence of activities or actions named as a plan. Such actions will be maintained until the corresponding motivation is fulfilled or canceled. A motivation can be further decomposed into sub-motivations and their corresponding activities are linked as an activity chain. A plan is constructed by dynamically computing or by searching the preliminarily established plan library. Similar to other procedures, planning can use many classic algorithms. For instance, an agent in traffic simulation can use dynamic programming to calculate his travel route according to his known congestion information.

Apart from the explainable rational deliberation cycle that models our cognitive System 2, a second implicit cycle is also drawn in the figure, corresponding to System 1 in cognitive science (formed by the lower double dot dashed line in the figure). This cycle is somewhat direct as it models human experienced decision-making. The "perception, learning, reasoning, action" cognitive loop is built on an ANN (especially DNN), which implicitly encodes the agent's endogenous knowledge. Due to the adaptive learning ability of DNN, the cycle can dynamically imitate particular decision patterns from the environment and from others. Usually, reinforcement such as Q learning is also added to this process so that the agent interactively improves its responsive strategies to specific situations. In general, reasoning of the second decision cycle only involves numerical computation and is thus less complex than the uncertain logic reasoning where many possible reasoning paths are heuristically searched. This has biological foundations. In real human cognition, rational deliberation represented by logic reasoning is more energy consuming and much slower than his intuitive decision. For example, if you come across a mathematical theorem for the first time, trying to prove its correctness. You will spend a great period of time thinking with your own knowledge repository. When you are familiar with that theorem later, however, you may probably draw the conclusion as long as you see its assumptions. Although the proof steps can be reproduced via your achieved knowledge, you are inclined to omit such a trivial process. The example tells us that human's explicit knowledge in System 2 tends to be converted into his implicit knowledge in System 1 since it saves energy. When the conclusion is not consistent with one's expectations, the conversion can reversely take place, stimulating brain to check or repair the logic reasoning paths in System 2. Therefore, agent with the cognitive model also has transformational mechanisms between the two decision cycles.

At the end of this section, we will describe the overall information flow in the interaction of parallel human system. During the computation and prescription, each agent constantly repeats his decision-making process, which starts with observation and interaction. The received messages from other agents are unpacked in the interaction module and sent to the working memory and learning procedure. The perception from the environment is sent to these two components as well. Inputs of such two channels will update the working memory that concerns about current problems. The learning procedure, influenced by the emotion and personality, gives new procedural knowledge to update the reasoning step. After the module update, the agent will check his social norm, emotion and personality, and his current physical state to conduct reasoning based on his memories and generate multiple motivations. The motivations are sorted according to the attention which means that the most concentrated one is arranged at the top of the motivation queue and will be processed in priority. Each motivation is used as the input for planning. The generated plans will send the information that the agent wants to express to others to the interaction module and will be executed via actuation. Finally, physical state may be updated after the actuation.

4.10   Conclusions and Discussions

CA is a fundamental structure that characterizes the formation of our mental recognition for objective world and the generation of particular decisions. It provides a feasible path from the macroscopic parallel population to the microscopic parallel human. Admittedly, using this kind of architecture to manage individual knowledge is optional, as modeler can directly put all the perception-action rules into a single "pool" which is deemed as the agent's total memory. Yet such a recipe, though possibly effective, may enhance difficulty in development especially when the agent has numerous productive rules. In such an extreme case, programmers have to clarify reasoning chains and debug unpredictable exceptions among thousands of rules. And the "one-pool" solution will undoubtedly reduce the computational efficiency since the search process involves a large number of candidates. Therefore, developers are strongly recommended to adopt CA, as illustrated in this chapter, to categorize different rules in their applications.

In this chapter, we explain the origin of CA research and briefly summarize classic architecture for several application domains. In addition, a hybrid decision-making model named Two-layered integrated DEcision Cycle (TiDEC) is proposed to characterize human cognitive components and information flow. In contrast with most existing work, TiDEC integrates the symbolic reasoning with emergent empirical decision. It also bridges the explicit cognitive System 2 with the implicit cognitive System 1. In this sense, TiDEC gives a more fine-grained model for human deliberation. Based on the structure, the next two chapters will address the knowledge acquisition and exploitation for decision achievement.

References

1 J. Ferber. Simulating with Reactive Agents. In E. Hillebrand and J. Stender (eds.), Many Agent Simulation and Artificial Life, Ohmsha, 1994, 36(6): 8–28.

2 M. Scheutz and B. B. Logan. Affective vs. Deliberative Agent Control. Proceedings of the 8th International Conference on Artificial Life (ICAL 2003), 2003.

3 S. Russell and P. Norvig, Artificial Intelligence: A Modern Approach. Prentice Hall, 1995.

4 A. Newell. Unified Theories of Cognition. Cambridge, MA: Harvard University Press, 1990.

5 R. Sun. Desiderata for Cognitive Architectures. Philosophical Psychology, 2004, 17(3): 341–373.

6 S. Adams, I. Arel, J. Bach, et al. Mapping the Landscape of Human-Level Artificial General Intelligence. AI Magazine, 2012, 33(1): 25–42.

7 J. R. Anderson, D. Bothell, M. D. Byrne, S. Douglass, C. Lebiere and Y. Qin. An Integrated Theory of the Mind. Psychological Review, 2004, 111(4): 1036–1060.

8 M. Georgeff, B. Pell, M. Pollack, et al. The Belief–Desire–Intention Model of Agency. In J. P. Muller, A. S. Rao and M. P. Singh (eds), Intelligent Agents V: Agent Theories, Architectures, and Languages—Proceedings of the 5th International Workshop, ATAL'98, Springer, 2003, 1555: 1–10.

9 M. Lloyd-Kelly, P. C. R. Lane and F. Gobet. The Effects of Bounding Rationality on the Performance and Learning of CHREST Agents in Tileworld. Research and Development in Intelligent Systems XXXI: Incorporating Applications and Innovations in Intelligent Systems XXII, 2014: 149–162.

10 R. Sun. Memory Systems within a Cognitive Architecture. New Ideas in Psychology, 2012, 30(2): 227–240.

11 H. B. Richman and H. A. Simon. Simulations of Classification Learning using EPAM VI. Complex Information Processing Working Paper 552, Department of Psychology, Carnegie Mellon University, 2002. http://www.pahomeschoolers .com/epam/cip552.pdf.

12 H. B. Richman, H. A. Simon and E. A. Feigenbaum. Simulations of Paired Associate Learning using EPAM VI. Complex Information Processing Working Paper 553, Department of Psychology, Carnegie Mellon University, 2002. http:// www.pahomeschoolers.com/epam/cip553.pdf.

13 D. K. Mitchell. Workload Analysis of the Crew of the Abrams V2 SEP: Phase I Baseline IMPRINT Model. Technical Report, ARL-TR-5028, Army Research Laboratory, USA, 2009.

14 U. Faghihi and S. Franklin. The LIDA Model as a Foundational Architecture for AGI. In P. Wang and B. Goertzel (eds), Theoretical Foundations of Artificial General Intelligence. Atlantis Press, 2012: 103–121.

15 S. Franklin, T. Madl, S. Strain, et al. A LIDA Cognitive Model Tutorial. Biologically Inspired Cognitive Architectures, 2016, 16: 105–130.

16 B. Goertzel and C. Pennachin. The Novamente Artificial Intelligence Engine. In B. Goertzel and C. Pennachin (eds), Artificial General Intelligence. Berlin Heidelberg, Springer-Verlag, 2007: 63–129.

17 B. Goertzel, C. Pennachin, N. Geissweiller, et al. An Integrative Methodology for Teaching Embodied Non-Linguistic Agents, Applied to Virtual Animals in Second Life. Proceedings of the 1st Conference on Artificial General Intelligence, 2008: 161–175.

18 B. G. Silverman, M. Johns, J. Cornwell, et al. Human Behavior Models for Agents in Simulators and Games: Part I—Enabling Science with PMFserv. Presence: Teleoperators and Virtual Environments, 2006, 15(2): 139–162.

19 J. E. Laird. The SOAR Cognitive Architecture. Cambridge, MA, USA: MIT Press, 2012.

20 D. P. Benjamin, D. Lyons and D. Lonsdale. ADAPT: A Cognitive Architecture for Robotics. Proceedings of International Conference on Cognitive Modeling, ICCM 2004, Pittsburgh, Pennsylvania, USA, 2004: 337–338.

21 R. Arrabales, A. Ledezma and A. Sanchis. Simulating Visual Qualia in the CERA-CRANIUM Cognitive Architecture. In C. Hernandez, R. Sanz, J. Gomez-Ramirez, L. S. Smith, A. Hussain, A. Chella and I. Aleksander (eds.), From Brains to Systems. New York, Springer, 2011.

22 R. Arrabales, A. Ledezma and A. Sanchis. CERA-CRANIUM: A Test Bed for Machine Consciousness Research. International Workshop on Machine Consciousness, Towards a Science of Consciousness, 2009.

23 J. Martinez-Gomez, R. Marfil, L. V. Calderita, et al. Toward Social Cognition in Robotics: Extracting and Internalizing Meaning from Perception. Workshop of Physical Agents, 2014.

24 A. Romero-Garces, L. V. Calderita, J. Martinez-Gomez, et al. The Cognitive Architecture of a Robotic Salesman. Proceedings of Conference of Spanish Association of Artificial Intelligence, 2015.

25 N. Hawes, J. L. Wyatt, M. Sridharan, et al. The Playmate System. In H. I. Christensen, G.-J. Kruijff and J. L. Wyatt (eds), Cognitive Systems. Berlin Heidelberg, Springer-Verlag, 2010: 367–393.

26 K. Sjoo, H. Zender, P. Jensfelt, et al. The Explorer System. In H. I. Christensen, G.-J. Kruijff and J. L. Wyatt (eds), Cognitive Systems. Berlin Heidelberg, Springer-Verlag, 2010: 395–421.

27 G. Maffei, D. Santos-Pata, E. Marcos, et al. An Embodied Biologically Constrained Model of Foraging: From Classical and Operant Conditioning to Adaptive Real-World Behavior in DAC-X. Neural Networks, 2015, 72: 88–108.

28 D. Vernon, C. von Hofsten and L. Fadiga. The iCub Cognitive Architecture. In D. Vernon, C. von Hofsten and L. Fadiga (eds), A Roadmap for Cognitive Development in Humanoid Robots. Berlin Heidelberg, Springer-Verlag, 2011: 121–153.

29 V. Tikhanoff, A. Cangelosi and G. Metta. Integration of Speech and Action in Humanoid Robots: iCub Simulation Experiments. IEEE Transactions on Autonomous Mental Development, 2011, 3(1): 17–29.

30 R. Brandon. A Developmental Agent for Learning Features, Environment Models, and General Robotics Tasks. Frontiers in Computational Neuroscience, 2011, 5: 3–8.

31 U. Faghihi, P. Fournier-Viger and R. Nkambou. CELTS: A Cognitive Tutoring Agent with Human-like Learning Capabilities and Emotions. In A. Pena-Ayala (ed.), Intelligent and Adaptive Educational-Learning Systems. Berlin Heidelberg, Springer-Verlag, 2013: 339–365.

32 G. Pezzulo. DiPRA: A Layered Agent Architecture Which Integrates Practical Reasoning and Sensorimotor Schemas. Connection Science, 2009, 21(4): 297–326.

33 S. L. Epstein and S. Petrovic. Learning a Mixture of Search Heuristics. In Y. Hamadi, E. Monfroy and F. Saubion (eds), Autonomous Search. Berlin Heidelberg, Springer-Verlag, 2012: 97–127.

34 N. Slam, W. Wang, G. Xue, et al. A Framework with Reasoning Capabilities for Crisis Response Decision-Support Systems. Engineering Applications of Artificial Intelligence, 2015, 46: 346–353.

35 G. M. Edelman. Learning in and from Brain-Based Devices. Science, 2007, 318(5853): 1103–1105.

36 A. Sloman and B. Logan. Building Cognitively Rich Agents Using the Sim_Agent Toolkit. Communications of the Association of Computing Machinery, 1999, 43(2): 71–77.

37 D. R. Hofstadter and M. Mitchell. The Copycat Project: A Model of Mental Fluidity and Analogy-Making. In D. Hofstadter and the Fluid Analogies Research group, Fluid Concepts and Creative Analogies. Basic Books, 1995, Chapter 5: 205–267.

38 J. Hawkins and S. Ahmad. Why Neurons Have Thousands of Synapses, a Theory of Sequence Memory in Neocortex. Frontiers in Neural Circuits, 2016, 10(177): 23.

39 D. Wyatte, S. Herd, B. Mingus, et al. The Role of Competitive Inhibition and Top-Down Feedback in Binding During Object Recognition. Frontiers in Psychology, 2012, 3: 182.

40 S. Schaat, K. Doblhammer, A. Wendt, et al. A Psychoanalytically-Inspired Motivational and Emotional System for Autonomous Agents. Proceedings of 39th Annual Conference of the IEEE Industrial Electronics Society, 2013: 6648–6653.

41 D. Martin, M. Rincon, M. C. Garcia-Alegre, et al. ARDIS: Knowledge-Based Architecture for Visual System Configuration in Dynamic Surface Inspection. Expert Systems, 2011, 28(4): 353–374.

42 D. Kieras. Modeling Visual Search of Displays of Many Objects: The Role of Differential Acuity and Fixation Memory. Proceedings of 10th International Conference on Cognitive Model, 2010.

43 A. L. Rothenstein and J. K. Tsotsos. Attentional Modulation and Selection—An Integrated Approach. PLoS ONE, 2014, 9(6): e99681.

44 K. R. Thorisson, O. Gislason, G. R. Jonsdottir, et al. A Multiparty Multimodal Architecture for Realtime Turntaking. Proceedings of International Conference on Intelligent Virtual Agents, 2010.

45 H. Schultheis and T. Barkowsky. Casimir: An Architecture for Mental Spatial Knowledge Processing. Topics in Cognitive Science, 2011, 3(4): 778–795.

46 M. Conforth and Y. Meng. CHARISMA: A Context Hierarchy-Based Cognitive Architecture for Self-Motivated Social Agents. Proceedings of the International Joint Conference on Neural Networks, San Jose, CA, 2011: 1894–1901.

47 B. F. Gore, B. L. Hooey, C. D. Wickens, et al. A Computational Implementation of a Human Attention Guiding Mechanism in MIDAS v5. Proceedings of International Conference on Digital Human Modeling, 2009.

48 J. From, P. Perrin, D. O'Neill, et al. Supporting the Commander's Information Requirements: Automated Support for Battle Drill Processes Using R-CAST. Proceedings of the IEEE Military Communications Conference MILCOM, 2011.

49 G. L. Zacharias, A. X. Miao, C. Illgen, et al. SAMPLE: Situation Awareness Model for Pilot in-the-Loop Evaluation. Conference on Situation Awareness in the Tactical Air Environment, 1998.

50 F.-Y. Wang. Building Knowledge Structure in Neural Nets Using Fuzzy Logic. In M. Jamshidi (ed.), Robotics and Manufacturing: Recent Trends in Research, Education and Applications. New York, NY, ASME (American Society of Mechanical Engineers) Press, 1992.

5

Evolutionary Reasoning

The decision-making model TiDEC elucidated in Chapter 4 provides a well-defined container that traceably maintains diverse knowledge. Components in such architecture can be viewed as sequential slots in decision cycles given an environment perception. This chapter will go deeper, delving what concrete knowledge used to achieve particular decisions. Overall, our main objective is to seek a feasible way to computationally simulate individual's decision-making. Such type of computable mental models can be injected into humanoid agents, leading to a more human-like mode in perception, thinking, and interaction. These agents with higher humanoid intelligence lay an implement foundation of more humanized services for our daily life. Usually, human deliberation reflects two related facets – rationality and irrationality. The former refers to the inclination of achieving expected maximum reward (or minimum loss) during one's decision, while the latter may weakly obey such a principle [1]. This book will restrict our discussions into the rational decision. The problem involves two entangled aspects – learning and reasoning, and it may not be suitable to talk about them in a separate way. However, simultaneous focus on these two facets without distinction may hinder our discussions. Thus in Chapter 5, we will firstly address the reasoning issue and then the learning aspect to acquire one's knowledge repository in the next chapter.

We begin in Section 5.1 by discussing knowledge representation, which is the fundamental "bricks" of our cognitive "building." Some classic approaches are compared in this part, and fuzzy logic is selected specifically to complete the task. In Section 5.2, we explain the process of reasoning. The reasoning follows the bottom-up emergent principle of complex biological systems. It is built upon evolutionary computing. As a key point of emergent intelligent decisions, this section exploits generative causal methods to expand the heterogeneity of decision sequence candidates. Expansion of heterogeneity enlarges the searching scope of decision space, providing more diverse initial solutions that may lead to more intelligent final results. Section 5.3 concentrates on the second key point of

Parallel Population and Parallel Human: A Cyber-Physical Social Approach,
First Edition. Peijun Ye and Fei-Yue Wang.
© 2023 The Institute of Electrical and Electronics Engineers, Inc. Published 2023 by John Wiley & Sons, Inc.

evolutionary reasoning – the fitness function. Since the arbitrary setting of fitness function may bring individual bias in traditional evolutionary computing, this section introduces inverse reinforcement learning to adaptively and automatically determine the fitness functions. However, our method differentiates from such techniques in that we are able to handle decision sequence with time series dependence.

5.1 Knowledge Representation

Knowledge representation is a comprehensive and fundamental issue. Before approaching this problem, it is necessary to illuminate what is knowledge. As the synthetic population with social organizations in Chapter 3, using certain social relationships to depict two individuals' link is a specific kind of knowledge. More formally, knowledge refers to the information that describes a collection of things with their mutual relationships. Such things can be the concrete matter or physical objects existing in real world (which we call entity in this chapter), and the abstract concepts in our imagination (which we call concept here). An abstract concept may be a mental reflection of actual entities in real world. Yet it may also be a purely imaginary result of our mental processing (e.g. theoretical models, laws from our study). When the concept corresponds to actual entities, each of those entities is also called the instance of the concept. The name used to label a particular concept is called terminology. It is just a symbol or an oral word for our daily communication but is not semantically relevant to its referred entity. For instance, the "sun" may not refer to that huge fireball in the sky in our commonsense. We can let this terminology correspond to a flying bird outside the window. Though this seems weird and few people would recognize such a reference, it is syntactically feasible in theory! This phenomenon manifests that the syntactic accuracy and semantic correctness of our natural language are not consistent. For such a reason, we need to ensure that the terminology strictly conforms to the common sense of its users.

The relationships between entities and/or concepts can be stored in various forms like formula, tuple, and table, and they are typically categorized into two classes. One is called state, which describes attribute values of a specific entity. For example, we use the expression "Is(Tom, Expert)" to state that "Tom is an expert." Here "Is" is called predicate. "Tom" and "Expert" are terminologies. The statement points out the membership between the human entity "Tom" and the concept "Expert." The other class of relationships is called action, which stands for a particular temporal process. Unlike the state relationship where attribute values may probably keep steady for a certain period, action process is accompanied by the state transfer of entities. For example, the expression

"Walk_in(Tom, building 3)" states that "Tom walks into building 3." The action predicate "Walk_in" brings a spatial change from outside to inside of the building. In some literature, state expression is simplified by using the attribute value directly, as "Expert(Tom)" for "Is(Tom, Expert)" mentioned before. When the provider of an action is clear, the action expression is also simplified, as "Walk_in(building 3)" for "Walk_in(Tom, building 3)." In cognitive science, state relationships are referred to be declarative knowledge (stored in the working memory), while action relationships are defined as procedural knowledge (maintained in the reasoning module as shown in Chapter 4).

Using predicate to represent relationships is a popular way to complete such a task. However, other forms are applicable as well. This elicits different types of knowledge representation. A major genre that attracts numerous research in recent years is the knowledge graph, which is a foundation of semantic web. As its name suggests, knowledge graph uses a graph structure to characterize the relationships. Figure 5.1 gives a segment of Thai food knowledge graph. As can be seen, the entity or concept is denoted by nodes and relationships are abstracted as edges. Note that the edges are directed, meaning that the relationships are one-sided, with their inversions not correct. Seven pieces of knowledge are contained in this example:

1. Sebastian is allergic to nuts;
2. Sebastian eats vegetable Thai curry;
3. Vegetable Thai curry is based on coconut milk;
4. Vegetable Thai curry is a Thai dish;
5. Nut is a sub-class of snack;
6. Thai dish is from Thailand;
7. Thai dish is made from the nutty.

The above knowledge is stated via natural language. It is usually represented as triples for machine processing by only indicating the subject, predicate, and object/property. Hence, the corresponding triples look like ⟨*SebastianAllergicToNut*⟩,

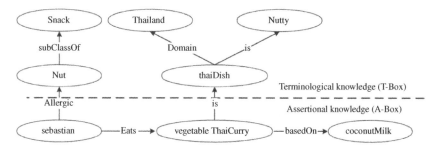

Figure 5.1 A segment of Thai food knowledge graph.

⟨*SebastianEatvegetableThaiCurry*⟩, etc. The knowledge can be further categorized into two types, assertional knowledge and terminological knowledge. Assertional knowledge describes the facts, and world states that may vary from time to time. It is stored in the A-Box of a knowledge graph. Terminological knowledge extracts those general rules that are applicable for a class of concepts. For example, the rule "Thai dish is from Thailand" almost holds for all of the Thai dishes at any time. It is an abstraction of human's experience and more instructive. Terminological knowledge is stored in the T-Box of a knowledge graph. In recent studies, knowledge graph is typically embedded into a latent space, which is called knowledge graph embedding or representation learning and can leverage the advantages of emerging technology for its construction [2, 3]. There are mainly three advantages for this operation. First, a low-dimensional latent space can effectively reduce the sparsity of the graph structure. It is able to compress the original representation so as to cut down requirements of computational memory. Second, the embedding can be easily combined with deep neural network, realizing a fast learning in dynamic contexts. This could avoid the long-term update after the graph established. Third, a unified latent space plays a general "container" of various rules from different data. It is a basis of data fusion from multimodal sources. A detriment of latent learning may be the loss of semantic explanation when the entity and relationship are converted into embedded vectors. Such a "black box" model makes it difficult to understand its decisions. Generally, two aspects of knowledge graph embedding are focused: translational embedding and graph neural networks. Translational embedding exerts its powerful ability to adaptively capture structures information of knowledge graphs. While being studied constantly, it is viewed as the cornerstone of embedding learning since it is proposal [4]. Graph neural network, an emerging technique, is specially designed for graph structure data. It is regarded as a promising method in the task of knowledge representation learning [5]. In addition, the latest research is not limited to triples but uses more abundant and available resources to promote knowledge representation [6, 7]. Detailed discussions about knowledge graph are beyond the scope of this book. We refer the readers to [8] for more details.

While the knowledge graph is intuitive for human users, it is not very suitable for machines, as the maintenance of graphical structure is inefficient for strict reasoning. For this reason, we choose the logic form to represent the knowledge. Actually, knowledge graph can be equivalently transformed into logic rules. And the latter form has a more rigorous mathematical underpinning. In semantic network, the international community for open standards of next-generation web, World Wide Web Consortium (W3C), recommends the Ontology Web Language for knowledge representation, which is founded on description logic. Therefore, for our insightful discussions, logic is still an appropriate tool. In a sequential decision-making, if every step of reasoning has semantic support, the decision sequence is interpretable and we call it the explicit knowledge. If the decision is achieved by some latent variables without understandable semantic meanings, we call it implicit knowledge. Intuitively, these two kinds of knowledge correspond to the human's rational deliberation and empirical decision, which are modeled as the symbolic system and artificial neural network in TiDEC. One fatal problem of classic symbolic system lies in its weakness of representing uncertainty. Its basic restriction behind is the binary truth values of classic logic. To avoid such a limitation, we choose fuzzy logic to model explicit knowledge. Consider a fuzzy rule system:

$$\text{Rule}: \ IF \ x_1 = s_1 \ \text{``and''} \ \ldots \ \text{``and''} \ x_n = s_n \ THEN \ D(\underline{s}) - fs \tag{5.1}$$

where $\underline{x} = (x_1, \ldots, x_n)$ is an input signal vector from the universe $U \subset \mathbb{R}^n$. Here, the whole set of entities and concepts is called the universe of discourse. $\underline{s} = (s_1, \ldots, s_n) \in S_1 \times S_2 \times \cdots \times S_n$ is a linguistic variable vector defined on the universe of discourse. As a convention in this book, we use capitals for variables and lowercase letters for specific values. For instance, when S_1 means the height of a person, its values may include "Tall," "Medium," and "Short." Notation "$\times$" stands for the Cartesian product. "and" is the logical operator, meaning that the expression is true if and only if its every item holds true. $D(\underline{s})$ is an atomic predicate formula containing linguistic values. fs is the firing strength of the rule, computed by:

$$fs = \mu_{s_1}(x_1) \wedge \mu_{s_2}(x_2) \wedge \cdots \wedge \mu_{s_n}(x_n) \tag{5.2}$$

where $\mu_{s_n}(x_n)$ is the membership degree of $x_n \in s_n$. In general, when $\underline{s}$ gets different linguistic values, Eq. (5.1) stands for a group of rules. The total number of the rules is calculated by $|S_1| \cdot |S_2| \ldots |S_n|$ ($|S_n|$ means the cardinality of the set S_n).

By fuzzification, Eq. (5.1) can be regarded as the transformation from raw perceptual signals to basic declarative beliefs. It is an initial state for the subsequent rational deliberation which can be modeled as a reasoning chain, given an axiomatic procedural knowledge base. Acquisition of such procedural knowledge base will be discussed in Chapter 6, and here we just assume its existence. A reasoning step in deliberation is written as:

$$\begin{aligned}
\text{Rule 1}: \ &IF \ d_1\left(\underline{s}\right) \ \text{``and''} \ \ldots \ \text{``and''} \ d_m\left(\underline{s}\right) \ \text{``and''} \ a\left(\underline{s}\right) \ THEN \ e_1\left(\underline{s}\right) - fs_a \\
\text{Rule 2}: \ &IF \ d_1\left(\underline{s}\right) \ \text{``and''} \ \ldots \ \text{``and''} \ d_m\left(\underline{s}\right) \ \text{``and''} \ a\left(\underline{s}\right) \ THEN \ e_2\left(\underline{s}\right) - fs_a \\
&\cdots \\
\text{Rule R}: \ &IF \ d_1\left(\underline{s}\right) \ \text{``and''} \ \ldots \ \text{``and''} \ d_m\left(\underline{s}\right) \ \text{``and''} \ a\left(\underline{s}\right) \ THEN \ e_R\left(\underline{s}\right) - fs_a
\end{aligned} \tag{5.3}$$

where $d_i\left(\underline{s}\right), e_j\left(\underline{s}\right) \in D \ (i = 1, \ldots, m, \ j = 1, \ldots, R)$ are all atomic predicate formulas. They indicate current and succeeding world states, respectively. $a\left(\underline{s}\right) \in A(\underline{s})$ means the action/behavior adopted for $d\left(\underline{s}\right)$ under current situation.

$fs_a \in [0, 1]$ is the activation strength (also named as firing strength) of Rule i. Its computation is similar to Eq. (5.2):

$$fs_a = fs[d_1(\underline{s})] \wedge fs[d_2(s)] \wedge \cdots \wedge fs[d_m(s)] \wedge fs[a(s)] \tag{5.4}$$

$fs[d]$ stands for the activation strength of preceding rule with the conclusion being d. And $fs[a]$ is the activation strength of action a, computed by an action function:

$$fs[a] = g_A(\langle d, a \rangle, u_a) \tag{5.5}$$

$\langle d, a \rangle$ means a decision history in a temporal space. When the history only involves last step, Eqs. (5.3)–(5.5) degrade into a Markov process. u_a is a stochastic noise variable that models individual's preference for action selection. Actually, Eq. (5.3) characterizes possible world states after action $a(\underline{s})$ applied. It is a split of the following rule:

$$d_1(\underline{s}) \text{ "and" } \ldots \text{ "and" } d_m(\underline{s}) \text{ "and" } a(\underline{s}) \Rightarrow e_1(\underline{s}) \text{ "and" } \ldots \text{ "and" } e_R(\underline{s}) \tag{5.6}$$

Equation (5.6) indicates that when all the condition terms $d_i(\underline{s})$ and $a(\underline{s})$ hold, then we have all the conclusion terms $e_j(\underline{s})$. Note that the activation strength of each rule in Eq. (5.3) is equal given a linguistic variable vector $\underline{s}$.

In classic logic, it is proved that any formula in predicate logic (also called first-order logic) can be rewritten as a conjunctive expression like

$$d_1(\underline{s}) \text{ "and" } \ldots \text{ "and" } d_m(\underline{s})$$

While fuzzy logic (also called multi-valued logic) is a generalization of predicate logic, in that it expands the truth value from a binary discrete set $\{0, 1\}$ to a continuous interval $[0, 1]$, Eq. (5.3) still holds for any scenario in the latter form. Therefore, knowledge representation using Eqs. (5.1)–(5.4) has a comprehensive applicability. In human rational thinking, reasoning is a discrete process and can be modeled as a manipulation for linguistic variables of all the concerned concepts/entities, given a particular set of axioms. This process is actually the repetition of Eq. (5.3). According to the causal relationship of each step, all of the activated rules construct a reasoning chain which can be drawn as Figure 5.2:

$$A \Longrightarrow D \text{ (and } C) \Longrightarrow F \text{ (and } B) \Longrightarrow Z$$

Facts with related linguistic variables are stored in the working memory in the figure, while the procedural rules with firing strength are dynamically maintained in the reasoning module, as TiDEC architecture indicated in Chapter 4. Different from traditional fuzzy control where the result of reasoning is inversely mapped into a continuous control signal by defuzzification, the human reasoning here is

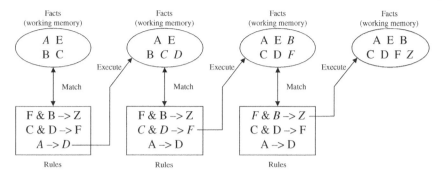

Figure 5.2 A reasoning chain using procedural knowledge.

to make a discrete action choice in his possible options. Suppose that the last step of a reasoning chain composed of Eq. (5.3) achieves action candidates like

$$\{\langle a_1\left(\underline{s}\right),\ e_1\left(\underline{s}\right)\rangle - fs_1, \langle a_2\left(\underline{s}\right),e_2\left(\underline{s}\right)\rangle - fs_2, \ldots, \langle a_R\left(\underline{s}\right),e_R\left(\underline{s}\right)\rangle - fs_R\}$$

where $e_i\left(\underline{s}\right)$ is the final state. fs_i is the activation strength and $a_i\left(\underline{s}\right)$ is the corresponding action. The rational decision will be

$$a^*\left(\underline{s}\right) = \arg\ \max_{a_i(\underline{s})}\ fs_i \tag{5.7}$$

Putting the details aside, human rational deliberation is concisely modeled as a classification issue with Eqs. (5.1), (5.3), and (5.7)

$$\mathcal{F}(\underline{x}):\ U \subset \mathbb{R}^n \to C = \{1, \ldots, R\}$$

5.2 Evolutionary Reasoning Using Causal Inference

Once the factual beliefs and production rules are given, all the reasoning paths are determined. This means that the agent's deliberation trajectories as well as final decisions to each input signal are predefined in advance, albeit computation of each path is difficult or even impossible in some extremely large-scale scenarios. The predefined trajectories seem not plausible with reality, since human deliberation is more extensive than a closed space. On the one hand, knowledge can be remolded, reconstructed, and recombined in one's mental world, and we refer to such operations with their corresponding reasoning as the deliberative experiments. For most people, deliberative experiments have endowed them with capacity that they can imagine not only what happened in the past and what will happen in the future but also what did not happen and what might happen [9–11]. On the other hand, in addition to learning, mutation of existing knowledge, reflected as the re-organization of reasoning chain, is a second source of intelligence from the view of complex biological systems. Otherwise, we may evolve too slowly to achieve today's smart society. The fact that we only live on one timeline does not restrain ourselves from envisioning events on alternative timelines, as manipulation of knowledge units often elicits divergent branches of the event's succeeding developments. It is the final results from these possible branches that bring us regret for the past or expectation for the future. Essentially, the mutual exclusive timelines of an event's development partially stem from a causal inference ability – counterfactual reasoning – enlightened by developmental [12–15], comparative [16–18], and clinical psychology [19–21], as well as cognitive neuroscience [22–24]. However, most of these studies have concentrated on characteristics of counterfactual reasoning or its influenced factors. Few of them provide a computational approach to simulate such a process. To our knowledge, counterfactual reasoning is mostly applied in computer vision to synthesize specific genre of images [25, 26]. How to represent this mechanism in sequential decision still remains to be investigated. To formulate the complex human deliberative experiments, this section follows the classic emergent cognitive paradigm and proposes evolutionary reasoning using generative counterfactual knowledge. It would be a computational foundation of simulating human rational thinking. There are several advantages brought about by this approach. First, compared with the generic algorithm or other evolutionary methods for complex adaptive systems, counterfactual generation is introduced as a new mutation mechanism, which expands the knowledge heterogeneity but restricts the new one into a more plausible scope. Second, without numeric encoding and decoding, evolutionary reasoning of the knowledge always carries semantic information throughout the whole searching process so that the explainable decision sequence can be directly obtained. This is quite beneficial to those scenarios where interpretability is necessary (like clinical diagnostics or judicial trials).

The evolutionary reasoning is composed of three steps: initial solution generation, mutation, and selection. To make our discussion more clear, we use a unified notation to represent a T-step reasoning chain $\tau = \{\langle d_1, a_1 \rangle, \langle d_2, a_2 \rangle, \ldots, \langle d_T, e_T \rangle\}$. Unlike traditional Markov process, the decision step is dependent on its previous sequence. The dependence is estimated by the firing strength function of each step fs_i according to experience data. Initial solution generation starts by using a group of decision chains as a training dataset. Such a dataset can be acquired by conducting psychological tests for typical people or simply choosing rule combinations with certain firing strengths. To sufficiently exploit the information of these sample decision chains, the generated initial solutions need to reproduce their implicit distribution without simply duplicating the reasoning paths. We use generative adversarial network (GAN) to complete the task. The GAN consists of two artificial neural networks, generator and discriminator (as Figure 5.3). Raw signal with a desired state is fed into the generator network to get a synthesized

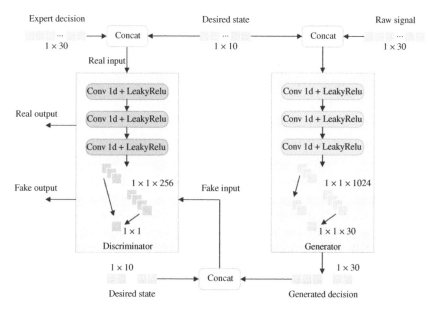

Figure 5.3 Initial solution generation using GAN.

decision sequence. Both synthesized and real sample decisions, also with the desired state, are used as inputs for the discriminator network. The discriminator tries to differentiate the input by evaluating whether it comes from a real sample or the generator. According to [27], this alternative optimization will elicit a well-trained generator that can fit the distribution of sample decisions while keeping subtle implicit noise. The detailed implementation can be referred in [28].

The second step of evolutionary reasoning is mutation. Now let us return to Eqs. (5.3) and (5.5). Assume that the distribution elicited by action function g_A is $P\{g_A; \{\langle d_i, a_i \rangle\}_{i=0}^{t-1}, a_t, u_t\}$, then given a decision history and an action a_t, the posterior of u_t is $P\{u_t | \{\langle d_i, a_i \rangle\}_{i=0}^{t-1}, a_t : g_A\}$. To expand the searching space, we construct a counterfactual reasoning chain as a result of mutation. The construction derives from a mandatory intervention called the "do" calculator which arbitrarily sets the action to be a particular one without considering influence from other variables. The reasoning step after intervention is represented as:

$$\text{Rule } i : \quad IF \ d_t \ \text{"and"} \ do\{a_t = a'\} \ THEN \ d_{t+1} - fs_{a_t} \tag{5.8}$$

According to [29], the world state transition is activated by the procedural rule:

$$\text{Rule } i : \quad IF \ d_t \ \text{"and"} \ a' \ THEN \ d_{t+1} - fs_{a_t} \tag{5.9}$$

This would result in a mutated decision chain from $\langle d_1, a_1, \dots, d_t, a \rangle$ to $\langle d_1, a_1, \dots, d_t, a' \rangle$. By continuing forward, the reasoning path would be different

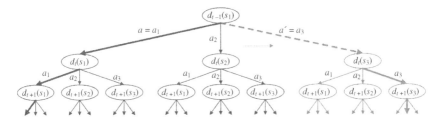

Figure 5.4 Mutated reasoning path by counterfactual reconstruction.

from the original trajectory. As illustrated in Figure 5.4, the arbitrary selection action a_3 leads to a change from $\langle d_{t-1}(s_1), d_t(s_1), d_{t+1}(s_1)\rangle$ (bold solid line) to $\langle d_{t-1}(s_1), d_t(s_3), d_{t+1}(s_3)\rangle$ (bold dashed line). Note that the above counterfactual mutation involves only one reasoning step. Yet such a single arbitrary action leads to a totally different decision chain. This is clear in the above latter decision chain, where the partial reasoning sequence starting from $d_t(s_3)$ is determined by original procedural knowledge base and does not contain any more counterfactual action.

Now let us go back to the action function g_A and intervention. The posterior $P\{u_t|\{\langle d_i, a_i\rangle\}_{i=0}^{t-1}, a_t : g_A\}$ is usually calculated via typical methods like maximum likelihood or Bayesian estimation with observed decision data. The hypothesis behind is that the observed action $a_t = a$ is most likely to be adopted under the estimated u_t. In other words, the counterfactual action $a_t = a'$ is nonstationary. However, the relatively "rare" reasoning characterizes different decision modes of individuals and does make sense in our evolutionary deliberation. Iteratively, the "single-point" mutation can be conducted for k times, leading to a multiple counterfactual step reasoning chain. By setting a suitable fitness function, the solution can be optimized a decision problem.

The third step of evolutionary reasoning is selection. This step determines which path is eligible to elicit a desired state of the system's later evolution. Given an objective state d_o, define a reasoning chain $\tau_k = \{\langle d_i, a_i\rangle\}_{i=0}^{t_k}$ as an eligible candidate if its final state $d_{t_k} = d_o$. It means that if the state transitions go along the chain, it will achieve our objective with a certain activation strength. Note that τ_k may be a part of other longer reasoning chains. Yet it is not necessary to concern about its following steps since the desired state has already been achieved. For a simple notation, we arbitrarily define the final action a_{t_k} as a $\langle null\rangle$ operation so that our eligible candidate can be represented like τ_k. As illustrated before, the uncertain reasoning may result in several possible final states even starting with a same initialization. Conversely, the objective may be also derived from multiple initial states, which implies a group of different eligible candidates. As a consequence, we need to introduce additional criterion to determine a unique reasoning chain for behavioral prescription. Our criterion exploits a linear combination of the activation strength (fs) and length of chain ($len(\tau_k)$), computed as:

$$fit(\tau_k) = \lambda \cdot fs + (1 - \lambda) \cdot \frac{len(\tau_k)}{L}$$

where L is a normalization constant and $\lambda \in [0,1]$ is a regularization parameter.

To test our evolutionary reasoning method, we conduct an experiment on mathematical theorem proving. As a reflection of human rational deliberation, theorem proving provides us an ideal scenario to investigate one's decision-making trajectories (shown by the multiple proof steps) for a desired goal (described by the conclusion). Our test is based on the Geometry3K open dataset, which contains about 3000 mathematical geometry problems [30]. The overall process of our problem-solving is illustrated in Figure 5.5. Each problem in the dataset is described by an image with a text paragraph of statements. Through a neural

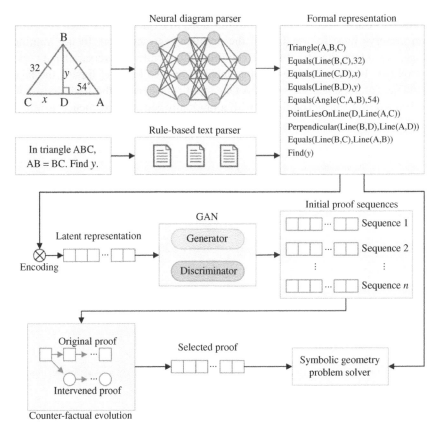

Figure 5.5 Process of geometry problem-solving.

diagram parser and a rule-based text parser, the problem is converted into a formal representation, where relations of the geometric elements (like Line, Angle, etc.) are described by predicate logic rules. For evolutionary reasoning, the problem is further sent to a pretrained GAN after latent encoding. Then, the GAN network generates a group of proof sequences that are treated as initial solutions. By counterfactual interventions, these solutions are reconstructed at a random intervention point according to expert reasoning step from the given proof knowledge base. And the final optimal proof sequence is selected after several generations of evolution. For validation, both the selected optimal solution and the formal representation will be sent to the Symbolic Geometry Problem Solver to test whether the generated proof sequence is feasible.

In the encoding stage, the top 1000 words with the highest frequency in the whole dataset are selected to construct a word dictionary. And each problem is converted into a 1000-dimensional vector using one-hot encoding. Since 1000 dimension is still large for the solution sequence, the encoded vector is further indexed by the nonzero elements and embedded in 10 dimensions. Such encoding can preserve most information of the problem representation. In the training stage, we adopt the structure of conditional generative adversarial network, cGAN (see Figure 5.6). The training depends on two kinds of inputs, the fake sequences and the real sequences. A fake input concatenates the 10-dimensional embedded problem as conditions with a randomly generated sequence as initial

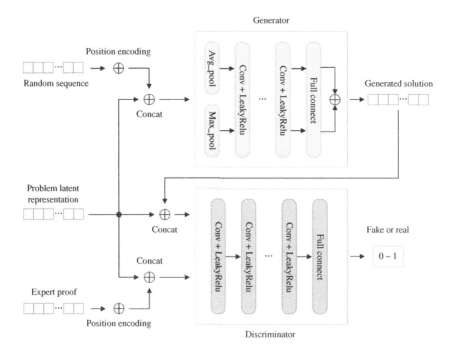

Figure 5.6 Training of conditional generative adversarial network.

solutions. The fake input is fed into the generator to get a generated solution with 30 maximum steps. By contrast, a real input concatenates the same embedded conditions with an expert proof directly drawn from the predefined knowledge base which contains 17 theorems. The generated and real solutions are sent to the discriminator, the output of which is a binary number to judge the authenticity of its input. The training gradually leads the generated solutions to approximate the real ones.

In the evolution stage, counterfactual reasoning is used to explore and optimize the solution sequences. The "facts" here are existing proofs from expert knowledge base and already-validated solutions, which reflect the response modes of human expert when encountering particular problems. The contextual dependence between theorems in a solution sequence implies their endogenous causal relationships. And the "counter facts" provide potential different reasoning paths with the implicit causal dependence retained. Such a counterfactual operation can be viewed as an intervention to recombine the causality. The intervention, though not validated so far, can infer a possible intuition for searching. It actually imposes heuristic directions of exploration while avoiding the inefficiency of completely random searching. For a given solution $\{\langle d(i)\rangle\}_{i=1}^{m}$ (as Figure 5.7), suppose that the intervention occurs at the position of theorem $d(k)$. It endows the successive node with a selected theorem $s(k+1)$ after learning the regularity from expert sequences. The computation of $s(k+1)$ is

$$s(k+1) = \arg\max_{s} P[d(k)|s] + \mu \cdot h[d(k)|s]$$

where $P[d(k)|s]$, calculated from the expert knowledge base, means the probability of cause $d(k)$ conditioned on the result s. $h[d(k)|s]$ is the penalty item that can be determined by human expert or the property of s itself (such as a function of its visited frequency). μ is a hyperparameter. Since $P[d(k)|s]$ cannot be directly computed from the knowledge base, we further use Bayesian theorem to convert it as:

$$P[d(k)|s] = \frac{P[s|d(k)] \cdot P[d(k)]}{\sum_{a} P(s|a)} \propto \frac{P[s|d(k)]}{\sum_{a} P(s|a)} \tag{5.10}$$

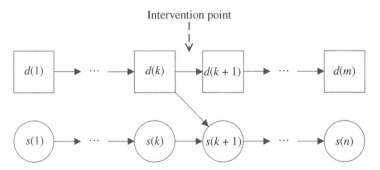

Figure 5.7 Training of conditional generative adversarial network.

Therefore, we have

$$s(k+1) = \arg\max_s \frac{P[s|d(k)]}{\sum_a P(s|a)} + \mu \cdot h[d(k)|s]$$

The intervened solution is $[\{\langle d(i)\rangle\}_{i=1}^{k}, \{\langle s(i)\rangle\}_{i=k+1}^{n}]$. In our experiment, the maximum number of reasoning steps in our experiment setting is 100. And if the solution cannot be achieved within this step limit, a guess with probability 0.25 will be introduced into each potential option.

The pseudocode of counterfactual evolutionary reasoning is as shown in Algorithm 5.1. In the main loop, the algorithm stochastically selects a solution, an intervention mode and an intervention point. Our intervention modes include uniform, probabilistic, and heuristic, which are used to determine the

---

Algorithm 5.1 Counter-Factual Evolutionary Reasoning (*IGS, N, IM, FF, SF*)

Input:

    IGS: initial generated sequences, *N*: number of generations,

    IM: intervention mode, *FF*: final fitness, *SF*: standard fitness;

Output:

    FTS: final theorem sequences.

  1: $Pop \leftarrow IGS, FF \leftarrow 0$;

  2: **repeat**

  3:     $p \leftarrow sample(Pop)$;

  4:     $inter\_mode \leftarrow sample(IM)$;

  5:     $inter\_pos \leftarrow sample(len(p), inter\_mode)$;

  6:     $d \leftarrow p[inter\_pos]$;

  7:     $P[d] \leftarrow \{ \ \}$;

  8:     **for** s that $P[d|s] > 0$ **do**

  9:         $P[d] \leftarrow P[d] \cup \{d : P[d|s]\}$;

10:     **end for**

11:     $s \leftarrow sample\_cand(P[d]); \triangleright p \neq s$

12:     $Child \leftarrow CF\_Intervention(p, s, inter\_pos); \triangleright$ Counter-Factual Inter.

13:     **if** $Fitness(Child) > SF$ **then**

14:         $Pop \leftarrow Pop \cup Child$;

15:     **end if**

16:     **if** $Fitness(Child) > FF$ **then**

17:         $FTS \leftarrow pop, FF \leftarrow Fitness(Child)$;

18:     **end if**

19: **until** N times

20: **return** *FTS*.

---

intervention point. Lines 7–12 conduct a random counterfactual intervention (by the function $CF_I ntervention$) according to Eq. (5.10) to get an intervened solution. Then, the algorithm checks whether the intervened solution is an improved one. The evolution is repeated for N times to return a final proof sequence. Our method is also compared with several previous approaches, and the preliminary results are listed in Table 5.1. As can be seen, the proof sequences generated by GAN outperform others in Ratio, Triangle, and Quad. But its overall performance is not as good as the original Inter-GPS solver. When the counterfactual evolution is introduced, five of nine metrics have reached the best performance, and the overall evaluation has increased about 4% compared to the original method. These results indicate that our evolutionary reasoning is effective in searching for optimal decision sequence in general.

Table 5.1 Results of counter factual reasoning experiment (%).

Method	All	Angle	Length	Area	Ratio
Q-only	25.3	29.5	21.5	28.3	33.3
I-only	27.0	26.2	28.4	24.5	16.7
Q+I	26.7	26.2	26.7	28.3	25.0
RelNet	29.6	26.2	34.0	20.8	41.7
FiLM	31.7	28.7	32.7	39.6	33.3
FiLM-BERT	32.8	32.9	33.3	30.2	25.0
FiLM-BART	33.0	32.1	33.0	35.8	50.0
Inter-GPS(No GT)	55.1	58.2	57.3	30.2	58.3
GAN	54.4	57.0	56.3	32.1	**58.3**
GAN + count. fact.	**59.5**	**58.3**	**71.5**	11.4	50.1

Method	Line	Triangle	Quad	Circle	Other
Q-only	21.0	26.0	25.9	25.2	22.2
I-only	24.7	26.7	30.1	30.1	25.9
Q+I	21.0	28.1	32.2	21.0	25.9
RelNet	29.6	33.7	25.2	28.0	25.9
FiLM	33.3	29.2	33.6	30.8	29.6
FiLM-BERT	32.1	32.3	32.2	34.3	33.3
FiLM-BART	34.6	32.6	37.1	30.1	37.0
Inter-GPS(No GT)	63.0	63.5	51.7	41.8	29.6
GAN	56.8	**65.6**	**52.4**	34.3	25.9
GAN + count. fact.	51.9	**73.3**	46.2	**42.0**	**88.9**

The bold values are the best performance in each column evaluation metric.

5.3 Learning Fitness Function from Expert Decision Chains

In Section 5.2, we use the proportion of valid steps in a decision chain as a fitness function. It seems plausible since optimizing such a fitness entails a correct direction to achieve a valid proof. However, this fitness setting may not be available in some complicated scenarios. For example, in intelligent driving, different drivers may have different preferences. Some of them prefer safety so that they "maximize" the distance between themselves and their surrounded vehicles. Others prefer travel time so that they pursue a fast speed to arrive their destinations as soon as possible. An even worse dilemma is that most drivers themselves could not accurately describe their appetites for risk. Therefore, setting a uniform fitness function is difficult and unreasonable. A possible solution for this dilemma is to learn fitness metrics directly from a set of expert decision sequences. Though the learning topic will be discussed formally in the Chapter 6, a preliminary glimpse of that factor is deserved to keep this section self-contained. Two issues are required to be clarified for the learning approach here. First, the direct learning from expert decisions is similar to inverse reinforcement learning. But again, we are dealing with reasoning chains composed of dependent steps. It is quite distinct from reinforcement learning where decision sequence is modeled as a Markov process. Moreover, reinforcement learning adopts probabilistic methods, leading a mutually exclusive transition of the world states. Rather, the world state transition in our evolutionary reasoning is fuzzy, which can be viewed as a "simultaneous" process resulting in a "mixed" state. Second, if possible, the learning expert decisions should be independent from the given samples for the GAN training, as explained in Section 5.2. If this condition is not satisfied, we can separate the given sample decisions into training set and learning set. The separation of training and learning sets will avoid homogeneous search between initial solution generation and final selection.

Consider a decision sequence $\tau_k = \{\langle d_i, a_i \rangle\}_{i=0}^{t_k}$. Let its fitness function be $fit(\tau_k)$. For the ith reasoning step, the probability of action a_t is $P\{a_t | \{\langle d_i, a_i \rangle\}_{i=0}^{t-1}, u_t : g_A\}$. The τ_k actually gives a reflection of one's maximum utilized decision preference. Therefore, the objective fitness function needs to take such a preference into account. In a general case, the form of $fit(\tau)$ is unknown. We exploit Gaussian distribution to learn the fitness via beta variational autoencoder (β-VAE) [31]. The structure of network is illustrated in Figure 5.8. The input and output of encoder are the given decision sequence τ_k and learned parameters of basic Gaussian distributions, respectively. While the input of decoder is sampled in the basic distributions as:

$$Sample = \sum_i (\mu_i + \sigma_i \cdot e_i)$$

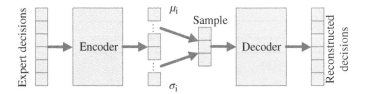

Figure 5.8 Beta variational autoencoder for fitness function learning.

where $e_i \sim N(0, 1)$. The output of decoder is defined as reconstructed decisions that are optimized as similar to original expert ones as possible. During training, the encoder and decoder are linked as a whole and its total loss function is set to be

$$loss = \frac{1}{t_k} \sum_{i=0}^{t_k} dist(a_i, \hat{a}_i) + \sum_{i=1}^{K} [\mu_i^2 + exp(\sigma_i) - \sigma_i - 1]$$

where

$$dist(a_i, \hat{a}_i) = \begin{cases} 0 & \text{if } a_i = \hat{a}_i \\ 1 & \text{otherwise} \end{cases}$$

stands for a "distance" between two actions. Note that such a distance can be defined arbitrarily. K is the predefined number of basic Gaussian distributions.

When the training of β-VAE-based model is well completed, the encoder actually establishes a mapping relationship from action sequence to continuous fitness. By contrast, the decoder converts a sampled fitness into an optimal decision, which is a by-product of our training. The achieved fitness function is implied in the encoder network and is approximated by a series of basic Gaussian distributions. The fitness value for a particular decision sequence is a sum of sampled ones. As a consequence, it may vary from time to time. This operation not only learns the maximum posterior of fitness according to expert decisions, but also characterizes the uncertainty of evaluation that different people view the same decision. The learning method is used in our experiment in Section 5.2, as an extension of validation. The experiments are similarly configured only by setting the fitness function learned from a part of reasoning sequences. To complete the learning, we use half of the given proof chains as the training samples for GAN and the other half as the expert sequences. The training samples and expert sequences are extracted by random sampling. Our results show that the fitness learning can roughly bring a similar accuracy as the original evolutionary reasoning (Table 5.2).

Table 5.2 Overall performance of reasoning with fitness learning.

Method	Inter-GPS(No GT)	EvoReason + FitLearn
Accuracy	55.07	58.9
Aver. steps for all prob.	39.97	39.94
Aver. steps for solved prob.	7.33	10.72
Aver. time for all prob.	57.13 s	45.76 s
Aver. time for solved prob.	10.64 s	15.73 s

5.4 Conclusions and Discussions

Evolutionary reasoning aims to simulate human's possible and heterogenous deliberation trajectories. Based on the architecture given before, this chapter first adopts fuzzy logic to represent one's decision knowledge. Then, we introduce causal inference in our algorithm. Specifically, the evolutionary mechanism involves two primary aspects, initialization of decision sequences via GAN and mutation via counterfactual reconstruction. In addition, we investigate the fitness function learning directly from expert sequences. Compared with inverse reinforcement learning where agent decides step by step with Markovian property, our method differentiates in that we directly handle full decision sequences with time series dependence. The proposed approach is tested on the Geometry3K open dataset, a novel benchmark of geometry theorem proving that is ideal to characterize expert's rational deliberation trajectories. Preliminary results show that the method is effective and achieves better overall accuracy as previous algorithms. Before closing this chapter, it is necessary to point out that GAN, counterfactual reconstruction, and fitness learning provided here are only particular implementations of these three phrases. Any techniques that are suitable for corresponding tasks can be exploited in this framework, and they should be still viewed as the evolutionary reasoning paradigm.

References

1 G. Askari, M. E. Gordji and C. Park. The Behavioral Model and Game Theory. Palgrave Communications, 2019, 5: 57.
2 Y. Lin, Z. Liu, M. Sun, Y. Liu and X. Zhu. Learning Entity and Relation Embeddings for Knowledge Graph Completion. Proceedings of the 29th Conference on Artificial Intelligence (AAAI 2015), Austin Texas, USA, Jan. 25–29, 2015: 2181–2187.

3 Z. Sun, Z. Deng, J. Nie and J. Tang. RotatE: Knowledge Graph Embedding by Relational Rotation in Complex Space. The 7th International Conference on Learning Representations (ICLR 2019), New Orleans, Louisiana, USA, May 6–9, 2019.

4 Z. Zhang, J. Cai, Y. Zhang and J. Wang. Learning Hierarchy-Aware Knowledge Graph Embeddings for Link Prediction. Proceedings of the 34th Conference on Artificial Intelligence (AAAI 2020), New York, USA, Feb. 7–12, 2020: 3065–3072.

5 Z. Wu, S. Pan, F. Chen, G. Long, C. Zhang and P. S. Yu. A Comprehensive Survey on Graph Neural Networks. IEEE Transactions on Neural Networks and Learning Systems, 2021, 32(1): 4–24.

6 S. Vashishth, S. Sanyal, V. Nitin and P. P. Talukdar. Composition Based Multi-Relational Graph Convolutional Networks. The 8th International Conference on Learning Representations (ICLR 2020), Virtual, Apr. 26–30, 2020.

7 K. Yang, S. Liu, J. Zhao, Y. Wang and B. Xie. COTSAE: Co-Training of Structure and Attribute Embeddings for Entity Alignment. Proceedings of the 34th AAAI Conference on Artificial Intelligence (AAAI 2020), New York, USA, Feb. 7–14, 2020: 3025–3032.

8 P. Ye and F.-Y. Wang. Artificial Intelligence: Principle and Technology. Tsinghua University Press, Beijing, 2020.

9 T. Suddendorf and M. C. Corballis. The Evolution of Foresight: What is Mental Time Travel, and is it Unique to Humans? Behavioral and Brain Science, 2007, 30: 299–313.

10 H. G. Jing, K. P. Madore and D. L. Schacter. Preparing for What Might Happen: An Episodic Specificity Induction Impacts the Generation of Alternative Future Events. Cognition, 2017, 169: 118–128.

11 J. Phillips, A. Morris and F. Cushman. How We Know What Not to Think. Trends in Cognitive Science, 2019, 23: 1026–1040.

12 T. McCormack, M. Ho, C. Gribben, et al. The Development of Counterfactual Reasoning About Doubly-Determined Events. Cognitive Development, 2018, 45: 1–9.

13 E. Rafetseder and J. Perner. Belief and Counterfactuality. Zeitschrift fur Psychologie, 2018, 226: 110–121.

14 A. Nyhout and P. A. Ganea. Mature Counterfactual Reasoning in 4-and 5-Year-Olds. Cognition, 2019, 183: 57–66.

15 A. Nyhout, L. Henke and P. A. Ganea. Children's Counterfactual Reasoning About Causally Overdetermined Events. Child Development, 2019, 90: 610–622.

16 T. Suddendorf, J. Crimston and J. Redshaw. Preparatory Responses to Socially Determined, Mutually Exclusive Possibilities in Chimpanzees and Children. Biology Letters, 2017, 13: 20170170.

17 A. Steiner and A. Redish. Behavioral and Neurophysiological Correlates of Regret in Rat Decision-Making on A Neuroeconomic Task. Nature Neuroscience, 2014, 17: 995–1002.

18 B. M. Sweis, M. J. Thomas and A. D. Redish. Mice Learn to Avoid Regret. PLoS Biology, 2018, 16: e2005853.

19 F. De Brigard, K. S. Giovanello, G. W. Stewart, et al. Characterizing the Subjective Experience of Episodic Past, Future, and Counterfactual Thinking in Healthy Younger and Older Adults. Quarterly Journal of Experimental Psychology, 2016, 69: 2358–2375.

20 A. Baskin-Sommers, A. M. Stuppy-Sullivan and J. W. Buckholtz. Psychopathic Individuals Exhibit but Do Not Avoid Regret During Counterfactual Decision Making. Proceedings of the National Academy of Sciences of the United States of America, 2016, 113: 14438–14443.

21 A. G. Broomhall, W. J. Phillips, D. W. Hine, et al. Upward Counterfactual Thinking and Depression: A Meta-Analysis. Clinical Psychology Review, 2017, 55: 56–73.

22 P. L. St. Jacques, A. C. Carpenter, K. K. Szpunar, et al. Remembering and Imagining Alternative Versions of The Personal Past. Neuropsychologia, 2018, 110: 170–179.

23 N. Parikh, L. Ruzic, G. W. Stewart, et al. What If? Neural Activity Underlying Semantic and Episodic Counterfactual Thinking. NeuroImage, 2018, 178: 332–345.

24 N. Bault, G. Pellegrino, M. Puppi, et al. Dissociation Between Private and Social Counterfactual Value Signals Following Ventromedial Prefrontal Cortex Damage. Journal of Cognitive Neuroscience, 2019, 31: 639–656.

25 L. Neal, M. Olson, X. Fern, et al. Open Set Learning with Counterfactual Images. Proceedings of 15th European Conference on Computer Vision (ECCV), Munich, Germany, Sep. 8–14, 2018: 620–635.

26 Z. Yue, T. Wang, H. Zhang, et al. Counterfactual Zero-Shot and Open-Set Visual Recognition. IEEE Conference on Computer Vision and Pattern Recognition, virtual, Jun. 19–25, 2021.

27 I. Goodfellow, J. Pouget-Abadie, M. Mirza, et al. Generative Adversarial Nets. Advances in Neural Information Processing Systems, 2014: 2672–2680.

28 M. Arjovsky, S. Chintala and L. Bottou. Wasserstein GAN. ArXiv:1701.07875, 2017. http://arxiv.org/abs/1701.07875.

29 L. Buesing, T. Weber, Y. Zwols, et al. Woulda, Coulda, Shoulda: Counterfactually-Guided Policy Search. arXiv preprint arXiv:1811.06272, 2018.

30 P. Lu, R. Gong, S. Jiang, et al. Inter-GPS: Interpretable Geometry Problem Solving with Formal Language and Symbolic Reasoning. Annual Meeting of the Association for Computational Linguistics, Bangkok, Thailand, Aug. 1–6, 2021.

31 I. Higgins, L. Matthey, A. Pal, et al. Beta-VAE: Learning Basic Visual Concepts with a Constrained Variational Framework. International Conference on Learning Representations (ICLR), Toulon, France, Apr. 24–26, 2017.

6

Knowledge Acquisition by Learning

The evolutionary reasoning paradigm elucidated in Chapter 5 provides a well-defined deductive process that traceably characterizes one's deliberation using diverse knowledge. Unlike traditional deductive reasoning in classic logic where all the paths for inference are determined once the knowledge base given, our evolutionary approach has introduced mutation factors that are able to increase the heterogeneity of the knowledge. This would expand the reasoning territory and may lead to new decision sequences. From cognitive science, it is a suitable way to model our insight which usually brings us novel ideas. Fitness learning also simulates the uncertainty of evaluation in our mind. It may vary from individual to individual and may even be time variant for the same person (according to his accumulation of experience). In this chapter, we will go to the other aspect – learning. Though this problem is preliminarily touched upon in Chapter 5, it is only an alternative method to achieve concrete fitness functions. By contrast, this chapter will focus on the acquisition of knowledge units. It constructs the fundamental "bricks" of root that the deliberative reasoning grounded. Rather than explaining the mechanism of concept formation or other meta-cognitive topics, the central issue here is to extract one's possible decision chains from his perceptual environment and his behavioral responses. This is, of course, a tough task since such two kinds of data can only provide very limited information. Furthermore, when the virtual agent is interactively assisting and cooperating with its human user counterpart, it is placed in a data stream environment, where human user's behavioral records are generated one by one. This is a further challenge for dynamic learning, as most of the existing techniques exploit batch operation to avoid the overwhelm of a single training record. These problems will be discussed in detail in the following.

The chapter is composed of four sections. Section 6.1 introduces some theoretical basis of learning. Section 6.2 explains knowledge acquisition in an offline mode. This is a traditional problem but we will use some latest techniques to achieve better performance. Section 6.3 addresses the online learning, which

Parallel Population and Parallel Human: A Cyber-Physical Social Approach,
First Edition. Peijun Ye and Fei-Yue Wang.
© 2023 The Institute of Electrical and Electronics Engineers, Inc. Published 2023 by John Wiley & Sons, Inc.

extracts knowledge dynamically through behavioral records in a data stream circumstance. This adaptive maintenance can supplement new procedural knowledge to the agent's knowledge base. Then it may result in quite different reasoning patterns due to the evolutionary mechanism built in Chapter 5. We mainly focus on two methodologies in this section – neural symbolic learning and explanation of deep learning. To test and validate our online learning method, Section 6.4 applies the proposed techniques to travel behavioral analysis. Comparative experiments indicate that our method can effectively acquire individual's decision knowledge from a data stream.

6.1   Foundation of Knowledge Repository Learning

As alluded before, one deficiency using fuzzy (or first-order) logic to simulate rational deliberation is that the rule base is completely dependent on prior knowledge. Once the rule base is given, the decision space is also fixed, which cannot reflect the adaptive learning characteristics of human users. With the breakthrough of machine learning especially the deep learning technologies in recent years, machines are becoming increasingly autonomous, making itself able to solve many problems adaptively. Therefore, how to exploit the learning ability from network-based approaches to enhance the agent's knowledge repository may be a feasible path for intelligence elevation. This path may also be a way to simulate human's learning mechanism from his experience in cognitive System 1 to interpretable logic in System 2. Before discussing the topic in more detail, let us first have a look at its theoretical feasibility.

Consider a knowledge system described in Chapter 5. The following theorem gives a basis of one-step learning using neural network (NN).

Theorem 6.1.1   *Assume a one-step fuzzy logic system is represented as Eq. (5.1),* $F_1(\underline{x}) : U \subset \mathbb{R}^n \longrightarrow C = 1, \ldots, R$. *Let $\varepsilon > 0$ be an arbitrary real valued constant, then there is a sum*

$$NN_e(\underline{x}) = \sum_{i=1}^{N} \alpha_i \sigma(\underline{a}_i^T \underline{x} + b_i) \tag{6.1}$$

and a set $U' \subset U$ so that $\mathbb{M}(U') > 1 - \varepsilon$ and

$$|F_1(\underline{x}) - NN_e(\underline{x})| < \varepsilon, \quad \forall \underline{x} \in U'$$

where $\mathbb{M}(D)$ is the Lebesgue measure of U' and σ is a continuous sigmoidal function which satisfies $\lim_{x \to +\infty} \sigma(x) = 1$ and $\lim_{x \to -\infty} \sigma(x) = 0$.

Proof: Since $F_1(\underline{x})$ is measurable and $F_1(\underline{x}) \leq R < +\infty$, there is a continuous function $\mathcal{H}(\underline{x})$ and a set $U' \subset U$ with $\mathbb{M}(U') > 1 - \varepsilon$ so that $F_1(\underline{x}) = \mathcal{H}(\underline{x}), \forall \underline{x} \in U'$

according to Lusin's theorem [1]. By universal approximation theorem [2, 3], there is a finite sum of

$$NN_e(\underline{x}) = \sum_{i=1}^{N} \alpha_i \sigma(\underline{a}_i^T \underline{x} + b_i)$$

so that $|F_1(\underline{x}) - NN_e(\underline{x})| < \varepsilon, \ \forall \underline{x} \in U'$. $\square$

The above theorem indicates that a one-step fuzzy logic system can be approximated with arbitrary precision by the multi-input–single-output(MISO) network of Eq. (6.1). Specifically, when $C = \{0, 1\}$, $F_1(\underline{x})$ is equivalent to a binary classification network with a single-hidden layer and a one-hot encoded output. The following theorem shows the fact that the subsequent reasoning step can be also approximated.

Theorem 6.1.2 *Consider a one-step reasoning system given by Eq. (5.3), $F_2(D)$: $[0, 1]^m \rightarrow [0, 1]^R$. Let $\varepsilon > 0$ be an arbitrary real valued constant, then there is a sum*

$$NN_e(D) = \sum_{i=1}^{N} \alpha_i \sigma(\underline{a}_i^T D + b_i) \tag{6.2}$$

so that

$$|F_2(D) - NN_e(D)| < \varepsilon, \quad \forall D \in D_1 \times D_2 \times \cdots \times D_m$$

where σ is also a continuous sigmoidal function with $\lim_{x \to +\infty} \sigma(x) = 1$ and $\lim_{x \to -\infty} \sigma(x) = 0$.

Proof: Since each inference rule in Eq. (5.3) is independent, $F_2(D)$ can be viewed as a combination of R unit mappings. For each unit mapping $[0, 1]^m \longrightarrow [0, 1]$, construct an $(m + 1)$-dimensional function

$$F'_2(d_1, \ldots, d_m, d_{m+1}) = (d_1, \ldots, d_m, F_2(d_1, \ldots, d_m))$$

Thus F'_2 is a function defined in $[0, 1]^{m+1}$. By the universal approximation theorem [2], there is a finite sum in the form of Eq. (6.2) so that

$$|F'_2 - NN_e(D)| < \varepsilon', \quad \forall D \in [0, 1]^{m+1}$$

where $0 < \varepsilon' < \varepsilon$. Therefore, the original mapping $F_2(D) : [0, 1]^m \longrightarrow [0, 1]^R$ is bounded by

$$|F_2 - NN_e(D)| < \max_{\varepsilon'} \varepsilon' < \varepsilon$$

The proof is completed. $\square$

The theorem proves that one-step reasoning in the linguistic domains defined by membership functions is learnable using artificial NNs. On this basis, we can easily achieve a similar conclusion for K-step ($1 < K < +\infty$) reasoning.

Theorem 6.1.3 *For a reasoning chain composed of K steps by Eq. (5.3), there exists a multilayer feed forward network that can approximate to it with any given precision $\varepsilon > 0$.*

Proof: The proof is intuitive by using induction. Theorem 6.1.2 provides a one-step situation, which is recorded as the approximation of $F_0(D) : [0,1]^{m_0} \to [0,1]^{m_1}$. Assume the first $(K-1)$ step reasoning is $F_0 \circ F_1 \circ\circ\circ F_{K-1} : [0,1]^{m_0} \to [0,1]^{m_{K-1}}$, and there exists a finite sum NN_{K-1} so that

$$\left| F_0 \circ F_1 \circ\circ\circ F_{K-1} - NN_{K-1} \right| < \varepsilon_1$$

where

$$NN_{K-1} = \sum_{i=1}^{N_{K-1}} \alpha_i^{K-1} \sigma(\underline{a}_{K-1,i}^T \cdots + b_i^{K-1})$$

Let $F_K : [0,1]^{m_{K-1}} \longrightarrow [0,1]^{m_K}$ be the Kth step reasoning. Then there is a finite sum NN_e like Eq. (6.2) satisfying

$$\left| F_K - NN_e \right| < \varepsilon_2$$

Thus, the K step chain is $F_0 \circ F_1 \circ\circ\circ F_{K-1} \circ F_K : [0,1]^{m_0} \longrightarrow [0,1]^{m_K}$. Again, consider a unit mapping $F'_K : [0,1]^{m_{K-1}} \longrightarrow [0,1]$, we have a finite sum that

$$\left| F_0 \circ F_1 \circ\circ\circ F_{K-1} \circ F'_K - NN_e(NN_{K-1}) \right|$$

$$= \left| F_0 \circ F_1 \circ\circ\circ F_{K-1} \circ F_K - \sum_{i=1}^{N_K} \alpha_i^K \sigma(\underline{a}_{K,i}^T NN_{K-1} + b_i^K) \right| < \varepsilon' < \varepsilon$$

Thus for $F_0 \circ F_1 \circ\circ\circ F_{K-1} \circ F_K : [0,1]^{m_0} \longrightarrow [0,1]^{m_K}$,

$$\left| F_0 \circ F_1 \circ\circ\circ F_{K-1} \circ F_K - NN_e(NN_{K-1}) \right|$$

$$= \left| F_0 \circ F_1 \circ\circ\circ F_{K-1} \circ F_K - NN_K \right| < \max_{\varepsilon'} \varepsilon' < \varepsilon$$

The proof is completed. □

The three theorems provided before have constructed our basis of rule learning using multilayer networks. It implies a feasible path to adaptively acquire deliberative knowledge represented by fuzzy logic. With the breakthrough of deep learning techniques in recent years, this path has been greatly broadened, as latest intelligent algorithms are able to autonomously extract particular feature representations or complex nonlinear mappings. However, what sort of networks or learning methods is suitable still depends on specific application scenarios. In the following sections, we will address typical cases.

6.2 Knowledge Acquisition Based on Self-Supervised Learning

As already seen in Section 6.1, there are theoretical foundations for fuzzy logic learning using artificial NNs. Such a learning paradigm brings us two primary benefits. One is the exploitation of self-learning ability from NNs, which can directly and automatically extract rules from data sources under very weak priors. The other, based on evolutionary reasoning proposed before, is the generation of multimode deliberative processes with explicit semantics and interpretability. This provides us traceable and understandable decisions for the analysis of one's behaviors. In Chapter 5, it is clear that the evolutionary reasoning itself is able to expand reasoning paths. This advantage is particularly remarkable when counterfactual modeling is introduced, leading to the branches of inference chain increased reasonably and greatly. These derived inference chains can be regarded as reliable stretches of the fact-based basic reasoning chains in essence. With this notion in mind, a natural question, then, is how to get the basic chain of such fact-based reasoning. Answers could be sought from traditional psychology where a small number of subjects are investigated through a questionnaire or other experiments to achieve their deliberation trajectories. A well-known example comes from Berg et al., who reported an investment game that became the proto-typical trust game in the subsequent works [4]. They conducted the experiment by endowing two players with US\$10 each. In stage 1 the first mover decides how much money to pass to an anonymous second mover. All money passed is tripled. In stage 2, the second mover decides how much to return to the first mover. In the original experiment, out of 32 first movers, 30 sent positive amounts and only 2 sent 0, whereas, out of 28 players who received amounts greater than US\$1, and 12 returned US\$0 or US\$1, 12 returned more than their paired player sent them. Decision reasons for each participant were also recorded for further analysis. And the results clearly departed from the Nash equilibrium outcome that would be reached by perfectly rational and selfish players. This experiment has been replicated many times since then, showing that these results are quite robust.

Admittedly, the "Experiment, Induction, Modeling, Validation" traditional approach gives us an alternative to acquire decision knowledge. Yet this option has several salient problems and may probably not be applicable for real systems. On the one hand, selection of subjects is inclined to be arbitrarily determined by the test organizer. They may not be representative and typical. For the study of large-scale complex social systems, subjects in psychological experiments usually account for quite a small part of the whole studied group. This often brings sampling bias, leading to the inaccurate cognitive models that do not reflect behavioral differences among individuals. On the other hand, the final achieved decision knowledge by traditional approach is "static." It can hardly characterize the dynamic cognitive process that human's reasoning and decision-making patterns in reality usually evolve as his knowledge and skills gradually accumulates (such accumulation typically comes from his learning, imitation, socialization, etc.). The stated problems above may be probably overcome by using machine learning techniques. Under the circumstance of big user data, intelligent algorithms can discover sufficient rules at a very low cost. This actually increases the scale of experiments at the data level and thus elevates our model's accuracy. In the rest of the section, we will talk about its feasibility and propose an off-line knowledge mining method using self-supervised learning.

Given a collection of user data, the objective of deliberation learning is to acquire heterogeneous deliberative patterns as well as ultimate behaviors of different individuals. Specifically, it is composed of perception learning and reasoning learning. In human cognition, perception is an assimilation that internalizes the surrounding environmental signals into abstract representations in the brain. It maps the visual, audio, tactile and/or olfactory inputs into mental symbols or concepts. Limited by the human physiological structure, such abstract representations are often qualitative (discrete) but quantitative (continuous). An intuitive example is shown in Figure 6.1, with three system states as nodes and four directed links as transfer directions and conditions. For this representation of the world, human individuals are accustomed to concentrating on the stable states (illustrated by nodes) with their tipping points rather than the dynamics in a particular state. In other words, we care more about whether ice, water, or boiling water is in the container than what its current temperature is. So perception learning aims to simulate the physical to mental conversion. It should be noted that, however, machines do not have similar representational characteristics as their human counterparts. They are much better at dealing with continuous cases. To this end, we use representation learning to complete the task. Take the visual input as an example. The learning NN is drawn in Figure 6.2, where the raw image is sent to convolutional layers with subsequent feed-forward layers. The final output Z is the latent encoded representation. The learning details are explained as follows.

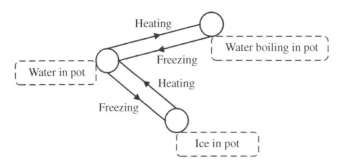

Figure 6.1 An example of abstract representation.

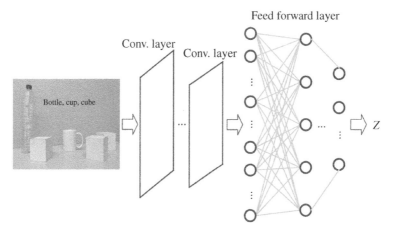

Figure 6.2 Neural network structure for perception learning.

Given an image i sampled from an offline data set D, denote the conversion from learning neural network to be PN. As a preliminary operation, the raw image i is first transformed by random crops or color distortion, etc. For simplicity, the transformed image is still denoted as i. The output code for i is $z = PN(i)$. In classic training, images are fed into the network in a batch mode as $X = [x_1 \cdots x_n] \in \mathbb{R}^{m \times n}$. m is the dimension of input image after transformation and n is the batch size. Then the output batch is $Z = [z_1 \cdots z_n] \in \mathbb{R}^{d \times n}$ where d is the compressed dimension of latent representation. We denote by Z_i the ith column vector in Z and $Z_{:,j}$ the row vector composed of each value at dimension j in all column vectors in Z. To exploit the autonomous learning ability, the loss function is composed of three parts. The first term is the variance regularization which is defined as

$$v(Z) = \frac{1}{d} \sum_{i=1}^{d} \max \left\{ 0, \ \gamma - \sqrt{Var(Z_{:,j}) + \varepsilon} \right\} \tag{6.3}$$

where γ is the target value standard deviation and ε is a small scalar preventing numerical instabilities. $Var(Z_{:,j})$ is computed by

$$Var(Z_{:,j}) = \frac{1}{m-1} \sum_{j=1}^{m} \left(Z_{:,j} - \overline{Z}_: \right)^2 \tag{6.4}$$

$\overline{Z}_:$ means the row average of Z. The second term is the covariance measurement defined as

$$c(Z) = \frac{1}{d} \sum_{i \neq j} \left[Cov(Z)_{i,j} \right]^2 \tag{6.5}$$

where $Cov(Z)$ is the covariance of Z computed by

$$Cov(Z) = \frac{1}{n-1} \sum_{i=1}^{n} \left(Z_i - \overline{Z} \right) \left(Z_i - \overline{Z} \right)^T \tag{6.6}$$

The third term of loss function is invariance defined as

$$s(Z, Z') = \frac{1}{n} \sum_i \|Z_i - Z'_i\|^2 \tag{6.7}$$

Z and Z' mean the outputs of two different batches, respectively. Hence the total loss function to be optimized is

$$L(Z, Z') = \alpha \cdot [v(Z) + v(Z')] + \beta \cdot [c(Z) + c(Z')] + \lambda \cdot s(Z, Z') \tag{6.8}$$

α, β, λ are hyperparameters to adjust the weights of each loss. Clearly, the three terms in the above equation stand for different considerations that are set to control the network training. The variance regularization arbitrarily introduces a target value γ to compulsively control for a positive deviation among different dimensions of learning results. It is an essential guarantee to avoid the collapse of latent representation. That is without this term, the latent code would degenerate to all zeros due to the inertia of neural network learning. The covariance measurement attempts to make each dimension of learning results orthogonal to others. That is to enhance the amount of information as much as possible. The invariance term minimizes the encoded distance between two batches. The intuition behind such an operation is that two sample batches of the same concept should result in the same latent representation. To achieve this goal, at first data augmentation needs to be conducted to guide the learning into a specific concept. We will discuss this step later in our experiment scenarios.

6.3 Adaptive Knowledge Extraction for Data Stream

In Section 6.2, we investigate the knowledge acquisition in an offline mode. Though plenty of decision-making knowledge can be mined with the support of big user data, such a learning paradigm still has some problems in practice. A typical defect is that sparse decision knowledge in batch processing mode is easy to be overwhelmed by dominant ones. Thus, this sort of knowledge loss is very likely to take place in our learning. For example, consider an online shopping scenario where we need to build a recommendation system to recommend customized products to various users. And our offline data set contains the item selection records from 100 users given the same page, among which 99 chose "beer" while only one chooses "diapers." According to the theory of machine learning, the learner would achieve a distribution that fits these training data.

Therefore, the recommendation system would give "beer" as advice in a high probability. The "diapers" option is rare and may never take place. Two detriments may be brought by such a kind of knowledge loss. First, because of this insensitivity, batch processing mode needs to accumulate a certain amount of new data to complete the knowledge update. This is obviously not enough for highly dynamic systems, leading to the optimization result temporarily invalid. In addition, the loss of sparse knowledge also causes a decrease of knowledge heterogeneity, which elicits the shrink of evolutionary reasoning space. It further reduces the system intelligence for optimization. For these reasons, we have to develop an adaptive method for dynamic knowledge extraction under the data stream condition, to avoid sparse decision loss. In the following, we concentrate on two lines of work: neural-symbolic learning and explanation of deep learning.

6.3.1 Neural-Symbolic Learning

Neural-symbolic learning tries to unify the symbolic reasoning and the neural network learning. With such a framework, logic and network models are studied together as integrated models of computation. This paradigm has biological foundations in cognitive science. In neural computing, it is widely assumed that our mind is an emergent property of the brain. Psychological knowledge of the world under this connectionism is implicitly encoded in the state of neural networks. And intelligent behavior is produced among the interactions of such relatively simple neural connections. Therefore, the artificial neural network analogically offers an appropriate representational language for artificial intelligence as well. It takes the abstract structure of the biological brain and try to "reproduces" the process of human cognition from bottom up. By adopting a hierarchical structure, the bottom level of the artificial neural network simulates the human cortex and neurons, while the top level simulates the active consciousness [5]. On the other hand, logic is firmly established as a fundamental tool in the modeling of deliberation and behavior [6, 7]. It is able to naturally process symbolic rules in language understanding and reasoning. A part from classic logic such as propositional and predicate logic, there are derivatives that have had even more significant impact in both academia and industry. For example, temporal logic introduces time index so that the truth values of the same rules may vary from time to time. This additional axis allows to characterize the gradual update of our mental knowledge repository. Modal logic extends conditions and has become a specification and analysis of knowledge and communication in multiagent or distributed systems [8]. As Allen Newell and Herbert Simon in their ACM Turing Award Lecture summarize, a physical symbol system has the necessary and sufficient means for general intelligent actions and it exercises its intelligence in problem solving by searching [9].

In neural-symbolic learning, both logic and network models are formally equivalent, especially for physically realizable and implementable systems (i.e. physical finite state machines) rather than strictly abstract computational models. The two models are not only considered equivalent concerning computability in practice but also in the classical dimensions of analysis (i.e. interchangeability except for a polynomial overhead) from a tractability perspective [10]. There is an existence result showing that no substantial difference in representational or problem-solving power exists between dynamical systems with distributed representations and symbolic systems with nonmonotonic reasoning capabilities [11]. In the research community, neural-symbolic learning is constantly studied in the context of machine learning research ever since McCulloch and Pitts proposed one of the first neural systems for Boolean logic in 1943 [12]. The field gained further research later in the 1990s and early 2000s. Scholars proposed logical programming systems for logical inference [13] and neural frameworks for knowledge representation and reasoning [14, 15]. Through meticulously designed neural architectures, the symbolic reasoning and neural computing are fused to achieve the ability of logical inference. There are also symbolic learning frameworks for nonclassical logic, abductive reasoning, and normative multiagent systems [16]. Yet they mostly focus on hard logic reasoning. A deficiency of such frameworks compared with deep learning lies in the learning representations and generalization ability. It makes them weak in reasoning over large-scale, heterogeneous, and noisy data. With the rise of deep learning, research on neural symbolic learning becomes less attractive during the 2010s [17]. Yet since the deep neural network is a kind of "black box" model that lacks semantic reasoning, neural symbolic learning gradually regains more attention in recent years [18].

Albeit many fruitful researches have emerged, there are still some major challenges for neural-symbolic learning in particular for the predicate logic. First, the learning results should be a set of lifted rules that are applicable to general objects instead of being tied with specific ones. This requirement guarantees that the achieved knowledge is abstract enough for a class of things rather than the propositional logic. Second, the learning system should both handle high-order relations and quantifiers, which exceeds the scope of traditional graph neural networks. For instance, the learning system needs to investigate three variables (a, b, c) to apply the transitivity rule of relation $r : \exists b\, r(a, b) \wedge r(b, c) \Rightarrow r(a, c)$, while the graph-structured networks usually represent the relation via an edge between node a and node c. Third, the learning system should avoid scale explosion of the extracted rules. Unlike traditional methods such as inductive logic programming where the number of logic rules grows exponentially, this requirement would timely perform knowledge reduct in order to keep the increasing speed of rule number not too fast [19]. Fourth, the learning system should recover rules based on as few priors as possible. This is also for the deficiency of traditional inductive logic programming, which usually relies on the predefined hand-coded and task-specific rule templates to restrict the size of searching space. In the following, we introduce a neural-symbolic learning method to deal with these challenges. The method is originally proposed as neural logic machines that can learn Horn clauses (a form of predicate logic) from data [20]. The basic idea behind is that logic operations such as logical ANDs and ORs can be efficiently approximated by neural networks, and the wiring among neural modules can realize the logic quantifiers.

To characterize the uncertainty of rules, logic predicates are represented as a probabilistic tensor. Assume that the universe of discourse includes m objects $\underline{s} = \{s_1, \ldots, s_m\}$, and an r-ary predicate with r variables is denoted as $d(x_1, \ldots, x_r)$. $d(x_1, \ldots, x_r)$ can be grounded on the object set $\underline{s}$, leading to a tensor $d^{\underline{s}}$ of dimension $[m^{\underline{r}}] \triangleq [m, m-1, \ldots, m-r+1]$, where the value of each entry $d^{\underline{s}}(s_{i_1}, \ldots, s_{i_r})$ of the tensor represents whether d is True under the grounding $\{x_1 = s_{i_1}, \ldots, x_r = s_{i_r}\}$. For a clear discussion, we define $d(s_{i_1} = x, s_{i_2} = x) \triangleq d(x)$ when $i_1 = i_2$. Therefore, without loss of generality, we can safely assume $i_j \neq i_k$ for any pair of (j, k) in $d^{\underline{s}}(s_{i_1}, \ldots, s_{i_r})$. Let $C^{(r)}$ be the number of r-ary predicates. We add a dimension to integrate the predicates. Thus, the m grounded tensor is extended to be the shape of $[m^{\underline{r}}, C^{(r)}] \triangleq [m, m-1, \ldots, m-r+1, C(r)]$. In particular, the grounded tensors are $[m, C^{(1)}]$ and $[m, m-1, C^{(2)}]$ dimensional when the unary and binary predicates are considered, respectively. A maximum arity B is set to control the length of dimensions. Taking a probabilistic view, the value of each element in grounded tensor ranges from 0 to 1, meaning the probability being True of the corresponding predicate expression with objects. In this way, all premises, conditions, conclusions, and intermediate results are stacked together and encoded by such probabilistic tensors.

After defining the encoding pattern, the next step is to model the logic rules using neural operators. The main objective is to develop a neural computing method to automatically learn rules that are both lifted and able to deal with multi-ary relational data. The overall structure of the neural network is illustrated as shown in Figure 6.3. In the input layer, all grounded tensors with zero to B arities are grouped as conditions. This determines the breadth of each layer for intermediate states, which contains $(B+1)$ computational units (vertically arranged). Each computational unit is implemented as a multilayer perceptron (MLP) and deals with a type of grounded tensor with particular predicates. The output layer encodes the conclusions of logic rules, which stand for the final world states. Through forward pass and back propagation, the network can transform rule-based reasoning sequences into the computation of MLP. Therefore, new reasoning rules may be achieved via the update of MLP weights. Just as the maximum dimension of the ground tensors, we set the maximum length of reasoning sequences to be L.

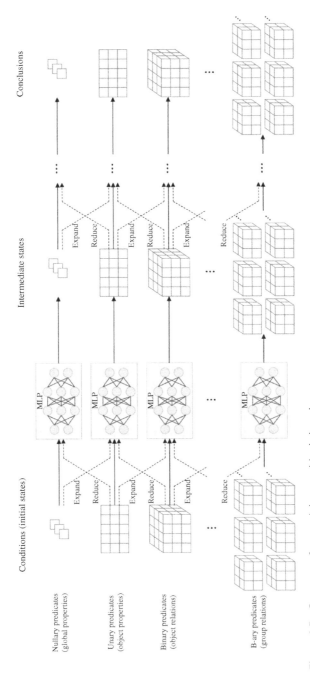

Figure 6.3 Structure of network in neural logic learning.

Two specific implementations are considered in the above neural logic learning: Boolean logic rules, which are lifted and include Boolean operations (AND, OR, NOT) over a set of predicates, and quantifiers (∃ and ∀), which bridge different kinds of predicates and generalize the extracted knowledge. The Boolean logic rule looks like the form

$$\hat{d}(x_1, \dots, x_r) \longleftarrow Express(x_1, \dots, x_r) \tag{6.9}$$

where *Express* stands for a Boolean expression with predicates over all variables $(x_1, \dots, x_r)$, and $\hat{d}$ is a conclusive predicate. Suppose there are k predicates $D = \{d_1, \dots, d_k\}$ in the expression *Express*. As defined before, the grounded tensor is of $[m^r, k]$ dimension. If $\hat{d}$ is given, then the number of all grounded arrangements for $Express(x_1, \dots, x_r)$ with the same subset of objects is $r! \times k$. For instance, if d_i is a ternary predicate $(r = 3)$, the grounded arrangements with objects $\underline{s} = \{s_1, s_2, s_3\}$ are $d_i(s_1, s_2, s_3)$, $d_i(s_1, s_3, s_2)$, $d_i(s_2, s_1, s_3)$, $d_i(s_2, s_3, s_1)$, $d_i(s_3, s_1, s_2)$, and $d_i(s_3, s_2, s_1)$, for $i = 1, \dots, k$. As a consequence, the input tensor for r-ary predicates in Figure 6.3 is of $[m^r, r! \times k]$ dimension. Its output after MLP computation is

$$\hat{d}(s_{i_1}, \dots, s_{i_r}) = \sigma[MLP(d_{1,1}(s_{i_1}, \dots, s_{i_r}), \dots, d_{k,r!}(s_{i_1}, \dots, s_{i_r})); \theta]$$

where σ is the sigmoid activation function and θ is the trainable network parameter. For any combination of mutually exclusive indexes $\{i_1, \dots, i_r\} \in \{1, \dots, m\}$, the MLP keeps the same. Hence, the size of θ is independent of the number of objects m. For the quantifiers (∃ and ∀), two operations, expansion and reduction, are introduced to model their properties. The expansion operates like

$$\forall x_{r+1} \, d'(x_1, \dots, x_r, x_{r+1}) \longleftarrow d(x_1, \dots, x_r) \tag{6.10}$$

Here $x_{r+1} \notin \{x_1, \dots, x_r\}$. By adding such a new variable, the expansion establishes a new predicate d' from d. Such variable addition is repeated for $(m - r)$ times for each predicate since we have m objects at most. As a consequence, the shape of the output tensor for a set of $C^{(r)}$ r-ary predicates is $[m^{r+1}, C^{(r)}]$. The reduction operation, on the contrary to expansion, reduces a variable modified by the quantifiers, which seems like

$$d'(x_1, \dots, x_r) \longleftarrow \forall x_{r+1} \, d(x_1, \dots, x_r, x_{r+1}) \tag{6.11}$$

The universal quantifier can be changed into existential quantifier, leading to a second reduction mode

$$d'(x_1, \dots, x_r) \longleftarrow \exists x_{r+1} \, d(x_1, \dots, x_r, x_{r+1}) \tag{6.12}$$

Here we provide an example.

$$Popular(y) \longleftarrow \forall x \, Likes(x, y) \text{ (From Eq. (6.11))}$$

$$Delicious(y) \longleftarrow Eatable(y) \wedge Popular(y) \text{ (From Eq. (6.9))}$$

The first rule means that "if everyone likes y, then y is popular." The second rule means that "if y is popular and eatable, then it is delicious." The reduction eliminates the variable x_{r+1} for a set of $C^{(r+1)}$ $(r+1)$-ary predicates. The computation takes the maximum (or minimum) element along the dimension of x_{r+1} for both types of quantifiers. By stacking the two result tensors, it converts the input of dimension $[m^{r+1}, C^{(r+1)}]$ into the output of dimension $[m^r, 2C^{(r+1)}]$. The expansion and reduction operations are drawn in Figure 6.3 with dashed lines. Let $O_i^{(r)}$ be the output of MLP that deals with r-ary predicates in layer i. Since the maximum width of the network is $(B+1)$, r ranges from 0 to B. As drawn in Figure 6.3, the input tensor for the r-ary MLP in layer $(i+1)$ is composed of three parts from layer i: the result from r-ary MLP, the expansion of output from $(r-1)$-ary MLP and the reduction of output from $(r+1)$-ary MLP. Their dimensions are $[m^r, C^{(r)}]$, $[m^r, C^{(r-1)}]$, and $[m^r, 2C^{(r+1)}]$, respectively. Thus, the input for the r-ary MLP in layer $(i+1)$ is

$$I_{i+1}^{(r)} = Concat[Expand(O_i^{(r-1)}), O_i^{(r)}, Reduce(O_i^{(r+1)})]$$

where $I_{i+1}^{(r)}$ is of shape $[m^r, C^{(r-1)} + C^{(r)} + 2C^{(r+1)}]$.

Neural-symbolic learning combines symbolic reasoning with neural network in an elegant way. It provides a feasible approach to extract probabilistic rules from data. In an online mode, the data gradually come record by record or batch by batch. Each record/batch brings an update of network via back propagation, and the updated parameters may elicit different probabilities of the same rule set. Therefore, the significant rules with dominant probabilities will be adaptive to the training data.

6.3.2 Explanation of Deep Learning

While neural-symbolic learning is able to effectively acquire "new" knowledge, explanation of deep learning gives another thought to complete such tasks. As can be viewed in Section 6.3.1, the predicates and objects have to be very meticulously encoded so that the weight parameters in specific layers precisely correspond to logic rule structures. Such requirements have imposed extremely strict constraints on the network architecture, which limits the application of the method. In contrast, explanation of deep learning relaxes this demand and may have more comprehensive applicable scenarios. Some related work is also conducted in previous researches to achieve this goal. Most of them investigate how the attributes and elementary operations derive the final decisions including decision tree and automatic rule extraction. For instance, Frosst and Hinton proposed a soft decision tree to hierarchically model the deep neural network for interpretable classification knowledge [21]. Another method of automatic rule extraction is the KT method which goes through each neuron, layer-by-layer, and applies an if-then rule by finding a threshold [22, 23]. Here we introduce a classic representation called DeepRED [24, 25], which uses RxREN [26] for pruning and C4.5 algorithm [27] for creating a parsimonious decision tree. DeepRED is applied for a multiclass classification task. Assume we have n training records $X = [x_1, \ldots, x_n]$, each x_j associated with one class $y_v \in \{c_1, c_2, \ldots, c_u\}$. Denote the input values of neural network as $i = \{i_1, \ldots, i_m\}$ and the output values as $o = \{o_1, \ldots, o_u\}$, one for each possible class. The hidden layers are abbreviated as $h_i \in \{h_1, \ldots, h_k\}$ while the hidden layer h_i consists of the neurons $h_{i,1}, h_{i,2}, \ldots, h_{i,H_i}$ (in the case of a single-hidden-layer neural network, the hidden neurons are written as $h_1, \ldots, h_H$). For convenience, we set $h_0 = i$ and $h_{k+1} = o$ and let $h_i(x)$ denote the specific layer values for input instance x. DeepRED produces intermediate rule sets $R_{a \to b}$ that include rules that describe layer b by means of terms based on layer a. A rule r: IF body THEN head is constituted by a set of terms in the body (conditions on attribute values) and an assignment term in the head. The general process of DeepRED is as follows: the algorithm extracts rules for each class output one after another. For each class, it processes every hidden layer in a descending order. DeepRED extracts rules for each hidden layer that describes its behavior based on the preceding layer. In the end, all rules for one class are getting merged such that we arrive at the rule set $R_{i \to o}$.

Algorithm 6.1 provides the pseudo code of DeepRED. The algorithm starts like the original implementation by using C4.5 to create decision trees consisting of split points on the activation values of the last hidden layer's neurons and the regarding classifications in the trees' leaves. To exemplify this approach, without loss of generality, an NN with k hidden layers. As a result of the first step, a decision tree that describes the output layer by split points on values regarding h_k is obtained, i.e. the rule set $R_{h_k \to o}$. The data to run C4.5 on are generated by feeding the training data to the NN and recording the outputs of the hidden neurons (line 8). In the next step, the algorithm processes the next shallower hidden layer h_{k-1} rather than directly referring to the input layer. For every term present in one of the rules in $R_{h_k \to o}$, we need to apply the C4.5 algorithm to find decision trees that describe layer h_k by means of h_{k-1} and can be transformed to the rule set $R_{h_{k-1} \to h_k}$ (line 10). The algorithm also implements a procedure to prevent itself from performing redundant runs of C4.5 since we only learn a decision tree for terms which were not already extracted (line 6). The terms in $R_{h_k \to o}$ are directly used to differentiate positive and negative examples for the regarding C4.5 runs (line 9). The iteration proceeds in the same manner until arriving at decision trees/rules that describe terms in the first hidden layer h_1 by terms consisting of the original inputs to the NN, i.e. $R_{i \to h_1}$. At this time, we have rule sets that describe each layer of the NN by their respective preceding layer, i.e. the sets of intermediate rules $R_{i \to h_1}, R_{h_1 \to h_2}, \ldots R_{h_{k-1} \to h_k}, R_{h_k \to o}$. To get a rule set $R_{i \to o}$ that describes the NN's outputs by its inputs, these rules need to be merged. This merging process proceeds layer-wise (loop starting at line 14). First, DeepRED substitutes the terms in $R_{h_k \to o}$ by the regarding rules in $R_{h_{k-1} \to h_k}$ to get the rule set $R_{h_{k-1} \to o}$. And unsatisfiable intermediate rules and redundant terms are deleted. This happens to reduce computation time and memory usage drastically. Next, the rule sets $R_{h_{k-1} \to o}$ and $R_{h_{k-2} \to h_{k-1}}$ are merged. The algorithm goes through all the layers step by step until arriving at rules that describe the classification/outputs according to the inputs to the NN, which is the result we were looking for. Though the original DeepRED algorithm developed for a batch training sample, it is also suitable for a data stream situation by setting the batch size $n = 1$.

Algorithm 6.1 Pseudo Code of DeepRED

Input:

    Neural network $h_0, h_1, \ldots, h_k, h_{k+1}$, training records $X = [x_1, \ldots, x_n]$;

Output:

    Set of rules representing the NN.

1: **for** each class $y_v \in \{c_1, c_2, \ldots, c_u\}$ **do**

2:    $R^v_{h_k \to o} \leftarrow$ IF $h_{k+1,v} > 0.5$ THEN $\hat{y} = y_v$;

3:    **for** each hidden layer $j = k, k-1, \ldots, 1$ **do**

4:      $R^v_{h_{j-1} \to h_j} \leftarrow \emptyset$;

5:      $T \leftarrow$ extractTermsFromRuleBodies($R^v_{h_j \to h_{j+1}}$);

6:      $T \leftarrow$ removeDuplicateTerms(T);

7:      **for** each $t \in T$ **do**

8:        $x'_1, \ldots, x'_n \leftarrow h_j(x_1), \ldots, h_j(x_n)$;

9:        $y'_1, \ldots, y'_n \leftarrow t[h_{j+1}(x_1)], \ldots, t[h_{j+1}(x_n)]$;

10:       $R^v_{h_{j-1} \to h_j} \leftarrow R^v_{h_{j-1} \to h_j} \cup C4.5(<x'_1, y'_1 >, \ldots, <x'_n, y'_n >)$

11:      **end for**

12:    **end for**

13:    **for** each hidden layer $j = k, k-1, \ldots, 1$ **do**

14:      $R^v_{h_{j-1} \to o} =$ mergeIntermediateTerms($R^v_{h_{j-1} \to h_j}, R^v_{h_j \to o}$);

15:      $R^v_{h_{j-1} \to o} =$ deleteUnsatisfiableTerms($R^v_{h_{j-1} \to o}$);

16:      $R^v_{h_{j-1} \to o} =$ deleteRedundantTerms($R^v_{h_{j-1} \to o}$);

17:    **end for**

18: **end for**

19: **return** $R^1_{i \to o}, R^2_{i \to o}, \ldots, R^u_{i \to o}$.

Overall, the rule extraction by DeepRED is built on internal neurons with interpretable meanings layer by layer. Such operations may not be able to exploit the powerful learning ability of deep neural network so that the acquired rule base might be less accurate. As is well known, the learning ability grows with the

Figure 6.4 Adaptive
learning neural network.

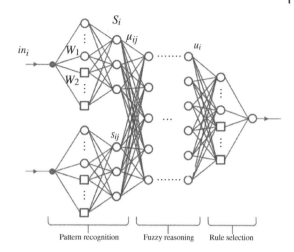

depth of network such as AlexNet [28], VGGNet [29], and ResNet [30]. Therefore, we resort to a novel adaptive learning paradigm to dynamically acquire decision knowledge.

The learning network is shown in Figure 6.4, which is composed of three parts with their names marked. The pattern recognition network accepts the system states as its inputs and fuzzifies them into the values of predefined linguistic variables. In principle, any type of existing fuzzification approach can be adopted in this network [31]. The fuzzification is implemented as a three-layered neural network with an input layer, a hidden layer, and an output layer. Yet its depth can be further extended for a more accurate approximation. In the input layer, the variables (in_i in the figure), discrete or continuous, can be either the latent representation from perception learning explained before or the original value of attributes concerned. The hidden layer is split into several parts, each of which encodes the membership function of a specific attribute and converts the input into linguistic values (we use s_{ij} to denote the jth value of the linguistic variable S_i). Linguistic values are represented as the neurons in the output layer, where each output stands for the membership of the value (μ_{ij} in the figure). The fuzzy reasoning network is a deep NN, which is the main container of the acquired knowledge. This deep NN treats the outputs of pattern recognition network as its input. In the output layer, each neuron represents a response candidate (also called a classification in some literature) of the agent or AI system. The ith response candidate is denoted as u_i. The rule selection network plays a role of de-fuzzification, which selects a specific strategy as the response. Despite most usual de-fuzzification methods like center-of-area or weighted combination are applicable in this network [32], the simplest way might be the softmax selection.

To interpret the knowledge implicated in the deep NN, one can extract explicit rules according to the connected weights. In the data stream learning, every output neuron in fuzzy reasoning network corresponds to a post-condition of an If ... Then ... rule, with the output value r_i as its firing strength. In this sense, the number of neurons in the fuzzy reasoning output layer equals the size of (discrete) decision space as well as the rule base. For u_i, the precondition is a combination of linguistic variables, so that the rule is written as Eq. (5.1):

$$IF\ x_1 = s_1\ \text{``and''}\ \ldots\ \text{``and''}\ x_n = s_n\ THEN\ u_i - fs_i$$

where S_i are the linguistic variables and s_i are their specific values determined by the membership functions. Note that preconditions of some rules may not cover the whole linguistic variables. In such case, the fuzzification outputs of the missing variables are expected to be zeros (or computationally small numbers).

Since the fuzzy reasoning network is fully connected, the preconditions of a particular rule can be adaptively changed during dynamic learning. For example, suppose one of our initial rules is denoted as

$$IF\ S_1 = s_{12}\ \text{``and''}\ S_2 = s_{23}\ THEN\ U = u_5$$

Given an appropriate input signal $(in_1\ in_2\ in_3)^T$ that makes $\mu_{12} \approx 1$, $\mu_{23} \approx 1$, and other $\mu_{ij} \approx 0$, the deep NN will output $u_5 \approx 1$. As the training goes on, the connected weights between pattern recognition and fuzzy reasoning networks may gradually change. When the membership value of another linguistic variable, say s_{32}, increases to a certain threshold with the same given input signal ($\mu_{32} \approx 1$), the rule becomes

$$IF\ S_1 = s_{12}\ \text{``and''}\ S_2 = s_{23}\ \text{``and''}\ S_3 = s_{32}\ THEN\ U = u_5$$

Clearly, the preconditions expanded.

The classic fuzzy set theory does not restrict the type of membership function. For continuous case, the theoretical basis in Section 6.1 guarantees that any membership function can be approximated by a traditional NN. Sigmoid function is usually adopted as the activations. This type of neurons is drawn as circles in Figure 6.4. For discrete membership functions, however, things could be worse. To make the proposed NN more general, we introduce a special type of neurons with the sigmoid basis functions (SBFs) as their activations in the pattern recognition and rule selection networks. The SBF is defined as

$$\varphi_k(x) = \begin{cases} 0, & x < 0 \\ (1 - e^{-x})^k, & x \geq 0 \end{cases}$$

The following theorem indicates that the three-layered NN with SBF neurons can approximate to discrete membership functions.

Theorem 6.3.1 *For a compact set D, let $f : D \to R$ be a bounded continuous and analytic function, except at $x = c_i$ $(i = 1, \ldots, n)$ where f has n finite jumps and is continuous from the right in each jump. For any given $\varepsilon > 0$, there exists a function*

$$F(x) = g(x) + \sum_{i=1}^{n} \sum_{k=0}^{N} a_{ik} \cdot \varphi_k(x - c_i)$$

such that

$$|F(x) - f(x)| < \varepsilon$$

where g(x) is a continuous function on the Nth derivative domain of D.

Proof: We prove by the induction of n. For $n = 1$, Ref. [33] provides a simple proof. Now let us assume that $n = m$, there is a function

$$F_m(x) = g(x) + \sum_{i=1}^{m} \sum_{k=0}^{N} a_{ik} \cdot \varphi_k(x - c_i)$$

such that

$$|F_m(x) - f(x)| < \varepsilon_m, \quad \forall \varepsilon_m > 0$$

For $n = m + 1$, without loss of generality, assume $0 < c_1 < \cdots < c_m < c_{m+1} < 1$. Let

$$f(x) = \begin{cases} f_1(x), & x \in [0, c_{m+1}) \\ f_2(x), & x \in [c_{m+1}, 1] \end{cases}$$

where $f_1(x)$ contains m jumps and $f_2(x)$ is continuous. Given $\forall \varepsilon_{m+1} > 0$, we are always able to choose $F_m(x)$ such that

$$|F_m(x) - f(x)| < \varepsilon_m < \varepsilon_{m+1}, \quad x \in [0, c_{m+1})$$

When $x \in [c_{m+1}, 1]$, Cybenko's Approximation Theorem tell us there exists a linear sigmoidal combination such that [2]

$$\left| \sum_{k=0}^{N} a_{m+1,k} \cdot \varphi_k(x - c_{m+1}) - f_2(x) \right| < \varepsilon_{m+1}$$

Let

$$F_{m+1}(x) = F_m(x) + \sum_{k=0}^{N} a_{m+1,k} \cdot \varphi_k(x - c_{m+1})$$
$$= g(x) + \sum_{i=1}^{m+1} \sum_{k=0}^{N} a_{ik} \cdot \varphi_k(x - c_i)$$

Then we have

$$|F_{m+1}(x) - f(x)| < \varepsilon_{m+1}, \quad x \in [0, 1] \qquad \square$$

As every membership function has finite jumps, the theorem guarantees that our proposed hybrid NN can be applied for any type of membership function with a given accuracy. Like the traditional NN, the new network training also relies on backpropagation and can be conducted in a separate mode or joint mode. The separate mode is mainly suitable for offline learning, which is performed in the initialization stage to fit the historical data. Given an initial membership function, the training of the pattern recognition network actually aims to update all of its connection weights so that it can approximate to that of membership function. To this end, we train the network with stochastic samples drawn from the objective function. Let in_i be a continuous input signal and s_j be its linguistic value after the fuzzification. The reference output is constructed as the vector with $\mu_j = 1$ and $\mu_k = 0$ $(k \neq j)$. Thus, by using gradient descent with the loss function

$$E = \frac{1}{2}\sum_j (\Delta\mu_j)^2 = \frac{1}{2}\sum_j (\mu_j - \hat{\mu}_j)^2$$

we are able to re-weight the connections between the second and third layers. For the input weights W_1 that connects the input and hidden sigmoid neurons, the training is similar with the back propagated error being a linear combination

$$\Delta hn_{2,i} = \sum_j w(hn_{2,i}, s_j) \cdot \Delta\mu_j$$

where $hn_{2,i}$ stands for ith hidden neuron in the second layer; $w(hn_{2,i}, s_j)$ means the weight from $hn_{2,i}$ to s_j, and $\Delta\mu_j$ means the output error of s_j. For the input weights W_2, the back propagated error is calculated in the same way. But we need to check the sign of the input $(in_i - c_i)$ if the membership function has a jump at c_i. The gradient for the hidden neuron with $\varphi_k(x)$ activation is

$$\frac{\partial E}{\partial w(in_i, hn_{2,k})} = \begin{cases} 0, & in_i < c_i \\ \frac{\partial \varphi_k(in_i - c_i)}{\partial(in_i - c_i)} \cdot \Delta hn_{2,k} \cdot in_i, & in_i \geq c_i \end{cases}$$

Therefore, the weights in W_2 are updated as

$$w(in_i, hn_{2,k}) \leftarrow w(in_i, hn_{2,k}) - \gamma \cdot \frac{\partial E}{\partial w(in_i, hn_{2,k})}$$

where γ is a learning rate. The training of the rule selection network can be conducted analogously, through an approximation to the initial de-fuzzification function. In contrast with the pattern recognition and rule selection networks, the training of deep fuzzy reasoning network depends on the input and output of historical business data. There are two cases here:

1. The input and output are both discrete. It means the fuzzy reasoning network can be trained separately, with the discrete linguistic values as the input vector and the discrete classifications as the output vector. Like the pattern recognition

network, the input and output vectors are constructed by setting the element pertinent to the given label to be one and others to be zeros. Obviously, this is especially suitable for the initialization according to a given initial rule base.

2. Either the input or output is continuous. This refers to that at least one element in the input or output vector is continuous. If the input is continuous, the linguistic values are not directly achievable. Thus, we need to combine the pattern recognition and fuzzy reasoning networks as a whole. The backward training process starts from the discrete output vector u_i to the continuous input vector in_i. This may change the weights of pattern recognition network and in essence modify our initial membership function. If the output is continuous, similar operations are carried out by combing the fuzzy reasoning and rule selection networks. And if the input and output are both continuous, we treat the three networks as a whole.

In the above second case, the training of two or three networks as a whole is referred to as the joint mode. This mode is more comprehensively applicable since DL mostly fit data in a continuous space in practice. The training is suitable for both off-line and online learning. In the on-line learning, the update will gradually change the weights of each network, modifying not only the implied knowledge but also the membership functions for fuzzification and de-fuzzification. Therefore, the extracted rule base from the deep NN also dynamically fit the time-variant input sample.

6.4 Experiment on Travel Behavior Learning

To test and validate our proposed method, the novel NN is applied to disaggregate travel demand analysis to adaptively learn and predict significant travel patterns of urban citizens. The traditional approach for traffic demand prediction is based on the travel survey, which investigates the daily travel patterns from a sample of residents. While the survey can reflect the actual travel demand to some extent, it is too expensive financially and in time cost to conduct frequently. This makes the investigated travel demand not dynamically match the time variant actual state. As such, we would like to adaptively estimate the dynamic travel demand using the proposed deep NN. We resort to multiagent system to complete this task. Figure 6.5 shows the abstract map, which characterizes the central area of Chengdu in China, covering about $19.2\,\mathrm{km}^2$ with 37 nodes and 112 links. In our application, the agent decision variables consist of two parts: the personal attributes which involve the age interval, income level, vehicle ownership and the travel plan which contains departure time and trip origin–destination (OD). In essence, they are the linguistic variables (S_i) in the proposed deep NN. To set

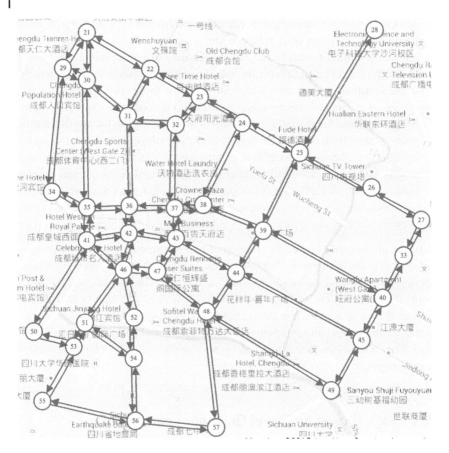

Figure 6.5 Abstract road network.

the values of the linguistic variables, we split the age into 8 intervals, the income level into 5 intervals and the time into 72 intervals. The values of each variable are listed in Table 6.1 and triangular membership functions are initially used as Figure 6.6 shows [34]. Note that the OD pair is represented as the node ID.

We use the active taxi information as the training and testing data, which comes from 13,608 taxies in three days. To avoid potential biases, the entire data sets are all from the same weekday. Each record provides the terminal ID, vehicle number, GPS position, head direction, speed, and time stamp as shown in Table 6.2. The first two days are used for training and the last day is for testing. Before experiment, three types of noise are removed from the data set:

1. Incomplete records, in which some items are missing. As long as the concentrated items are complete, the record is retained in the data set.

Table 6.1 Agent decision linguistic variables.

Var.	Values
Age interval	≤20, 21–30, ... , 71–80 , >80
Income level	Very low, low, mid., high, very high
Vehicle ownership	True, false
Time interval	6:00–6:15, ... , 23:46–24:00
OD pair	(21,22), (21,23), ... , (56,57)

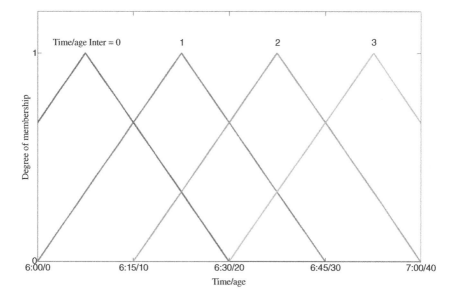

Figure 6.6 Initial membership function.

Table 6.2 Taxi data records.

Ter. ID	Veh. num.	Lon.	Lat.	Dir.	Speed	Time
200102181	CA-TC408	104.05	30.61	0.0	9.5	2014/8/1 13:21:30
101180078	CA-TZ602	104.08	30.63	356.0	8.3	2014/8/1 21:07:08
101360016	CA-TC321	104.10	30.62	100.0	17.7	2014/8/1 15:37:51

2. Abnormal records, which are obviously wrong in the actual situations. For example, the record with a 100 km/h speed is impossible since the speed limit in urban area is 60 km/h. The malfunction of GPS device may also bring abnormal records where the latitude and longitude are both zeros.
3. Duplicate records. Duplicate results may arise due to transmission problems. For this kind, only one record is retained and other duplicates are removed.

After the data cleaning, we have 151,445,240 records for training and 75,212,870 records for testing. For each vehicle, the original GPS information is uploaded every 10 seconds and is converted into links through map matching. The converted links are connected to construct trajectories. A particular path is extracted as the longest trajectory that does not contain cycles since the records do not have pickup and drop-off flags. For example, if a taxi has a trajectory like Figure 6.7, which manifests the vehicle sequentially went through the nodes

$$26 \rightarrow 25 \rightarrow 24 \rightarrow 38 \rightarrow 39 \rightarrow 25 \rightarrow 28$$

Then OD pairs are set to be (25, 39) and (24, 25), with the paths $26 \rightarrow 25 \rightarrow 24 \rightarrow 38 \rightarrow 39$ and $39 \rightarrow 25 \rightarrow 28$.

A second data source is the basic synthetic population. We use Chinese census sample and annual statistics to generate the initial population at the community level [35, 36]. The disaggregate sample involves 3373 households and 10,515 individuals, accounting for 1.02‰ of the total target population. To limit the research scope, we restrict the personal attributes to age, income, and vehicle status of the household. The final synthetic population contains 405,758 individuals with 136,127 households, distributed a little larger than the studied area in order to fully cover the abstract road network.

Our experiments are composed of three stages, network training, rule extraction, and travel behavior prediction. The pattern recognition network has 5 input neurons and 1419 output neurons. Accordingly, the fuzzy reasoning DNN has 1419 input neurons, 14,895 output neurons, and two hidden layers with 122 and 262 neurons. The rule selection network has 14,895 inputs with only one output. In the training stage, the pattern recognition network is pretrained by the initial membership function. After that, the first two days' trajectory data set is used to train the whole NN. The training sample is generated by a two-step operation. First, a trajectory record is read to get the time, OD, and the actual path. Then a synthetic individual in the origin node is stochastically drawn to get the age, income level, and vehicle ownership. The two parts of attributes are integrated as the input and the actual path is used as the output reference. Since the time variable is continuous, the network has continuous input and discrete output. Therefore, joint training mode is adopted in our learning. The training samples with time stamps come one by one in a chronological order to simulate the online learning process. For each sample, we first generate a path selection using its

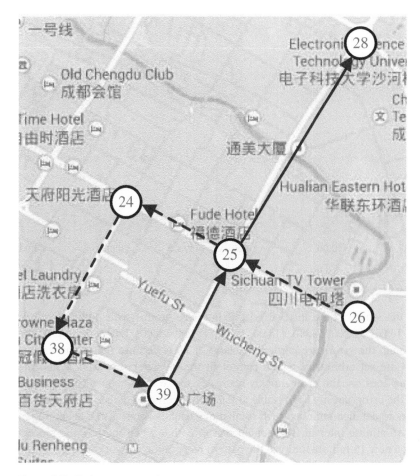

Figure 6.7 Trajectory with a loop.

input based on the current network and calculate the error according to the sample path. Then the weights among neurons are updated via back propagation.

As a comparative study, a representative method, DeepRED, is also implemented to extract explainable rules in our experiments. Each experiment is conducted for five times, and the average training errors are drawn in Figure 6.8 (our proposed neural network is referred as FNN here). The training error is computed by

$$e = \sum_i \left| a(u_i) - a(\hat{u}_i) \right|$$

where $a(u_i)$ stands for the activation strength of the sample path (real label), and $a(\hat{u}_i)$ stands for the activation strength of NN predicted path. As can be

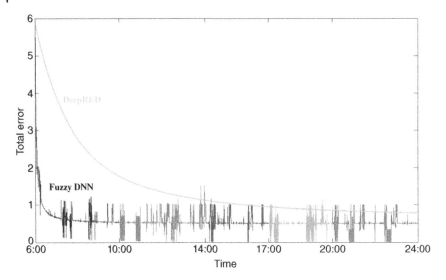

Figure 6.8 Neural network training error.

seen, the studied time interval is split into five groups with different colors: [6:00, 10:00], [10:00, 14:00], [14:00, 17:00], [17:00, 20:00], [20:00, 24:00]. At the beginning, the errors are particularly large. This is because the initial weights of NN are set arbitrarily, which cannot fit the behavior very well. When the training goes on, the error quickly decreases to 0.6 after about 600 iterations. Then the errors mostly keep stable at 0.5 with a certain number of oscillations. In a more detailed analysis, such oscillations usually occur at the beginning of every 15-minute interval. A potential reason is that when the training process enters a new 15-minute interval, the pattern recognition network will fuzzify the input time signal into a new linguistic value. However, the NN does not contain the knowledge of such input at this time, since it never met similar samples before. Therefore, this will lead to large errors when it tries to "predict" the sample paths. After a short term of fitting, the NN can approximate the travel behavior distribution so that the error becomes stable. Compared with our Hybrid DNN, the errors from DeepRED are larger and decrease much more smoothly. It is because the DeepRED network is not able to handle data stream records. Thus, its training samples are stochastically drawn from all the time intervals, which avoid the accuracy of oscillations. Clearly, our network outperforms DeepRED with about 16% improvement in an overall aggregate error.

The second stage, rule extraction, aims to transform the NN knowledge into agent decision rules. After the training, the output of fuzzy reasoning network will provide each path candidate an activation strength for a given input vector. The de-fuzzification in rule selection network will choose a particular path as the ultimate decision. Figure 6.9 shows an example, in which the test input vector is $(613, 1, 27, 8.2, 0)^T$. Note the time 613 means the number of seconds past from 6:00. Each linguistic value with its degree of membership after fuzzification is marked below the output neuron in pattern recognition network. In the figure, the uppermost neuron represents *TimeInter* = 0 with the membership degree being 0.93. Through forward propagation, the fuzzy reasoning deep NN endows each path

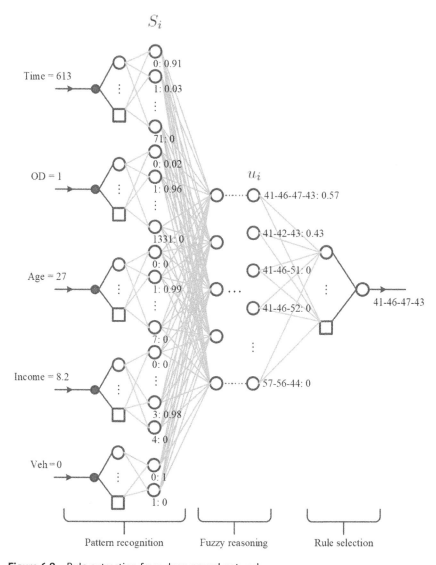

Figure 6.9 Rule extraction from deep neural network.

with an activation strength (also marked in the figure). Clearly, the uppermost path has a dominant activation strength 0.57. The rule selection network finally outputs the 41-46-47-43 as its ultimate decision. Taking the linguistic value with maximum membership degree as the preconditions, the rule in Figure 6.9 can be extracted as

$$If \quad TimeInter = 0 \wedge OD = 1 \wedge AgeInter = 1$$
$$\wedge\, Income = 3 \wedge Veh = 0$$
$$Then \quad U = 41\text{-}46\text{-}47\text{-}43$$

For readability, this is equivalent to

$$If \quad TimeInter = 6\text{:}00\text{--}6\text{:}15 \wedge OD = (41, 43)\wedge$$
$$AgeInter = 21\text{--}30 \wedge Income = High \wedge Veh = F$$
$$Then \quad Path = 41\text{-}46\text{-}47\text{-}43$$

The above example also indicates that whatever the membership function is, part of the knowledge will be lost during de-fuzzification. For example, if the top two paths in Figure 6.9 have 0.8 and 0.2 activation strengths, respectively, the rule selection network will achieve similar final decision. To explain the knowledge more accurately, we can directly extract the outputs of the fuzzy reasoning network as post-conditions. This operation will elicit a group of rules for every linguistic input. For simplicity, we store the top three rules (if has) with the largest activations for each input type. The total size of our rule base is 13,954. Table 6.3 lists a segment where the activations strengths in the brackets have been normalized. As can be seen, for the given identical input variables, the path selection results change with time interval. In the morning rush hours, travelers mostly choose the route 49-45-40-39-44 dominantly. Few of them travel through 49-45-44 and 49-48-44. The reason for the use of such long-distance path might be a congestion in the urban central area or a traffic guidance for the object path. In contrast, travel behaviors between the same OD pair in the evening nonrush hours return to a normal state, mainly distributed on the two shortest paths with nearly equivalent

Table 6.3 Some extracted rules.

Time	OD	Age	Inc. Lv	Veh. own.	Path
9:00–9:15	(49,44)	20–30	Mid.	False	49-45-40-39-44(0.97)
9:00–9:15	(49,44)	20–30	Mid.	False	49-45-44(0.02)
9:00–9:15	(49,44)	20–30	Mid.	False	49-48-44(0.01)
20:15–20:30	(49,44)	20–30	Mid.	False	49-48-44(0.52)
20:15–20:30	(49,44)	20–30	Mid.	False	49-45-44(0.48)

Table 6.4 Rules with adaptively varied preconditions.

Time	OD	Age	Inc. Lv	Veh. own.	Path
19:30–19:45	(51,48)	31–40	Mid.	False	51-54-56-57-48(0.87)
19:30–19:45	(51,48)	31–40	Mid.	False	51-46-47-48(0.13)
19:30–19:45	(51,48)	31–40	Mid.	True	51-54-56-57-48(0.95)
19:30–19:45	(51,48)	31–40	Mid.	True	51-46-47-48(0.05)
21:45–22:00	(51,48)	31–40	Mid.	False	51-54-56-57-48(1.0)
21:45–22:00	(51,48)	31–40	Mid.	True	51-54-56-57-48(1.0)

activations. This phenomenon clearly manifests that the post-conditions of the acquired rules are adaptively variable during our deep learning process.

As alluded in Section 6.3, the rule pre-conditions can be also adaptively changed through learning. One instance from our rule base looks like Table 6.4. Reflected by the different activation strengths in the first four rows, the travel paths in the evening rush hours rely on the vehicle ownership. In contrast, the rules represented by the last two rows indicate that in a later time interval, the decision is independent from such an attribute. To show more clearly, we can conduct a knowledge reduction for the last two rows to get

$$If\ TimeInter = 63 \land OD = (51, 48)$$
$$\land AgeInter = 3 \land Income = 2$$
$$Then\ U = 51\text{-}54\text{-}56\text{-}57\text{-}48$$

where the vehicle ownership attribute is deleted.

The third stage of our experiment is the travel behavior prediction, in which the testing data are used to validate whether the extracted rules can predict the travel patterns of the same weekday. Specifically, the artificial traffic flow is generated based on an identical synthetic population. For each input state, we gradually import one, two, and three (if it has) rules with the largest activation strengths. The prediction errors are shown in Figures 6.6–6.12. The points are absolute errors computed by

$$e\{r|t,o,d\} = |p\{r|t,o,d\} - \hat{p}\{r|t,o,d\}| = \left| \frac{N\{r|t,o,d\}}{\sum_p N\{r|t,o,d\}} - \frac{\hat{N}\{r|t,o,d\}}{\sum_p \hat{N}\{r|t,o,d\}} \right|$$

where $N\{r|t,o,d\}$ and $\hat{N}\{r|t,o,d\}$ represent the real and generated total travel number in the path r, time interval t and OD pair (o, d). Obviously, the overall errors are mostly below 100%, and the average error (represented as polygonal lines) of our fuzzy DNN is slightly lower than the DeepRED in each time group.

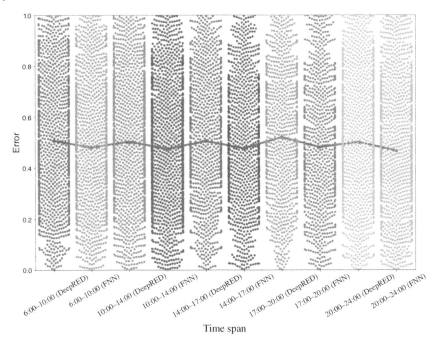

Figure 6.10 Traffic prediction errors with one dominant rule.

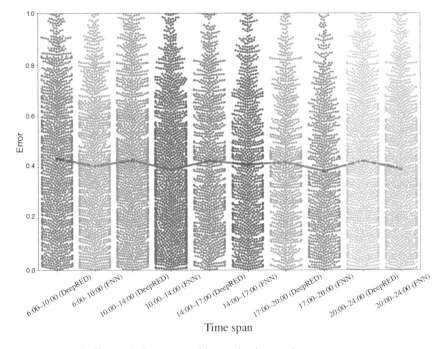

Figure 6.11 Traffic prediction errors with two dominant rules.

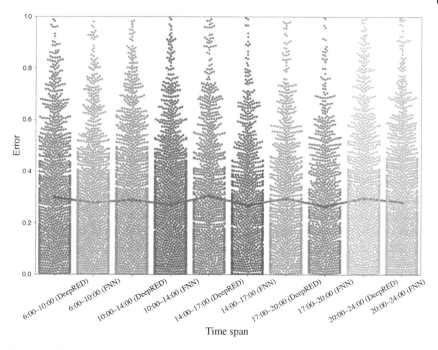

Figure 6.12 Traffic prediction errors with three dominant rules.

To quantitatively investigate the results, some other statistical metrics are listed in Table 6.5. The three metrics, mean absolute error (MAE), relative mean square error (RMSE), and R square (R^2) are computed as

$$MAE : \frac{1}{m} |p\{r|t, o, d\} - \hat{p}\{r|t, o, d\}|$$

$$RMSE : \sqrt{\frac{1}{m} \sum_{r,t,o,d} (p\{r|t, o, d\} - \hat{p}\{r|t, o, d\})^2}$$

$$R^2 : \frac{(\sum_{r,t,o,d} p\{r|t, o, d\} \cdot \hat{p}\{r|t, o, d\})^2}{[\sum_{r,t,o,d}(p\{r|t, o, d\})^2][\sum_{r,t,o,d}(\hat{p}\{r|t, o, d\})^2]}$$

From the table, the MAEs decrease with the exploited rules growing. This is intuitive in that the more travel rules used, the more accurate the traffic predictions are. The RMSE also decreases with more decision rules imported. Such metric measures the degree of error dispersion and suggests that the travel prediction ability gets more stable. The R square reveals that our extracted rules can significantly interpret the traffic flow patterns. And the interpretability increases with the number of rules.

Table 6.5 Statistical metrics of travel behavior prediction.

Metrics	MAE		RMSE		R^2	
Experiment	DeepRED	FNN	DeepRED	FNN	DeepRED	FNN
a (1 rule)	0.506	0.475	0.572	0.544	0.762	0.785
b (2 rules)	0.425	0.396	0.497	0.469	0.832	0.852
c (3 rules)	0.295	0.272	0.369	0.344	0.909	0.923

6.5 Conclusions and Discussions

Knowledge acquisition is an important topic for decision making. This chapter focuses on the transformation of user data into fuzzy rules. By exploiting the learning ability of neural network, the knowledge implied in the connection weights can be endogenously transformed into agent decision rules. This is unlike the traditional methods where input perturbation, hidden neuron analysis, and external surrogate are used to investigate the primary features of NN processing. Our proposed approach is applied in urban travel behavior learning. Computational experiments based on actual traffic data indicate that the extracted rules can reconstruct and predict the traffic patterns at a satisfactory level.

The NN in this chapter involves a part of neurons that adopt SBFs as their activations. This hybrid structure, as proved by the theorem, can approximate to the membership functions with finite jumps. However, the conclusion holds on the condition that these jumps are already known. Unfortunately, such a condition is seldom satisfied in a general case where the sequentially arrived training samples do not reveal the characteristics of the functions behind. Therefore, how to deal with the discrete membership functions without prior knowledge is a worth exploring.

The values of MAE in the experiments manifest that there might be significant travel patterns in urban transportation, as they can be reconstructed by exploiting a few primary rules. This phenomenon enlightens us to identify and construct dominant rule base. Moreover, by combining derivatives of such basic rules, we might generate various traffic flows which are slightly different from the reality but still distribute near the actual ones. For instance, we can arbitrarily change the time interval linguistic values of particular rules to investigate what will emerge when the dominant behaviors take place in a different period. This modification, in essence, considers a reasonable combination of travel templates at the bottom level, and thus can be deemed as potential alternatives of the actual traffic flows. We will return to address this issue in Chapter 8 for computational experiments.

References

1 M. B. Feldman. A Proof of Lusin's Theorem. American Mathematics Monthly, 1981, 88: 191–192.

2 G. Cybenko. Approximation by Superpositions of a Sigmoidal Function. Mathematics of Control, Signals, and Systems, 1989, 2(4): 303–314.

3 Z. Lu, H. Pu, F. Wang, et al. The Expressive Power of Neural Networks: A View from the Width. Proceedings of Advances in Neural Information Processing Systems, Curran Associates, 2017, 30: 6231–6239.

4 J. Berg, J. Dickhaut and K. McCabe. Trust, Reciprocity, and Social History. Games and Economic Behavior, 1995, 10: 122–142.

5 D. A. Medler. A Brief History of Connectionism. Neural Computing Surveys, 1998, 1: 61–101.

6 R. Kowalski. Computational Logic and Human Thinking: How to be Artificially Intelligent. Cambridge University Press, 2011.

7 L. M. Pereira. Turing is Among Us. Journal of Logic and Computation, 2012, 22(6): 1257–1277.

8 R. Fagin, J. Halpern, Y. Moses and M. Vardi. Reasoning About Knowledge. MIT Press, 1995.

9 A. Newell and H. A. Simon. Computer Science as Empirical Inquiry: Symbols and Search. Communications of the Association for Computing Machinery, 1976, 19: 113–126.

10 I. van Rooij. The Tractable Cognition Thesis. Cognitive Science, 2008, 32: 939–984.

11 H. Leitgeb. Interpreted Dynamical Systems and Qualitative Laws: From Neural Networks to Evolutionary Systems. Synthese, 2005, 146: 189–202.

12 W. S. McCulloch and W. Pitts. A Logical Calculus of The Ideas Immanent in Nervous Activity. The Bulletin of Mathematical Biophysics, 1943, 5(4): 115–133.

13 A. S. A. Garcez and G. Zaverucha. The Connectionist Inductive Learning and Logic Programming System. Applied Intelligence, 1999, 11(1): 59–77.

14 A. Browne and R. Sun. Connectionist Inference Models. Neural Networks, 2001, 14(10): 1331–1355.

15 I. Cloete and J. M. Zurada. Knowledge-Based Neurocomputing. The MIT Press, 2000.

16 A. S. Garcez, L. C. Lamb and D. M. Gabbay. Neural-Symbolic Cognitive Reasoning. Springer-Verlag, Beilin Heidelberg, 2009.

17 Y. LeCun, Y. Bengio and G. Hinton. Deep Learning. Nature, 2015, 521(7553): 436–444.

18 Y. Bengio. From System 1 Deep Learning to System 2 Deep Learning. The 33rd Conference on Neural Information Processing Systems (NeurIPS), Vancouver, Canada, Dec. 8–14, 2019.

19 R. Evans and E. Grefenstette. Learning Explanatory Rules from Noisy Data. Journal of Artificial Intelligence Research, 2018, 61: 1–64.

20 H. Dong, J. Mao, T. Lin, C. Wang, L. Li and D. Zhou. Neural Logic Machines. The 7th International Conference on Learning Representations, New Orleans, LA, USA, May 6–9, 2019.

21 N. Frosst and G. Hinton. Distilling a Neural Network into a Soft Decision Tree. arXiv:1711.09784 [cs.LG], 2017. https://arxiv.org/abs/1711.09784.

22 L. Fu. Rule Generation from Neural Networks. IEEE Transactions on Systems, Man, and Cybernetics, 1994, 24(8): 1114–1124.

23 J. Cozar, A. Fernandez, F. Herrera, et al. A Metahierarchical Rule Decision System to Design Robust Fuzzy Classifiers Based on Data Complexity. IEEE Transactions on Fuzzy Systems, 2019, 27(4): 701–715.

24 J. R. Zilke, E. L. Mencia and F. Janssen. DeepRED—Rule Extraction from Deep Neural Networks. In T. Calders, M. Ceci and D. Malerba (eds), Discovery Science. Cham, Springer, 2016: 457–473.

25 J. R. Zilke. Extracting Rules from Deep Neural Networks. Master's Thesis, Technische Universitat Darmstadt, 2016.

26 M. G. Augasta and T. Kathirvalavakumar. Reverse Engineering the Neural Networks for Rule Extraction in Classification Problems. Neural Processing Letters, 2012, 35(2): 131–150.

27 J. R. Quinlan. C4.5: Programs for Machine Learning. Morgan Kaufmann Publishers, Inc. 1993.

28 A. Krizhevsky, I. Sutskever and G. E. Hinton. ImageNet Classification with Deep Convolutional Neural Networks. 26th Conference on Neural Information Processing Systems, Lake Tahoe, NV, USA, Dec. 3–8, 2012.

29 K. Simonyan and A. Zisserman. Very Deep Convolutional Networks for Large-Scale Image Recognition. International Conference on Learning Representations, San Diego, CA, USA, May 7–9, 2015.

30 K. He, X. Zhang, S. Ren and J. Sun. Deep Residual Learning for Image Recognition. Proceedings of the IEEE Conference on Computer Vision and Pattern Recognition (CVPR), 2016: 770–778.

31 O. N. A. Sayaydeh, M. F. Mohammed and C. P. Lim. Survey of Fuzzy Min-Max Neural Network for Pattern Classification Variants and Applications. IEEE Transactions on Fuzzy Systems, 2019, 27(4): 635–645.

32 J. Chachi. A Weighted Least Squares Fuzzy Regression for Crisp Input-Fuzzy Output Data. IEEE Transactions on Fuzzy Systems, 2019, 27(4): 739–748.

33 R. R. Selmic and F. L. Lewis. Neural-Network Approximation of Piecewise Continuous Functions: Application to Friction Compensation. IEEE Transactions on Neural Networks, 2002, 13(3): 745–751.

34 Z.-J. Wang. A Goal-Programming-Based Heuristic Approach to Deriving Fuzzy Weights in Analytic Form from Triangular Fuzzy Preference Relations. IEEE Transactions on Fuzzy Systems, 2019, 27(2): 234–248.

35 P. Ye, X. Hu, Y. Yuan, et al. Population Synthesis Based on Joint Distribution Inference without Disaggregate Samples. The Journal of Artificial Societies and Social Simulation, 2017, 20(4): 16.

36 P. Ye and X. Wang. Population Synthesis using Discrete Copulas. IEEE International Conference on Intelligent Transportation Systems (ITSC 2018), Maui, Hawaii, USA, Nov. 4–7, 2018: 479–484.

7

Agent Calibration and Validation

Chapter 5 and Chapter 6 have discussed the facets of reasoning and learning for human decision. They have formed the basis of an agent's behavior generation. Before applying to reproduce the actual behaviors of population in complex social systems, calibration of the agent models is an essential stage, which aims to adjust the parameter values under various situations. For our cognitive reasoning model elucidated in Chapters 5 and 6, as the activation strength of actions is predefined, the main parameter to be calibrated is the rule activation strength. It numerically determines the systemic state transfer. In multiagent systems, the parameters of a specific reasoning chain need to be calibrated step by step, since there are numerous combinations of parameter values if we only have the start and end states. We shall talk about agent calibration and validation methods in this chapter. Section 7.1 addresses what is calibration and why it is required before the model use. Then from Sections 7.2–7.5, four typical methods are introduced in detail. They are calibrations based on optimization, machine learning, cybernetics, and variational auto-encoder, among which the former two are applicable in an offline mode and the latter two are usually running online. Our discussion will show a sketch map of this filed.

7.1 Model Calibration for Agent

Multiagent system is a useful tool in the study of markets, industries, organizations, or other complex systems by evolving many heterogeneous agents that exhibit bounded rationality and explicitly interact in a decentralized fashion. The recent tremendous improvement in computing capabilities has increasingly made it easier to implement. For researchers, the extreme flexibility of agent models in accommodating alternative modeling assumptions – including various forms of individual behavior, interaction/decision patterns, and institutional arrangements – has allowed them to explore the positive and normative consequences

Parallel Population and Parallel Human: A Cyber-Physical Social Approach,
First Edition. Peijun Ye and Fei-Yue Wang.
© 2023 The Institute of Electrical and Electronics Engineers, Inc. Published 2023 by John Wiley & Sons, Inc.

of departing from the often oversimplifying assumptions characterizing most mainstream analytical models. From the positive, descriptive side, multiagent system has been successfully applied to a long list of both micro and macro issues including innovation and technological change, market dynamics, finance, industrial dynamics, organization theory, growth and development, international trade, macroeconomic dynamics and business cycles, evolution of institutions, social norms and networks, and political economy. It has also been applied to shed light on the area of economic policy and market design. Here the agent approach is proving to be extremely fruitful. This is primarily because agents, especially humanoid agents, facilitate the construction and evaluation of policy measures in alternative institutional arrangements (market structure and auction types); behavioral and expectation-formation hypotheses for the agents involved (consumers, firms, government, unions, and market traders); and interaction patterns (global versus local, social networks).

A common theme informing both applied (positive, normative) analysis and methodological research concerns the relationships between agents and "real behavioral data." By real behavioral data, we mean not only standard empirical evidence (e.g. data sets, stylized behavioral modes) but also qualitative and quantitative evidence regarding the setup of the system and agents' cognitive repertoires gathered from laboratory experiments, case studies, and inductive analyses. After all, one of the main justifications for using agent models in complex systems, either as complements or substitutes of mainstream neoclassical models, relies in their capability to go beyond the constraints imposed by standard building blocks and to provide the micro-foundations based on "empirically sound" assumptions. At the same time, agent models also have to confront empirical evidence and be better able to reproduce and explain existing observations. The interplay between agents and "real behavioral data" concerns all stages of model development and analysis and becomes crucial in assessing the success of agent models. We use the expression empirical validation to stand for the procedure through which the modeler assesses the extent to which the model's outputs approximate reality, typically described by one or more "stylized behaviors" drawn from empirical research. More generally, however, to "empirically validate" a given agent can involve the appraisal of how "realistic" the set of model assumptions are (e.g. the behavioral rules employed by the agents in the model), or the evaluation of the impact of alternative designs and/or policy measures.

The most adopted procedure for the development of an agent model is the indirect calibration approach [1]. It is composed of four separate steps. The first consists of the identification of some real-world stylized behaviors of interest that the modeler wants to explain. In the second, one specifies the model, the timeline of events, the micro-level dynamics which embody the individual agents' deliberation, the set of parameters, and the set of random disturbances. Validation and the hypothesis testing are performed in the third step in order to compare model's output with the observations obtained from real-world behaviors. Finally, there could be a fourth step, where the multiagent model is employed for computational experiments for system evolutionary analysis, implemented by changing some of the behavioral dynamics (e.g. like capital requirements for macroprudential policy [2]) or some of the environmental parameters (e.g. tax rates for fiscal policies [3]). In what follows, we will explore these four steps in more detail.

The starting point of most agent models is the identification of a set of micro and macro stylized behaviors/facts and empirical regularities (e.g. static or dynamic correlations, empirically observed distributions, etc.). For the sake of generality, let us define as a stylized behavior any possible type of measurable action sequences that can be investigated by means of some social experiments or more generally by statistical techniques. In such action sequences, the causal generating mechanism, or data generating process, is unclear or too complex to be explained by a simple, low-dimensional system of dynamic equations. Examples of micro and macro stylized behaviors that have been empirically identified and replicated by means of agents in different fields encompass fat-tailed distributions of returns, long-run coexistence of heterogeneous investing rules in economic activities, etc.

After having singled out a set of possibly interlinked stylized behaviors, one can try to find an explanation of the underlying causal forces, i.e. learning and describing the exact form of the real-world data generation process, or at least a sufficiently accurate approximation of it. This is the ultimate objective of any agent model. The great advantage of agent models in contrast with traditional ones derives from its generative bottom-up approach genuinely rooted in evolutionary, complex-system theories [4]. This indeed allows the researcher to keep into account the complex dynamics of a system that is populated by heterogeneous and boundedly rational agents possessing a partial and possibly biased amount of information about the global system in which they live. However, agents are adaptive and learn in order to survive and prosper in such an uncertain framework following some forms of "bounded rationality" satisfying principle [5]. Obviously, also when agents are developed to approximate the real-world human counterparts, the number of degrees of freedom is high and different researchers can follow alternative routes according to their different expertise, backgrounds, and theoretical hypothesis about the underlying generating process.

After the modeler has specified the behavioral dynamics of the actors populating the system, the agent takes the form of a high-dimensional, discrete-time stochastic process. Indeed, a part of the artificial intelligence community has strongly relied on Markov processes theory and on statistical physics tools in order to reduce the dimensionality of the model and eventually – under specific circumstances – to analytically solve the simplest model [6]. But in general, as their complexity is high, agents are usually simulated by means of extensive

Monte Carlo (MC) exercises in which the random seed is modified along the MC dimension. Once such MC exercises are performed and the synthetic data collected, the researcher can verify whether the model is able to generate reasonable behaviors, which are not statistically significantly different from the ones previously observed in real world. Naturally, all these reasonable behaviors can be related to micro and macro variables.

Once the agent model has been validated and proved to be able to account for the micro and macro empirical regularities under study, it can then be employed as a virtual laboratory. Indeed, the impact of different management strategies or policies in alternative scenarios can be studied by (i) varying some parameters, in particular those related to policy-maker interventions or to some broad institutional setting (e.g. tax rates); (ii) modifying initial conditions related to agents' state variables (e.g. income distribution, vehicular allocation ratio); (iii) changing some agents' behavioral rules and interaction patterns (accounting e.g. for different market set-ups); and (iv) introducing macro and/or micro heterogenous shocks (e.g. emergent events or climate-damages shocks). These can be interpreted as exogenous environmental changes, which allow a researcher to evaluate their effects in a fully controllable experiment, where treatment effects can be easily identified, and endogeneity issues are almost absent.

By linking the virtual agent and its corresponding human user, controllable computational experiments can be conducted in an online mode, and the local behavioral prescription for the human participant is dynamically pushed to influence his deliberations and decisions. The background global experiments could investigate how to decompose the global objective into local ones for human participants. Even some of these local behavioral prescriptions might be nonoptimal (e.g. nonshortest travel path for a part of travelers), their aggregate results conform to the desired global equilibrium. Moreover, recent tremendous improvement in computational power has been able to support the constant online experiments throughout the task. And it results in an interactive "detection, experiment, prescription" cycle for real-time optimization.

7.2 Calibration Based on Optimization

As alluded in Section 7.1, calibration and validation (also called estimation in some literature) typically refer to the process that the agent is adjusted to keep its output approximate to realistic stylized behaviors within an acceptable error. Such stylized behaviors in a quantitative way are often represented by empirical evidence gathered from social experiments, case studies, inductive analyses, or more directly, by a set of aggregate statistics. Limited by the sample scale, the empirical evidence usually covers only a small part of population. Thus calibration based on this type of data cannot avoid bringing sample bias which causes the emergent behaviors very likely to deviate from the actual system. As such, using the aggregate statistics directly is considered to be more convincing since it is easier to control for macro phenomenon reproduction. Naturally, minimization of the distance between the aggregation of agents' output and the actual observed counterpart is a feasible direction. According to this idea, the calibration process can be viewed as an optimization problem

$$\theta^* = \arg\min_{\theta} D(Y^R, Y^A, \theta)$$

where Y^R, Y^A, θ stand for the selected moments from realistic data, the selected moments from artificial results and the parameter set, respectively. D is the distance function of the real and artificial moments. The consistency and efficiency of the parameter estimation strongly depend on how well the moment functions approximate. In most cases, however, the moment function is completely unknown, and the aggregation of Y^A from heterogeneous agents does not have analytical forms either. Thus, it is usually calculated by simulation techniques, such as the Monte Carlo simulation, stochastic searching with heuristics, and evolutionary computing. Accordingly, these approaches lead to similar methods like the generalized method of moments (GMM) [7], method of simulated moment (MSM) [8], simulated minimum distance (SMD) [9–11], and simulated maximum likelihood (SML) [12]. Here we take the SML as an example to introduce the calibration in detail.

The method is originally developed for economic behaviors. Consider an asset pricing model with one risky and one risk-free asset. The wealth dynamics of each agent is of the following form

$$W_{t+1} = RW_{t+1} + (p_{t+1} + y_{t+1} - Rp_t)z_t \tag{7.1}$$

where W_{t+1} denotes the total wealth at time $t + 1$. The risk-free asset is perfectly elastically supplied at a fixed gross rate $R = 1 + r$, i.e. r stands for the constant risk-free interest rate. p_t and $\{y_t\}$ denote the ex-dividend price per share of the risky asset at time t and its stochastic dividend process, respectively. Lastly, z_t represents the amount of shares of the risky asset purchased at time t. The utility of each agent is given by an exponential-type constant absolute risk aversion (CARA) utility function $U(W) = -\exp(-aW)$, where $a > 0$ is a risk-aversion parameter. The Walrasian auction scenario for setting the market clearing price is assumed, i.e. p_t makes demand for the risky asset equal to supply and agents are "price takers." Suppose there are $H \in \mathbb{N}$ different trading strategies available to agents. Let E_t, V_t denote the conditional expectation and conditional variance operators. $E_{h,t}, V_{h,t}$ then represent beliefs of agent class $1 < h < H$ that uses trading strategy h about the conditional expectation and conditional variance of wealth based on a publicly available information set $\mathcal{F}_t = \{p_t, p_{t-1}, \ldots; y_t, y_{t-1}, \ldots\}$. For analytical tractability, beliefs about the conditional variance of excess returns are assumed to be constant, i.e. $V_{h,t}(p_{t+1} + y_{t+1} - Rp_t) = \sigma^2$, implying conditional variance of total wealth $V_{h,t}(W_{t+1}) = z_t^2 \sigma^2$. Assuming myopic mean-variance maximization, the optimal demand for the risky asset $z_{h,t}$ for each agent class h solves:

$$\max_{z_t} \left\{ E_{h,t} \left[W_{t+1} \right] - \frac{a}{2} V_{h,t} \left[W_{t+1} \right] \right\} \tag{7.2}$$

Therefore,

$$E_{h,t} \left[p_{t+1} + y_{t+1} - Rp_t \right] - a\sigma^2 z_{h,t} = 0 \tag{7.3}$$

$$z_{h,t} = \frac{E_{h,t} \left[p_{t+1} + y_{t+1} - Rp_t \right]}{a\sigma^2} \tag{7.4}$$

Let $n_{h,t}$ denote fractions of agents of classes $h \in 1, \ldots, H$ at time t satisfying $\sum_{h=1}^{H} n_{h,t} = 1$. Let $z_{s,t}$ be the overall supply of outside risky shares per all agents. The Walrasian temporary market equilibrium for the risky asset then yields

$$\sum_{h=1}^{H} n_{h,t} \cdot z_{h,t} = \sum_{h=1}^{H} n_{h,t} \cdot \left\{ \frac{E_{h,t} \left[p_{t+1} + y_{t+1} - Rp_t \right]}{a\sigma^2} \right\} = z_{s,t} \tag{7.5}$$

In a specific case of zero supply of outside risky shares, $z_{s,t} = 0$, $\forall t$, the market equilibrium satisfies:

$$Rp_t = \sum_{h=1}^{H} n_{h,t} \cdot \left\{ E_{h,t} \left[p_{t+1} + y_{t+1} \right] \right\} \tag{7.6}$$

In a completely rational market assuming all agents identical with homogeneous expectations, p_t is completely determined by fundamentals and Eq. (7.6) thus reduces to $Rp_t = E_t \left[p_{t+1} + y_{t+1} \right]$. The price of the risky asset is then given by the discounted sum of its future dividend cash flow:

$$p_t^* = \sum_{k=1}^{\infty} \frac{E_t \left[y_{t+k} \right]}{(1+r)^k} \tag{7.7}$$

where p_t^* denotes the fundamental price depending upon the stochastic dividend process $\{y_t\}$. The fundamental price provides an important benchmark for asset valuation under rational expectations based on economic fundamentals. In a specific case of an independent identically distributed (i.i.d.) process, $\{y_t\}$, $E_t \{y_{t+1}\} = \bar{y}$ is a constant. All agents are then able to derive p_t^* by the simple formula:

$$p_t^* = \sum_{k=1}^{\infty} \frac{\bar{y}}{(1+r)^k} = \frac{\bar{y}}{r} \tag{7.8}$$

For the subsequent analysis, it is convenient to work with the deviation x_t from p_t^* instead of price levels:

$$x_t = p_t - p_t^* \tag{7.9}$$

A key point of the model is the existence of heterogeneous beliefs about future prices. Beliefs can be represented as the procedural knowledge (reasoning rules) elucidated in Chapters 5 and 6. But here we model it via an analytical form since our discussion focuses on the method of parameter calibration. The method can be easily extended into more complex scenarios – the reasoning rules. Assume beliefs of individual agent classes are:

$$E_{h,t}\left(p_{t+1} + y_{t+1}\right) = E_t\left(p_{t+1}^* + y_{t+1}\right) + f_h(x_{t-1}, \dots, x_{t-L}), \quad \forall\, h, t \tag{7.10}$$

where $E_t\left(p_{t+1}^* + y_{t+1}\right)$ denotes the conditional expectation of the fundamental price based on the information set $\mathcal{F}_t$. f_h is a deterministic function which can differ across agent classes h and represents an "h-type" trading strategy, and L indicates the number of lags. The beliefs about future dividends flow following Eq. (7.10) is

$$E_{h,t}\left(y_{t+1}\right) = E_t\left(y_{t+1}\right), \quad h = 1, \dots, H \tag{7.11}$$

are the same for all agents and equal to the true conditional expectation. On the other hand, agents' heterogeneous beliefs about future price abandon the perfect rationality paradigm, which is crucial step toward the heterogeneous agent modeling. f_h allows individual agents believe that the market price will differ from the fundamental value p_t^* and thus the form of beliefs:

$$E_{h,t}\left(p_{t+1}\right) = E_t\left(p_{t+1}^*\right) + f_h(x_{t-1}, \dots, x_{t-L}), \quad \forall\, h, t \tag{7.12}$$

allows prices to deviate from their fundamental value.

The heterogeneous market equilibrium from Eq. (7.6) can thus be reformulated in the deviations form and conveniently used in empirical and experimental testing. Combining Eqs. (7.9), (7.10) and $\sum_{h=1}^{H} n_{h,t} = 1$, we obtain:

$$Rx_t = \sum_{h=1}^{H} n_{h,t} \cdot E_{h,t}\left[x_{t+1}\right] = \sum_{h=1}^{H} n_{h,t} \cdot f_h(x_{t-1}, \dots, x_{t-L}) \equiv \sum_{h=1}^{H} n_{h,t} \cdot f_{h,t} \tag{7.13}$$

where $n_{h,t}$ represent values related to the beginning of period t, before the equilibrium price deviation x_t is observed. The actual market clearing price p_t might then be calculated simply using Eq. (7.9).

Beliefs of agents are updated during evolution according to endogenous adaptive belief system and exogenous factors. In economic behaviors, the exogenous factors are driven by the market forces. The adaptive belief system is an expectation feedback system in which variables depend partly on the known values and partly on the future expectations. The profitability measures for strategies $h \in 1, \dots, H$ are derived from past realized profits as:

$$U_{h,t} = (x_t - Rx_{t-1}) \frac{f_{h,t-1} - Rx_{t-1}}{a\sigma^2} \tag{7.14}$$

Market fractions $n_{h,t}$ of agent classes $h \in 1, \ldots, H$ are derived under the discrete choice probability framework using the multinomial logit model:

$$n_{h,t} = \frac{\exp(\beta U_{h,t-1})}{\sum_{h=1}^{H} \exp(\beta U_{h,t-1})} \tag{7.15}$$

where the lagged timing of $U_{h,t-1}$ ensures that all information for updating of market fractions $n_{h,t}$ is available at the beginning of period t and $\beta \geq 0$ is the intensity of choice parameter measuring how fast are agents willing to switch between different trading strategies.

With the notion that only very simple forecasting rules can have a real impact on equilibrium prices because complicated strategies are unlikely to be understood and followed by a sufficient number of traders, trading strategies thus have a simple linear form:

$$f_{h,t} = g_h x_{t-1} + b_h \tag{7.16}$$

where g_h denotes the trend parameter and b_h is the bias parameter of the trading strategy h.

The first agent class is fundamentalists. They believe that the asset prices are determined solely by economic fundamentals according to the efficient market hypothesis. Therefore, the price can be simply computed as the present value of the discounted future dividends flow. Fundamentalists also believe that prices always converge to their fundamental values. In the heterogeneous agent model, fundamentalists comprise the special case of Eq. (7.16) with $g_h = b_h = f_{h,t} = 0$. The fundamental strategy has completed past market prices and dividends in its information set $F_{h,t}$. The fundamentalists' demand also reflects the market actions of other agent classes, but fundamental traders are not aware of the fractions $n_{h,t}$ of other trading strategies. Fundamentalists might pay costs $C \geq 0$ to obtain market information and to understand how economic fundamentals work. However, some scholars mostly set $C = 0$ to keep simplicity of the analysis [13]. Another agent class represents chartists. They believe that asset prices can be partially predicted taking various patterns observed in the past data into account, e.g. using simple technical trading rules and extrapolation techniques. If $b_h = 0$, trader h is called a pure trend chaser if $0 < g_h \leq R$ and a strong trend chaser if $g_h > R$. Next, the trader h is called a contrarian if $-R \leq g_h < 0$ or a strong contrarian if $g_h < -R$. If $g_h = 0$, trader h is considered to be purely upward biased if $b_h > 0$ or purely downward biased if $b_h < 0$. Combined trading strategies with $g_h \neq 0$ and $b_h \neq 0$ are certainly also possible.

Given the multiagent model explained before, now let us go on to the agent calibration. Let us assume the process (x, v), $x : t \rightarrow \mathbb{R}^k$, $v : t \rightarrow \mathcal{V}_t$, $t = 1, \ldots, \infty$ with time-varying $\mathcal{V}_t$ and we have T realizations $\{(x_t, v_t)\}_{t=1}^{T}$. Let us further assume the time series $\{x_t\}_{t=1}^{T}$ are generated by a fully parametric model:

$$x_t = q_t(v_t, \varepsilon_t, \theta), \quad t = 1, \ldots, T \tag{7.17}$$

where a function $q : v_t, \varepsilon_t, \theta \rightarrow \mathbb{R}^k$, $\theta \in \Theta \subseteq \mathbb{R}^l$ is an unknown parameter vector, and ε_t is an i.i.d. sequence with known distribution $\mathcal{D}_\varepsilon$, which is (without loss of generality) assumed not to depend on t or θ. In general, the processes (x, v) can be nonstationary and v_t is allowed to contain other exogenous variables than lagged x_t. We also assume the model to have an associated conditional density $c_t(x|v; \theta)$, i.e.

$$C(x \in A|v_t = v) = \int_A c_t(x|v; \theta)dx \tag{7.18}$$

For any Borel set $A \subseteq \mathbb{R}^k$.

Let us now suppose that $c_t(x|v; \theta)$ from Eq. (7.18) does not have a closed-form representation. In such a situation, we are not able to derive the exact likelihood function of the model in Eq. (7.17) and thus a natural estimator of θ, the maximizer of the conditional log-likelihood

$$\tilde{\theta}_{ML} = \arg\max_{\theta \in \Theta} \mathcal{L}_T(\theta), \quad \mathcal{L}_T(\theta) = \sum_{t=1}^{T} \log c_t(x_t|v_t; \theta) \tag{7.19}$$

is not feasible. In such situation, however, we are still able to simulate observations from the model in Eq. (7.17) numerically. The method presented allows us to compute a simulated conditional density, which we further use to gain a simulated version of the MLE.

To obtain a simulated version of $c_t(x_t|v_t; \theta)$ $\forall t \in < 1, \dots, T >, x \in \mathbb{R}^k, v \in \mathcal{V}_t$, and $\theta \in \Theta$, we firstly generate $N \in \mathbb{N}$ i.i.d. draws from $\mathcal{D}_\varepsilon, \varepsilon_i{}_{i=1}^N$, which are used to compute:

$$X_{t,i}^\theta = q_t(v_t, \varepsilon_i, \theta), \quad i = 1, \dots, N \tag{7.20}$$

These N simulated i.i.d. random variables, $\{X_{t,i}^\theta\}_{i=1}^N$, follow the target distribution by construction: $X_{t,i}^\theta$ $c_t(\cdot|v_t; \theta)$, and therefore can be used to estimate the conditional density $c_t(x|v; \theta)$ with kernel methods. We define:

$$\hat{c}_t(x_t|v_t; \theta) = \frac{1}{N} \sum_{i=1}^{N} K_\eta(X_{t,i}^\theta - x_t) \tag{7.21}$$

where $K_\eta(\psi) = K(\psi/\eta)/\eta^k, K : \mathbb{R}^k \rightarrow \mathbb{R}$ is a generic kernel and $\eta > 0$ is a bandwidth. Under regularity conditions on c_t and K, we get:

$$\hat{c}_t(x_t|v_t; \theta) = c_t(x_t|v_t; \theta) + O_P(1/\sqrt{N\eta^k}) + O_P(\eta^2), \quad N \rightarrow \infty \tag{7.22}$$

where the last two terms are $O_P(1)$ if $\eta \rightarrow 0$ and $N\eta^k \rightarrow \infty$. Having obtained the simulated conditional density $\hat{c}_t(x_t|v_t; \theta)$ from Eq. (7.21), we can now derive the simulated MLE of θ:

$$\hat{\theta}_{SMLE} = \arg\max_{\theta \in \Theta} \hat{\mathcal{L}}_T(\theta), \quad \hat{\mathcal{L}}_T(\theta) = \sum_{t=1}^{T} \log \hat{c}_t(x_t|v_t; \theta) \tag{7.23}$$

The same draws are used for all values of θ and we may also use the same set of draws from $\mathcal{D}_\varepsilon(\cdot), \{\varepsilon_i\}_{i=1}^N$, across t. Numerical optimization is facilitated if $\hat{\mathcal{L}}_T(\theta)$ is continuous and differentiable in θ. Considering Eq. (7.21), if K and $\theta \to q_t(v, \varepsilon, \theta)$ are $s \geq 0$ continuously differentiable, the same holds for $\hat{\mathcal{L}}_T(\theta)$. Under the regularity conditions, the fact that $\hat{c}_t(x_t|v_t; \theta) \xrightarrow{P} c_t(x_t|v_t; \theta)$ implies that also $\hat{\mathcal{L}}_T(\theta) \xrightarrow{P} \mathcal{L}_T(\theta)$ as $N \to \infty$ for a given $T \geq 1$. Thus, the simulated MLE, $\hat{\theta}_{SMLE}$, retains the same properties as the infeasible MLE, $\tilde{\theta}_{ML}$, as $T, N \to \infty$ under suitable conditions.

Overall, there are several advantages and disadvantages of the simulated MLE estimator. Starting with the former, the estimator works whether the observations x_t are i.i.d. or nonstationary because the density estimator based on i.i.d. draws is not affected by the dependence structures in the observed data. Second, the estimator does not suffer from the curse of dimensionality, which is usually associated with kernel estimators. In general, high-dimensional models, i.e. with larger $k \equiv dim(x_t)$ as we smooth only over x_t here, require larger number of simulations to control the variance component of the resulting estimator. However, the summation in Eq. (7.23) reveals an additional smoothing effect and the additional variance of $\hat{\mathcal{L}}_T(\theta)$ caused by simulations retains the standard parametric rate $1/N$.

Conversely, the simulated log-likelihood function is a biased estimate of the actual log-likelihood function for fixed N and $\eta > 0$. To obtain consistency, we need $N \to \infty$ and $\eta \to 0$. Thus, the parameter η needs to be properly chosen for given sample and simulation size. In the stationary case, the standard identification assumption is:

$$\mathbb{E}[\log c(x_t|v_t; \theta)] < \mathbb{E}[\log c(x_t|v_t; \theta_0)], \quad \forall \theta \neq \theta_0 \tag{7.24}$$

Under stronger identification assumptions, the choice of the parameter η might be less important and one can prove the consistency of the estimator for any fixed $0 < \eta < \bar{\eta}$ for some $\bar{\eta} > 0$ as $N \to \infty$ [14]. In practice, this still requires us to know the threshold level $\bar{\eta} > 0$ but from the theoretical viewpoint this ensures that parameters can be well identified in large finite samples after a given $\bar{\eta} > 0$ is set. Moreover, it suggests that the proposed methodology is fairly robust to the choice of η. Later studies show that simulated MLE performs indeed well using a broad range of bandwidth choices [15].

Before end of this section, we now have a glimpse of the asymptotic properties of the method. As the theoretical convergence of the simulated conditional density toward the true density is met, we would expect the $\hat{\theta}_{SMLE}$ to have the same asymptotic properties as the infeasible $\tilde{\theta}_{ML}$ for a properly chosen sequence $N = N(T)$ and $\eta = \eta(N)$. Fortunately, $\hat{\theta}_{SMLE}$ is proved to be first-order asymptotic equivalent to $\tilde{\theta}_{ML}$ under a set of general conditions, allowing even for nonstationary and mixed discrete and continuous distribution of the response variable. Further, using additional assumptions, including stationarity, they provide results regarding the higher order asymptotic properties of $\hat{\theta}_{SMLE}$ and derive expressions of the bias and variance components of the $\hat{\theta}_{SMLE}$ compared to the actual MLE due to kernel approximation and simulations. Therefore, a set of general conditions, satisfied by most models, need to be verified so that $\hat{c} \to c$ sufficiently fast to ensure asymptotic equivalence of $\hat{\theta}_{SMLE}$ and $\tilde{\theta}_{ML}$. The regularity conditions and its associated conditional density that satisfy these general conditions for uniform rates of kernel estimators are defined in [16].

The kernel K from Eq. (7.21) has to belong to a broad class of so-called bias high-order or bias-reducing kernels, e.g. the Gaussian kernel satisfies this condition if $r \geq 2$, where r is the number of derivatives of c. Higher r causes faster rate of convergence and determines the degree of $\hat{c}$ bias reduction. Moreover, general versions of conditions usually required for consistency and well-defined asymptotic distribution (asymptotic normality) of MLEs in stationary and ergodic models are imposed on actual log-likelihood function and the associated MLE to ensure the actual $\tilde{\theta}_{ML}$ in Eq. (7.19) is asymptotically well-behaved.

7.3 Calibration Based on Machine Learning

Section 7.2 addresses agent calibration using optimization method. They mostly deal with this problem by minimizing an arbitrarily defined distance between the real and artificial moments. As the objective function directly relates the evaluation criterion, this calibration method is easy to control. However, since the moment selection is arbitrary, different choices may result in different parameter estimations. This section will discuss a second approach, using machine learning techniques. This line of work introduced a surrogate modeling approach to facilitate parameter space exploration and sensitivity analyses. Its spatial interpolation estimates the agent response over the full parameter space from finite samples, to generate the best unbiased predictor through knowledge of the true variogram or true degree of spatial dependence in the data. It also shows that reducing computational time can be achieved in a meaningful way by efficiently training a surrogate model over multiple rounds to approximate the mapping between the agent's perception and its response to a user-defined calibration criterion.

The main idea of the calibration is to propose an iterative algorithm to efficiently approximate a surrogate model for any agent using a limited budget $B \in \mathbb{N}$ of evaluations. Once this budget is reached, the surrogate's approximation is completed, and it is available to provide a nearly costless approach to predict the original agent's response. In all generality, one can represent an agent model as a mapping $m : I \to O$ from a set of input parameters I into an output set O. The set of parameters can be conceived as a multidimensional space spanned by the support of each parameter. Usually, the number of parameters go from 1 or 2 to few dozens, as in large decision models. The output set is generally larger, as it corresponds to time-series realizations of a very large number of states and actions. This rich set of outputs allows a qualitative validation of agent models based on their ability to reproduce the statistical properties of empirical data (e.g. cross-correlations and relative volatilities of statistical trend), as well as micro distributional characteristics (e.g. distribution of group size). Beyond stylized behaviors, the quantitative validation of an agent model also requires the calibration/estimation of the model on a (generally small) set of aggregate variables (e.g. the growth rates of system scale, average interactions of agents etc.). In practice, such a quantitative calibration consists in the determination of input values such that the output satisfies certain calibration conditions, coming from, e.g. a statistical hypothesis test or the evaluation of a likelihood or loss function. This is in line with the method of optimization. The assessment of a model's output is carried out by computing a specific indicator, which is called the calibration measure. We consider two settings here. The first is the binary outcome where calibration measure might take just two values: 1 if a certain property (or set of properties) on the output is satisfied, or 0 otherwise. For example, we might want to test whether a financial multiagent system shows excess kurtosis in the distribution of simulated returns. The second is real-valued outcome, where calibration measure is a real-valued number providing a quantitative assessment of a certain property of the model. For example, we might want to compute excess kurtosis of simulated data.

Clearly, one would like to find the set of input parameters $x \in I$ such that the calibration measure satisfies certain conditions, which we call calibration criteria. The choice of such criteria is crucial, as it determines the fitness of the model with the empirical data or properties of interest. In this sense, simulated moment and distance function defined in Section 7.2 are the calibration measure and calibration criterion here. To continue our discussion, consider a set of non-normal time-series realizations of a multiagent system. Further, assume that non-normality is measured through negative skew and excess kurtosis, which are then identified as our calibration measures. Once the agents generate the time series, both the skew and kurtosis are computed. In the classification outcome setting, the calibration criterion might simply require the presence of both excess kurtosis and negative skew. In the real-valued outcome setting, instead, the calibration criterion might involve the comparison of the computed calibration measures with specified thresholds, with the empirical counterparts or with the same quantities computed for other parameter combinations. In particular, if we choose a calibration criterion requesting that the distance between simulated and actual observed skew and kurtosis be lower than all previously evaluated points, we would obtain the standard calibration problem of minimizing some loss function over the parameter space. In the following, positive and negative calibrations will be defined and then the surrogate training will be elucidated.

Definition 7.3.1 (Positive and Negative Calibration). A positive calibration is a parameter vector $x \in I$ such that model's output satisfies the calibration criterion, whereas one gets a negative calibration if the opposite occurs.

Assume that the calibration criterion takes the form of a simple sign test of the skew and the excess kurtosis. Positive calibrations must show a negative sign on the skew and positive one on the excess kurtosis. All other combinations of skew and kurtosis are negative calibrations. "Positive" and "negative" are what we call labels of the points in the parameter space. Then, the objective is to find all positive calibrations conditioned on a limited budget $B \in \mathbb{N}$ of evaluations. Positive calibrations may exist in multiple locations of the parameter space, potentially including those that are difficult-to-interpret conditions. Although agents are not designed to mirror every facet of system behaviors, they must provide reasonable results for those they have been designed for. Ultimately, one should assume that positive calibrations lie along several regions of the parameter space and may not sit solely along regions that are contiguous, or related to a meaningful interpretable phenomenon. In fact, it is usually supposed that there exist an increasing number of equivalent positive calibrations with the growing complexity of agent models. Finding these regions can be relevant, from the researcher's perspective, to evaluate the model's reliability and application domain.

An intuitive notion is that the topology of agent's response can be characterized by a smooth transition between regions of positive and negative calibrations. Unfortunately, this might also not be the case. Positive calibrations may exist in several regions of the space without much structure. It does not guarantee that neighboring points in the parameter space provide the same system dynamics as the baseline parameter setting. The multi-agent system might exhibit "knife-edge" properties, where the response can be described as having a discontinuous and clustered topology [17]. Taken this into account, one of the goals for surrogate calibration is to avoid assumptions on the response surface that is either smooth or non-smooth, contiguous or non-contiguous.

Overall, the surrogate training requires three preliminary settings:

1. Selection of the surrogate algorithm. A machine learning algorithm is essential to act as a surrogate for the original agent model. This selection should be very careful to avoid forcing unrealistic assumptions on the agent response by the machine learning model.
2. Selection of a fast uniform sampler. A sampling procedure to draw samples from the parameters space is also necessary in order to train the surrogate.
3. Selection of the surrogate performance measure. The user must choose an indicator to evaluate the performance of the surrogate.

With all the preliminary settings completed, the surrogate training proceeds in six steps. The training begins by first drawing a relatively large "pool" of parameter combinations, where each combination is a vector containing a value for each parameter. The drawing can adopt any standard sampling routine such as quasi-random Sobol sampling [18]. In contrast with other popular sampling techniques (Monte Carlo and Latin Hypercube sampling), Sobol sequences possess uniformity properties. Further, standard design of experiments is computationally expensive in high dimensional spaces and shows little or no advantage over random sampling. The pool constructed in this stage dictates the ability of the algorithm to learn a good surrogate model. As there is a trade-off between the approximation of the parameter space by the pool and the speed to obtain it, it is recommended to adopt faster sampler given the high computational cost of running the models.

After the parameter pool is constructed, in the second step, an initial set of samples is chosen at random from the pool. Evaluating these initial samples consists in running the selected parameter combinations through the agent model and use its output(s), together with the selected calibration measure and calibration criteria, to determine which of these combinations are positive or negative calibrations. The two steps constitute the initialization phase of calibration procedure.

In step III, a meta-model is learned over the initial labeled values in order to build the surrogate. Specifically, we approximate a surrogate by building a set of decision trees here to fit the labeled parameter combinations. The decision trees are implemented as XGBoost, which exploits the gradient boosting in machine learning for regression and classification problems. In the calibration, it ensembles simpler decision trees to aggregately improve the overall label prediction of points in the pool. Similar to other boosting methods, XGBoost builds the model in a stage-wise fashion but it further generalizes them by allowing optimization of an arbitrary differentiable loss function.

Step IV uses the surrogate model to predict the response over the parameter combinations in the pool, i.e. real-valued responses in the case of a calibration measure and a category in the case of a calibration criterion. Then, a small subset of unlabeled combinations is drawn from the pool in step V. These combinations are evaluated in the agent model, labeled according to the application of the calibration criterion and added to the set of labeled combinations within the pool in step VI. It is required to investigate two issues at this stage. One is how many new points should be sampled and the other is how to select them. Some studies show that the total number of additionally drawn parameter vectors is the logarithm of the budget [19]. Concerning the selection of new data points, the algorithm randomly chooses parameter combinations among those points with positive predictions. The procedure gradually increases true positives, while reducing false ones. If there are no new positive predictions in the current round, new points are added to the set of labeled combinations. In the absence of probabilities that predict a positive label, we use the uncertainty sampling [20]. Such method concentrates on the entropy of the distribution of existing labels, so that the sampling frequency of parameter combinations that are difficult to label correctly can be increased. By doing this, we can reduce the discrepancy between the regions that contain a manifold of interest (which are frequently sampled by the algorithm) and those where the surrogate tends to fail (which are more informative from the perspective of machine learning). Steps IV–VI are repeated until the budget of evaluations is reached.

The surrogate calibration shares with iterative Monte Carlo recursive sampling. By sampling predicted positive calibrations from a non-stationary approximation of the distribution of positive and negative calibrations in the parameter space, it aggregates informative samples for accurate predictive inference. On the other hand, other iterative Monte Carlo methods such as the Metropolis Hastings algorithm iteratively and directly sample the distribution at random, traversing along a Markov chain in hypothesis until enough samples have been generated to reach the stationary distribution. This elicits several differences. First, the surrogate approach does not assume that a Markov chain underlies the sample sequence. Second, as each additional set of labeled samples changes the computation in each round, it does not assume that the approximated distribution is stationary over rounds. Third, there is no statistical priori made on the parameter distribution. Finally, the surrogate method deems a pool of unlabeled combinations from the parameter space as a proxy for the full population. It predicts the values of unlabeled combinations in the pool and then samples from the predictions, conditioned on a positive prediction. By contrast, classic iterative Monte Carlo methods directly complete the sampling and evaluation in each round. The total workflow of surrogate calibration is illustrated as Figure 7.1.

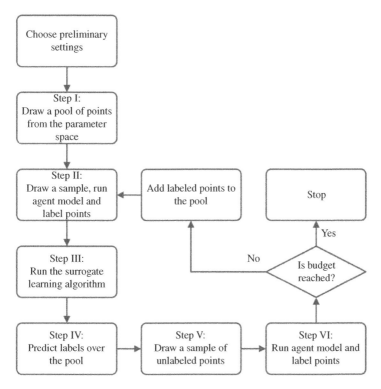

Figure 7.1 Workflow of surrogate calibration.

7.4 Calibration Based on Cybernetics

Given a set of empirical data or stylized behaviors, calibration based on optimization and machine learning is able to explore the parameter space and
ultimately determine their appropriate values. However, this approach is an
off-line process which would be conducted in a batch mode. It is not suitable for
dynamic scenarios, as the intermittent running of calibration may lose its time
validity in real-time simulation and the latest change of agent behavior which
should be reflected by adjusting the parameter values may be overwhelmed by the
large amount of historical data (particularly in the machine learning paradigm).
In addition, moment based optimization and surrogate learning both need a
heuristic search in the feasible parameter space. Thus, the model has to be run in
several cycles for parameter sampling and evaluation. This trial-and-error process
requires extensive computation especially when the number of parameters is
relatively large. To alleviate these problems, this section introduces a new calibration method based on cybernetics, which starts from the dynamics of the macro
multi-agent system and "inversely" calculates the parameter values. The overall
calibration process is illustrated as Figure 7.2. The main idea can be summarized
as follows. During each time step, the aggregate agent number of each state is
detected to construct a macro state transfer equation. Such an equation is solved
together with several previous steps to determine the state transfer matrix. Then,
agent micro state transfer probability is set to be the corresponding matrix element, so that its micro decision parameters can be calibrated via this constraint.
In the micro parameter computation, the mean-field approach from statistical
physics is used, which aims to use a mixed state to approximate the exogenous
dependencies for a given agent, and thus simplifies its interactions with the whole
system. In the following, the method is elaborated in two stages – the macro state
transfer computation and the micro parameter calibration.

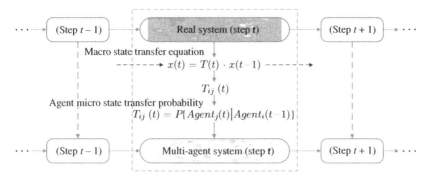

Figure 7.2 Dynamic calibration of multi-agent system.

Let us first address the macro state transfer computation. Consider a multi-agent system with a set of agents $A : \{a_i\}, i = 1, \ldots, |A|$. The notation $|A|$ means the cardinality of the set A. That is the number of agents in set A. The micro state of each agent is defined by a set of attributes which are represented as $< Nei(t), W(t) >$, where t is the time index, $Nei(t)$ represents the attributes that depend on his "neighbors" in his social networks (we call them social attributes), $W(t)$ represents the rest attributes that do not depend on his "neighbors" (we call them individual attributes). To model the randomness of one's state, a time variant stochastic factor $\xi(t)$ is usually added in practice. Therefore, each agent can be written as $a_i = a(t, Nei, W, \xi)$. Here we write the time index separately, but this does not change the attributes' time-variant property. To simplify the analysis, assume that all the attributes have finite discrete values, which can be also realized for continuous attributes by a piece-wise discretization.

Example 7.4.1   Consider a scenario of inter-city population migration. Assume the attributes related to one's migration behavior are age, city, income, location of family members and location of friends. Then we have $Nei(t) = \{famLoc(t),\ friLoc(t)\}$ which are determined by the agent's "neighbors" (here refer to his family members and friends) from social networks, and $W(t) = \{age(t), city(t)\}$ which are his individual attributes. To model the randomness, assume the variable $age(t)$ follows a stochastic process $\xi(t)$ such as the Gaussian process that can be achieved through the census statistical results. Thus each agent's age is computed by $\xi(t)$. Given a time index t, $Nei(t)$ and $W(t)$ will take a group of specific values in their feasible spaces, say $(t, famLoc, friLoc, age, city, \xi)$. Therefore, each agent a_i can be represented as $a_i = a(t, Nei, W, \xi) = a(t, famLoc, friLoc, age, city, \xi)$.

Define each combination of attribute values as a state. Based on the previous assumption, each agent has finite possible micro states, since the attributes $(famLoc, friLoc, age, city)$ are all discrete and have finite values. Let these states be ordered and N be the number of the states. In the aggregate (macro) level, define the system state as a vector $x(t) = \left[x_1(t) \ \cdots \ x_N(t)\right]^T$, where $x_i(t) \in \mathbb{R}$ stands for the expected number of agents with the ith micro state. Then the system state equation is represented as

$$\begin{cases} x(t) = T(t) \cdot x(t-1) \\ x(0) = x_0 \end{cases} \tag{7.25}$$

x_0 is the initial state of the system. $T(t) \in \mathbb{R}^{N \times N}$ is the state transfer matrix whose cell in the ith row and jth column is denoted as $T_{ij}(t)$. $T_{ij}(t)$ means the aggregate transfer probability from the agent micro state j to i. For system observation, let

$$y(t) = O[x(t)]$$

be the M-dimensional vector of detected metrics. Here we consider a linear measurement

$$y(t) = B(t) \cdot x(t) \tag{7.26}$$

where $B(t) \in \mathbb{R}^{M \times N}$ is called a measurement matrix. Denote the actual observation from the realistic system as $\hat{y}(t)$. The performance of the multi-agent system is defined as

$$J = \sum_{t=1}^{K} J(t) = \sum_{t=1}^{K} [y(t) - \hat{y}(t)]^T \cdot V \cdot [y(t) - \hat{y}(t)] \tag{7.27}$$

where K is the total number of observed steps and the positive symmetric matrix V represents the importance of each metric. Equations (7.25)–(7.27) can be viewed as a discrete calculus of variation problem.

The macro state transfer model above is intuitive. However, agent usually has quite a lot of possible states in practice, which means the dimension of $x(t)$ is very large. Hence, we need to compress the state space so that its computational complexity can be adaptive to limited computational resources. Given a time index t, let historical macro states be $X(t) = [x(0) \cdots x(t)]$. In particular, we use principal components analysis (PCA) to extract optimal projection axes

$$X(t) = P(t) \cdot Z(t) \tag{7.28}$$

where $P(t) \in \mathbb{R}^{N \times r}$ are principle component vectors and $Z(t) = [z(0) \cdots z(t)] \in \mathbb{R}^{r \times t}$ are the coordinate vectors. Subscribe the above decomposition into Eq. (7.25), the macro state transfer is converted into

$$\begin{cases} z(t) = P^\dagger(t) \cdot T(t) \cdot P(t) \cdot z(t-1) \\ z(0) = P^\dagger(0) \cdot x_0 \end{cases} \tag{7.29}$$

$P^\dagger(t)$ is the Moore–Penrose inverse of $P(t)$. Here, the number of principle components r is selected according to the available computational resources. The linear measurement in Eq. (7.26) is converted accordingly

$$y(t) = B(t) \cdot P(t) \cdot z(t) \tag{7.30}$$

By minimization of the performance, optimal trajectory z^* is obtained from Euler equation

$$\begin{cases} \frac{\partial J(t)}{\partial z(t)}|_{z=z^*} = 2[B(t)P(t)]^T V[B(t)P(t)z^*(t) - \hat{y}(t)] = 0 \\ z(0) = P^\dagger(0) \cdot x_0 \end{cases}$$

Since $B(t)$ and V are not zeros, $z^*(t)$ needs to solve by $B(t)P(t)z^*(t) = \hat{y}(t)$. By Eq. (7.29), this elicits

$$B(t) T(t) P(t) z(t-1) = \hat{y}(t), \quad \forall t = 1, \ldots, K \tag{7.31}$$

Note that in each step, we have r equations with $N \times N$ unknown variables (the cells of $T(t)$). In most applications, there is $r \leq M < N$ which means the feasible set of $T(t)$ is infinite if Eq. (7.31) has no contradictory equations. To solve $T(t)$ uniquely, our basic idea is to jointly consider observations from more than one step. Mathematically, if $K \geq \lceil N^2/r \rceil$ in Eq. (7.31), and for the first $\lceil N^2/r \rceil$ steps, $T(t) = T$ is assumed to be time-invariant, then there are

$$B(t) \cdot T \cdot P(t) \cdot z(t-1) = \hat{y}(k), \quad \forall t = 1, \dots, \lceil N^2/r \rceil \tag{7.32}$$

where notation $\lceil \cdot \rceil$ stands for the ceiling function. For every step $t \in \{1, \dots, \lceil N^2/r \rceil\}$, we have r equations. Thus the total number of equations in (7.32) is $r \cdot \lceil N^2/r \rceil \geq N^2$. On the other hand, all the unknown variables are contained in T which has $N \times N$ cells. Therefore, T can be solved numerically by the combination of the all equations from (7.32).

In theory, the lower bound $\lceil N^2/r \rceil$ gives the minimum observation steps for uniquely calculation of T. However, this is not a sufficient condition. If the rank of $B(t)$ in Eq. (7.32) is not full, then $\lceil N^2/r \rceil$ steps may not be enough and more observations are required. For $t > \lceil N^2/r \rceil$, $T(t)$ is computable analogously from step $(t - \lceil N^2/r \rceil)$ to step t, which means we maintain a $\lceil N^2/r \rceil$-step time window.

Basically, the joint consideration of multiple step observations aims to increase the constraint equations, so that $T(t)$ can be computed. However, this is not the only way to achieve such a goal. Rather, we are able to convert the equation solving into an optimization problem by introducing a suitable objective function. A typical metric is a particular distance like the Frobenius norm, and the optimization problem is

$$T^*(t) = \arg \min_{T(t)} \|T(t) - T(t-1)\|_F$$
$$s.t. \quad B(t)T(t)P(t)z(t-1) = \hat{y}(t)$$

where the solution $T^*(t)$ minimizes the variation between two adjacent state transfer probabilities.

We now come to the second stage – micro parameter calibration. Obviously, either the combination of multiple step observations or the conversion into an optimization problem can lead to a reasonable solution $T(t)$. And as mentioned before, $T_{ij}(t)$ represents the transfer probability from agent micro state $j \to i$. In the micro level, each agent from state j to i depends on four aspects: (i) the current values of his individual attributes; (ii) the current values of his social attributes and ultimately, the states of his neighbors; (iii) the agent's decision-making model or algorithms together with their parameters; and (iv) the stochastic factors. Thus, the conditional probability can be further written as

$$T_{ij}(t) = T\left\{a\left[t, Nei(t), W = w_j, \Theta(t), \xi\right] \mid a\left[t-1, Nei(t-1),\right.\right.$$
$$\left.\left. W = w_i, \Theta(t-1), \xi\right]\right\} \tag{7.33}$$

Here $\Theta(t)$ stands for the parameter set of decision-making algorithms, and the stochastic factors are assumed to be independent and identically distributed (i.i.d.).

Example 7.4.2 Continue with the previous example of inter-city population migration. If an agent has a state (state j)

$$a = a\left(t-1, famLoc = \{a_1.city, a_2.city, a_3.city\}\right.$$
$$friLoc = \{a_4.city, a_5.city, a_6.city\}, age = 26, city = Beijing, \xi\right)$$

which implies that he has three family members $\{a_1, a_2, a_3\}$ and three friends $\{a_4, a_5, a_6\}$. He will stochastically choose a city among all the locations of himself, his family members and his friends. The probabilities are $\Theta = p_0, p_1, \dots, p_6$ with $p_0 + p_1 + \cdots + p_6 = 1$ (This decision-making algorithm seems quite simple but is enough to explain our method). Suppose $a_1.city = Shanghai$, then from Eq. (7.30) the state transfer probability

$$T_{ij}(t) = T\left\{a\left[t, famLoc, friLoc, age = 27, city = Shanghai, \Theta, \xi\right]\right.$$
$$\left| a\left[t-1, famLoc, friLoc, age = 26, city = Beijing,\right.\right.$$
$$Theta = \{p_0, \dots, p_6\}, \xi\right]\right\} = p_1$$

Equation (7.30) establishes a link between the transfer probabilities of the system aggregate state and the agent micro state. Since the aggregate state is usually identifiable, such a link provides us a reasonable basis for the inference of agent decision parameters, $\{p_0, p_1, \dots, p_6\}$ in our above example. Given a ξ and w_i in step t, an agent's decision parameters depend on the states of his own and those of his "neighbors." While the individual attributes can be computed efficiently, the difficulty lies in the iterative check of his social networks. This is also the most complicated step in traditional ABM calibration, as social network scales may be quite large and may vary from agent to agent. For instance, in our above example, the agent may have four family members and five friends, which leads to the parameter set $\Theta = \{p_0, p_1, \dots, p_9\}$.

To model the social impact of neighbors, we propose to use a mean-field method to approximate one's exogenous impacts via an expectation equation. Consider all the agents that are with individual state w_i, written as $\{a \in A | a(t-1, w_i)\}$. The kth agent in this set, $a_k(t-1, w_i)$, has a set of neighbors $NB_k\left(t-1, w_i\right) = \{a_{k,1}, \dots, a_{k,|NB_k|}\}$. Let $z_k\left(t-1, w_i\right) = \{z_{k,1}, \dots z_{k,N}\}$ be the frequencies where $z_{k,i} > 0$ stands for the number of agents with the ith micro state (recall that there are totally N states). We introduce a virtual neighbor to approximate all the neighbors of the agent set $\{a \in A | a(t-1, w_i)\}$. Such a virtual neighbor has a mixed state of a distribution on all the micro states. It gets the ith micro state with a probability of $\frac{\sum_k z_{k,i}}{\sum_i \sum_k z_{k,i}}$ ($i = 1, 2, \dots, N$).

Example 7.4.3 Still continue with the previous example of inter-city population migration. Assume there are three agents with individual attributes $\{age = 26,$ $city = Beijing\}$, say $\{a_1, a_2, a_3\}$. And their neighbors are $\{a_{1,1}, a_{1,2}, a_{1,3}\}$, $\{a_{2,1}, a_{2,2},$ $a_{2,3}, a_{2,4}\}$, and $\{a_{3,1}, a_{3,2}, a_{3,3}, a_{3,4}, a_{3,5}\}$. As in our decision-making model, only the attribute city influences the agent's migration behavior. We assume their locations are $\{Beijing, Tianjin, Shanghai\}$, $\{Shanghai, Tianjin, Shanghai, Shanghai\}$, and $\{Tianjin, Tianjin, Beijing, Tianjin, Beijing\}$. Then a virtual neighbor with a distribution $\{Beijing : \frac{3}{12}, Tianjin : \frac{5}{12}, Shanghai : \frac{4}{12}\}$ is introduced to approximate the exogenous impacts for $\{a_1, a_2, a_3\}$. Therefore, for each agent in $\{a_1, a_2, a_3\}$, his migration destination will be $\{Beijing : p_0, Beijing :$ $\frac{3}{12}(1-p_0), Tianjin : \frac{5}{12}(1-p_0), Shanghai : \frac{4}{12}(1-p_0)\}$. The probabilities here are slightly changed so that the influences of different social networks can be distinguished. By Eq. (7.33), the parameter p_0 can be calibrated via the aggregate transfer probability $T_{ij}(t)$.

As can be seen, the mean-field approach uses aggregate social network distributions as a common pattern to approximate one's dependencies on others. Compared with the machine learning surrogate methods, where the multi-agent system is treated as a "black box" and must be repeatedly run with heuristically sampled parameters, our method investigates endogenous social patterns of the system and needs to be run only once. This "warm-start" calibration dynamically maintains a group of state equations from multi-step time window in memory, thus avoid the iterations of the whole system. Furthermore, in contrast with the traditional calibration methods, the mean filed approach goes deeper into the model by distinguishing the individual and social attributes. Such a more detailed perspective may bring a potential improvement of the agent model accuracy.

The two stages of our calibration based on cybernetics have been elaborated before. To conduct a deeper analysis, we would like to investigate the convergence of such method. The convergence is built upon the following assumptions:

1. Given all the interacting agents as a whole, the overall evolutionary trajectory of the system from a given initial state is invariant (but may involve some oscillations) in law for permutation of the agents without any exogenous force imposed;
2. For each given agent, the external forces that impact his evolution (or more specifically, his state transfer) all come from his social neighbors, and each neighbor in a particular type of social network imposes an equal contribution.

The first assumption is intuitive, which means the whole system is self-autonomous and all the interactions among agents are its internal forces that cannot change the systemic dynamics. The second assumption simplifies the social influences by treating all the neighbors equally. It can be easily extended as in reality one can have friends with different intimacies that lead to distinct personal impacts. Based on these assumptions, the following proposition indicates that the time-invariant version $T(t) = T$ will converge to the agent micro state transfer probability asymptotically.

Proposition 7.4.4 *Given a multi-agent system as Eqs. (7.25)–(7.27), let $Prob\{i|j\}$ be the agent micro state transfer probability from state j to state i at time t, and NA be the total number of agents, then there is $T_{ij} \longrightarrow Prob\{i|j\}$, s. t. NA $\longrightarrow +\infty$.*

Proof: Let $Freq\{s = a\} = \frac{NA\{s=a\}}{NA}$ be the frequency of the agent in state $\{s = a\}$. According to the law of large number, there is

$$\lim_{NA \to \infty} \frac{NA\{s = a\}}{NA} = \lim_{NA \to \infty} Freq\{s = a\} = Prob\{s = a\}$$

Therefore, in the calibration

$$T_{ij}(t) = \frac{NA\{s(t) = i, s(t-1) = j\}}{NA\{s(t-1) = j\}} = \frac{\frac{NA\{s(t)=i, s(t-1)=j\}}{NA}}{\frac{NA\{s(t-1)=j\}}{NA}}$$

$$= \frac{Freq\{s(t) = i, s(t-1) = j\}}{Freq\{s(t-1) = j\}}$$

By $NA \to \infty$, we have

$$\lim_{NA \to \infty} T_{ij}(t) = \lim_{NA \to \infty} \frac{Freq\{s(t) = i, s(t-1) = j\}}{Freq\{s(t-1) = j\}}$$

$$= \frac{Prob\{s(t) = i, s(t-1) = j\}}{Prob\{s(t-1) = j\}} = Prob\{i|j\} \qquad \square$$

Based on Proposition 7.4.4, T_{ij} can be viewed as an approximation of $Prob\{i|j\}$. This is the theoretical basis of our calibration. By using the mean-field approximation, the agent number in state i is actually computed by the expectation

$$x_i(t, \Theta) = \mathbb{E}_{Nei \sim NE} \left[T_{ij}(\Theta, Nei) \right] \cdot x_j(t-1, \Theta)$$

$$= \left[\sum_{Nei} T_{ij}(\Theta, Nei) \cdot \frac{x_j(t-1, \Theta)\{Nei\}}{x_j(t-1, \Theta)} \right] \cdot x_j(t-1, \Theta)$$

$$= \sum_{Nei} T_{ij}(\Theta, Nei) \cdot x_j(t-1, \Theta)\{Nei\}$$

where $x_j(t-1, \Theta)\{Nei\}$ means the number of agents with neighbor state $\{Nei\}$. The above formula indicates that our introduced virtual neighbor can approximate to the aggregation of the actual agent state transfer.

To validate the proposed calibration method, two computational experiments on Chinese nationwide population evolution and urban travel demand analysis are conducted. As a comparison, machine learning surrogate and optimization are also implemented as benchmarks. In the first population evolution experiment,

Table 7.1 Individual attributes.

Attributes	Values	Num. of values
Gender	Male, female	2
Age	0–5, ..., 95–100, ≥100	21
Residential city	Beijing, Shanghai, ...	361
Ethnic group	Han, MengGu, ...	58
Registration province	Beijing, Tianjin, ...	32
Marital status	Married, unmarried	2
Procreative status	Has child, not have child	2

annual population from 2000 to 2010 is selected to be simulated. Three types of data sources are used as the inputs. The first type is statistical marginal/partial joint frequencies from the fifth national census in 2000. Individual attributes are listed in Table 7.1. The second sort of input data is the disaggregate population sample, including 1,180,111 records. Each record covers both individual and household attributes (with private information omitted). These two types of inputs are used to generate the basic synthetic population in 2000. Noted that different from the reference, we have further fine-grained the spatial distribution of population in a city level. The third type of input data is the annual statistical yearbooks of 361 cities, which provide the average income, birth rate, death rate and other demographic characteristics. This information is used as the observed metrics in Eq. (7.26).

In the experiment, each agent decides whether to migrate to other cities by four decision factors: income, locations of other family members, his registration place, and his ethnic group [21]. SI_{Income}, the income of the agent, is initialized according to the normal distribution with the parameters being local income level. The personal income is only applicable for the employees and increases with the predefined regional economic growth. SI_{reg} represents the satisfaction of registration, which is calculated according to the well-known Schelling's model [22]:

$$SI_{reg} = \begin{cases} 1, & \textit{Locally Registered} \\ \frac{1}{dist(ResCity,RegCity)}, & \textit{Otherwise} \end{cases}$$

where *dist* means the distance between the agent's residential place and registration place. k is a constant that keeps $k/dist(ResCity, RegCity) \leq 1$. In particular, we set

$$k = \min_{ResCity \neq RegCity} dist(ResCity, RegCity)$$

Similarly, SI_{eth} means the satisfaction of ethnic group, which is only applicable for minorities and computed as

$$SI_{eth} = 1 - \frac{\#\langle ResCity \rangle}{|\langle City \rangle|}$$

where # means the rank of proportion of the same ethnic group in his residential city and $| \cdot |$ means the total number of cities. SI_{fam} is the agent's satisfaction from family members

$$SI_{fam} = \frac{|mem_{loc}|}{|mem|}$$

where $|mem_{loc}|$ is the number of members in the same city and $|mem|$ represents the total number of members.

Based on the four satisfactions, each agent will compute the relative satisfaction

$$S_i = SI_i - SAve_i - \delta_i$$

where the subscript i represents income, family, registration, or ethnic group factor. $SAve_i$ stands for the average level of his friends. Positive S_i means the agent is satisfied with current situation, while negative S_i means unsatisfied. δ_i is the tolerance which is randomly drawn from $(-0.1, 0.1)$. If the agent is radical, which means low tolerance of dissatisfaction, δ_i will be a positive real number. This indicates that his S_i is easier to reach negative. When the agent is conservative, δ_i will be a negative number and the situation is vice versa. The final decision is achieved by

$$S = \alpha \cdot S_{income} + \beta \cdot S_{fam} + \gamma \cdot S_{regist} + (1 - \alpha - \beta - \gamma) \cdot S_{ethnic}$$

where S_{income} is directly perceived and $S_{fam}, S_{regist}, S_{ethnic}$ are computed as before. The parameters $\alpha, \beta, \gamma, (\alpha + \beta + \gamma) \in [0, 1)$ quantitatively characterize one's attention that which aspects are more focused in his decision process. Like S_i, the sign of final satisfaction S determines whether the agent chooses to migrate (positive for stay and negative for migration). The parameters α, β, γ, $(\alpha + \beta + \gamma) \in [0, 1)$ are to be calibrated in our experiments.

During each iteration, the dynamic calibration using mean-field approach involves four steps: (i) collect aggregate population number in each city, which is the state vector $x(t - 1)$ in Eq. (7.28); (ii) given statistical observation $\hat{y}(t)$, solve the state transfer matrix $T(t)$ numerically. Here we let $x(t - 1)$ and $\hat{y}(t)$ have the same dimensions, thus $B(t) = I$ (Identity matrix); (iii) considering the birth and death rates, the system state equation Eq. (7.25) is rewritten as:

$$x(t) = T(t)x(t - 1) = Mig(t)x(t - 1) + Bir(t)x(t - 1) - Dea(t)x(t - 1)$$

where $Mig(t)$, $Bir(t)$, $and Dea(t)$ are the migration, birth, and death probabilities. In this formula, each row of $Mig(t)$ will be strictly normalized with a 1.0 sum. $Bir(t)$ and $Dea(t)$ are both diagonal matrices which represent each city's population increment; and (iv) for every city, collect each agent's exogenous dependencies from his social networks, and compute a universal mixed distribution. The exogenous dependencies here are represented as the four satisfactions of one's friends. And the universal approximation is the average satisfaction of all the agents in a given city. Then by Eq. (7.33), the parameters can be determined numerically.

To limit the complexity of computation, the scale factor is set to be 1000. That means the evolutionary system contains about 1.2 million agents with each agent mapping 1000 people in reality. For comparison, we also use decision tree as the surrogate to approximate the ABM system. Uniform sampling scheme is adopted to search the parameter values in the space: $\alpha, \beta, \gamma, (\alpha + \beta + \gamma) \in (0, 1)$. The parameter points are shown in Figure 7.3, in which the step length is set to be 0.1. The step length is determined according to our computational resources. The smaller step length is, the more simulations we need to run. As the 0.1 step length brings 84 parameter combinations and a more fine-grained search would lead to an unacceptable computational time, such a value is suitable.

After learning, the optimal values are $(0.3, 0.5, 0.1)$, with the relative error points drawn in Figure 7.4. The results are the average of 20 experiments. The relative error is computed as

$$err = \frac{1}{C} \sum_{i=1}^{C} \frac{|ActNum_i - SynNum_i|}{ActNum_i}$$

where *ActNum_i* and *SynNum_i* stand for actual number and synthetic number of population in the *i*th city. C is the city number. In the upper sub-figure, errors

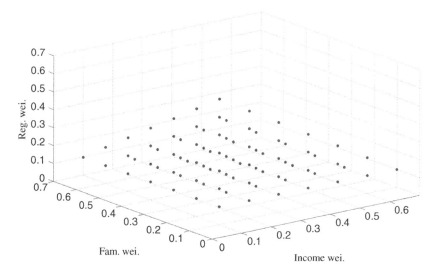

Figure 7.3 Parameter sample points.

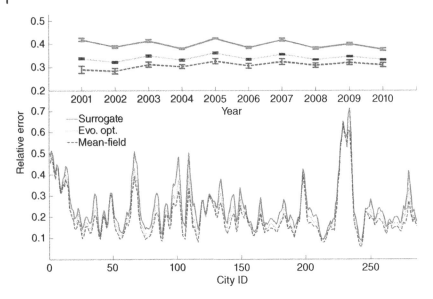

Figure 7.4 Relative error of three calibration methods for population evolution.

are aggregated by the each year, while the bottom sub-figure shows the errors aggregated by the each city. Clearly, error points are all scattered between 28% and 42%. Our method, however, gets lower average errors but larger standard deviations, which are quantitatively listed in Table 7.2. While the proposed method reduces annual errors by 3% around, its computational performance is far better than the other two (less than 1/3 of evolutionary optimization in Table 7.3). The basic reason is that our mean-field method is a dynamic calibration that is conducted during simulation, whereas the other two approaches iteratively run the ABM to heuristically search for optimal parameters. The latter trial-and-error process requires running the system many times and thus takes an expensive computational cost.

Our second experiment concentrates on a much smaller scaled scenario – urban traffic demand analysis by multiagent simulation. The experiment is based on the actual detected data from Chengdu, as configured in Chapter 6. Our studied time is from 6:00 to 24:00, which is split into 72 15-minute intervals. For each interval, all the travel paths between a given origin and destination node pair (OD pair) are computed. The most frequent three paths are used as the travel path candidates for each agent with the same OD pair. Therefore, given an OD pair represented as node *orig* and *dest*, each agent needs to select paths according to the following probability distributions

$$P\{path_1|orig, dest, k\} = \alpha_{orig-dest}$$
$$P\{path_2|orig, dest, k\} = \beta_{orig-dest}$$
$$P\{path_3|orig, dest, k\} = \gamma_{orig-dest}$$

Table 7.2 Average error and standard deviation of population evolution.

	Sur.		Evo. opt		Mean-field	
	Ave. (%)	Std.	Ave. (%)	Std.	Ave. (%)	Std.
2001	41.80	0.0063	33.72	0.0034	28.98	0.0156
2002	38.72	0.0054	32.16	0.0031	28.35	0.0118
2003	41.23	0.0057	34.84	0.0041	31.14	0.0107
2004	37.84	0.0032	33.05	0.0039	30.20	0.0082
2005	42.25	0.0020	36.15	0.0042	32.57	0.0115
2006	38.38	0.0046	33.36	0.0032	30.58	0.0102
2007	41.64	0.0065	35.49	0.0026	32.32	0.0122
2008	38.05	0.0050	33.17	0.0021	30.78	0.0097
2009	39.89	0.0057	34.59	0.0027	31.93	0.0104
2010	37.54	0.0055	33.15	0.0027	30.94	0.0090

Table 7.3 Computational performance of population evolution.

	Cal. and sim. time per exp.	Environment
Surrogate	18H 15M 16S	Software: Repast 2.6 (Java Version)
		OS: Windows 7 (x64)
Evo. opt.	15H 51M 40S	CPU: Intel Core i7-4790
		(8 cores, 3.6 GHz)
Mean-field	4H 55M 10S	RAM: 8 GB

where $path_i(i = 1, 2, 3)$ means the top 3 path candidates between *orig* and *dest*, and k is the time interval. Note that $\alpha_{orig-dest} + \beta_{orig-dest} + \gamma_{orig-dest} = 1$ ($\alpha, \beta, \gamma > 0$) which indicates that we ignore the other paths between the OD pair.

In aggregate level, link traffic counts are the observed measurement $\hat{y}(t)$ in Eq. (7.31). The population numbers in all traffic zones (related with nodes) are the state vector $x(t - 1)$. $B(t) = B$ is the path to link measurement matrix, determined by the road network topology and parameters (α, β, γ). For example, assume that in our abstract road network, the top 3 path candidates from node 21 to node 32 are $path_1$: 21-22-23-32, $path_2$: 21-29-30-31-32, and $path_3$: 21-30-31-32, with path selection probability ($\alpha_{21-32}, \beta_{21-32}, \gamma_{21-32}$). The first element of $\hat{y}(t)$ gives the traffic counts in link (30, 31). Then first row of $B(t)$ will start by $(\beta_{21-32} + \gamma_{21-32}, \dots)^T$, since ($\beta_{21-32} + \gamma_{21-32}$) of travel demand from node 21 to node 32 contributes to the flow in link (30, 31). $B(t)$ is also called the traffic assignment matrix. Therefore, $T(t)x(t - 1)$ in Eq. (7.31) actually stands for the origin-destination demand vector between all OD pairs, and $T(t) = \{t_{ij}(t)\}$ is the travel proportion from node j to i. Given enough observation steps, we are able to solve (α, β, γ) and $T(t)$ numerically via heuristic search, and further calibrate the agent parameters $(\alpha, \beta, \gamma, t_{ij})$.

Figure 7.5 shows the average errors of five experiments. The time intervals are numbered from 1 (6:00–6:15) to 72 (23:45–24:00) as the coordinates of X axis. Each error is computed similarly as population evolution

$$err = \frac{1}{L} \sum_{i=1}^{L} \left| \frac{ActCount_i - SynCount_i}{ActCount_i} \right|$$

where $ActCount_i$ and $SynCount_i$ are the observed link traffic counts from real system and the detected traffic counts from our agent-based system. L is the number of observed links. As can be seen, the errors decrease quickly at the beginning of simulation and then stay stable with weak oscillations. The reason of such phenomenon might be the vehicle numbers are quite small in the early morning, so that even a small deviation brings a large relative error. As travel demand increases, the errors keep stable at about 5%. Overall, our mean-field calibration receives a slightly higher accuracy than the machine learning surrogate approach, with the average errors being 6.14% and 7.06%. Figure 7.6 illustrates the root mean squared errors (RMSE), which also indicates that the mean-field method out performs the surrogate method. The average RMSE are 2352 and 2501, respectively, about 6% decrease in general.

For computational performance, the running time is listed in Table 7.4, where all of the experiments are run on the platform Simulation of Urban Mobility (SUMO) [23]. Clearly, mean-field calibration costs about 26 hours, while

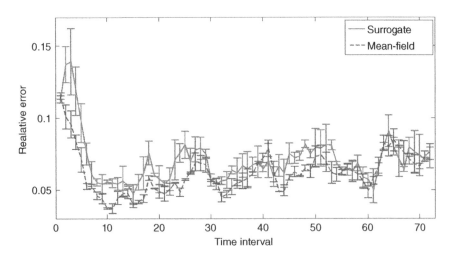

Figure 7.5 Relative error of two calibration methods for traffic demand analysis.

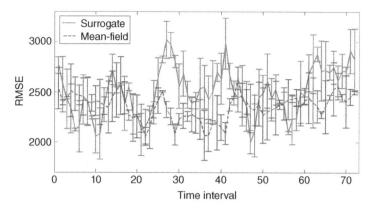

Figure 7.6 RMSE for traffic demand analysis.

Table 7.4 Computational performance of travel demand analysis.

	Surrogate	**Mean-field**
Cal. and sim. time per exp.	29 hour 36 min. 02 sec.	26 hour 01 min. 40 sec.
Environment	Software: SUMO 1.3.1 + Java 1.8 OS: Windows 7 (x64) CPU: Intel Core i7-4790 (8 cores, 3.6 GHz) RAM: 8 GB	

surrogate search takes nearly 30 hours. The reason behind still lies in the iterative trial-and-error process in surrogate calibration. In particular, eight parameter combinations that satisfy $\alpha \geq \beta \geq \gamma$ and $\alpha + \beta + \gamma = 1$ are attempted for every time interval, which leads to a replicate running of the ABM for surrogate learning. In general, our method only accounts for 88% of the surrogate method, meaning that a 12% improvement.

7.5 Calibration Using Variational Auto-Encoder

In Section 7.4, PCA is used to extract main state variables so that the transfer probability matrix is computed efficiently. While such a method has a certain effect on the calibration as proved by experiments mentioned before, one of its deficiencies lies in the determination of principal components. The basic idea of PCA is to project the state variables onto orthogonal axes so that the data information can be characterized by much fewer principal dimensions. The bridge between original data and projected principal representations is a linear transformation. Therefore, PCA can only decompose the linear correlations among samples, which limits its application in a high-order complicated scenario. To tackle this problem, we use variational auto-encoder (VAE) in this section to improve our calibration. VAE is one of the emerging techniques that is able to extract complex relationships among sample instances. The primary objective is to approximate the target distribution given by training samples (unknown) through a combination of predefined parameterized distributions, assuming that the training records are independent and identically distributed (i.i.d) in the target distribution (the i.i.d assumption is also a fundamental premise of the whole machine learning field). Parameters of the predefined distributions can be learned by a meticulously designed neural network. In such a way, the training data is well fitted with a model that can be further used to predict new instances. In practice, the predefined distributions are usually set to be Gaussian.

We still begin with the system model in Section 7.4 given by Eqs. (7.25)–(7.27). Since solving the state transfer probability is an underdetermined problem, we incorporate further constraints to relax it into an optimization for a unique solution as

$$T^*(t) = \arg\min_{T} \|B(t)T(t)x^*(t-1) - \hat{y}(t)\|_2 + \lambda\|t\|_1, \quad s.t.\ 0 \le T_{ij}(t) \le 1$$

(7.34)

where λ is a regularization parameter. Here, we use the L_2 and L_1 norms, but other types of norms are also applicable. The structure of our VAE neural network is illustrated in Figure 7.7, where the encoder learns a compressed representation in a latent space while the decoder completes an inverse task. At first, the system state vectors from adjacent time steps are encoded to achieve their embedded representations. This process relies on an encoder network with shared parameter values. Then, the state transfer equation in latent space is solved given the

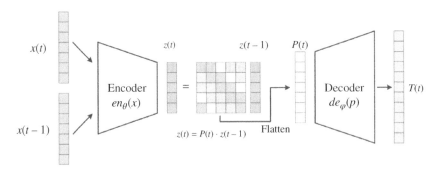

Figure 7.7 Structure of VAE network.

embedded states $z(t)$ and $z(t-1)$. Estimation of the latent state transfer probability is similar as $T(t)$:

$$P^*(t) = \arg\min_P \|P(t)z(t-1) - z(t)\|_2 + \lambda\|P(t)\|_1, \quad s.t.\ 0 \le P_{ij}(t) \le 1$$

$$(7.35)$$

As the dimension of compressed representation is much lower than the original one, such an optimization takes far less computational time to get a result. The achieved $P(t)$ is then flattened to the decoder, which transforms the latent state transfer probabilities into the original space. As such, $T_{ij}(t)$ is calculated in an efficient way. The training of the VAE network involves forward computation and backward propagation. The forward computation is explained in the last paragraph, as an "encoding, latent transfer probability solving, and decoding" process. Since the decoding step finally reconstructs state transfer probabilities in the original space, the backward propagation exploits a "real" label by directly solving Eq. (7.34). We adopt the loss of mean squared error as

$$loss = \mathbb{E}_{x \sim D(x)}[\|T(t) - T^*(t)\|_2]$$

where $D(x)$ is the training data set.

To analyze the VAE calibration method, we develop an agent-based simulation system based on the SUMO platform, and an external calibrator as explained in Section 7.4. The framework of our experiment system is illustrated in Figure 7.8.

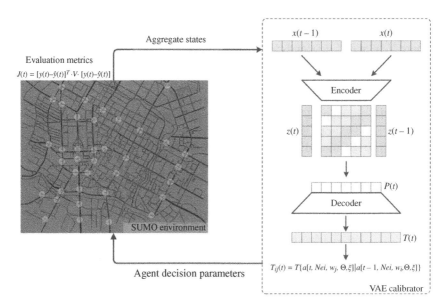

Figure 7.8 Framework of the VAE calibration system.

In every calibration interval, the SUMO simulation environment collects the number of agents in each micro state and sends aggregate results to the VAE calibrator. The calibrator computes the agent state transfer probabilities via a pre-trained VAE network and returns to the SUMO system. Then the simulation system changes each agent's travel parameters according to its received results. For evaluation, a certain number of sensors are set in the observable links to compare calibrated link flows with corresponding observed ones.

The data preprocessing before computational experiments is similar as before, including the deletion of three types of records: the abnormal records, the duplicates and the records from malfunctioned detectors. Our experiment time is still from 6:00 to 24:00, taking every 15 minutes as a calibration cycle. For each cycle, the calibrator estimates the total traffic flow between a given origin and destination node pair (OD pair). This estimation is according to Eq. (7.35) via the agent numbers $x(t-1)$ from SUMO and the pretrained VAE network. Then, the calibrator searches all the travel paths between a given origin and destination node pair (OD pair) and computes the path selection probability of each agent. The computation is as

$$T_{ij}(t) = \sum_k T_k\{a[t, Nei, W = j, \Theta, \xi] | a[t-1, Nei, W = i, \Theta, \xi]\}$$

where T_k means the assignment probability of the kth path from node i to node j. To get a unique solution, we further set each T_k to be proportional to the taxi path

$$\frac{T_k\{a[t, Nei, W = j, \Theta, \xi] | a[t-1, Nei, W = i, \Theta, \xi]\}}{\sum_k T_k\{a[t, Nei, W = j, \Theta, \xi] | a[t-1, Nei, W = i, \Theta, \xi]\}} = \frac{N_k\{W = j | W = i\}}{\sum_k N_k\{W = j | W = i\}}$$

where $N_k W = j | W = i$ stands for the number of taxi trajectories through path k.

The computational experiments are conducted for five times with identical settings. We use the same amount of data to train our VAE model and test the ultimate calibration effect. Figure 7.9 shows the training error of our VAE network, where the MSE loss is adopted. As can be seen, the loss gets nearly 240% at the beginning and rapidly drops while the training goes on. It decreases to nearly zero at the 120-th epoch around. The error curve also indicates that our training of VAE is steady as it is monotonic without oscillation.

Figure 7.10 shows the mean average errors (MAE) of five experiments. The time intervals are numbered from 1 to 72 as the coordinates of X axis, with each index standing for a 15-minute time span. Each error point is computed by

$$MAE = \frac{1}{L} \sum_{i=1}^{L} \left| \frac{ActCount_i - SynCount_i}{ActCount_i} \right|$$

where $ActCount_i$ and $SynCount_i$ are the observed link traffic counts from real system and the detected traffic counts from our SUMO simulation. L is the number of observable links. We also include two previous calibration methods, machine

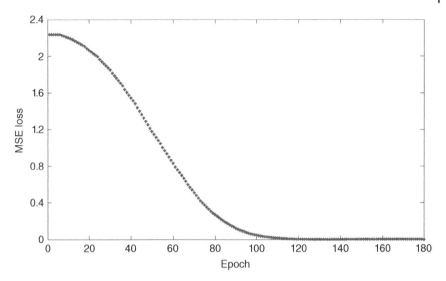

Figure 7.9 Training error of VAE network.

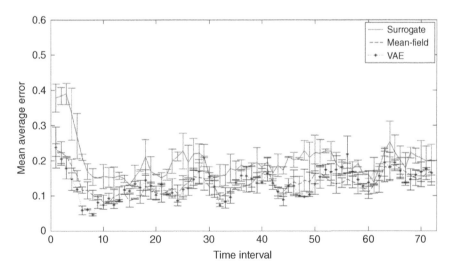

Figure 7.10 Mean average errors of calibration for traffic demand prediction.

learning surrogate and mean-field, as the comparative benchmarks. Clearly, the overall MAE of surrogate method is about 6% larger than the other two. And their errors all decline rapidly at the beginning of simulation and then keep stable with weak oscillations. This is because that the vehicles in the early morning are too few, so that even a small deviation will bring a large relative error. With the grown

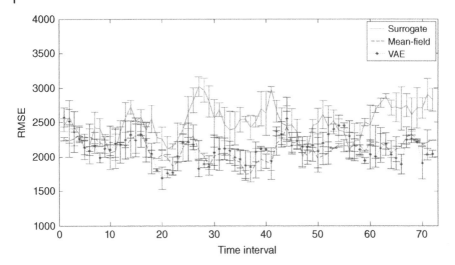

Figure 7.11 RMSE of calibration for traffic demand prediction.

of travel demand, the errors keep stable at about 16%. However, while the proposed VAE method achieves a similar overall accuracy as the mean-field approach (about 13%), it suffers from greater oscillations.

Figure 7.11 illustrates the RMSE of the three methods. Similarly, the surrogate approach gets the worst overall performance with such indicator being about 2500. By contrast, mean field and VAE are 2123 and 2156, respectively, which shows a slight elevation. And the VAE model in this metric is also less stable than mean field. We further investigate the computational performance that is listed in Table 7.5. For running time, the surrogate calibration takes about 26 hours while mean-field calibration costs about 23 hours. The reason behind lies in the iterative trial-and-error process in surrogate calibration, whereas the mean-field method can dynamically conduct simulation and calibration. By contrast, our

Table 7.5 Computational performance of three calibration methods.

	Surrogate	Mean-field	VAE
Cal. and sim. time per experiment	26 hour 03 min.	22 hour 54 min.	18 hour 27 min.
Environment	Software: SUMO 1.3.1 + Python 3.6 OS: Windows 10 (x64) CPU: Intel Core i5-9400 (8 cores, 2.9 GHz) GPU: Nvidia GeForce GTX 1660 Ti (6 GB) RAM: 16 GB		

VAE method requires only 18.5 hours to complete the calibration with simulation. This reflects that the latent encoding of state variables can effectively reduce the computational complexity and thus lead to an efficient calibration. In general, our method brings about 19% improvement in the efficiency.

7.6 Conclusions and Discussions

While multiagent system provides a useful tool to analyze the endogenous dynamics of distributed systems, the parameter calibration remains to be one of its drawbacks, as the micro parameters are difficult to measure in the real system. This chapter concentrates on calibration methods of agent behavioral model. After elucidating two classic approaches, simulated moments optimization and surrogate machine learning, we further propose a novel method based on cybernetics, which adopts the systemic perspective of the agents. Different from traditional ones, the new method can dynamically calibrate the parameters online by linking agent micro behaviors to the macro system state transfer. Mean-field approach is further introduced to compute an aggregate expected state to approximate one's complex dependencies on other agents. This operation accelerates the computational performance to a certain extent, but it can only decompose the linear correlations among training samples based on PCA, which limits its application in a high-order complicated scenario. We further introduce a VAE to deal with more complex associations. Our methods are tested and validated in two computational experiments on Chinese nationwide population evolution and urban travel demand analysis. After careful calibration of the agent model, we are able to conduct computational experiments through its evolutionary reasoning and learning.

References

1 P. Windrum, G. Fagiolo and A. Moneta. Empirical Validation of Agent-Based Models: Alternatives And Prospects. Journal of Artificial Societies and Social Simulation, 2007, 10(2): 8.

2 L. Popoyan, M. Napoletano and A. Roventini. Taming Macroeconomic Instability: Monetary and Macro-Prudential Policy Interactions In An Agent-Based Model. Journal of Economic Behavior & Organization, 2017, 134(C): 117–140.

3 G. Dosi, M. Pereira, A. Roventini, et al. When More Flexibility Yields More Fragility: The Micro Foundations of Keynesian Aggregate Unemployment. Journal of Economic Dynamics & Control, 2017, 81: 162–186.

4 D. J. Farmer and D. Foley. The Economy Needs Agent-Based Modelling. Nature, 2009, 460: 685–686.

5 H. A. Simon. Bounded Rationality and Organizational Learning. Organization Science, 1991, 2(1): 125–134.

6 R. S. Sutton and A. G. Barto. Reinforcement Learning: An Introduction (2nd Edition). MIT Press, Cambridge, MA, 2018.

7 S. Alfarano, T. Lux and F. Wagner. Estimation of Agent-Based Models: The Case of an Asymmetric Herding Model. Computational Economics, 2005, 26(1): 19–49.

8 S.-H. Chen, C.-L. Chang and Y.-R. Du. Agent-Based Economic Models and Econometrics. The Knowledge Engineering Review, 2012, 27(2): 187–219.

9 M. Gilli and P. Winker. A Global Optimization Heuristic for Estimating Agent Based Models. Computational Statistics & Data Analysis, 2003, 42(3): 299–312.

10 P. Winker, M. Gilli and V. Jeleskovic. An Objective Function for Simulation Based Inference on Exchange Rate Data. Journal of Economic Interaction and Coordination, 2007, 2: 125–145.

11 A. Fabretti. On the Problem of Calibrating An Agent Based Model For Financial Markets. Journal of Economic Interaction and Coordination, 2013, 8(2): 277–293.

12 J. Kukacka and J. Barunik. Estimation of Financial Agent-Based Models with Simulated Maximum Likelihood. FinMaP-Working Paper, Financial Distortions and Macroeconomic Performance, Kiel University, Germany, 2016.

13 W. A. Brock and C. H. Hommes. Heterogeneous Beliefs and Routes to Chaos in A Simple Asset Pricing Model. Journal of Economic Dynamics & Control, 1998, 22: 1235–1274.

14 F. Altissimo and A. Mele. Simulated Non-Parametric Estimation of Dynamic Models. The Review of Economic Studies, 2009, 76(2): 413–450.

15 D. Kristensen and Y. Shin. Estimation of Dynamic Models with Nonparametric Simulated Maximum Likelihood. Journal of Econometrics, 2012, 167(1): 76–94.

16 D. Kristensen. Uniform Convergence Rates of Kernel Estimators with Heterogeneous Dependent Data. Econometric Theory, 2009, 25: 1433–1445.

17 S. Gualdi, M. Tarzia, F. Zamponi, et al. Tipping Points in Macroeconomic Agent-Based Models. Journal of Economic Dynamics and Control, 2015, 50: 29–61.

18 W. J. Morokoff and R. E. Caflisch. Quasi-Random Sequences and Their Discrepancies. SIAM Journal on Scientific Computing, 1994, 15(6): 1251–1279.

19 S. Ross, G. J. Gordon and J. A. Bagnell. A Reduction of Imitation Learning and Structured Prediction to No-Regret Online Learning. Proceedings of the 14th International Conference on Artificial Intelligence and Statistics, Ft. Lauderdale, FL, USA, April 11–13, 2011.

20 D. D. Lewis and W. A. Gale. A Sequential Algorithm for Training Text Classifiers. Proceedings of the 17th Annual International ACM SIGIR Conference on Research and Development in Information Retrieval, Dublin, Ireland, Jul. 3–6, 1994.

21 H. Fujita, A. Gaeta, V. Loia, et al. Resilience Analysis of Critical Infrastructures: A Cognitive Approach Based on Granular Computing. IEEE Transactions on Cybernetics, 2019, 49(5): 1835–1848.

22 T. Schelling. Models of Segregation. American Economic Review, 1969, 59(2): 488–493.

23 D. Krajzewicz, J. Erdmann, M. Behrisch, et al. Recent Development and Applications of SUMO—Simulation of Urban MObility. International Journal On Advances in Systems and Measurements, 2012, 5(3&4): 128–138.

8

High-Performance Computing for Computational Deliberation Experiments

Up to now, we have talked about most methodologies in the construction of virtual humans and their aggregation – artificial population. These methodologies together with related technologies pave a feasible way for creating a cyber system that can interact and prescribe its realistic counterparts for a better human–machine interaction (HMI) and social management. Such optimization builds upon a series of computational experiments that aim to evaluate prescriptive strategies. Depending on the granularity, the experiments investigate either the group behaviors under particular incentives for social management or the possible deliberation trajectories given specific perception signals for HMI (which we call the computational deliberation experiments). The experiments may be quite computationally expensive when the number of agents or the size of one's knowledge base (KB) is large. With the support of big data in a dynamic scenario, this elicits a necessity of computational acceleration by using related techniques to achieve time valid results. A natural solution for such problem is to exploit high-performance computing (HPC) paradigm. This chapter discusses some of its details for the implementation of our computational deliberation experiments. In particular, Section 8.1 presents the overview of two popular paradigms of HPC, the cloud computing and supercomputing. Sections 8.2 and 8.3 will then show the implementation details via each path, respectively.

8.1 Computational Acceleration Using High-Performance Computing

As we are in the era of big data, our virtual human and artificial population system must deal with numerous information, ranging from human activity signals from wearable sensors, multiple sorts of images and texts from social media, to economic or travel behaviors from daily life. The continuous exponential data growth

Parallel Population and Parallel Human: A Cyber-Physical Social Approach,
First Edition. Peijun Ye and Fei-Yue Wang.
© 2023 The Institute of Electrical and Electronics Engineers, Inc. Published 2023 by John Wiley & Sons, Inc.

elevates the complexity of the system, bringing a strong need to find efficient solutions for aspects of efficient computation such as data storage, real-time processing, knowledge extraction, and abstract model training. HPC approaches have been proposed in order to boost processing speeds, which mainly resort to the joint use of a cluster of computing units (like central processing unit, graphics processing unit, or computational machinery). The alliance of distributed units can coordinate computing power from each one, leading to a remarkable promotion of the aggregate computation. Accordingly, several technologies are currently available that exploit multiple levels of HPC (e.g. multicore, many core, cluster, etc.) [1, 2]. They trade-off aspects such as performance, cost, failure management, data recovery, maintenance, and usability in order to provide solutions adapted to every application. For example, a preference for speed at the expense of a low fault tolerance and vice versa.

Basically, there are two commonly used cluster computing frameworks for related tasks. One is the cloud computing which conforms to the Google technological paradigm of big data analysis. Representative in this research line is Apache Spark, a popular platform from UC Berkley that exploits in-memory computation for solving iterative algorithms and can integrate traditional clusters such as Hadoop [3]. The other is the supercomputing which efficiently exploits multicore clusters architectures via OpenMP/MPI communication protocol. The message passing interface (MPI) paradigm is widely used in meteorological prediction, life science, and so on [4]. The main differences between these two frameworks are fault tolerance support and data replication. Spark deals with them effectively but with a clear impact on speed. Instead OpenMP/MPI provides a solution mostly oriented to computing speed but susceptible to faults, in particular, if used in commodity hardware. We will briefly introduce them in the following.

8.1.1 Spark with Hadoop

Spark is a state-of-the-art framework for high-performance cloud computing designed to efficiently deal with iterative computational procedures that recursively perform operations over the same data, such as supervised machine learning algorithms. It is designed to overcome the deficiency of distributed computing on Hadoop, which is another open-source software platform from Apache for distributed big data processing over commodity cluster architectures [5]. As the basis of Spark, Hadoop is a framework that allows for the distributed processing of large data sets across clusters of computers using simple programming models. It is designed to scale up from single servers to thousands of machines, each offering local computation and storage. Rather than relying on hardware to deliver high availability, the framework itself is designed to detect and handle failures at the application layer, so delivering a highly available service on top of a cluster of computers, each of which may be prone to failures. Different from the traditional solution for big data processing where high-performance servers with large memories and advanced CPU/GPUs are resorted to, the basic idea of Hadoop is to construct a cluster that can rival servers using cheap and easily available machines. Such advantage from cost and convenience of system deployment have expanded its application scenarios especially for small and medium corporations with limited budgets. Hadoop has three main components: (i) a Hadoop distributed file system (HDFS) with high-throughput data access; (ii) a MapReduce programming model that separates data processing in mapping for performing data operations locally, shuffling for data redistribution over the network and reduction for data summarization; and (iii) a cluster manager (YARN) in surveillance of the available computing resources and job scheduling.

HDFS is a highly fault-tolerant distributed file system that provides high-throughput data access and is suitable for storage of massive (PB-level) data files. Its overall structure is shown in Figure 8.1. Data are stored in the form of blocks, and several blocks may comprise a file. HDFS has three important roles: NameNode, DataNode, and Client. NameNode can be regarded as the administrator of HDFS. It is responsible for managing the namespace of file

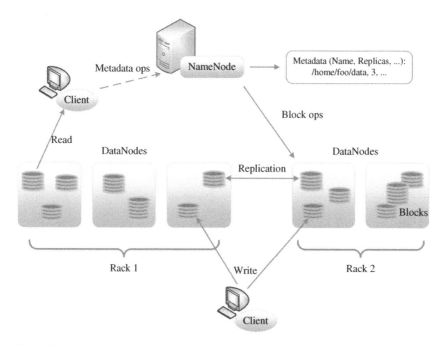

Figure 8.1 Structure of Hadoop distributed file system.

system, the configuration of cluster, and the replication of data block storage. The NameNode maintains the Metadata of file system in memory, which includes descriptions of the files, data blocks, and DataNodes. DataNodes are basic units for file storage. They keep blocks in local file systems and periodically send the block Metadata to the NameNode. Client represents an application program for user terminals that needs to acquire data from HDFS files.

The general architecture of Hadoop system built upon HDFS is illustrated in Figure 8.2. There is a Master node in the cluster, which is a container for NameNode and JobTracker, and a collection of Slave nodes, which perform decomposed computational tasks. The main function of JobTracker is to start, track, and schedule the task execution of each Slave. Each Slave node typically runs in a DataNode and maintains TaskTrackers to conduct Map and Reduce tasks based on user requirements and local data.

A second important component of Hadoop system is the MapReduce programming model. It provides those engineers with little experience on distributed computing a simplified programming environment to develop suitable applications. As its name indicated, the programming model derives from the idea of functional programming and consists of two core operations – Map and Reduce. Map aims to decompose a job into multiple tasks, whereas Reduce is designed to aggregate the temporary intermediate records of such tasks to obtain the final result. The central concept here is to divide the input data into different logical blocks. Each piece is independently processed by a Map operation in parallel. The achieved results are then shuffled and sorted into different collections in a specific way (ascending or descending). These collections are eventually grouped and sent to Reduce operations for further processing. As drawn in Figure 8.3, the Map tasks convert input records into key-value pairs. Their outputs are recombined into sorted sets, each of which is sent to a separate Reduce task. A specific Reduce task processes

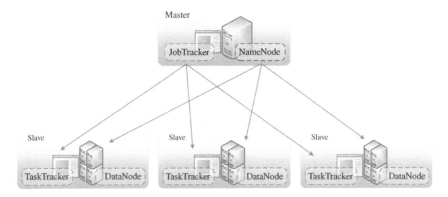

Figure 8.2 Architecture of Hadoop.

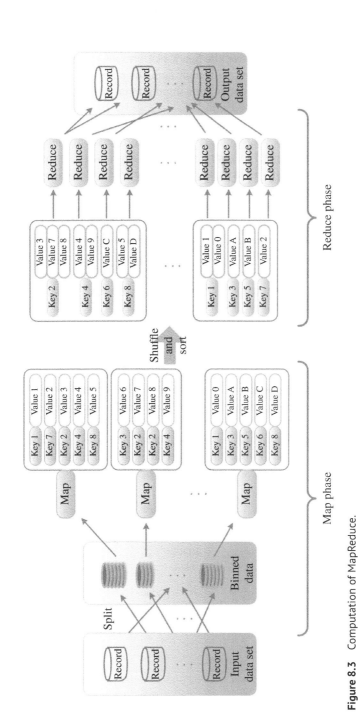

Figure 8.3 Computation of MapReduce.

the records associated with a same key from Map operations to achieve the final outputs. Based on Hadoop cluster, the Spark platform also retains the high efficiency of distributed computing with high fault tolerance and large-scale data processing ability. It is a good option for computational experiments in complex scenarios.

MapReduce provides a well-built distributed programming model. It greatly simplifies the development of cloud computing, so that such a big data technique is increasingly applied to a variety of applications. With the help of such functional programming framework, engineers only need to decompose the logic of their codes and abstract them into Map and Reduce (or Sort as discussed later in this chapter) functions. This simplification allows engineers to focus on application-oriented logic without considering its implementation details in programming. However, there are still some drawbacks about the MapReduce computing. One major deficiency is that the model is only fit for batch data that are prestored on the disk. In a nutshell, computational process of Hadoop can be drawn in Figure 8.4, where many intermediate records are generated between the Map and Reduce phases. The intermediate records are all maintained in disk, leading to a repeated visit to the hardware. Such frequent I/O operations inevitably become a bottleneck in Hadoop computation, which results in a relatively poor performance particularly in an iterative task. Spark can be viewed as an improvement targeted on this deficiency of Hadoop. Basically, Spark is still a distributed programming model that is similar to MapReduce. It is based on the principle of maintaining data in memory rather than in disk as it is done by Hadoop and other well-known approaches (such as Apache Mahout) that require data reloading and incur considerable latencies [6]. Experiments have shown Spark outperforms by up to two orders of magnitude conventional MapReduce jobs in terms of speed [7]. This benefit comes from the design of

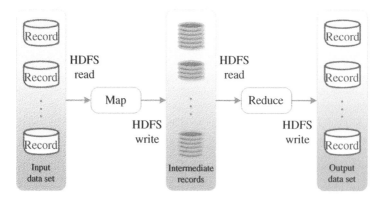

Figure 8.4 Hadoop computational process.

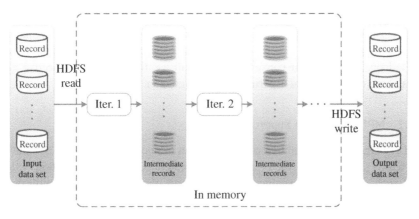

Figure 8.5 Spark computational process.

in-memory data processing as illustrated by Figure 8.5. In contrast to the two-step computing of Hadoop, Spark launches the data read/write only in the first and last iterations and is able to conduct multiple constant and efficient iterative computing in memory. The data read/write is also based on HDFS since Spark does not include a file system. This is why Spark is usually deployed on Hadoop. To better support the continuous computation, Spark adopts data-oriented view and encapsulates data units as resilient distributed datasets (RDDs). RDD is a distributed, immutable, and fault-tolerant memory abstraction that collects a set of elements in which a set of operations can be applied to either produce other RDDs (transformations) or return values (actions). Each RDD has five core properties: (i) dependency, a variable that gives the parents of the current RDD; (ii) compute, a method that defines the interface of how current RDD generated; (iii) partition, a variable that contains the indexes of the raw data sharding (mainly stored in memory but can be also in HDFS); (iv) partitioner, a method that determines the mode of RDD data partition (there are two modes: the Hash Partitioner for key-value records and the Range Partitioner for others); and (v) preferred location, a variable that gives physical location preference for raw data sharding. For application, engineers only need to focus on the first two properties. As Spark deems the continuous iterative computation to be a series of data transformation, the dependency specifies where the current RDD comes from (data source), while the compute property defines how the current RDD is achieved (operation). In this way, Spark extends the two-step MapReduce computation. Map and Reduce are only two sorts of operators in the operator set. As a unified data abstraction, RDD can reside in memory, disk, or in their combination. They are only computed on actions following a lazy evaluation (LE) strategy, in order to perform minimal computation and prevent unnecessary memory usage. RDDs are not cached in memory by default, therefore, when data are reused, a persist method is needed to avoid reloading. As can be seen, Spark is compatible with all the key-value data structure and MapReduce operation in Hadoop. Therefore, for convenience, we still use the Hadoop perspective to discuss our computational experiments in this chapter.

8.1.2   MPI/OpenMP on Supercomputing

MPI is a language-independent communication protocol for distributed computing which supports both the point-to-point and collective communications [8]. MPI goals are high performance, scalability, and portability. It is currently the dominant model used in supercomputing and is a popular communication standard that provides portability among heterogenous programs running on distributed memory systems [9]. However, the protocol does not currently support fault tolerance since it mainly addresses the high performance rather than data management [10]. Another MPI drawback is that it is not suitable for small grain level of parallelism, for example, to exploit the parallelism of multicore platforms for shared memory multiprocessing. OpenMP, by contrast, is an application programming interface (API) that supports multiplatform shared memory multiprocessing programming on most processor architectures and operating systems [11, 12]. It has become the standard for shared memory parallel computation for its high performance. The user-friendly interface of OpenMP allows developers to easily reconstruct complex algorithms into distributed forms, which cannot be done for MPI since the code must be heavily re-engineered in order to obtain relevant performance improvements. A deficiency of OpenMP is that it is not suitable for distributed memory systems. Therefore, later researches seek to cope with this issue by extending this API, making it compatible with the MPI standard. Consequently, the popular tools based on such extensions allow the combination of granularity in two levels: small grain parallelism with OpenMP and large grain parallelism with MPI-based extension [13].

The MPI interface is meant to provide essential virtual topology, synchronization, and communication functionality between a set of processes in a language-independent way, with language-specific syntax (bindings), plus a few language-specific features. It provides several features for the programmer to decide what functionality to use in their application programs. The first is the communicator object that connects groups of processes in the MPI session. Each communicator gives each contained process an independent identifier and arranges them in an ordered topology. MPI also has explicit groups, but these are mainly good for organizing and reorganizing groups of processes before another communicator is made. MPI has single-group intra-communicator operations and bilateral intercommunicator communication. Communicators can also be partitioned into multiple subcommunicators, where each process joins one of the colored subcommunicators by declaring itself to have that color. The second is the point-to-point basics, which allows one specified process to send a message to a second specified process. Point-to-point operations, as these are called, are particularly useful in patterned or irregular communication, for example, a data-parallel architecture in which each processor routinely swaps regions of data with specific other processors between calculation steps, or a master-slave architecture in which the master sends new task data to a slave whenever the prior task is completed. MPI specifies mechanisms for both blocking and nonblocking point-to-point communication mechanisms, as well as the so-called "ready-send" mechanism whereby a send request can be made only when the matching receive request has already been made. The third feature of MPI is its collective basics involving communication among all processes in a process group (which can mean the entire process pool or a program-defined subset). A typical function is the broadcast function, which takes data from one node and sends it to all processes in the process group. A reverse operation for broadcast is the MPI reduce function, which takes data from all processes in a group, performs an operation (such as summing), and stores the results on one node. MapReduce is often useful at the start or end of a large distributed calculation, where each processor operates on a part of the data and then combines it into a result.

MPI point-to-point communication typically involves message passing between two, and only two, different MPI tasks. One task is performing a send operation, and the other task is performing a matching receive operation. There are different types of send and receive routines used for different purposes. Common routines include synchronous send, blocking send/blocking receive, nonblocking send/nonblocking receive, buffered send, combined send/receive, and "Ready" send. Any type of send routine can be paired with any type of receive routine. MPI also provides several routines associated with send-receive operations, such as those used to wait for a message's arrival or probe to find out if a message has arrived. In a perfect environment, every send operation would be perfectly synchronized with its matching receive. However, this is rarely the case in practice, where the MPI implementation must be able to deal with storing data when the two tasks are out of synchronization. Take the following two cases as examples. The first situation is that a send operation occurs five seconds before the receive is ready. Then where is the message while the receive is pending? The second one is that multiple sends arrive at the same receiving task which can only accept one send at a time. Then what happens to the messages that are "backing up"? The specific MPI implementation decides what happens to data in these types of cases. Typically, a system buffer area is reserved to hold data in transit. As illustrated in Figure 8.6, the data from the sender application is passed through the network that connects multiple processors and establishes communications

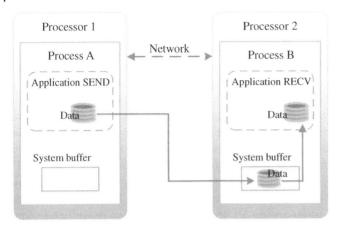

Figure 8.6 Data buffered at message passing.

between processes resided on them. The message is first put into the system buffer of the destination process and later read by the receiving application. The system buffer space has several properties. First, it is opaque to the programmer and managed entirely by the MPI library. Second, it only has a finite resource that can be easily exhausted. Third, it is able to exist on the sending side, the receiving side, or both. Fourth, it allows send/receive operations to be asynchronously executed. This property may greatly improve the program performance. MPI also provides an address space that the user can manage. This space is called the application buffer.

Most of the MPI point-to-point communications can be used in either blocking or nonblocking mode. A blocking send will only "return" after it is safe to modify the application buffer for reuse. Here, safe means that modifications will not affect the data intended for the receive task. Safe does not imply that the data was actually received – it may very well be sitting in a system buffer. A blocking send can be either synchronous, which means there is handshaking occurring with the receive task to confirm a safe send, or asynchronous if a system buffer is used to hold the data for eventual delivery to the receive. A blocking receive only "returns" after the data has arrived and is ready for use by the program. Nonblocking send and receive modes behave similarly, but they will return almost immediately. They do not wait for any communication events to complete, such as message copying from user memory to system buffer space or the actual arrival of message. It simply "request" the MPI library to perform the operation when it is able. The user cannot predict when that will take place. Therefore, it is unsafe to modify the application buffer until a confirmation of the fact that the requested non-blocking operation was actually performed by the library. To do this, MPI provides a "wait" operation for the task. Compared with the blocking mode, nonblocking communications are primarily used to overlap computation with communication and exploit possible performance gains. The message passing mechanism built in MPI guarantees that messages will not overtake each other. In other words, if a sender sends two messages, say Message 1 and Message 2, in succession to the same destination, and both match the same receive. The receive operation will receive Message 1 before Message 2. If a receiver posts two receives, say Receive 1 and Receive 2, in succession, and both are looking for the same message. Then Receive 1 will receive the message before Receive 2. However, these order rules do not apply if there are multiple threads participating in the communication operations. MPI does not guarantee fairness. It is up to the programmer to prevent "operation starvation." Take Figure 8.7 as an example. Task 1 sends a message to task 3. And task 2 also sends a competing message that matches the receive of task 3. Then only one of the sends will complete.

Collective communications of MPI includes three types of operations (see Figure 8.8). The first is synchronization where processes wait until all members of the group have reached the synchronization point. The second is data movement in which the message is broadcast and scattered/gathered in an all to all style. The third is collective computation (reductions) where one member of the group collects data from the other members and performs an operation (such as min, max, add, and multiply) on that data. Collective communications must involve all processes within the scope of a communicator. And the user is able to define additional communicators as well. Unexpected behavior, including program failure, may occur even if one task in the communicator does not participate. Therefore, it is the programmer's responsibility to ensure that all processes within a communicator participate in any collective operations. Collective communications do not take message tag arguments. The operations within subsets of processes are accomplished by first partitioning the subsets into new groups and then attaching the new groups to new communicators.

In general, cloud computing and MPI for supercomputing are two mainstreams of HPC that can accelerate our computational deliberation experiments. They

Figure 8.7 Fairness of messages in MPI.

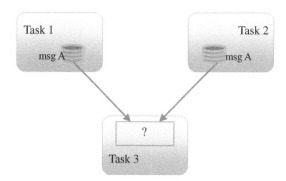

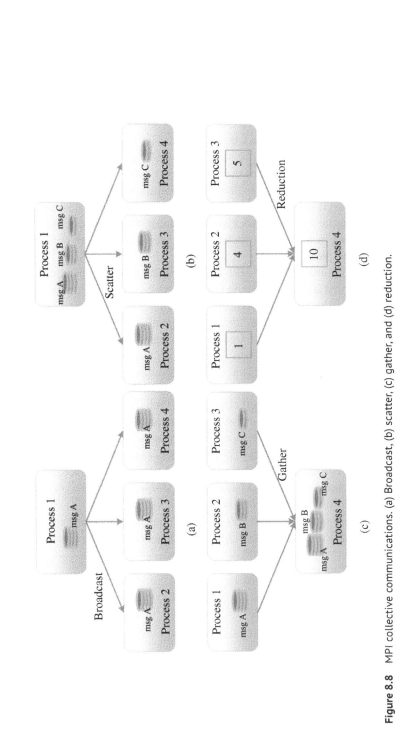

Figure 8.8 MPI collective communications. (a) Broadcast, (b) scatter, (c) gather, and (d) reduction.

both have pros and cons to our comparative study. First, cloud computing offers a distributed file system with failure and data replication management. This paradigm provides the programmers a more user-friendly mode by hiding irrelevant general technical implementations, so that the applications are easier to develop. By contrast, MPI focuses on task decomposition and computation itself, rather than the data management. Second, the easy to use of cloud computing is at the expense of its computational performance. In other words, MPI for supercomputing is in most cases faster than cloud computing. According to some comparative research, Spark and Hadoop are far from achieving state-of-the-art MPI technologies performance in machine learning tasks [14]. Third, cloud computing allows the addition of new nodes at runtime, while MPI does not support such system reconstruction. By virtually separating the applications and computational resources, the former paradigm endows the system with greater dynamic scalability. Fourth, cloud computing typically provides a set of tools for data analysis before and after the computation. These tools are constantly supported by dominant corporations, active research communities, outstanding individual engineers, etc. Yet in MPI environments, such kind of useful software needs to be developed all by the programmer himself. Therefore, in summary, we can say that cloud computing is application oriented while MPI is computation oriented.

8.2 Computational Deliberation Experiments in Cloud Computing

After learning the technical paths about cloud computing and supercomputing, this section will specifically discuss how to implement large-scale computational deliberation experiments on cloud computing platforms. Let us return to the reasoning model given in Chapter 5, where the reasoning chain is expanded by evolutionary mutation using counterfactual interventions. As illustrated by the inference tree in Figure 8.9 (same as Figure 5.4), given an initial state of the world,

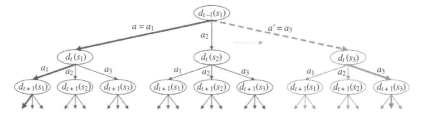

Figure 8.9 Mutated reasoning path by counterfactual reconstruction.

computational complexity will increase exponentially with the depth that the state node reached. When the tree is wide or the reasoning chain is long, it brings difficulties for practical use. Two potential solutions may ease such problem. One is to introduce dynamic pruning, reducing a part of branches timely as the reasoning proceeded. In such a way, the pruning restrains the inference within a "narrow" belt of the original inference tree, so that the knowledge evolution will not cover the whole possible search space. For example, for each reasoning step, we only select the top k branches to continue according to the activation strengths of the rules. The other solution, more directly, resorts to the distributed computing to calculate each reasoning branch in parallel and aggregate them finally. This acceleration speeds up the computation at the expense of memory in essence. For comparison, the pruning method is hard to predict the activation strengths of deep nodes in the early stage. It is very likely to result in the removal of optimal branches so that the ultimate reasoning is of low accuracy. In contrast, distributed computing retains reasoning information as much as possible. It is more inclined to achieve desirable decisions, which elicits the motivation of the work in this section.

Assume that we have a KB with its replicant stored in each data node of the cloud computing platform. Here we ignore the knowledge management and only concentrate on the reasoning implemented by MapReduce model. For a clearer discussion, the two steps of reasoning in Figure 8.9 are demonstrated first and then we come to a theoretical talking for general cases. Our distributed reasoning is composed as follows.

1. Initialization. Operations of Map and Reduce in this stage are shown in Figure 8.10. In the Map phase, records of initial state and KB rules are generated. Each record is a key value pair and will be manipulated by an independent Map function. For the initial state, the record keeps its linguistic variables as the key, leaving the value part empty (or represented by a null notation). For each rule in KB that is conditioned by the initial state, a record is generated with the state transfer being the key and the corresponding action being the value. The Map operation will distinguish these two types of records, by keeping the initial state records as the same and recombining the rule records with their common condition as the keys and their different conclusions together with activation strengths as the values. The outputs of Map operation will be shuffled and sorted. According to the computational mechanism of cloud, records with the same key will be assigned to the same group and sent to a reduce task for further processing. Therefore, since all of the output records have the same key, $d_{t-1}(s_1)$, they are dealt by one Reduce operator, which represents different state transfers as keys and those transfers with activation strengths as values. Finally, it can be viewed in the figure that all of the possible state transfers with their corresponding activation strengths

are kept and there is no other path from $t-1$ to t. Thus, the reasoning step is completed.

2. Forward reasoning. Overall, operations of this stage are similar to the previous ones. But there are some minor distinctions (see Figure 8.11). The inputs for Map operators are still composed of two parts, records of the final outputs from the last round and records of the related rules from KB. Here we only take the first output record from last round for example. The related rules in KB are those conditioned by its conclusion part, $d_t(s_1)$. In Map operations, the input record generated from last round is reconstructed by setting its conclusion of original key as the new key and the value as the same. The Map of related rules are similar to the initialization stage. Like before, all of the outputs of Map have the same key. They will be processed by one Reduce operator, leading to a forward expansion of every reasoning chain. In particular, the Reduce operator will start from the current reasoning chain by checking every record's value part. Then each state of other record values are added to this original chain, respectively, to generate new output records. The Reduce function will also calculate the transferred activation strengths by Eq. (5.4)

$$fs_{t+1}(a_1, a_1) = fs_t(a_1) \wedge fs_{t+1}(a_1)$$

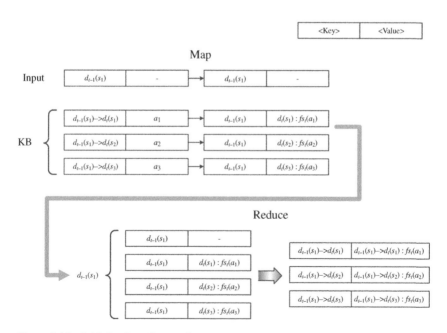

Figure 8.10 Initialization of reasoning.

After this round, the reasoning path goes one step further, containing every possible expansion. Therefore, the computation is still completed. Note that the above reasoning is only for one output from initialization. The other two are analogical as illustrated in Figure 8.12.

3. Iteration. Our algorithm will repeat the previous forward reasoning stage until no related rules from KB can be queried as the input for Map.

For the above distributed reasoning based on MapReduce, another two issues need to be explained here in order to avoid computation failure. First, in forward reasoning, Reduce function must strictly distinguish whether the received records are from last round chains or from KB queries. It also needs to remove the duplicate rules for KB queries. This requirement prevents generating duplicate reasoning paths, which will lead to unnecessary Maps of the next iteration. Second, if a particular Reduce operator receives multiple records of reasoning chains, each of them should be expanded in the form of "current chain $->$ rule conclusion." In other words, the expansion is required to start from reasoning chains but related rules. This condition avoids generating reasoning loops, which means a chain that contains duplicate states. These two situations may occur in scenarios where different reasoning chains have a common state variable. To see it clearly, let us come to an example as Figure 8.13. The input records manifest that the two initial states $d_{t-1}(s_1)$ and $d_{t-1}(s_2)$ both transfer to a common state $d_t(s)$. Thus, their related rules from KB queries are the same. By shuffling and sorting, the Reduce operator

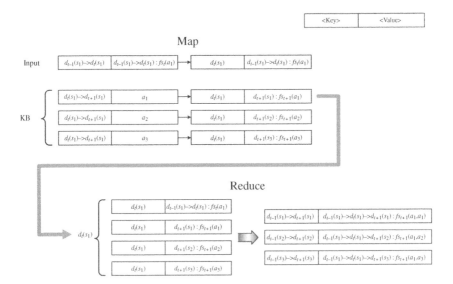

Figure 8.11 Forward reasoning step (part 1).

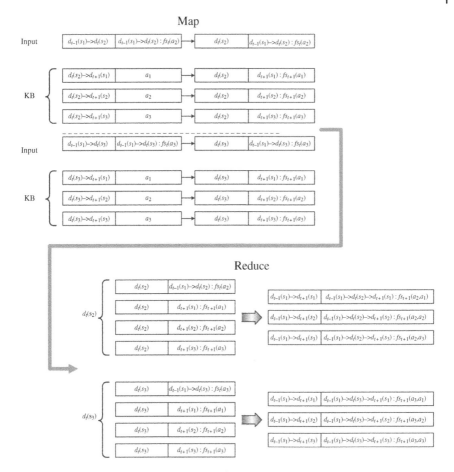

Figure 8.12 Forward reasoning step (part 2).

receives duplicate records which are shaded in the figure. Such duplicates need to be removed, and the two reasoning chains need to be expanded, respectively, via the rules. The final outputs are six different records as shown. Accordingly, reasoning tree of this process is drawn in Figure 8.14.

Now we are going to present some theoretical analysis on our algorithm. Generally, assume that the reasoning chain is $\langle d_i, a_i \rangle_{i=0}^{t-1}$ after t iterations, and further assume there are $n(d_{t-1})$ rules that are conditioned by d_{t-1}. Denote $R_{(t-1) \to j} = \left\{ d_{t-1} \overset{a_j}{\to} d_j \right\}$, $j \in 1, 2, \dots, n(d_{t-1})$ to be the jth expanded rule. Since a_j is a possible action for the world state d_{t-1}, we can define a new $\hat{d}_j$ as the aggregation of $\langle a_j, d_j \rangle$. $R_{i \to}$ is the rule set that is conditioned by d_i and $R_{\cdot \to j}$ is the

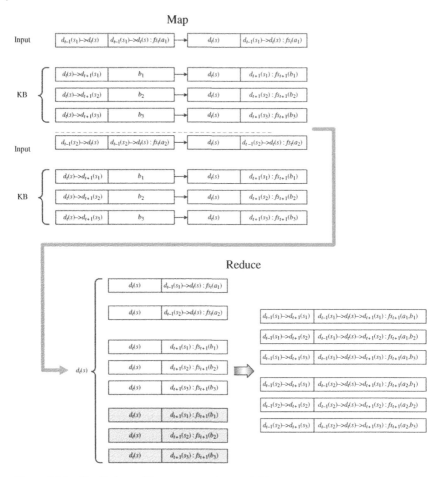

Figure 8.13 MapReduce with a common state variable.

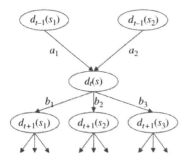

Figure 8.14 Reasoning tree with a common state variable.

rule set that is concluded by $\hat{d}_j$. A proof for the completeness of the inference is given below.

Definition 8.2.1 (Reachability). Let $\underline{s} = (s_1, \dots, s_n) \in S_1 \times S_2 \times \dots \times S_n$ be the value of input linguistic variable vector. The result state d is said to be $\underline{s}$ reachable if d can be obtained through finite steps of reasoning with a positive activation strength given a KB. Otherwise d is $\underline{s}$ unreachable.

Theorem 8.2.1 (Completeness). *Given a KB and an initial state $\underline{s}$, the following conclusions hold according to the iterative reasoning steps demonstrated by Figures 8.10–8.13:*

(1) Any $\underline{s}$ reachable state is included in the output records;
(2) Any $\underline{s}$ unreachable state is not included in the output records.

Proof:
(1) Assume that an $\underline{s}$ reachable state $\hat{d}_k$ is not in the outputs. By definition of reachability, there is a reasoning chain $\underline{s} \to \hat{d}_1 \to \dots \to \hat{d}_{k-1} \to \hat{d}_k$ supported by the KB. Consider $\hat{d}_{k-1}$ in two cases.

   (a) If $\hat{d}_{k-1}$ is included in the $(k-1)$th iteration's outputs, then a record generated by Map in the kth iteration for $\underline{s} \to \hat{d}_1 \to \dots \to \hat{d}_{k-1}$ will be

   $$\hat{d}_{k-1} | \underline{s} \to \hat{d}_1 \to \dots \to \hat{d}_{k-1}$$

   where the key-value parts are separated by notation |. Other outputs of Maps are the rule set conditioned by $\hat{d}_{k-1}, R_{(k-1) \to}$. Accordingly, records aggregated by the Reduce with the key $\hat{d}_{k-1}$ will expand the reasoning chain as

   $$\underline{s} \to \hat{d}_1 \to \dots \to \hat{d}_{k-1} \to \hat{d}_j, \ j \in \{1, 2, \dots, n(\hat{d}_{k-1})\}$$

   Because $\hat{d}_k$ is not in the output records, we have $k \notin \{1, 2, \dots, n(\hat{d}_{k-1})\}$. Therefore, $\hat{d}_{k-1} \to \hat{d}_k \notin R_{(k-1) \to}$. and thus $\hat{d}_{k-1} \to \hat{d}_k \notin KB$. This is contradicted with the fact that there is a reasoning chain $\underline{s} \to \hat{d}_1 \to \dots \to \hat{d}_{k-1} \to \hat{d}_k$ supported by the KB, which implicates $\hat{d}_{k-1} \to \hat{d}_k$ in the KB.

   (b) If $\hat{d}_{k-1}$ is not included in the $(k-1)$th iteration's outputs, then let $k := k-1$ and go back to the reasoning step $\hat{d}_{k-2} \to \hat{d}_{k-1}$. This process is iteratively conducted. Once an intermediate state in the reasoning chain is in the outputs, the proof is completed according to Case (a). If all the intermediate states are not in the outputs, we will arrive at the initial state $\underline{s}$, indicating that $\underline{s}$ is not in the outputs and thus $\underline{s} \notin KB$. This is contradicted with that $\hat{d}_k$ is $\underline{s}$ reachable.

(2) Assume $\hat{d}_k$ is $\underline{s}$ unreachable and is in the outputs. According to our MapReduce algorithm, each output record corresponds to a reasoning chain from the initial state to the current expanded linguistic state. Therefore, if $\hat{d}_k$ is in the outputs, its corresponding reasoning chain $\underline{s} \rightarrow \hat{d}_1 \rightarrow \cdots \rightarrow \hat{d}_{k-1} \rightarrow \hat{d}_k$ has already provided a reachable path from $\underline{s}$ to $\hat{d}_k$, which is contradicted with the assumption. □

As illustrated by our example before, a reasoning chain is reflected by a path in its inference tree and vice versa. Theorem 8.2.1 guarantees that our MapReduce inference is completed, that is, the inference tree covers all reachable variable nodes in KB. Note that Theorem 8.2.1 does not enforce the finiteness of KB, but in practice this property is generally satisfied. In the case of finite KB, the following theorem shows a condition for the halt of computation.

Theorem 8.2.2 (Halt Condition). *Our MapReduce computation as Figures 8.10–8.13 will halt if and only if there is no loop in the inference tree (Figure 8.9) rooted by the initial state.*

Proof: "⇒": We prove by contradiction. First, note that a loop in a reasoning chain is like the form $\hat{d}_m \rightarrow \cdots \rightarrow \hat{d}_{m+n} \rightarrow \hat{d}_m$, a directed path from state $\hat{d}_m$ to itself. Assume the MapReduce computation halts after T iterations, and there is a loop $L : \hat{d}_m \rightarrow \cdots \rightarrow \hat{d}_{m+n} \rightarrow \hat{d}_m$ in its inference tree. Consider the outputs of the Tth iteration.

(a) If the final output records contain a state from L, denoted by $\hat{d}_k$, $k \in m$, $m+1, \dots, m+n$, then according to our algorithm, related rules from KB query in the $(T+1)$th iteration are vacant. Therefore, KB does not contain any rule conditioned by $\hat{d}_k$, which is contradictory with $\hat{d}_k \rightarrow \hat{d}_{k+1}$, $k \in m, m+1, \dots, m+n-1$ or $\hat{d}_{m+n} \rightarrow \hat{d}_m$ in L.

(b) If the final output records do not contain any state from L, then consider the outputs of the $(T-1)$th iteration. If any state in L is still not included, then our examination goes on to its previous iteration. The examination will result in either of the following cases. One is that the outputs of every iteration always do not contain any state from L, which elicits the initial state $\underline{s}$ not included as well. It means the inference tree excludes any part of L (if not, the reasoning should have generated records of corresponding states by Theorem 8.2.1). The other is some outputs concluded by states from L. Suppose the output concluded by a state from L, $\hat{d}_k$, $k \in m, m+1, \dots, m+n$, first comes from the $(T-t)$th iteration by our backward examination. The Maps in iteration $(T-t+1)$ check the KB to achieve the rule set conditioned by $\hat{d}_k$, $R_{k\rightarrow}$. Since the rules given by L are also rules in KB, $R_{k\rightarrow}$ must contain $\hat{d}_k \rightarrow \hat{d}_{k+1}$, which means the upcoming Reduce operation will expands reasoning chain with $\hat{d}_k \to \hat{d}_{k+1}$. Thus, the $(T-t+1)$th iteration receives a reasoning chain $\underline{s} \to \hat{d}_1 \to \cdots \to \hat{d}_k \to \hat{d}_{k+1}$ with $\hat{d}_{k+1}$ from L as well. This is contradictory with the assumption that $\hat{d}_k$ is the first state in L in our backward examination.

"$\Leftarrow$": Because KB is finite, the derived inference tree is also finite, containing a finite number of nodes. Since there is no loop in the tree, the path length from root (initial state) to any other node (state) is also finite. Suppose the longest path involves L edges. By Theorem 8.2.1, our computation halts after L iterations at most. □

Before the end of this section, we give the pseudo code of our MapReduce algorithm in Algorithm 8.1. The outputs of Maps are prefixed by "KB." Function *GetCondMatchRules* queries the rules from KB conditioned by d_k. Function

---

Algorithm 8.1 Fuzzy Reasoning Using MapReduce

Input:
  Key—Value pair: $s \to d_k | s \to d_1 \to \cdots \to d_k - \{a\}$;

Output:
  Reasoning Chain.
  Map(Key, Value)

1: $R_{i\to}. \longleftarrow$ GetCondMatchRules(KB, d_k);
2: Emit($d_k, s \to d_1 \to \cdots \to d_k - \{a\}$);
3: **for** each $r \in R_{i\to}.$ **do**
4: Emit(d_k, "KB:"$+r$); //set a KB flag
5: **end for**
  Reduce(Key, Iterator Values)
6: InRec $\longleftarrow \{\ \}$; Rules $\longleftarrow \{\ \}$;
7: **for** each value in Values **do**
8: **if** value.StartsWith("KB:") **then**
9:   Rules $\longleftarrow$ Rules + value;
10: **else**
11:   InRec $\longleftarrow$ InRec + value;
12:   Rules $\longleftarrow$ RemoveRedun(Rules);
13:   InRec $\longleftarrow$ ExtendChain(InRec, Rules);
14: **end if**
15: **end for**
16: **for** each rec in InRec **do**
17: Emit($s \to$ Key, rec);
18: **end for**

RemoveRedun removes duplicate rules. Function *ExtendChain* expands every input reasoning chain.

8.3 Computational Deliberation Experiments in Supercomputing

Benefited from the good design of system architecture with proper underlying implementations, distributed reasoning based on cloud computing is intuitive. In most cases, programmers only need to decompose their application workflow into Map and Reduce tasks and write corresponding functions. However, this is not the only paradigm that can accelerate our computational experiments. Supercomputing based on MPI is a second choice that exploits faster computational speed. We shift our focus to such field in this section. Overall, supercomputing splits the computational task into multiple processes (or threads) and simultaneously runs these processes on different computing nodes. The running processes are independent with respective memories. When their data need synchronization, the supported MPI protocol requires the programmers to manually implement communications among processes.

In MPI computing, while every process can be treated in a peer-to-peer way, we still adopt a master-slave mode for our computational deliberation experiments. The reason behind is twofold. On the one hand, as the deliberation experiments may produce a number of reasoning paths with various lengths, their corresponding processes may terminate at different time as well. Therefore, it is necessary to set a global daemon to synchronize the computation results and monitor their terminations. On the other hand, our optimal behavior prescription that will be addressed in Chapter 9 is based on all of the reasoning results. Thus, a master process can continue to perform such a task after all the reasoning processes completed. These two sorts of processes will be explained in detail.

The overall sequence chart is illustrated in Figure 8.15. The master process is unique and global. It can communicate with every slave. The master process is set to monitor and control the whole progress of the entire experiment, including its initialization, start, pause, and termination. It creates a few slave processes in the early stage of experiment, sending the KB to them for their subsequent reasoning, but receives registration request from every slave process that is ever existed. The reasoning path generated by each slave is also returned to the master, so that the whole results can be aggregated for later behavioral prescriptions. By such a kind of global registrations, all the reasoning slaves are tracked to guarantee that the final result is globally optimal. In the figure, only four slaves are drawn, but in practice, there may be more depending on the actual situation. Slave process is dynamically created when the reasoning encounters a branch in searching its inference

Master

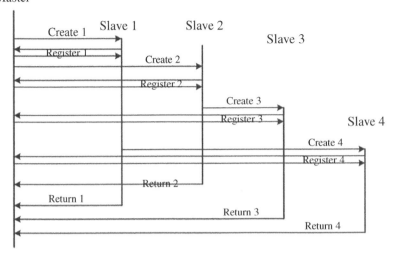

Figure 8.15 Sequence chart of supercomputing.

tree. It can be created either by the master or by another slave. However, all the slaves are registered to the global master after their initializations and thus treated in a peer-to-peer way. Computations of different salves are independent, each of which performs a forward reasoning to generate a reasoning chain. When a slave process reaches a leaf node in the inference tree, it terminates the computation by returning its generated reasoning chain to the master.

There are three types of messages in the above computation, the initialization, registration, and return messages. The initialization message is used to create a new slave process, including the information of master for registration, current world state, tailored KB for its subsequent reasoning, etc. Registration messages are bidirectional, from slaves to master and vice versa. The slave to master message sends basic information of the slave process to register. After receiving the basic information, the master assigns an ID which is globally unique and sends it back. The termination message returns the reasoning chain generated by the slave process. And the master stores the result for its further optimization. During the experiment, the master process will receive numerous reasoning chains as our reasoning goes on.

Figure 8.15 is designed to be the paradigm that each generated chain is returned to the master and then the master usually writes the results into database. But note this is not the only technical path. An alternative is the distributed visit to database where each slave process directly saves its reasoning result into the database. Accordingly, the master needs to check all the results in a distributed way after confirming all the slaves terminated, and the distributed database needs to be set process or thread safe. This paradigm can alleviate the communication burden of return messages. In addition, pruning techniques can be introduced into the reasoning experiments to avoid the generation of a large number of slaves. When the reasoning encounters a branch in the inference tree, the algorithm may heuristically determine whether to prune the subtree from current node. If so, the algorithm will select only one child node to proceed its reasoning and will not create a new slave for other child nodes. Let us see an example in Figure 8.16. Suppose slave 1 starts at node $d_{t-1}(s_1)$. When its reasoning proceeds to node $d_t(s_1)$ and encounters a branch with two child nodes, it chooses one child, say the node $d_{t+1}(s_1)$, to expand its reasoning chain, and is assumed to create a new slave process, say slave 2, to begin the reasoning of other nodes. If our algorithm adopts pruning policy by heuristically cutting off the node $d_{t+1}(s_2)$ together with the subtree rooted by it, there is no need to create slave 2 for further processing. Thus, the computational complexity will be seriously reduced. One issue to be noticed is that the pruning is required to take place in the middle or late stages of reasoning, because early pruning will lead to the cut of a major part in inference tree and make the upcoming behavioral guidance lose its global optimality. However, calculation of optimal pruning strategies without any priori is difficult. We need to seek a balance between the reasoning width with the optimality of its related result and computational efficiency.

To test our distributed reasoning, we conduct a simulated experiment of travel decisions within the second Ring Road of Jinan city, Shandong Province, China, which is about 570.81 km [15]. The predefined KB includes representations of travel mental repository that is composed of 419 intersections, 330 links, 163 residential areas, 88 office buildings, 59 schools, 19 shopping malls, 21 hospitals, 37 restaurants, 13 leisure and entertainment places, and 10 sports fields. To clearly

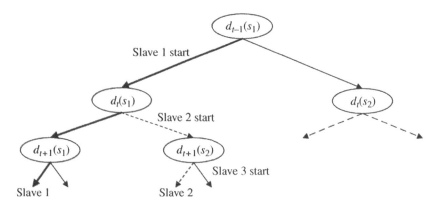

Figure 8.16 Pruning to reduce slaves.

investigate the acceleration of computation, we simulated the travel behaviors of 300,000 people based on the distributed deliberation reasoning from 6:00 a.m. to 12:00 a.m. Daily travel patterns of individual agent are modeled as an activity chain, and each travel plan involving selection of destination, travel mode, and departure time is dynamically generated by computational deliberation reasoning. Our experiment is first conducted on a cloud computing platform that contains six nodes configured as Table 8.1. As the speed up is widely used to measure the performance of distributed computing, we define a similar metric to test our algorithm:

$$Su = \frac{T_s}{T_d}$$

where T_s is the time spent to complete the computational experiment on a single node and T_d is the time to complete the experiment on distributed nodes. Obviously, a larger speed up means less running time for a same scaled computational task and thus a better performance of the algorithm. Here, we adopt the time cost from Node 2 to be the single node criterion T_s because its configuration is popular and representative.

We conduct seven groups of computational experiments, each of which runs five times to reduce the impact of stochastic factors. Average performances are summarized in Table 8.2. The first and second groups of experiments use only one node to investigate the single-node performance. As configuration of Node 1 is superior to Node 2, their related results show that Node 1 reduces about 26% computational time than Node 2. In addition, the experiment with 300,000 population lasts for several hours, indicating that the time validity of results can hardly be satisfied if the system scale increases further. In Experiment 3, nearly 2 (1.95) speed-up is achieved with two nodes, while this metric grows to nearly 3 (2.88) when three nodes are used. The ratio of speed up and computing nodes is nearly

Table 8.1 Configurations of computational nodes.

Node number	Core count	Memory	Operation system	Type
#1	4	4.00G	XP 64bit	Desktop
#2	2	1.00G	XP 32bit	Desktop
#3	2	1.00G	XP 32bit	Desktop
#4	2	1.00G	XP 32bit	Laptop
#5	1	1.00G	XP 32bit	Laptop
#6	1	1.00G	XP 32bit	Laptop

Table 8.2 Computational performance of nodes.

No.	Nodes	MR time (h)	MR Su	MPI time (h)	MPI Su
1	#1	6.52	—	3.95	—
2	#2	9.11	1.00	5.33	1.00
3	#1,2	5.80	1.57	2.74	1.95
4	#1,2,3	4.41	2.07	1.85	2.88
5	#1,2,3,4	5.73	1.59	2.59	2.06
6	#1,2,3,4,5	4.98	1.83	2.06	2.59
7	#1,2,3,4,5,6	4.24	2.15	1.72	3.10

linear which verifies the validity of our distributed algorithms. By contrast, experiments 5 and 6 do not achieve expected speed-ups even they use more nodes than experiment 4. This is because with the number of nodes grown, more resources have been put into the communication and synchronization among nodes, leading to a decrease of each CPU's utilization. Moreover, potential load imbalance is also a possible cause for the nonmonotonic increase in speed up. Comparing the 4th and 7th experiments, the latter uses as twice nodes as the former, but this only elevates its performance by 4–8% around. Thus, the elevation of speed up by adding mode nodes is limited for this computational task, and experiment 4 has achieved a better efficiency. For the MapReduce cloud computing, we underline that even if in-memory data processing reduces the gap between this paradigm and MPI computing, we are still far from achieving the latter's performance. Its speed-ups in all tested scenarios are lower than MPI. As a concluding remark, when conducting distributed deliberation experiments, the computational paradigm and the number of nodes for deployment need to be carefully considered to obtain a desired performance.

8.4 Conclusions and Discussions

HPC is a direct way to accelerate the computational deliberation experiments, particularly for a large knowledge repository where numerous reasoning trajectories are required to be checked. In this chapter, we concentrate on two popular distributed computing paradigms – MapReduce cloud computing and MPI supercomputing. Theoretical analysis on the completeness and halt condition of our designed algorithms is given, showing that the computing paradigm can always achieve accurate and full reasoning chains. The distributed algorithms are tested in a travel simulation experiment with 300,000 population supported by customized computational nodes. The results demonstrate that MPI computing outperforms MapReduce overall, but the latter possesses data management and is easy for users. In addition, a careful consideration needs to be given to which paradigm and how many nodes are suitable to achieve a desired performance, since the communication and synchronization cost will grow with the scale of clusters.

References

1 K. Olukotun. Beyond Parallel Programming with Domain Specific Languages. Proceedings of 19th Symposium on Principles and Practice of Parallel Programming, Orlando, FL, USA, Feb. 15–19, 2014: 179–180.

2 Y. You, S. L. Song, H. Fu, et al. MIC-SVM: Designing a Highly Efficient Support Vector Machine for Advanced Modern Multi-Core and Many-Core Architectures. Proceedings of 28th IEEE International Parallel and Distributed Processing Symposium, Phoenix, AZ, USA, May 19–23, 2014: 809–818.

3 M. Zaharia, M. Chowdhury, M. J. Franklin, et al. Spark: Cluster Computing with Working Sets. USENIX Conference on Hot Topics in Cloud Computing, Boston, MA, USA, Jun. 22, 2010: 10.

4 F. D. Natale, H. I. Ingolfsson, H. Bhatia, et al. A Massively Parallel Infrastructure for Adaptive Multiscale Simulations: Modeling RAS Initiation Pathway for Cancer. The International Conference for High Performance Computing, Networking, Storage, and Analysis, Denver, CO, USA, Nov. 17–22, 2019.

5 T. White. Hadoop: The Definitive Guide. O'Reilly Media, Inc., 2012.

6 H. Karau, A. Konwinski, P. Wendell, et al. Learning Spark. O'Reilly Media, 2015.

7 R. S. Xin, J. Rosen, M. Zaharia, et al. Shark: SQL and Rich Analytics at Scale. Proceedings of ACM SIGMOD International Conference on Management of Data, New York, USA, Jun. 23–28, 2013: 13–24.

8 W. Gropp, E. Lusk, N. Doss, et al. A High-Performance, Portable Implementation of the MPI Message Passing Interface Standard. Parallel Computing, 1996, 22(6): 789–828.

9 S. Sur, M. J. Koop and D. K. Panda. High-Performance and Scalable MPI Over InfiniBand with Reduced Memory Usage: An In-Depth Performance Analysis. Proceedings of ACM/IEEE Conference on Supercomputing, Tampa, FL, USA, 2006: 105.

10 K. Sato, A. Moody, K. Mohror, et al. FMI: Fault Tolerant Messaging Interface for Fast and Transparent Recovery. Proceedings of 28th IEEE International

Parallel and Distributed Processing Symposium, Phoenix, AZ, USA, May 19–23, 2014: 1225–1234.

11 B. Chapman, G. Jost and R. Van Der Pas. Using OpenMP: Portable Shared Memory Parallel Programming. MIT Press, 2008.

12 L. Dagum and R. Menon. OpenMP: An Industry Standard API for Shared-Memory Programming. IEEE Computational Science & Engineering, 1998, 5(1): 46–55.

13 Intel. Intel Parallel Studio XE 2015 Sp2, 2015. https://software.intel.com/en-us/intel-parallel-studio-xe.

14 J. L. Reyes-Ortiz, L. Oneto and D. Anguita. Big Data Analytics in the Cloud: Spark on Hadoop vs MPI/OpenMP on Beowulf. Procedia Computer Science, 2015, 53: 121–130.

15 J. Li, S. Tang, X. Wang, et al. A Software Architecture for Artificial Transportation Systems—Principles and Framework. Proceedings of the 10th IEEE International Conference on Intelligent Transportation Systems, 2007, pp. 229–234.

9

Interactive Strategy Prescription

The building of artificial cognition system with its evolutionary deliberations has been elaborated from Chapters 2–7. The process, in an emergent way from the bottom up, simulates diverse possible paths of one's cognition and decision making. However, such massive computational deliberation experiments are not the end of our parallel human system. They need to be converged to specific operational strategies for particular scenarios. In a scientific sense, this step is essential to generate the intelligence of human complex deliberation system. And it also provides a feasible action candidate to prescribe one's behavior in complex systems. In this chapter, we focus on the interactive strategy prescription for human behaviors, which will bridge the artificial cognition system and actual human participants. Section 9.1 presents a hierarchical behavior prescription system that forms the basic structure of artificial to real feedbacks. The system is composed of three layers that stand for evaluations of aggregate behaviors in global, regional, and individual levels. The global objective might be the minimum of systemic running cost, the maximization of total utility of all the individuals, or the minimum gap of utilities among different groups of individuals, etc. Similarly, regional and individual objectives represent benefits of their respective levels. Here, the "regional" is a broad concept. Any group of individuals with specific common characteristics can be viewed in a same "region." By decomposing a global objective from expected states into lower levels, we are able to achieve appropriate behaviors for every human participant that can reversely lead to a systemic efficient running. With the hierarchical structure of prescription system, Section 9.2 considers one of its main issues – how to dynamically formulate the groups. The section presents a dynamic group detection using community discovery techniques from social network research. It can facilitate the construction of group prescription agents and thus their cooperation or confrontation. While the three-layered prescription is suitable for complex social systems, for a

Parallel Population and Parallel Human: A Cyber-Physical Social Approach,
First Edition. Peijun Ye and Fei-Yue Wang.
© 2023 The Institute of Electrical and Electronics Engineers, Inc. Published 2023 by John Wiley & Sons, Inc.

human-in-loop scenario that involves only few operators, we could directly evolve one's mental trajectories and return an optimal action by careful evaluations. This paradigm elicits Section 9.3, where a concrete evaluation is considered for strategy prescription based on content match. In Section 9.4, the prescription is further put into a dynamic environment, which takes the real-time interactions between human and machine into account. We deal with the related problem from the machine's perspective and introduce active learning to efficiently improve the mental model by generating specific interactive mode. This closes the dynamic loop of parallel human system, which constantly and iteratively performs "behavioral learning, massive deliberation experiments, strategy prescription."

9.1　Hierarchical Behavior Prescription System

As alluded in Chapter 1, the objective for social management is to keep the system running at an optimal equilibrium. However, although the optimal equilibrium does exist in theory, it is often not easily computable. Therefore, decomposing the overall objective into multiple local goals with an acceptable loss of optimality is an alternative for such a task. This section will propose a three-layered prescription system, as illustrated in Figure 9.1. The system is based on the techniques of mobile agents. At the top is the global evaluation agent, which includes a systemic optimization objective. The global objective can be set by default, such as the minimum of systemic running cost as mentioned before, or achieved from expert experience with human priori knowledge, or their combinations. Furthermore, some intelligent algorithms like imitation learning are applicable to get an objective directly through human experts' behaviors. In an online prescription case, it can be also a dynamic indicator from time to time. The evaluation agent estimates the match degree between the global objective and results from computational experiments. Inversely, it is able to guide the evolutionary direction of experiments according to evaluation results by heuristically setting the experiment parameters. Analogous to the pruning of the inference tree, this mechanism is important to the time validity as it shrinks the searching space of deliberation experiments. After the investigation of evolutionary decisions, the evaluation agent then selects actions from the strategy pool to generate behavioral plan. The plan is decomposed into partial ones of group levels and sent to their related group agents. Group prescription agents are collaborative to slightly adjust their received plans as required for a better accomplishment. Each group agent further decomposes its received subplan and then pushes them to individual agents, which are responsible for the concrete action prescription for a specific real individual.

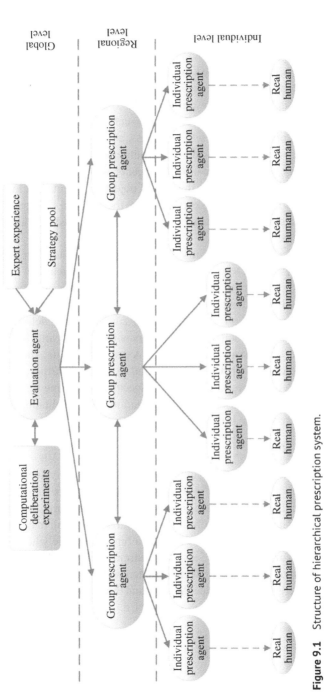

Figure 9.1 Structure of hierarchical prescription system.

The individual agents are placed at the bottom level, as symbiotic avatars of their human counterparts. Each individual agent bidirectionally corresponds to a real human user, eliciting a dynamic interaction of learning and prescription (here, we focus on the prescription while the learning will be discussed later in this chapter). Clearly, the system hierarchical framework aims to decompose a complicated general objective into different prescription tasks that are then distributed within components. Accordingly, the hierarchical structure endows the agents with different degrees of intelligence, which reduces as the level decreases. In other words, not all agents are responsible for simultaneously making strategic-level behaviors. Rather, regional task-oriented agents and individual prescription agents are organized to implement the overall objective. Agents in a higher level will consider more complicated tasks that involve the wider scope of people. Thus, their intelligent algorithms will be more complex as they need to deal with more complex situations.

Our prescription system first runs in a default mode. Each level of default agents is predetermined according to historical data. When the spatial and temporal behavioral patterns get changed, the evaluation agent may set up a switch by dispatching suitable prescription agents with appropriate strategies. Such a switch is founded on the indicator for computational deliberation and behavioral experiments. Compared with the new reasoning paths learned from human–machine interaction and historical accumulated data, the evaluation algorithm can determine whether it is required to adjust the expected strategies by dispatching updated prescription agents. Specifically, assume we have historical system states with their statistical distributions. The evaluation of current systemic evolutionary state is represented as a dot product

$$e_t = \begin{bmatrix} w^{rel} & w^{ext} & w^{mom} \end{bmatrix}^T \cdot \begin{bmatrix} \hat{\tau}_t^{rel} & \hat{\tau}_t^{ext} & \hat{\tau}_t^{mom} \end{bmatrix} \tag{9.1}$$

where $\hat{\tau}_t^{rel}$ is the relative state that is defined to be the percentile value of the historical state distributions at time t. $\hat{\tau}_t^{ext}$ is an indicator that stands for the occurrence of an extreme state. Extreme states are defined as the ones that rarely take place in a statistical sense. They are first determined by historical data and may get changed as the running states accumulated. So $\hat{\tau}_t^{ext}$ is a binary variable whose value can be either 1 if the current systemic state is an extreme state or 0 otherwise. $\hat{\tau}_t^{mom}$ is called the trend momentum factor. It is calculated via the difference between moving average convergence/divergence (MACD) and the exponential moving average (EMA) of MACD with a smaller time window, i. e.

$$\hat{\tau}_t^{mom} = \hat{\tau}_t^{macd} - f^{EMA}(\hat{\tau}_t^{macd}, n_1) \tag{9.2}$$

and

$$\hat{\tau}_t^{macd} = f^{EMA}(\hat{\tau}_t, n_2) - f^{EMA}(\hat{\tau}_t, n_3) \tag{9.3}$$

where $\hat{\tau}_t$ denotes the system state time t, $\hat{\tau}_t^{macd}$ denotes the value of MACD, and n_1, n_2, n_3 $(n_1 \le n_2 \le n_3)$ refer to the time window of EMA. The EMA function is defined as

$$f^{EMA}(\tau_t, n) = \frac{2}{n+1} \sum_{k=0}^{n} \left(\frac{n-1}{n+1}\right)^k \tau_{t-k} \qquad (9.4)$$

$\left[w^{rel} \ w^{ext} \ w^{mom}\right]$ is the weight vector that characterizes the contribution of each considered item. By the above definition of e_t, it is obvious that a greater e_t implicates a greater mismatch of the current system state and historic patterns, meaning a higher requirement for an operational switch of prescription agents. If e_t exceeds a given threshold η in practice, new prescription agents will be generated and a switch will take place.

The prescription switch can be triggered by either the regional or global layer of the system. The former, in a bottom-up way, stems from the deviation between individual/local states and those expected ones prescribed by strategies. The latter usually comes from the change of global objective, assigning new regional prescriptions if current expected strategies cannot fulfill the updated objective. The switch requests from regional level need to be sent up to global agent where the task decomposition will be recalculated to fit the new situation. Here, we focus on the evaluation of regional agent in the bottom-up mode. In this mode, each individual agent collects the measurement of its human user and transmits the results to its regional coordinating agent. The measurement is represented as

$$\left\{ user_{id}, \ \hat{\tau}_t^{rel}, \ \hat{\tau}_t^{ext}, \ \hat{\tau}_t^{mom}, \ \hat{\tau}_t^{ratio}, \ \hat{\tau}_t^{tran} \right\} \qquad (9.5)$$

where $user_{id}$ is the user identification. $\hat{\tau}_t^{rel}$, $\hat{\tau}_t^{ext}$, and $\hat{\tau}_t^{mom}$ are similarly defined as before. $\hat{\tau}_t^{ratio}$ is the ratio that users adopt prescribed actions in the last time step. $\hat{\tau}_t^{tran}$ is a transition type of the system macroscopic dynamics (MAP) at time t. That is

$$\hat{\tau}_t^{tran} = f^{MAP}(u_t^{ave}, \ \hat{\tau}_t^{ratio}, \ C) \qquad (9.6)$$

f^{MAP} is a clustering model to generate the MAP indicator. u_t^{ave} and $\hat{\tau}_t^{ratio}$ are the average utility of users and the action adoption rate within the region, respectively, at time t. In practice, $\hat{\tau}_t^{tran}$ is an accumulated indicator for a long period (such as a month) and is maintained in each time step. C is the number of clusters that stand for typical systemic dynamic patterns. Given a number of clusters C, $\hat{\tau}_t^{tran}$ is a function in the two-dimensional space spanned by u_t^{ave} and $\hat{\tau}_t^{ratio}$. Unsupervised clustering methods can be introduced on this metric to automatically discover different typical macroscopic dynamics. In particular, we use the k-means algorithm to characterize similarity via Euclidean distance. For each cluster of typical dynamics, a customized computational experiment started with such a historical trajectory is evolved to compute action candidates with activation strengths. Then, each action is prescribed with its probability to achieve the expected final system state.

9.2 Dynamic Community Discovery for Group Prescription

At the middle level of the three-layered prescription system are the regional agents, each of which represents a group of individuals. Generally, any collection of individuals with specific common characteristics can be viewed as a group. Such a kind of personalized partition for users is helpful to the customized strategy generation in the prescription system. In our view, setting a group level will bring at least three benefits. On the one hand, the regional layer can help engineers decompose the overall systemic objective from top to bottom. This is quite important since the global goal is sometimes abstract. Regional subgoals could be deemed as an initial refinement to keep that goal achieved. On the other hand, clustering of heterogenous individuals in a complex social system would aggregate the large number of different user demands into several categories. It is better to meet the user requirements coarsely in a bottom-up way. A third reward of group agents is that the computational complexity is effectively reduced, so that many intelligent algorithms such as distributed planning or adversarial game can get time-valid solutions in an online environment. Therefore, dynamically construct or reconstruct the groups is a vital issue for behavioral prescription.

The task to cluster users is consistent with the concept of community detection proposed by Newman and coworker [1], where users are modeled as nodes in a graph and their relationships are modeled as edges. Original methods for community division are based on the experience of engineers and certain heuristic rules. However, with the scale of users grown, artificial intervention is increasingly inefficient. The research community has developed many intelligent algorithms to complete this task. These methods are roughly composed of two stages. First, an evaluation criterion is given to explicitly define whether two specific nodes belong to the same cluster. Second, an algorithm is developed to assign all the user nodes to each community cluster according to the criterion. Depending on the number of communities assigned to each node, the community detection algorithms are further categorized into nonoverlapping methods (each user node belongs to only one community) and overlapping communities (a user node may be in multiple communities). Considering a specific user demand in our prescription, the former seems more appropriate as multiple communities may lead to conflict strategy prescriptions to the same individual. Therefore, we will explain the discovery process in detail below based on nonoverlapping methods.

Our discussion begins with mathematical notations. Let $F_{i \to j}$ be the impact from agent i to agent j. $d_{i \to j}$ is the topological distance from agent i to agent j. We deem the social network as a directed acyclic graph. Thus, $d_{i \to j}$ does not equal to $d_{j \to i}$. The capacity of information passing from agent i to j is denoted as $L_{i \to j}$. $N(i)$ is the collection of direct neighbors of agent i. Here a direct neighbor means the agent is directly connected to i in their social network. Define the information acceptance capacity of an agent as

$$O_i^{in} = \sum_{j \in N(i)} L_{j \to i}$$

and the information diffusion capacity as

$$O_i^{out} = \sum_{j \in N(i)} L_{i \to j}$$

The impact factor F is computed by the following formula

$$F_{i \to j} = f\left(\frac{L_{i \to j}}{O_i^{out} \cdot O_j^{in}}, d_{i \to j}\right)$$

$F_{i \to j}$ characterizes the unidirectional impact from i to j. However, when agents i and j are in the same group, the algorithm needs to treat them equally. In other words, the result of classification of i and j should be independent from the sequence of their assignment. So we further define a bidirectional impact factor

$$F_{ij} = g\left(\frac{L_{i \to j}}{O_i^{out} \cdot O_j^{in}}, \frac{L_{j \to i}}{O_i^{in} \cdot O_j^{out}}, d_{i \to j}, d_{j \to i}\right)$$

We propose three basic principles for dynamic community discovery.

1. Users with similar demands are grouped together in principle;
2. Dominant user nodes with high centralities should be classified in the same group as far as possible on condition that their information propagations are at the same level and their demands are similarly satisfied;
3. In order to keep computational loads balanced in distributed computing, scales of different groups should not vary too much, and each group needs to contain a certain number of agents (in other words, the size of a group should not be too small).

Given a topological social network, we introduce a modularity function to characterize the coupling degree of nodes within a cluster. The modularity function is computed as

$$Q^t = \frac{1}{m} \sum_{ij} (L_{i \to j}^t - P_{i \to j}^t) \delta(i, j)$$

$$P_{i \to j}^t = O_i^{out} \cdot O_j^{in} \cdot f(d_{i \to j})$$

$$f^t(d_{i \to j}) = \frac{\sum_{ij | d_{i \to j} = d} L_{i \to j}^t}{\sum_{ij | d_{i \to j}} O_i^{out} O_j^{in}}$$

In the above formulas, $m = \frac{1}{2} \sum_{ij} L_{i \to j}$. t is the time index. $\delta(i, j)$ is an indicator function. Its value is 1 if i and j belong to the same cluster and 0 if i and j are in different clusters. $P_{i \to j}$ can be viewed as an expected probability of connection within a cluster. $f^t(d_{i \to j})$ can be viewed as an information passing density.

Based on the modularity function defined earlier, the dynamic community discovery algorithm is given by Algorithm 9.1. The whole computation can be roughly separated into three parts. Part 1 is the initialization including Lines 1 and 2. Part 2 is the dynamic adjustment of cluster assignment from Lines 3

Algorithm 9.1 Agent Community Clustering

Input:

> n, number of agents; L, impact matrix; D, distance matrix; ε, convergence threshold;

Output:

> Agent groups.

1: Initialization by setting each agent as an independent cluster, indexed as $i = 1, \ldots, n$. Let the flag of community reconstruction flag $C_{flag} = False$;

2: Compute the impact matrix L;

3: **for** $i = 1$ to n **do**

4:     Find $N(i) = \{I_1, I_2, \ldots, I_m\}$ according to the distance matrix D;

5:     **for** $j = 1$ to m **do**

6:         Reclassify node i into the cluster of its neighbor node I_j;

7:         Calculate the increment of modularity function, V_{ij};

8:     **end for**

9:     Find $V_{imax} = \max_{j \in \{1, \ldots, m\}} V_{ij}$ and $j^* = \arg\max_{j \in \{1, \ldots, m\}} V_{ij}$;

10:     **if** $V_{imax} > \varepsilon$ **then**

11:         $C_{flag} = True$;

12:         Reclassify node i into the cluster of its neighbor node I_{j^*};

13:     **else**

14:         Leave the cluster of node i unchanged;

15:     **end if**

16: **end for**

17: **if** $C_{flag} == False$ **then**

18:     **return** the assigned agent groups;

19: **else**

20:     Reconstruct the social network by collapsing each community into a single node in the new network and normalize their distances;

21:     The impact factor between each node pair in the new network is the sum of impact factors between their corresponding communities in the original network;

22:     Go to Line 3.

23: **end if**

to 16. Such an adjustment is conducted by investigating whether the potential variation of modularity function exceeds the given convergence threshold. If not, the algorithm will stop and return the currently assigned agent groups. Part 3 involves Lines 17–23, which reconstruct the original social network as a new simplified one. This step abstracts a community as a new node so that the computational complexity will be greatly reduced. In Line 7, the increment of modularity function after reclassification of node i to the cluster of node j (denoted as c) is calculated by

$$\Delta Q^t = \frac{1}{m} \left[k_{i \to c}^{in(t)} + k_{c \to i}^{out(t)} - O_i^{out} \sum_{j \in c} O_j^{in} f^t(d_{i \to j}) - O_i^{in} \sum_{j \in c} O_j^{out} f^t(d_{i \to j}) \right]$$

where $k_{i \to c}^{in(t)}$ is the aggregate connections (impact) from i to c and vice versa for $k_{c \to i}^{out(t)}$. Rather than re-computation of the modularity function itself, the calculation of its local increment can greatly accelerate the dynamic node assignment.

9.3 Strategy Prescription Based on Content Match

Sections 9.1 and 9.2 give a hierarchical architecture of our prescription system, with global, regional, and individual levels. The agent group construction is also discussed from the perspective of community discovery. The setting of regional level is particularly for the complex social management, whereas in the human–machine interaction scenario that involves only a few participants, the agent group may degenerate into a single person. This section will talk about the prescription for individual levels. For the strategy prescription given in Eq. (9.6), its basic thought is to discretize the evolutionary space of the system's possible trajectories via state clustering. By treating the centroid of each cluster as the representative of its trajectory set, its related prescription template is well established and stored, so that our system in an online mode can directly use it rather than dynamic generation. Obviously, this discretization with precalculated prescriptions reduces the computational complexity. A necessary step to do this is to calculate the "distance" between the current system's evolutionary trajectory and every cluster template to determine which kind of strategies will be used to prescribe user's behavior. This section will elaborate a content-based method to complete the task.

The primary task of prescription is to push the most appropriate actions to meet the user's demand and to result in an expected evolutionary path of the system. The appropriation is defined as the degree of similarity between historical system states and arbitrary ones from computational experiments. In content-based prescription, it is required to characterize the system state using a common set of features. For instance, in a transportation system, the features may be traffic delay, queue length, average speed, etc. Then, the distance between system state and clusters can be computed by representing them with these features. The whole algorithm is explained as follows.

Step 1. Given a set of features, let the current system state be denoted as $a = \begin{bmatrix} a_1 & \cdots & a_m \end{bmatrix}^T$. Similarly, the centroid state of a specific cluster can be also represented as $b = \begin{bmatrix} b_1 & \cdots & b_m \end{bmatrix}^T$.

Step 2. Use a particular metric to compute the similarity between the two vectors. Here we adopt Euclidean distance, and the similarity is defined as

$$sim(a, b) = \frac{1}{1 + \sqrt{\sum_i (a_i - b_i)^2}} \tag{9.7}$$

Step 3. At every iteration, use K nearest neighbor (KNN) algorithm to choose the top K clusters that are most similar to the current state [2]. By taking the average value of these K nearest centroids, a matching degree for every action candidate is

$$pred(a, c) = \frac{\sum_{b \in K} sim(a, b) \cdot r_{b,c}}{\sum_{b \in K} sim(a, b)}$$

Here, $r_{b,c}$ means the correlation between centroid b and its prescription action c.

Step 4. The last step obtains an ordered prescription list. Without loss of generality, we denote them as $(c_1, c_2, \ldots, c_n)$ in a descending order of *pred*, where $pred(a, c_1) \geq pred(a, c_2) \geq \cdots \geq pred(a, c_n)$. Use c_1 as the prescription strategy.

Clearly, the above prescription algorithm returns a strategy intuitively. Its decision making is semantically explainable so that we can understand the reason behind the prescription. However, one of its deficiencies lies in the "cold start" problem, which refers to the weakness and inaccuracy of clusters with their correlated action candidates. This problem can be resolved via offline computational experiments. By conducting large-scale experiments, we can get a good estimation of the cluster features.

For validation, our prescription system and algorithm are tested in a travel behavior prescription. The experiment scenario is in the central area of Qingdao in China, including about 263 traffic zones, 50 main roads, 20 variable message signs (VMS), etc. We build a parallel transportation system that is composed of the real system and an artificial system (see Figure 9.2). The two systems coevolve through agent calibration and strategy prescription. According to the census data, we synthesized 405,758 virtual travelers at the community level. Each agent chooses his travel schedule based on classic disaggregate selection method by

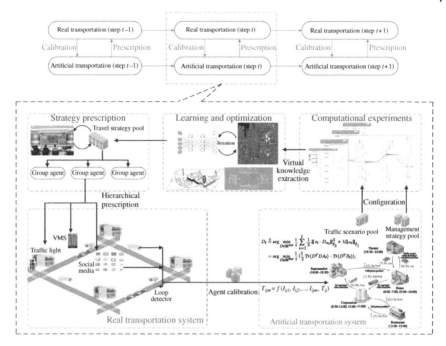

Figure 9.2 Travel behavior prescription in parallel transportation system.

considering travel distance, congestion level, and familiarity. By default, the travel path is determined by

$$p_l^e = \frac{\exp\left(c_e/L_l + d_e \cdot F_{el} + f_e/G_l\right)}{\sum_t \exp\left(c_e/L_t + d_e \cdot F_{et} + f_e/G_t\right)}$$

where p_l^e stands for the probability that agent e selects the lth path. L_l is the length of the path. F_{el}, a fuzzy variable ranging from 0 to 10, represents the agent's familiarity to the lth path. G_l, also a fuzzy variable ranging from 0 to 10, represents the overall congestion level of the lth path. c_e, d_e, and f_e are coefficients. In each step, the virtual travelers in the artificial system are calibrated using the methods introduced in Chapter 7. Then, computational deliberation experiments are conducted extensively, and the optimal management strategy is learned from the experiment results. By computing the similarities between the management strategy and the travel strategy pool, an expected optimal path for each traveler in the real system is pushed via official traffic websites, VMS, and applications in users' cell phones. Our preliminary test was conducted on 11 May 2020, and Figures 9.3–9.6 demonstrates the comparison of queue length before and after the travel behavioral prescription. It should be noted that 11 May and 18 May have similar traffic demand for the same weekday. For east direction, the queue lengths are decreased

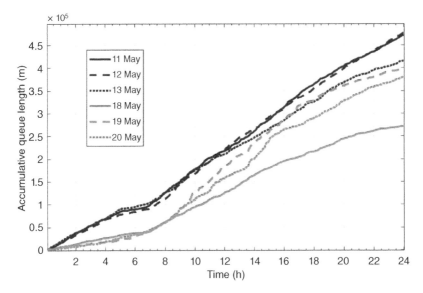

Figure 9.3 Queue length before and after travel behavioral prescription: east direction.

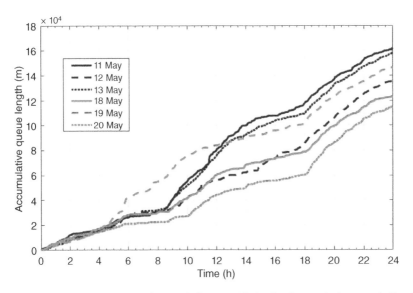

Figure 9.4 Queue length before and after travel behavioral prescription: south direction.

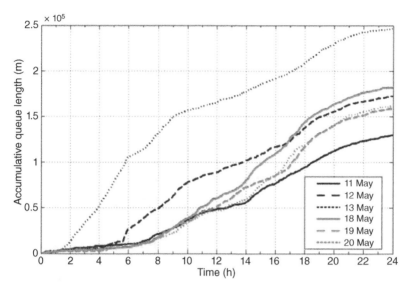

Figure 9.5 Queue length before and after travel behavioral prescription: west direction.

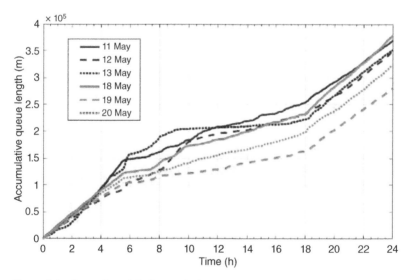

Figure 9.6 Queue length before and after travel behavioral prescription: north direction.

by 44.7%, 16.8%, and 8.7% in the whole day. In addition, customized recommendations served for more than 85,000 drivers, indicating that our travel behavioral prescription is effective and valid.

9.4 Active Learning in Strategy Prescription

Sections 9.1 to 9.3 talk about a prescription system that is applicable for complex social systems. The prescription aims to simulate the strategies from system manager that leads to an "optimal" global state of the system. In this section, we shift our focus to the behavioral prescription in complex human-in-loop systems. This kind of scenarios usually does not involve as many operators as the social ones. While rarely concerned with massive person-to-person connections, it requires to consider complex human–computer interactions. Compared with the social management, such a local objective of system running is much more microscopic, and we need to give a more detailed characterization of the human mental model. On the one hand, a set of detailed mental or cognitive beliefs of the world is a good foundation to support the accurate deliberation experiments, as human behaviors arise from his thinking and decision. Examining one's possible deliberation trajectories means capturing the causal source of his actions. On the other hand, traditional design often internalizes human operators as "components" of the system and strictly regulates their operations by the predetermined operational rules or instructions. It assumes that any eligible operators can "perfectly" undertake their assigned subtasks. Yet due to the heterogeneity of individual cognitions such as cognitive load, distraction, and knowledge level different operators will adopt strategies with different preferences even in a same operating position and situation. Such minor behavioral distinctions might result in subtle human errors that may accumulatively lead to fatal accidents, particularly in a scenario of frequent real-time interactions and high safety demand (like the manipulation of aerospace craft, the surveillance of nuclear power plant, and the control of high-speed railway). Therefore, it is necessary to monitor and dynamically "learn" the operator's physiological and mental beliefs (like the fatigue or risk preference) from his constant interactions, and further prescribe his actions to avoid human errors. With the promotion of machine intelligence, this task may be completed, at least to some extent, by developing automatic learning algorithms for one's mental knowledge. We adopt the active learning technique for this goal.

The main objective of active learning in constant and frequent human–machine interaction is to generate specific machinery states to query the operator for responsive actions. As its name inferred, such an approach aims to interactively acquire as much independent information as possible to exactly determine what decision trajectory is for a particular user. It helps us dynamically reconstruct one's mental map more accurately. The machinery state for query can be from either a snapshot that naturally emerges during the evolution of human–machine interaction or an arbitrarily synthesized one that is intended for active improvement of cognitive models. In the former case, our algorithm in each interaction cycle needs to determine whether the current ⟨state, action⟩ tuple should be considered as an instance to update the cognitive model. If not, the instance will be simply ignored after the interaction. In the latter case, the learning algorithm may reasonably synthesize a new state (either emerged before or not) to explore some uncertain hypotheses. Accordingly, the active learning can be run in two modes. One is to update the existing knowledge in the cognitive model according to the action response of an operator, such as calibrating the activation strengths of uncertain beliefs. This helps characterizing the heterogeneity in a more precise way since individual distinctions are mostly reflected as the different confidence of beliefs. The other is incremental learning, which adds new knowledge into the mental model so that it can cover more possible scenarios or provide more alternative responsive actions. The expansion of knowledge base will lead to more reasoning paths in computational deliberation experiments, making the prescribed strategy more optimal.

Leaving running mode aside, the ultimate goal of active learning in our prescription system is to reduce the uncertainty for the operator's behaviors. To this end, we introduce a hypothesis that given a behavioral prediction model, its uncertainty will be reduced the most if responsive action for the most uncertain state is queried [3, 4]. Various metrics of uncertainty are available depending on the problem and model. For our evolutionary reasoning and prescription method, where the activation strengths naturally accompany the prediction, all states that are query candidates are predicted, and the one with the highest entropy in the predicted action distribution should be selected. This policy is called entropy sampling, as entropy is a common metric of uncertainty. Formally speaking, let us return to our evolutionary reasoning and similarly define $\tau_k = \langle a_i, d_i \rangle_{i=0}^k$ as a decision sequence. The probability of action a_t in the tth reasoning step is $Pa_t | \langle a_i, d_i \rangle_{i=0}^{t-1}, u_t : g_A$, and the fitness function is denoted as $fit(k)$. Assume that after model initialization on a historical batch of data τ, our prescription agent has the possibility to query its user for his response at particular states chosen by the agent. In the $(k+1)$-th step, we are interested in choosing an eligible state to query the user so as to reduce the uncertainty of predicted behaviors while requiring significantly less data than purely random selection. This means the chosen state will be maximum informative to our current model. To this end, given an eligible tuple $\langle a_k, d_k = d \rangle \in A(\underline{s}) \times D(\underline{s})$, the distribution of action is

$$P\{a_{k+1} = a | \tau_k\} = g_A(a | \tau_k)$$

Thus, the entropy is

$$H(d) = -\sum_{a_{k+1} \in A(\underline{s})} g_A(a_{k+1}|\tau_k) \cdot \log\left[g_A(a_{k+1}|\tau_k)\right] \tag{9.8}$$

where $\tau_k = \langle a_0, d_0, \ldots, a_k, d_k = d\rangle$. If the query only considers one-step reasoning, then the prescription agent needs to select the state with maximum entropy

$$d_k^* = \arg\max_d H(d) \tag{9.9}$$

If the query considers multiple steps of reasoning, then we have

$$H\left(d_{k+1}\right) = -\sum_{a_{k+2} \in A(\underline{s})} g_A(a_{k+2}|\tau_{k+1}) \cdot \log\left[g_A(a_{k+2}|\tau_{k+1})\right] \tag{9.10}$$

where $\tau_{k+1} = \langle a_0, d_0, \ldots, a_k, d_k = d, a_{k+1}, d_{k+1}\rangle$. Since

$$g_A\left(a_{k+2}|\tau_{k+1}\right) = g_A\left(a_{k+2}|\tau_k, a_{k+1}, d_{k+1}\right) = \frac{g_A\left(a_{k+2}, a_{k+1}, d_{k+1}|\tau_k\right)}{g_A\left(a_{k+1}, d_{k+1}|\tau_k\right)}$$
$$= \frac{fs[d] \wedge g_A(a_{k+1}|\tau_k) \wedge g_A(a_{k+2}|\tau_k)}{fs[d] \wedge g_A(a_{k+1}|\tau_k)} \tag{9.11}$$

For all $d_{k+1} \in D(\underline{s})$, the expected entropy is

$$H(k+1) = -\sum_{a_{k+1} \in A(\underline{s})} \left[fs\left[d\right] \wedge g_A\left(a_{k+1}|\tau_k\right)\right] \cdot H\left(d_{k+1}\right)$$
$$= -\sum_{a_{k+1}, a_{k+2} \in A(\underline{s})} \left[fs[d] \wedge g_A(a_{k+1}|\tau_k) \wedge g_A(a_{k+2}|\tau_k)\right] \tag{9.12}$$
$$\cdot \log\left[\frac{fs[d] \wedge g_A(a_{k+1}|\tau_k) \wedge g_A(a_{k+2}|\tau_k)}{fs[d] \wedge g_A(a_{k+1}|\tau_k)}\right]$$

Recursively, we have

$$H(k+m)$$
$$= -\sum_{a_{k+1}, \ldots, a_{k+m+1} \in A(\underline{s})} \left[fs[d] \wedge \cdots \wedge g_A(a_{k+m+1}|\tau_k)\right] \tag{9.13}$$
$$\times \log\left[\frac{fs[d] \wedge \cdots \wedge g_A(a_{k+m+1}|\tau_k)}{fs[d] \wedge \cdots \wedge g_A(a_{k+m}|\tau_k)}\right]$$

Therefore, if the query considers the maximum entropy of m steps, its selected state is

$$d_k^* = \arg\max_d H(k+m)$$

Our active learning method in strategy prescription is tested in the cognitive visual reasoning task. In a complex human–machine interactive system, operators typically make specific actions to ensure the successful completion of the task. Their decisions rely on the state information as inputs from machines via visual, audio, olfactory, and other perception channels. Among the channels, visual perception is the most important source of external information acquisition. And the cognitive visual reasoning task can effectively simulate the human decision

Figure 9.7 An example of cognitive visual reasoning. (a) Problem and (b) candidates.

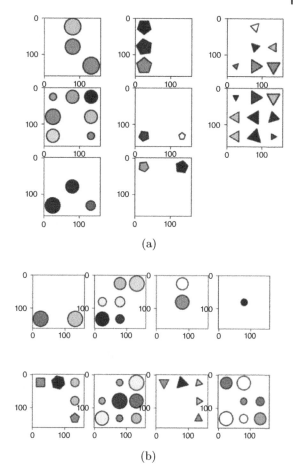

process based on visual signal inputs. Our experiment scenario is also set on the RAVEN data set, which provides synthetic tasks for relational and analogical visual reasoning [5]. As illustrated in Figure 9.7, each problem contains given eight images as inputs. Users need to select a suitable one from eight candidate images to complete the problem, so that the implicit decision rules could be satisfied. The decision rule involves seven attributes listed in Table 9.1, where the last four attributes correspond to the entities. In the example in Figure 9.7, the implicit rule is

$$Struct. = Sing. \text{ "and" } Comp. = Grid \text{ "and" } Layout = Dis.\_Nine$$

$$\text{"and" } Type = Dis.\_Three \text{ "and" } Size = Dis.\_Three$$

$$\text{"and" } Color = Dis.\_Three \text{ "and" } Angle = Prog.$$

For a particular testee, we build an artificial human as a prescription agent that is pretrained with given dataset. Then by dynamically choosing the type of

Table 9.1 Attributes of cognitive visual reasoning.

No.	Attr. name	Values	Num. of val.
1	Structure	Singleton, Left-Right, Up-Down, Out-In	4
2	Component	Grid, Left, Right, Up, Down, Out, In	7
3	Layout	Center_Sing., Dis._Four, Dis._Nine, Out_Center_Sing., In_Center_Sing., In_Dis._Four, Left_Center_Sing., Right_Center_Sing., Up_Center_Sing., Down_Center_Sing.	10
4	Type	Const., Prog., Arith., Dis._Three	4
5	Size	Const., Prog., Arith., Dis._Three	4
6	Color	Const., Prog., Arith., Dis._Three	4
7	Angle	Const., Prog., Arith., Dis._Three	4

problem, the agent actively interacts with the user, learning what he is good at and what he is weak in. The experiment is illustrated in Figure 9.8, where the artificial human iteratively selects a customized problem from the dataset for its user. There are two running modes for the agent, active learning and problem selection. In active learning, the artificial human provides the most uncertain problem according to its current deliberative knowledge. This can be viewed as an active query from machine to human user, which improves the most ambiguous part of the cognitive model. In problem selection by contrast, the artificial human does not try to improve the cognitive model but provides a "suitable" problem that the user is most likely to answer correctly, based on its learned knowledge. The two running modes are performed alternatively. Our aim is to elevate testee's accuracy by such active learning and computational deliberation experiments. To investigate the user's decision in detail, we separately examine the rule for each property. Figure 9.9 shows the rule recognition errors of human participants,

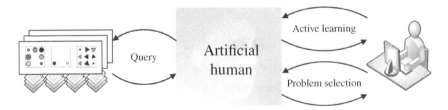

Figure 9.8 Experiment on cognitive visual reasoning.

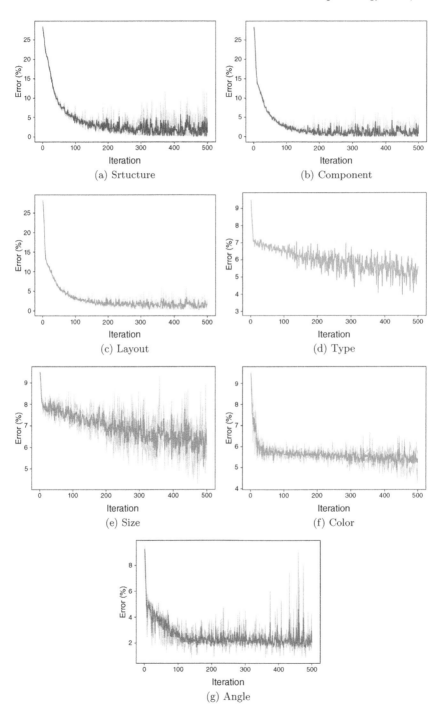

Figure 9.9 Recognition errors of human participants. (a) Structure, (b) component, (c) layout, (d) type, (e) size, (f) color, and (g) angle.

with each subfigure providing a particular attribute error. As can be seen, all the errors decrease with test iterations. In the early stage of experiments, visual reasoning problems are randomly given to the testees. Thus errors are relatively large. As active learning by human–machine interaction goes, our prescription agent gradually learns the user's preference and chooses the problems that he is good at according to computational deliberation experiments. This customization effectively leads to a decrease in the average errors and finally reaches a stable trend. Such a phenomenon could prove the effectiveness of our active learning method and preliminarily validate the thought of the parallel human approach. A second phenomenon is that the overall errors of image structure, component, and layout are smaller than those of other attributes. It is because these three attributes are global features, which can be more easily identified (the accuracies approach to 100%). By contrast, type, size, color, and angle are local properties of each entity. Their values are usually confused by users, especially when an image includes several entities, bringing a heavy cognitive load to limited perception channels of the testee.

9.5 Conclusions and Discussions

As the last step of our description–prediction–prescription loop, strategy prescription forms the kernel of the parallel population/human system. It also guarantees the execution of optimized strategies via artificial population/cognition modeling and computational deliberation experiments. This chapter elaborates the hierarchical architecture and computational flow of the prescription system. For the complex social management, we present a content-based prescription approach. By clustering the behaviors of extensive users, the system can match the similarity between specific individuals and centroids of clusters, so as to efficiently provide appropriate prescription strategies. For complex human-in-loop systems, we consider the cognitive heterogeneity of individual operators that derives from physiology, psychology, and social organization relations. The real-time human–machine interaction mechanism based on active learning is proposed to enhance the personalized setting of artificial cognition system and improve the accuracy of prescription strategy. And in the test on visual reasoning task, our active learning system can achieve good performance.

Admittedly, the study of strategy prescription has obtained only a few achievements. There are still many challenges to be further solved. For instance, in the content-based prescription, heterogeneous behavioral preferences are matched to the cluster center. This is a discretization operation in essence where all the possible values in the decision space are artificially represented by several cluster labels. Such a type of prescription may get poor performance in the fine-grained behavior patterns. Therefore, how to balance the accuracy of prescription with the efficiency of computational deliberation experiment is a problem worth considering. In our future work, we plan to improve the behavior prescription methods for heterogeneous individuals, and try to achieve more valuable results.

References

1 M. Girvan and M. E. Newman. Community Structure in Social and Biological Networks. Proceedings of the National Academy of Sciences of the United States of America, 2002, 99(12): 7821–7826.

2 R. M. Bell and Y. Koren. Scalable Collaborative Filtering with Jointly Derived Neighborhood Interpolation Weights. The 7th IEEE International Conference on Data Mining, Omaha, NE, USA, Oct. 28–31, 2007.

3 D. D. Lewis and W. A. Gale. A Sequential Algorithm for Training Text Classifiers. Proceedings of the International ACM SIGIR Conference on Research and Development in Information Retrieval, Dublin, Ireland, Jul. 3–6, 1994: 3–12.

4 Y. Yang, Z. Ma, F. Nie, et al. Multi-Class Active Learning by Uncertainty Sampling with Diversity Maximization. International Journal of Computer Vision, 2015, 113(2): 113–127.

5 C. Zhang, F. Gao, B. Jia, et al. RAVEN: A Dataset for Relational and Analogical Visual REasoNing. Proceedings of the IEEE Conference on Computer Vision and Pattern Recognition (CVPR), Long Beach, CA, USA, Jun. 16–20, 2019.

10

Applications for Parallel Population/Human

We have elucidated the framework, methodology, supporting techniques, and algorithms of our parallel population/human system. Some preliminary tests have been also conducted, for validation of specific algorithms. In this chapter, we will address the applications of the whole system in a higher level. There are four cases in this chapter, mainly from the population evolution to urban traffic guidance. These cases are representatives of our successful projects, which indicate that the parallel population/human system is effective for the management and control of complex social/engineering systems. We will start in Section 10.1 with a population evolution case. As a foundation of various applications, a multiagent system that characterizes the basic features of individuals is the first topic to be discussed. After that, three applications from urban transportation guidance are shown from Section 10.2 and 10.4. Qualitative and quantitative analyses have proved the validity of our system.

10.1 Population Evolution

With the framework proposed before, our development of cognitive artificial population system is composed of seven steps, namely basic synthetic population generation, agent cognitive architecture selection, knowledge representation and reasoning pattern determination, concrete domain knowledge and rules formulation, parameter calibration, validation, and computational experiments, as illustrated by Figure 10.1. During a full development process, it is suggested to take these steps sequentially. This section will adopt this paradigm to show the design and implementation in an application scenario – Chinese national population system. As one of the most populous country, Chinese population system is representative and complicated enough. Implementation of such system can test the validity of our system and reveal potential problems sufficiently.

Parallel Population and Parallel Human: A Cyber-Physical Social Approach,
First Edition. Peijun Ye and Fei-Yue Wang.

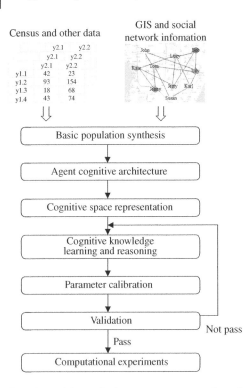

Census and other data

GIS and social
network infomation

Figure 10.1 Steps of artificial population development.

Based on this evolutionary system, results of computational experiments will be analyzed as well in this section.

We choose the nationwide population in 2000 as the basic synthetic population for simulation. This is partly because China periodically conducts its national census every 10 years, in the year number ended with 0. In 2000, the fifth census was taken, investigating tens of attributes about household and individual. The final official statistical results from National Bureau of Statistics published detailed geographical distributions and attribute structures that reflect the overall population's situation. In addition, we have collected a small proportion of disaggregate samples, each of which reveals an individual's attribute values with private information omitted. The sample set includes 1,180,111 records, accounting for 0.95% of the total population. Nonetheless, it provides a valuable seed of attribute correlations. This can improve the quality of synthetic population. According to the census data, the following individual attributes are considered in our model:

1. Gender (male and female)
2. Age (21 levels: 0–5, 6–10, …, 100 above)
3. Residential province (31 provinces)
4. Residential city (361 prefecture-level regions composing 31 provinces)

5. Ethnic group (57 levels: 56 groups plus 1 foreigners)
6. Residential type (urban, town, and village)
7. Education level (10 levels: infant, not educated, elementary school, ... , graduate)
8. Registration type (agricultural, non-agricultural, and no registration)
9. Registration province (32 levels: 31 provinces plus 1 no registration)
10. Marital status (married and unmarried)
11. Procreative status (has child and not have child)

Nationwide synthetic population is generated using Joint Distribution Inference (JDI) [1]. Social network of each individual is generated by randomly connecting himself with a certain number of other people that are in the same residential city or registered province.

In the second step, the integrated agent cognitive architecture proposed in Chapter 4 is adopted, while the third and fourth steps include five types of rules into the cognitive knowledge: marriage, social network, fertility, mortality, and migration. A person with qualified age is possible to find a spouse in his residential locations to form a family. The possibility, influenced by social norms, increases with his age until he is 40. Also, everyone is possible to get new friends and may be oblivious of an old friend. For fertility, every married female aged between 20 and 50 years and with no child will have a probability to give a new birth. The new child will be added to her family members after initialization, and the "mother" will change her procreative status into "Has Child." Mortality is similar. Every person has a probability to "die." Such probability relies on his age. To model reasonable migration flows in the cognitive level, we consider three factors: income, registration, and ethnic group. The ultimate satisfaction is computed as

$$s = \alpha \cdot s_{income} + \beta \cdot s_{regist} + (1 - \alpha - \beta) \cdot s_{ethnic}$$

where s_{income}, s_{regist}, and s_{ethnic} are three satisfaction levels of the factors; $\alpha, \beta \in (0, 1)$ are the intensity of attentions. When total satisfaction is smaller than a certain threshold, the agent cannot bear its current life and decides to migrate. To calibrate and validate the parameters, we use 10 years' data from Chinese Statistical Yearbook, that is the fertility rate, mortality rate, migration threshold, etc. After that, computational experiments using the validated system are designed to predict further evolution. The validated and prediction accuracies will be shown in the following.

The evolution is divided into three phases: population synthesis, model validation, and prediction. First, we focus on the accuracy of the basic population in 2000. The relative error of each city is computed as

$$err_{Pop} = \frac{\left| act_{Pop} - sim_{Pop} \right|}{act_{Pop}}$$

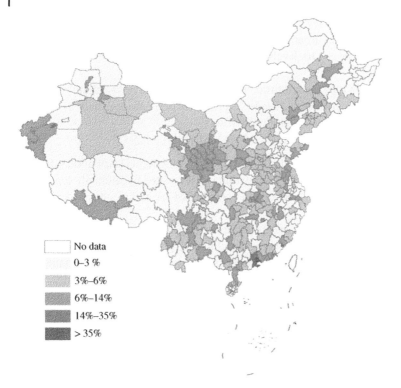

Figure 10.2 Relative errors of synthetic population.

where act_{Pop} and sim_{Pop} are actual and simulated person numbers. From Figure 10.2, we can see that most regions have no more than 15% errors. Eight cities pass this threshold, among which only two get larger than 35%. This indicates that our synthetic population fits the actual demographic structures very well.

Second, we investigate the calibration and validation accuracies, using the first 10 years' data (2001–2010). This tests the ability that our artificial population system "reproduces" the actual demographic trend. In the end of every year, simulated population number of each city is calculated to compare with the statistical ones. Limited by computational resources, the reduced scale is set to be 10,000. Figure 10.3 presents the annual errors of city population. It is clear that while simulation goes on, the total errors increase as well.

After validation, the artificial population system is used to predict the following five years' population distributions. The means and standard deviations are listed in Table 10.1. As is shown clearly, the errors stay relatively small and keep growing slowly and stably. This may be caused by the randomness of our model. As each step brings some random error, the accumulated error is growing. The standard

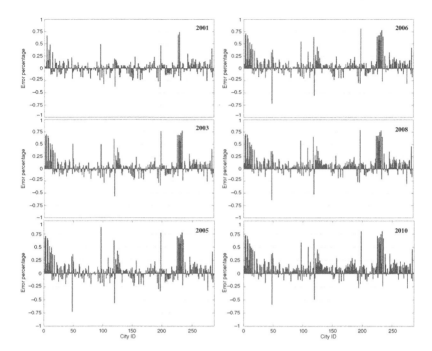

Figure 10.3 Annual relative errors of validated evolution.

Table 10.1 Means and standard deviations of prediction errors.

	2011	2012	2013	2014	2015
Mean (%)	17.07	17.62	18.55	19.46	19.93
Variance	0.1700	0.1688	0.1702	0.1673	0.1718

deviations seem to remain at the same level, which indicates that our prediction can track the trend of realistic population dynamics. In general, since the means and standard deviations are all below 20%, it manifests that our system is able to predict future population structures with a good accuracy.

As a comparison, the proposed model is also tested in the US population data set. However, the available US census data does not provide annual county statistics. Our experiment considers all the 3138 counties in US homeland (excluding Alaska, Hawaii, and Puerto Rico). Two types of data, annual disaggregate samples and statistics from 2000 and 2010 census, are used as inputs. The samples contain basic individual attributes like gender, age, ethnic group, marital status, and employment. The migration pattern is also recorded in the data. Therefore, we use

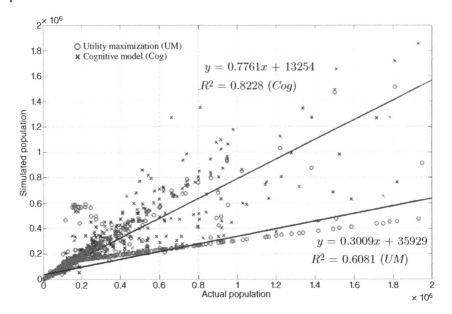

Figure 10.4 Results of 3138 counties from US homeland in 2010.

the samples to calibrated the model and evaluate the simulation results according to the 2010 overall census data. To test the performance of our system, the results are compared with the traditional utility maximization method. The experiment conducted on US population data set is shown as Figure 10.4. Obviously, neither regression line has a slope of 45 degrees, which means the models both bring some deviations in this case. However, the slope and goodness of fit of upper line (cognitive model) are closer to 1, meaning that the synthetic data by this model match the real census data more accurately overall. Intercepts in the axis of ordinate also indicate a smaller systemic error with the cognitive method than utility maximization. Therefore, from the perspective of statistics, the cognitive-based method can be viewed to have a better reconstruction capability. This partly manifests that the proposed model has a relatively better generalization performance.

10.2 Computational Experiments for Travel Behavior

Our second application is about the urban traffic demand analysis in Jinan. Based on the parallel population elaborated in Section 10.1, this use case mainly concentrates on computational experiments, which try to investigate various travel demand patterns. The synthetic travel demand with their elicited overall traffic state might be either someone emerged in history or some other situation that have

Figure 10.5 Abstract area of computational experiments for Jinan.

not seen before. In such a way, we are able to conduct experiments of urban transportation in certain extreme conditions, qualitatively, and quantitatively. Jinan is the capital of Shandong Province, a major economic province in the east coast of China. As a national coastal open city, it is the political, economic, cultural, scientific, educational, and financial center of the province. Our experiment scenario mainly builds on the area within the second Ring Road, covering the central area of the city (Figure 10.5). The abstract region contains a total of 420 activity places, including 163 residential areas, 86 workplaces, 59 schools, 19 malls, 21 hospitals, 37 hotels, 10 sport centers, and 13 recreational venues.

Given the land use and abstract road network, our artificial population scale is set to be 50,000, 80,000, 100,000, 120,000, 150,000, 180,000, and 230,000, respectively. By running the computational experiments, the statistical average speed in the road network during 6:00–14:00 weekdays is shown in Figure 10.6. As can be seen, with the increase of population scale, the overall traffic situation deteriorates constantly, and the time span for morning rush hour becomes longer as well. In a quantitative analysis, the worst average speed with 50,000 population is about 28 km/h while this metric drops significantly to only 10 km/h around when the population scale rises to 230,000. The morning peaks with different experiment configurations almost start at a same time of 7:30 a.m. Yet they required time to dissipate the congestions is quite different. In the case of 50,000 population, it takes

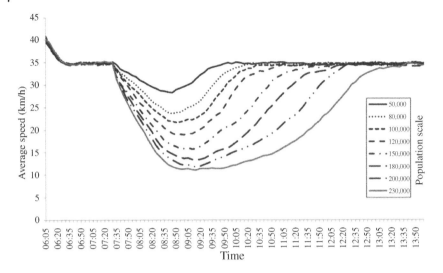

Figure 10.6 Average speed in road network with different population scale.

Table 10.2 Table of variance analysis.

Source	SS	df	MS	F	Prob > F
Columns	525.69	2	262.844	16.08	3.13835e−7
Error	3482.08	213	16.348		
Total	4007.77	215			

2.5 hours to end the rush hour while for 230,000 population, the dissipation time lasts for 5.5 hours in contrast. The latter extreme result indicates a great expense that has already seriously impacted social running. Such a large amount of travel cost will drag on people's normal lives and further harm the economic development of society.

Figure 10.7 further gives the cumulative probability distribution of the average speed with 50,000, 80,000, and 120,000 population scales. In addition, we mark 15% fractiles for each distribution, which is commonly used as an acceptable degree in urban traffic management. Clearly, the distributions are consistent with the trend of average speed mentioned before. When the population scale increases from 50,000 to 120,000, the average velocity in 15% fractile drops from 32.07 to 22.58 km/h, accounting for about 30%. The analysis of variance corresponding to Figure 10.7 is shown in Table 10.2. The results of the three population scales are significantly different in the statistical sense, and such a difference is more than

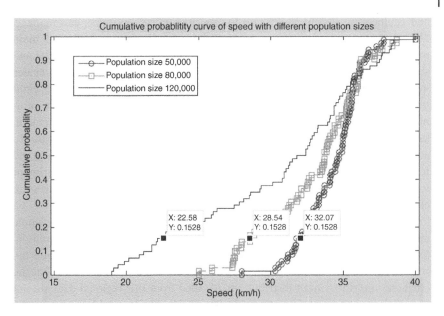

Figure 10.7 Cumulative probability distribution of average speed for different population scales.

99% confident. Our computational experiment results can be quantitative basis of prescriptions for the traffic management and control.

10.3 Parallel Travel Behavioral Prescription

After the pure computational experiments for travel behavioral analysis, we next step further to add the prescription into our applications. The use case in this section is from a second costal open city in eastern China named Qingdao. As a world regional trade center and an international tourist sight, its urban area is 3239 km^2, with 9.05 million population and 869.2 billion gross domestic product (Chinese Yuan) in 2014. As a frontier harbor that links China and the world's trade, Qingdao has constructed a basic traffic network with five vertical and six horizontal arterial highways. With the rapid increase of vehicles, seven major commercial and shopping districts become major traffic attraction blocks. The centralization of travel demand has seriously aggravated congestions which becomes a bottleneck of city development. Our project is the first application for group travel behavioral prescription in a whole city. Built upon the parallel population/human, our parallel traffic control and management system (PtMS) tries to interactively solve the dilemma that the urban transportation, as a complex social and engineering system, is difficult to experimentalize, optimize, and manage. The whole project covers Sinan, Sibei, and Licang districts, including 45 main roads, 76 secondary roads, and 49 key branches of the 7 major commercial and shopping centers. Driven by model and data in a hybrid way, the system provides infrastructure for intelligent management, control, and service. It involves eight primary functions on the signal control, situational monitoring, travel information collection, travel behavioral guidance, traffic regulation enforcement, safety management, command and dispatch, and service information release. To achieve the individual-oriented smart management, PtMS implements a closed feedback loop from traffic situational awareness, computational experiment for analysis, and to optimal travel behavioral prescription. The three stages are elaborated as follows.

The first stage is to construct artificial transportation system based on the whole city's population. The total scale of the target population is about 7.5 million. Similar to the synthetic population chapter, our available data source contains the regional overall cross-classification tables and the relevant Long Tables. But the attributes and their input distributions revealed from this regional data are not as sufficient as those of the nationwide. Specifically, the long tables only give the *Gender × District* frequencies of individuals whose age are beyond 15. Table 10.3 shows the attributes considered. The distributions of the short and long tables are listed in Table 10.4. Here we investigate several main streams of methods, sample-free fitting (SFF) [2], Markov chain Monte Carlo (MCMC) [3], and joint

Table 10.3 Attributes for the population of Qingdao.

Attributes	Num. of values	Values
Gender	2	Male, female
District	12	ShiNan, ShiBei, SiFang, HuangDao, LaoShan, LiCang, ChengYang, JiaoZhou, JiMo, PingDu, JiaoNan, LaiXi
Res. type	2	Urban, rural
Edu. Lv	10	Infant, Not Educated, Liter. Class, Pri. Sch., Jun. Mid. Sch., Sen. Mid. Sch., Polyteh. Sch., College, University, Graduate
Age interval	18	0–4, …, 85 and above

Table 10.4 Two types of tables used as the inputs and benchmark.

No.	Short Table (inputs)	No.	Long Table (benchmark)
1	*District × Res. Type*	1	*Gender × District* (for Age ≥ 15)
2	*Gender × District × Age Inter.*		
3	*Gender × District × Edu. Lv*		

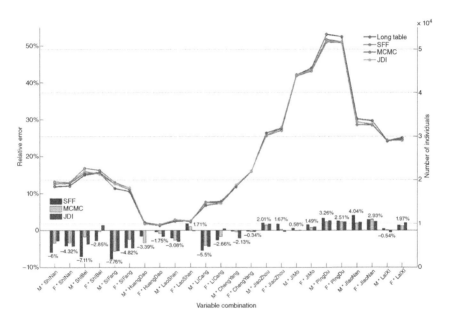

Figure 10.8 Frequency and relative error of Qingdao synthetic population (M, male; F, female).

distribution inference (JDI) [1], to generate the population. The population synthesis is repeated five times and a small proportion of each result is stochastically sampled according to the long table population scale. The sampled populations are evaluated, respectively, and the averaged final result is shown in Figure 10.8. As can be seen, the largest error is −7.76% and most of them are below 5%. The three RSSZm values are 18.6998 (SFF), 8.1140 (MCMC), and 10.2088 (JDI). It indicates that the latter two perform much better in general. As RSSZm measures the deviation between real and synthetic data, the results also manifest that it is better to adopt the population from JDI. The generated group travel behavior involves 1020 activity places in the studied districts, including 263 residential areas, 186 workplaces, 109 schools, 69 malls, 71 hospitals, 87 hotels, 60 sport centers, and 63 leisure/entertainment places. The abstract traffic network contains 424 light-controlled intersections, 1500 detectors, 350 traffic signs, 20 variable message signboard, 50 speed limited lanes, and 30 overpasses (see Figure 10.9).

The second stage is evolutionary computational experiments for the optimization of management and control strategies. Our experiments mainly focus on the following aspects:

(1) Impacts on urban traffic situation with different configurations of commuter time;
(2) Parking capacities of interested regions for a big event with various resizable parking lots;
(3) Overall traffic pressure and distribution of police in particular roads and intersections, with different time settings for big events;
(4) Temporal and spatial propagations of various major accidents;
(5) Crowd evacuation strategies under distinct public transportation lines and schedules;
(6) Impacts on traffic situation with different traffic control measures such as driving restriction and one-way driving;
(7) Analysis of public transport service capacity and its impacts on social transportation, with public transport priority strategy;
(8) Evolutionary traffic patterns under severe weather conditions such as snowing and hailing;
(9) Quantitative performance of signal control strategy in specific intersections;
(10) Performance test of other traffic management and control strategies.

In contrast to traditional traffic simulation that mostly concentrates on the moving dynamics of road vehicles but the endogenous factor of travel demand generation, our computational experiments are built upon individual travel behaviors as well as their couplings with environment and social factors (see Figure 10.10). In addition, computational experiments can investigate rare scenarios that have not observed but likely to occur in the future, such as the transportation under extreme weather conditions, or with the total vehicle number passing the city's capacity limit, etc.

The third stage is to prescribe individual travel behaviors according to optimal tested strategies. Two ways for behavioral prescription are exploited in our project. One is the real-time broadcast of regional traffic guidance information, including congestion states, travel time, accidents, travel restrictions, etc. The other is customized information via cell phone APP, including personalized navigation, real-time video surveillance, etc. Some additional services are also provided like the vehicle management record inquiry, violation record inquiry, driver license

(a)

(b)

Figure 10.9 Real and virtual maps of Qingdao artificial transportation system. (a) Artificial and (b) real.

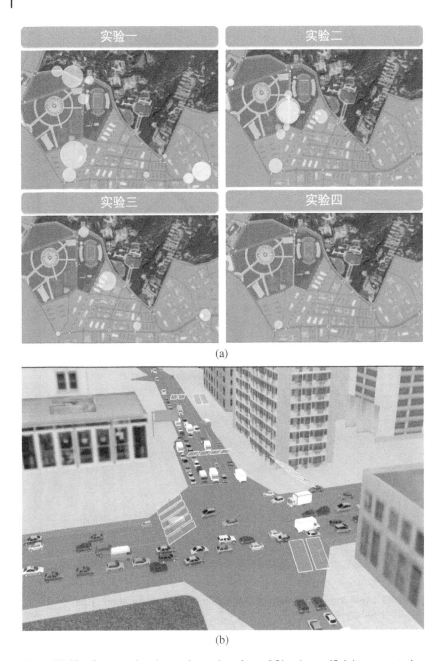

(a)

(b)

Figure 10.10 Computational experiment interface of Qingdao artificial transportation system. (a) Artificial and (b) real.

annual update, etc. After our system deployed, traffic situation in the main districts of Qingdao has been significantly improved. An application report from government indicates that the travel time in arterial roads decreases 20% in average while the number of stops decreases 45%. The congestion miles and travel time of key roads drop about 30% and 25%, respectively, leading to a 43.39% elevation of traffic efficiency. For individual prescription, our APP in cell phone has attracted more than 85,000 users with over 4.4 million visits after it deployed for only one month. Furthermore, more than 58,000 vehicles have been bound to inquire traffic violation records, and over 20,000 traffic violation reminders have been automatically pushed to the drivers.

10.4   Travel Behavioral Prescription for Sports Event

The last application in this chapter will address a scenario for Asian games. This use case also comes from a successful project that serves the 16th Asian Games in Guangzhou, China. As the largest international event held in Guangzhou, the quadrennial game also brings an opportunity to promote the city's reputation and economic development. More than 10,000 athletes from 45 countries and regions participate in 42 sports competitions, ranging from Archery to Chess. In addition, a huge number of spectators and visitors flood into the city, leading to a great challenge to its congested urban transportation. To tackle the problem, the government makes a policy for public transport priority and we develop a Parallel Public Transportation System (PPTS) to guarantee its implementation. The system is based on parallel population and is developed to model the area surrounding Guangzhou Tianhe sport center (Figure 10.11). Tianhe sport center is a primary cluster of venues for Asian Games. It includes Tianhe stadium, Tianhe gymnasium, Tianhe natatorium, Tianhe softball field, Tianhe tennis field, and Tianhe bowling hall. Adjacent to the sport center are central business district (CBD) and several malls. Even though there are 2 subway lines, 30 bus lines and 28 bus rapid transit (BRT) lines passing through this region, such a centralization of travel attraction still makes it face a high traffic pressure.

A part from the great travel demand, a second consideration for the government is the competition that may potentially cause mass traffic chaos. Therefore, it is treated as one of the most important tasks in preparation of the Asian Games. For the Tianhe sport center district, various evacuation plans have been made to deal with possible emergent situations. Yet these plans are mainly formulated via accumulated experiences from traffic engineers and managers, without a feasible way for quantitative validation. In this sense, computational experiments based on parallel population might be the only approach to tackle such an issue. Here

Figure 10.11 Abstract road network of PPTS.

we set two experiment scenarios for the eighth match day to investigate two evacuation plan candidates. As the match schedule listed in Table 10.5, our studied area accommodates about 10,000 spectators during day time and over 50,000 in the evening. Figure 10.12 shows the BRT schedules for four lines (B1, B2, B3, and B4) in the two evacuation plans. Compared with the normal schedule, the evacuation plans only add buses from 7:00 p.m. to 9:00 p.m. for the increase of evacuation demand. Our computational experiments are evaluated by collecting and analyzing different metrics of the results.

Figure 10.13(a) is the traffic flow trend for the whole day. Unlike traditional "M" curve with morning and evening peaks, this trend has additional peak hours from 20:00 to 21:00, which is caused by the football and badminton matches. The sudden stimulation of great travel demand brought by the end of matches in 20:00 is also verified by the average speed in Figure 10.13(c). This indicator shows an obvious drop from 20:00 to 21:00, meaning that the spectators' leaving causes a certain

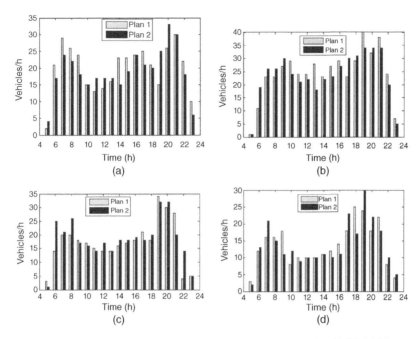

Figure 10.12 BRT schedule plans for the eighth match day. (a) B1, (b) B2, (c) B3, and (d) B4.

Table 10.5 Schedule for the eighth Match Day.

Competition	Time	Stage	Spectators	Location
Football	18:30–20:30	M/QF	30,000–50,000	Tianhe stadium
Badminton	19:30–21:30	M/W/F	5000–7000	Tianhe gymnasium
Water polo	09:00–11:10 14:30–17:10 19:30–22:10	M/P	3000–5000	Tianhe natatorium
Softball	13:00–15:00 15:30–17:30 18:00–20:00	W/P	3000–5000	Tianhe softball field
Soft tennis	09:30–17:00	M/W/SF/F	2000–3000	Tianhe tennis field
Bowling	09:00–12:00	M/W/F	<1000	Tianhe bowling hall

M, men; W, women; P, preliminary; QF, quarter final; SF, semi final; F, final.

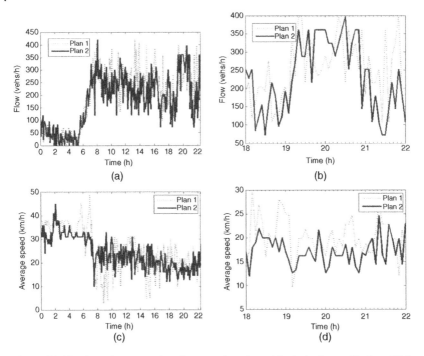

Figure 10.13 Experiment results of evacuation plans. (a) whole day traffic flow, (b) four hours traffic flow, (c) whole day average speed, and (d) four hours average speed.

Table 10.6 Analysis of variance for the whole day average speed.

Source	SS	df	MS	F	Prob > F
Columns	401.7	1	401.668	5.92	0.0153
Error	38,963.9	574	67.881		
Total	39,365.6	575			

degree of congestion. For a clearer view, four hours traffic flow and average speed are drawn in Figure 10.13(b) and Figure 10.13(d).

Further comparative analysis is conducted for the two evacuation plans. In Figure 10.4, the mean values of average speed for plans 1 and 2 are 28.5 and 26.38 km/h, respectively. The analysis of variance (ANNOV) is calculated in Table 10.6, which indicates that we cannot statistically reject the hypothesis $H_0 : AV_{plan1} = AV_{plan2}$ the confidence level 0.99. In other words, the evacuation effects of two plans are not significantly distinct in a statistical sense. Next, we

Table 10.7 Analysis of variance for the four hours average speed.

Source	SS	df	MS	F	Prob > F
Columns	210.18	1	201.184	16.79	8.71248e−05
Error	1201.5	96	12.516		
Total	1411.69	97			

restrict our time window from 18:00 to 22:00 for a more detailed comparison. The mean values of average speed in this time span drop to 20.16 and 17.23 km/h, respectively. The corresponding analysis of variance is given in Table 10.7. In contrast with the whole day situation, the result indicates that the hypothesis $H_0 : AV_{plan1} = AV_{plan2}$ can be rejected with the confidence level 0.9999, meaning that the evacuation effects of two plans differentiate from each other significantly.

We use average time occupancy and space density as two overall criteria to verify the effect of our system. After deployment of our PPTS, the average time occupancy drops from 27.8% to 22.6%, and the average space density drops from 36.2 to 31.3 vehs/km. While both of the indicators prove an effective traffic management after PPTS deployed, the improvement mainly comes from the time intervals with high travel demand. For example, the improvement of traffic situation in morning and evening rush hours is particularly notable. This implies that our system can be adaptive to the variation of travel demand and adjust its parameters in an automatic way.

10.5 Conclusions and Discussions

As a foundation of system analysis, experiment, optimization, control, and management, the parallel population and parallel human systems can be applied in many scenarios particularly for complex social and human–machine interactive systems. This chapter presents four application cases from population evolution and travel behavioral prescription. For complex social systems, the parallel population is a self-consistent system that plays a testbed for other kind of social systems, such as economics, public health, and military simulation. Thus, the first application starts from population evolution. The use case focuses on the endogenous dynamics of the population. On this basis, we further consider travel behavioral prescription by adding travel models into the individual agent. As a consequence, the following three applications investigate urban transportation as a representative scenario, from pure computational experiments, travel behavioral prescription, to evacuation for sports event. Quantitative analysis indicates that our system is effective and valid for urban transportation control and management.

While the use cases from real projects in this chapter mainly concern about computational social systems, the parallel population/human system is still applicable for complex human–machine interactive systems. In our population system, the individual agent is modeled with a cognitive architecture. By adding different knowledge and interactive rules from various domains, the multiagent system can be easily transferred into the manipulation of aerospace craft, the surveillance of nuclear power plant, the control of high-speed railway, etc. Such human–machine tight coupling systems are one of our future directions in validating the parallel humans.

References

1 P. Ye, X. Hu, Y. Yuan, et al.. Population Synthesis Based on Joint Distribution Inference Without Disaggregate Samples. Journal of Artificial Societies and Social Simulation, 2017, 20(4): 16.

2 J. Barthelemy and P. L. Toint. Synthetic Population Generation Without a Sample. Transportation Science, 2013, 47(2): 266–279.

3 B. Farooq, M. Bierlaire, R. Hurtubia, et al.. Simulation Based Population Synthesis. Transportation Research Part B: Methodological, 2013, 58: 243–263.

11

Ethical and Legal Issues of Parallel Population/Human

Chapters 2–10 have elaborated the parallel population and parallel human for cyber physical social systems. Our discussions mainly address the technical facets, ranging from the basic methodologies, possible implementations, to the typical applications. In this chapter, we will shift our views into the ethics, which is also an indispensable part of this book. As explained in the Introduction chapter, the parallel human system has exploited extensive techniques from AI. This characteristic determines that we should concentrate on the ethical issues pertinent to our system. The topic is more important for our parallel population/human system than for other intelligent ones because the former directly interacts with the real human users or groups. With the increase of the system intelligence through an accumulative learning, once the autonomy exceeded a certain threshold, behavioral computation and guidance may exclude the participation of human users, leading to unpredictable consequences. Therefore, it is essential to make a fruitful discussion on these issues, which may foresee particular ethical and legal problems that the system may encounter in its application, and design appropriate responses for those challenges.

Our discussion in this chapter will unfold in three directions. Section 11.1 elaborates the relationships between the parallel population/human and its individual users. Our central idea here is that the system is human centric, and the artificial system lies in an auxiliary position all through its life. Some concrete measures are also discussed in this section. Section 11.2 shifts the perspective from the technological system building to the use of human participants. We emphasize a supreme principle that the artificial system should have a very limited authority so that human users could reserve the final right to decide whether adopt the recommendations from artificial population as their behavior service. If the service from the artificial human system is adopted, the prescribed behaviors may take partial responsibilities when accidents or illegal activities occur. Various situations in this case are discussed in Section 11.3. Then the chapter concludes at last.

Parallel Population and Parallel Human: A Cyber-Physical Social Approach,
First Edition. Peijun Ye and Fei-Yue Wang.
© 2023 The Institute of Electrical and Electronics Engineers, Inc. Published 2023 by John Wiley & Sons, Inc.

11.1 Relationships Between the Parallel Population/Human and Its Individual Users

The overall structure of parallel population and parallel humans clearly shows that the system contains two weakly related closed loops. While these two loops are running independently, they are not in an equivalent status. Basically, the real human/population lies in a dominant place whereas the artificial counterparts play an auxiliary role. Our supreme principle is that the system, at any time of its running, can only be the assistant of its human users rather than performing autonomous decision makings by itself. Such a principle requires two essential facets in the system building. First, the artificial human needs to display key information for behavior selection when interacting with its human user. It is a digital secretary that helps human users filter out most useless information. Living in an age of information explosion, we are facing with substantial messages, both online and offline, for multiple decisions. Only a small part of them, however, are really useful for our decision making. The digital secretary thus can sift these useless and redundant messages out to alleviate people's cognitive load, raising the accuracy and efficiency of their decisions. Second, the key information conveyed by the artificial human should not missing any important clues that may possibly influence the user's final decisions. This can avoid the bias of the user's decision as much as possible. Here, the importance of information varies from person to person. For example, given a same battlefield situation map, a commander may concentrate on the overall distribution of troops while a soldier may focus on his surrounding local environment. The criterion depends on the cognitive model learned from the human participant, which has been discussed in Chapters 4 and 6.

Another principle that may facilitate better artificial systems is the intervention of the public in moral and ethical evaluations. As learning and reasoning algorithms are developed by human engineers, the running of our system reflects the data and operational flow designed by its designers. For some simple cases such as the autonomous driving, the artificial driver controls the steering wheel, the gas pedal, and the brake. We are able to predict the system's outputs, the steering angle, speed, and acceleration, in every input condition, and then their potential detrimental effects for the real driver and other travelers (such as the possible collision with pedestrians). In other more complicated cases, things could be worse, where the outputs may not be enumerated. For example, the artificial secretary may encounter different demands from its human user, ranging from planning a flight trip to booking a cup of latte based on his/her past experiences. The diverse behavior selection may bring much difficulty to analyze its potential subsequent effects. However, we are able to estimate its possible outputs, at least in part, from the output space, since all the behavior candidates are included in a predefined universe. Based on such estimations, impacts on user groups can also be evaluated in advance. Therefore, by introducing public moral and ethical evaluations, it is feasible to correct possible design "defects" that may result in adverse consequences on human users. Such an early intervention can guarantee the system development in a human compatible direction at the very beginning stage.

11.2 Authority of the Parallel Population/Human System

The supreme principle that the parallel systems are always human centric is applicable not only in the technological system building but also in the use of human participants. From the perspective of users, it is their own right to decide whether accept or partly accept the service from artificial humans. We introduce a three-tiered control to implement this principle. At the top, most is the user's authorization for the use of parallel humans. As the artificial system needs to constantly interact with human users during its running, it will inevitably access some user's behavioral records, which may reveal the user's preference and habits. Hence, just like the use of an application in cell phone, the users are permitted to totally reject the access of our system. Apart from totally rejecting or accepting the interaction with artificial humans, users can also partially adopt the service provided by our artificial system. Such a partial authorization is implemented in the second layer control. For human participants, taking part in the interaction in parallel population with a limited scope can be controlled both from the use and techniques. On the one hand, what kind of information or operational records can be collected depends on the user's choices. Such data is very helpful for the learning and reasoning of the artificial system. In the learning phase, user data is treated as the model's input and directly determines the significant features that impact one's particular behaviors. Thus, the range of input attributes has great influence on the model's final performance. By excluding some key features, the human user is able to prevent specific detrimental effects on himself. On the other hand, some emerging techniques such as the federated learning can also be exploited to protect the user's privacy. In contrast to classic centralized machine learning techniques where all the local datasets are uploaded to one server to train the model, and the classic decentralized approaches which often assume that local data samples are identically distributed, the federated learning is born to train a model across multiple decentralized edge devices or servers holding local data samples, without exchanging them. It enables multiple actors to build a common, robust knowledge base without sharing data, thus allowing to address critical issues such as data privacy, data security, data access rights and access to heterogeneous data. By exploiting the federated learning, the data of different users or the data of the same user in different devices (such as the cell phone, wearable devices, etc.) is not required to be exchanged, so that the personal privacy will be carefully protected. At the bottom of our three-tiered control implementation is the optional behavioral prescription. As elaborated in Chapter 5 and 9, the prescriptive strategy is recommended to its human user after the evolutionary experiments for deliberation reasoning and convergent evaluations. However, such prescriptions are "soft" but not mandatory. Whether adopt or to what extent to adopt such recommended strategies remains for the human users to decide. Through our three-tiered controlled implementations of the artificial population system, we are capable of effectively protecting the human users' privacy and ensuring the parallel system is always at a correct track to serve the human society.

11.3 Risk Management and Responsibility Identification

The auxiliary principle and the three-tiered controlled implementations have equipped our parallel system with ethical interventions. This allows our system to prevent the vast majority of possible hazards to the human society. In some very extreme cases, however, there might be also potential risks, leading to unforeseen dangers or even accidents. A well-known example is the fatal crash of Tesla automated vehicle in its assistant driving mode, Autopilot, in Mountain View, California, USA, 23 March 2018 [1]. The driving assistant mistakenly used the left lane line as a land mark, leading to a crash into the narrow concrete barrier. Struck by two following vehicles, it then caught on fire. This is not a single case in history. Similar accidents successively occurred later [2–4]. All these accidents have indicated that any latest and advanced system has the possibility for dangers. The most important is not to absolutely prevent the accidents but how to deal with them. Therefore, the risk management and responsibility identification, even if the user voluntarily accepts the service from the parallel system, are unavoidable issues in application. We address this issue in two cases. When critical information that may lead to illegal activities or dangers has not clearly shown to the user, for a given accident, the system developer is suggested to take the responsibility. By contrast, if such type of critical information related to the illegal activity or accident has clearly shown to the user, then the user is advised to be responsible. For example, when Lily, an animation designer, asks her artificial secretary about the popular cartoon characters. Her "Artificial Lily" gets some results by searching from the Internet and even the generation of additional ones according to classic characters. The artificial system then prescribes a collection of candidates with preferences based on Lily's past appetite. Lily chooses a cute one and applies it in the propagation of her corporation's product. Several days later, her corporation receives an attorney's letter, accused of using unauthorized cartoon characters. How about the responsibility identification in this case? According to the principle mentioned before, two situations need to be considered. If each candidate returned by the "Artificial Lily" is clearly attached with its source and a tip that its copy's re-use might raise legal problems, the human user, Lily, would take the responsibility. In contrast, if the source and tips of each candidate are missing or unclear, then the artificial system with its builders would be responsible. Undoubtedly, a clear definition of the boundaries of authority and responsibility helps to avoid moral hazards from both the developers and users of parallel systems. It guides a safe and efficient development as well as the usage of every artificial human. Of course, for the risk of an accident, there is currently no common identification of what kind of information is the key information. It depends on a case-by-case analysis.

11.4 Conclusions and Discussions

This chapter briefly talks about ethical and legal issues of our parallel population/human system. Our discussion addresses the technological aspect and the use of human participants. Our supreme principle is that the parallel systems are always human-centric all through its running life. This is reflected as the fact that the real human/population lies in a dominant place, whereas the artificial counterparts play an auxiliary role. We further build a three-tiered control to implement this principle, which considers the user's authorization at the top layer, the personal data access/privacy in the middle layer, and the (partially) acceptance of the prescribed behavior at the bottom layer. The three-tiered control implementation can ensure that the parallel system is always at a correct track to be human-centric, and prevent the vast majority of possible hazards to the human users. The risk management and responsibility identification are discussed as well. Ultimately, all these principles and measures would guarantee that the parallel population and parallel human are serving the human society, promoting the harmonious cooperations of human and machines as well as of people themselves via cyberspace.

References

1 The Tesla Team. An Update on Last Week's Accident. March 30, 2018. https://www.tesla.com/blog/update-last-week%E2%80%99s-accident. Retrieved October 20, 2022.

2 S. Sutton. Tesla driver killed after crash involving semi in western Delray Beach. WPTV 5 West Palm Beach, March 01, 2019. https://www.wptv.com/news/region-s-palm-beach-county/serious-crash-investigated-on-u-s-441-in-southern-palm-beach-county. Retrieved October 20, 2022.

3 AP News. Feds will investigate deadly Tesla crash in California. AP News, December 31, 2019. https://apnews.com/article/technology-business-los-angeles-us-news-california-6eae3986e7d9c1d00db7d52146cddf23. Retrieved October 20, 2022.

4 Ryan Bittan. Motorcyclist dies in crash with Tesla on auto-pilot. ABC 4, July 24, 2022. https://www.abc4.com/news/local-news/motorcyclist-dies-in-crash-with-tesla-on-auto-pilot/. Retrieved October 20, 2022.

Appendix A

Convergence for Multivariate IPF

Theoretical convergence of joint distribution inference (JDI) algorithm is investigated as follows. Our proof will be grounded on the iterative proportional fitting (IPF) method proposed by Deming and Stephan [1], whose convergence has been extensively investigated [2–4]. However, these related literatures have only considered two-dimensional case. This appendix will give a proof for a general case. In order to illustrate the main thought, three-dimensional case is first presented and then extended to a multivariate case.

Proposition A.1.1 (Three-dimensional case) *Suppose the marginals of three positive real variables (X_1, X_2, X_3) are $f(x_1), f(x_2),$ and $f(x_3)$. The result of kth iteration can be written as*

$$f^{(1)}(x_1, x_2, x_3)(k) = \frac{f(x_1, x_2, x_3)(k-1)}{\sum_{x_2, x_3} f(x_1, x_2, x_3)(k-1)} \cdot f(x_1) \quad (x_1 \text{ fitted})$$

$$f^{(2)}(x_1, x_2, x_3)(k) = \frac{f^{(1)}(x_1, x_2, x_3)(k)}{\sum_{x_1, x_3} f^{(1)}(x_1, x_2, x_3)(k)} \cdot f(x_2) \quad (x_2 \text{ fitted})$$

$$f^{(3)}(x_1, x_2, x_3)(k) = \frac{f^{(2)}(x_1, x_2, x_3)(k)}{\sum_{x_1, x_2} f^{(2)}(x_1, x_2, x_3)(k)} \cdot f(x_3) \quad (x_3 \text{ fitted})$$

$$f(x_1, x_2, x_3)(k) = f^{(3)}(x_1, x_2, x_3)(k)$$

Define L1 error as

$$L(k) = \sum_{x_1} \left| \sum_{x_2, x_3} f(x_1, x_2, x_3)(k) - f(x_1) \right| + \sum_{x_2} \left| \sum_{x_1, x_3} f(x_1, x_2, x_3)(k) - f(x_2) \right|$$

$$+ \sum_{x_3} \left| \sum_{x_1, x_2} f(x_1, x_2, x_3)(k) - f(x_3) \right|$$

Then the L1 error monotonously decreases during its iteration.

Parallel Population and Parallel Human: A Cyber-Physical Social Approach,
First Edition. Peijun Ye and Fei-Yue Wang.
© 2023 The Institute of Electrical and Electronics Engineers, Inc. Published 2023 by John Wiley & Sons, Inc.

Proof: When X_1, X_2, and X_3 are fitted in turn during the kth iteration, $L1$ errors are

$$L^{(1)}(k) = \sum_{x_2} \left| \sum_{x_1,x_3} f^{(1)}(x_1,x_2,x_3)(k) - f(x_2) \right| + \sum_{x_3} \left| \sum_{x_1,x_2} f^{(1)}(x_1,x_2,x_3)(k) - f(x_3) \right|$$

$$L^{(2)}(k) = \sum_{x_1} \left| \sum_{x_2,x_3} f^{(2)}(x_1,x_2,x_3)(k) - f(x_1) \right| + \sum_{x_3} \left| \sum_{x_1,x_2} f^{(2)}(x_1,x_2,x_3)(k) - f(x_3) \right|$$

$$L^{(3)}(k) = \sum_{x_1} \left| \sum_{x_2,x_3} f^{(3)}(x_1,x_2,x_3)(k) - f(x_1) \right| + \sum_{x_2} \left| \sum_{x_1,x_3} f^{(3)}(x_1,x_2,x_3)(k) - f(x_2) \right|$$

Similarly for the $(k+1)$th iteration:

$$L^{(1)}(k+1) = \sum_{x_2} \left| \sum_{x_1,x_3} f^{(1)}(x_1,x_2,x_3)(k+1) - f(x_2) \right|$$

$$+ \sum_{x_3} \left| \sum_{x_1,x_2} f^{(1)}(x_1,x_2,x_3)(k+1) - f(x_3) \right|$$

$$L^{(2)}(k+1) = \sum_{x_1} \left| \sum_{x_2,x_3} f^{(2)}(x_1,x_2,x_3)(k+1) - f(x_1) \right|$$

$$+ \sum_{x_3} \left| \sum_{x_1,x_2} f^{(2)}(x_1,x_2,x_3)(k+1) - f(x_3) \right|$$

$$L^{(3)}(k+1) = \sum_{x_1} \left| \sum_{x_2,x_3} f^{(3)}(x_1,x_2,x_3)(k+1) - f(x_1) \right|$$

$$+ \sum_{x_2} \left| \sum_{x_1,x_3} f^{(3)}(x_1,x_2,x_3)(k+1) - f(x_2) \right|$$

Consider the first item of $L^{(1)}$. There is

$$\sum_{x_2} \left| \sum_{x_1,x_3} f^{(1)}(x_1,x_2,x_3)(k) - f(x_2) \right|$$

$$= \sum_{x_2} \left| \sum_{x_1,x_3} f^{(1)}(x_1,x_2,x_3)(k) - \sum_{x_1,x_3} f^{(2)}(x_1,x_2,x_3)(k) \right| \qquad \text{(A.1)}$$

$$= \sum_{x_2} \left| \sum_{x_1,x_3} \left(f^{(1)}(x_1,x_2,x_3)(k) - f^{(2)}(x_1,x_2,x_3)(k) \right) \right|$$

Note that

$$f^{(2)}(x_1,x_2,x_3)(k) = \frac{f^{(1)}(x_1,x_2,x_3)(k)}{\rho(x_2)(k)}$$

where

$$\rho(x_2)(k) = \frac{\sum_{x_1,x_3} f^{(1)}(x_1,x_2,x_3)(k)}{f(x_2)}$$

Clearly, $\rho(x_2)(k)$ only depends on x_2. Thus, for a given x_2, each

$$f^{(1)}(x_1,x_2,x_3)(k) - f^{(2)}(x_1,x_2,x_3)(k) = \left(1 - \frac{1}{\rho(x_2)(k)}\right) \cdot f^{(1)}(x_1,x_2,x_3)(k)$$

has the same sign, and Eq. (A.1) can be written as

$$\sum_{x_2} \left| \sum_{x_1,x_3} \left(f^{(1)}(x_1,x_2,x_3)(k) - f^{(2)}(x_1,x_2,x_3)(k) \right) \right| \tag{A.2}$$
$$= \sum_{x_1,x_2,x_3} \left| f^{(2)}(x_1,x_2,x_3)(k) - f^{(1)}(x_1,x_2,x_3)(k) \right|$$

According to triangle inequality, it can be obtained immediately that

$$\sum_{x_1,x_2,x_3} \left| f^{(2)}(x_1,x_2,x_3)(k) - f^{(1)}(x_1,x_2,x_3)(k) \right|$$
$$\geq \sum_{x_1} \left| \sum_{x_2,x_3} \left(f^{(2)}(x_1,x_2,x_3)(k) - f^{(1)}(x_1,x_2,x_3)(k) \right) \right| \tag{A.3}$$
$$= \sum_{x_1} \left| \sum_{x_2,x_3} f^{(2)}(x_1,x_2,x_3)(k) - f(x_1) \right|$$

On the other hand,

$$\sum_{x_1} \left| \sum_{x_2,x_3} f^{(2)}(x_1,x_2,x_3)(k) - f(x_1) \right|$$
$$= \sum_{x_1} \left| \sum_{x_2,x_3} \left(f^{(2)}(x_1,x_2,x_3)(k) - f^{(1)}(x_1,x_2,x_3)(k+1) \right) \right| \tag{A.4}$$

where

$$f^{(1)}(x_1,x_2,x_3)(k+1) = \frac{f^{(2)}(x_1,x_2,x_3)(k)}{\rho(x_3)(k) \cdot \rho(x_1)(k+1)}$$

Note

$$\rho(x_3)(k) = \frac{\sum_{x_1,x_2} f^{(2)}(x_1,x_2,x_3)(k)}{f(x_3)}$$

only depends on x_3. And

$$\rho(x_1)(k+1) = \frac{\sum_{x_2,x_3} f^{(3)}(x_1,x_2,x_3)(k)}{f(x_1)}$$
$$= \frac{1}{f(x_1)} \cdot \sum_{x_2,x_3} \left[\frac{f^{(2)}(x_1,x_2,x_3)(k)}{\sum_{x_1,x_2} f^{(2)}(x_1,x_2,x_3)(k)} \cdot f(x_3) \right]$$

Obviously, $\sum_{x_1,x_2} f^{(2)}(x_1,x_2,x_3)(k)$ only depends on x_3. Denote $M^{(2)}(x_3) = \sum_{x_1,x_2} f^{(2)}(x_1,x_2,x_3)(k)$ for convenience. Thus

$$\rho(x_1)(k+1) = \frac{1}{f(x_1)} \cdot \sum_{x_2,x_3} \left[\frac{f^{(2)}(x_1,x_2,x_3)(k)}{\sum_{x_1,x_2} f^{(2)}(x_1,x_2,x_3)(k)} \cdot f(x_3) \right]$$

$$= \frac{1}{f(x_1)} \cdot \sum_{x_3} \left[\frac{f(x_3)}{M^{(2)}(x_3)} \cdot \left(\sum_{x_2} f^{(2)}(x_1,x_2,x_3)(k) \right) \right]$$

Again, $\sum_{x_2} f^{(2)}(x_1,x_2,x_3)(k)$ only depends on x_1 and x_3. We denote it as $N^{(2)}(x_1,x_3) = \sum_{x_2} f^{(2)}(x_1,x_2,x_3)(k)$ for convenience. Then

$$\rho(x_1)(k+1) = \frac{1}{f(x_1)} \cdot \sum_{x_3} \left[\frac{f(x_3)}{M^{(2)}(x_3)} \cdot \left(\sum_{x_2} f^{(2)}(x_1,x_2,x_3)(k) \right) \right]$$

$$= \frac{1}{f(x_1)} \cdot \sum_{x_3} \left(\frac{N^{(2)}(x_1,x_3)}{M^{(2)}(x_3)} \cdot f(x_3) \right)$$

As can be seen, $\rho(x_1)(k+1)$ is not relevant to x_2. Consequently, for any x_2, each

$$\sum_{x_3} \left(f^{(2)}(x_1,x_2,x_3)(k) - f^{(1)}(x_1,x_2,x_3)(k+1) \right)$$

$$= \sum_{x_3} \left(1 - \frac{1}{\rho(x_3)(k) \cdot \rho(x_1)(k+1)} \right) f^{(2)}(x_1,x_2,x_3)(k)$$

has the same sign, and Eq. (A.4) can be written as

$$\sum_{x_1} \left| \sum_{x_2,x_3} \left(f^{(2)}(x_1,x_2,x_3)(k) - f^{(1)}(x_1,x_2,x_3)(k+1) \right) \right|$$

$$= \sum_{x_1,x_2} \left| \sum_{x_3} \left(f^{(2)}(x_1,x_2,x_3)(k) - f^{(1)}(x_1,x_2,x_3)(k+1) \right) \right|$$

Also, the triangle inequality leads to

$$\sum_{x_1,x_2} \left| \sum_{x_3} \left(f^{(2)}(x_1,x_2,x_3)(k) - f^{(1)}(x_1,x_2,x_3)(k+1) \right) \right|$$

$$\geq \sum_{x_2} \left| \sum_{x_1,x_3} \left(f^{(1)}(x_1,x_2,x_3)(k+1) - f^{(2)}(x_1,x_2,x_3)(k) \right) \right| \tag{A.5}$$

$$= \sum_{x_2} \left| \sum_{x_1,x_3} f^{(1)}(x_1,x_2,x_3)(k+1) - f(x_2) \right|$$

From Eqs. (A.1)–(A.5), there is

$$\sum_{x_2} \left| \sum_{x_1,x_3} f^{(1)}(x_1,x_2,x_3)(k) - f(x_2) \right| \geq \sum_{x_2} \left| \sum_{x_1,x_3} f^{(1)}(x_1,x_2,x_3)(k+1) - f(x_2) \right|$$

Similarly, the second item of $L^{(1)}$ holds

$$\sum_{x_3} \left| \sum_{x_1,x_2} f^{(1)}(x_1,x_2,x_3)(k) - f(x_3) \right| \geq \sum_{x_3} \left| \sum_{x_1,x_2} f^{(1)}(x_1,x_2,x_3)(k+1) - f(x_3) \right|$$

Therefore, $L^{(1)}(k) \geq L^{(1)}(k+1)$. $L^{(2)}(k)$ and $L^{(3)}(k)$ can be proved analogously. $\square$

The general case is discussed later.

Proposition A.1.2 (Multivariate case) *Suppose that the marginals of n positive real variables $(X_1, \dots, X_n)$ are $f(x_1), \dots, f(x_n)$. Each variable in the kth iteration is fitted in turn as*

$$f^{(1)}(x_1, \dots, x_n)(k) = \frac{f(x_1, \dots, x_n)(k-1)}{\sum_{x_2,\dots,x_n} f(x_1, \dots, x_n)(k-1)} \cdot f(x_1), \quad (x_1 \text{ fitted})$$

$$f^{(2)}(x_1, \dots, x_n)(k) = \frac{f^{(1)}(x_1, \dots, x_n)(k)}{\sum_{x_1,x_3,\dots,x_n} f^{(1)}(x_1, \dots, x_n)(k)} \cdot f(x_2), \quad (x_2 \text{ fitted})$$

$$\vdots$$

$$f^{(n)}(x_1, \dots, x_n)(k) = \frac{f^{(n-1)}(x_1, \dots, x_n)(k)}{\sum_{x_1,\dots,x_{n-1}} f^{(n-1)}(x_1, \dots, x_n)(k)} \cdot f(x_n). \quad (x_n \text{ fitted})$$

Then the L1 error monotonously decreases during its iteration.

Proof: The $L1$ errors are

$$L^{(1)}(k) = \sum_{x_2} \left| \sum_{x_1,x_3,\dots,x_n} f^{(1)}(x_1, \dots, x_n)(k) - f(x_2) \right|$$

$$+ \dots + \sum_{x_n} \left| \sum_{x_1,\dots,x_{n-1}} f^{(1)}(x_1, \dots, x_n)(k) - f(x_n) \right|$$

$$\vdots$$

$$L^{(n)}(k) = \sum_{x_1} \left| \sum_{x_2,\dots,x_n} f^{(n)}(x_1, \dots, x_n)(k) - f(x_1) \right|$$

$$+ \dots + \sum_{x_{n-1}} \left| \sum_{x_1,\dots,x_{n-2},x_n} f^{(n)}(x_1, \dots, x_n)(k) - f(x_{n-1}) \right|$$

As the three-dimensional case, the first item of $L^{(1)}$ has

$$\sum_{x_2} \left| \sum_{x_1,x_3,\ldots,x_n} f^{(1)}(x_1,\ldots,x_n)(k) - f(x_2) \right|$$

$$= \sum_{x_2} \left| \sum_{x_1,x_3,\ldots,x_n} (f^{(1)}(x_1,\ldots,x_n)(k) - f^{(2)}(x_1,\ldots,x_n)(k)) \right|$$

$$= \sum_{x_2} \left| \sum_{x_1,x_3,\ldots,x_n} \left(1 - \frac{1}{\rho(x_2)(k)} \right) \cdot f^{(1)}(x_1,\ldots,x_n)(k) \right|$$

$$= \sum_{x_1,x_2} \left| \sum_{x_3,\ldots,x_n} \left(1 - \frac{1}{\rho(x_2)(k)} \right) \cdot f^{(1)}(x_1,\ldots,x_n)(k) \right|$$

$$\left(\text{Given } x_2, \text{ each } 1 - \frac{1}{\rho(x_2)(k)} \text{ has the same sign} \right)$$

$$\geq \sum_{x_1} \left| \sum_{x_2,\ldots,x_n} \left(1 - \frac{1}{\rho(x_2)(k)} \right) \cdot f^{(1)}(x_1,\ldots,x_n)(k) \right|$$

$$= \sum_{x_1} \left| \sum_{x_2,\ldots,x_n} f^{(2)}(x_1,\ldots,x_n)(k) - f(x_1) \right|$$

(triangle inequality)

On the other hand,

$$\sum_{x_1} \left| \sum_{x_2,\ldots,x_n} f^{(2)}(x_1,\ldots,x_n)(k) - f(x_1) \right|$$

$$= \sum_{x_1} \left| \sum_{x_2,\ldots,x_n} (f^{(2)}(x_1,\ldots,x_n)(k) - f^{(1)}(x_1,\ldots,x_n)(k+1)) \right|$$

$$= \sum_{x_1} \left| \sum_{x_2,x_3,\ldots,x_n} \left(1 - \frac{1}{\rho(x_3)(k) \ldots \rho(x_n)(k) \cdot \rho(x_1)(k+1)} \right) \cdot f^{(2)}(x_1,\ldots,x_n)(k) \right|$$

$$= \sum_{x_1,x_2} \left| \sum_{x_3,\ldots,x_n} \left(1 - \frac{1}{\rho(x_3)(k) \ldots \rho(x_n)(k) \cdot \rho(x_1)(k+1)} \right) \cdot f^{(2)}(x_1,\ldots,x_n)(k) \right|$$

$$(A.6)$$

This is because each

$$\sum_{x_3,\ldots,x_n} \left(1 - \frac{1}{\rho(x_3)(k) \ldots \rho(x_n)(k) \cdot \rho(x_1)(k+1)} \right) \cdot f^{(2)}(x_1,\ldots,x_n)(k)$$

has the same sign given x_1. Thus,

$$\sum_{x_1} \left| \sum_{x_2,\dots,x_n} f^{(2)}(x_1,\dots,x_n)(k) - f(x_1) \right|$$

$$\geq \sum_{x_2} \left| \sum_{x_1,x_3,\dots,x_n} \left(1 - \frac{1}{\rho(x_3)(k)\dots\rho(x_n)(k)\cdot\rho(x_1)(k+1)} \right) \cdot f^{(2)}(x_1,\dots,x_n)(k) \right|$$

(*triangle inequality*)

$$= \sum_{x_2} \left| \sum_{x_1,x_3,\dots,x_n} f^{(1)}(x_1,\dots,x_n)(k+1) - f^{(2)}(x_1,\dots,x_n)(k) \right|$$

$$= \sum_{x_2} \left| \sum_{x_1,x_3,\dots,x_n} f^{(1)}(x_1,\dots,x_n)(k+1) - f(x_2) \right|$$

Similarly, there is

$$\sum_{x_i} \left| \sum_{x_1,\dots,x_{i-1},x_{i+1},\dots,x_n} f^{(1)}(x_1,\dots,x_n)(k) - f(x_i) \right|$$

$$\geq \sum_{x_i} \left| \sum_{x_1,\dots,x_{i-1},x_{i+1},\dots,x_n} f^{(1)}(x_1,\dots,x_n)(k+1) - f(x_i) \right| \quad (i = 3,\dots,n)$$

Thus, $L^{(1)}(k) \geq L^{(1)}(k+1)$. Other $L^{(i)}(k) \geq L^{(i)}(k+1), (i = 2,\dots,n)$ can be proved analogously. □

References

1 W. E. Deming and F. F. Stephan. On a Least Squares Adjustment of a Sampled Frequency Table When the Expected Marginal Totals Are Known. The Annals of Mathematical Statistics, 1940, 11(4): 427–444. http://www.jstor.org/stable/2235722.

2 E. F. Stephan. An Iterative Procedure for Estimation in Contingency Tables. The Annuals of Mathematical Statistics, 1970, 41(3): 907–917.

3 O. Pretzel. Convergence of the Iterative Scaling Procedure for Non-Negative Matrices. Journal of the London Mathematical Society, 1980, 21(4): 379–384.

4 L. Ruschendorf. Convergence of the Iterative Proportional Fitting Procedure. The Annuals of Statistics, 1995, 23(4): 1160–1174.

Index

Parallel Population and Parallel Human: A Cyber-Physical Social Approach,
First Edition. Peijun Ye and Fei-Yue Wang.
© 2023 The Institute of Electrical and Electronics Engineers, Inc. Published 2023 by John Wiley & Sons, Inc.

IEEE Press Series on Systems Science and Engineering

Editor: MengChu Zhou, *New Jersey Institute of Technology*
Co-Editors: Han-Xiong Li, *City University of Hong-Kong*
Margot Weijnen, *Delft University of Technology*

The focus of this series is to introduce the advances in theory and applications of systems science and engineering to industrial practitioners, researchers, and students. This series seeks to foster system of systems multidisciplinary theory and tools to satisfy the needs of the industrial and academic areas to model, analyze, design, optimize, and operate increasingly complex man-made systems ranging from control systems, computer systems, discrete event systems, information systems, networked systems, production systems, robotic systems, service systems, and transportation systems to Internet, sensor networks, smart grid, social network, sustainable infrastructure, and systems biology.

1. *Reinforcement and Systemic Machine Learning for Decision Making*
   Parag Kulkarni

2. *Remote Sensing and Actuation Using Unmanned Vehicles*
   Haiyang Chao and YangQuan Chen

3. *Hybrid Control and Motion Planning of Dynamical Legged Locomotion*
   Nasser Sadati, Guy A. Dumont, Kaveh Akbari Hamed, and William A. Gruver

4. *Modern Machine Learning: Techniques and Their Applications in Cartoon Animation Research*
   Jun Yu and Dachen Tao

5. *Design of Business and Scientific Workflows: A Web Service-Oriented Approach*
   Wei Tan and MengChu Zhou

6. *Operator-based Nonlinear Control Systems: Design and Applications*
   Mingcong Deng

7. *System Design and Control Integration for Advanced Manufacturing*
   Han-Xiong Li and XinJiang Lu

8. *Sustainable Solid Waste Management: A Systems Engineering Approach*
   Ni-Bin Chang and Ana Pires

9. *Contemporary Issues in Systems Science and Engineering*
   Mengchu Zhou, Han-Xiong Li, and Margot Weijnen

Printed and bound by CPI Group (UK) Ltd, Croydon, CR0 4YY
27/10/2024

14580670-0001